HARD LESSONS

This publication has been assisted by an Ontario Heritage Book Award from the Ontario Heritage Foundation, an agency of the Ministry of Culture, Tourism and Recreation

HARD LESSONS
THE MINE MILL UNION IN THE CANADIAN LABOUR MOVEMENT

EDITED BY
MERCEDES STEEDMAN,
PETER SUSCHNIGG, AND DIETER K. BUSE

DUNDURN PRESS
TORONTO & OXFORD

Copyright © Institute of Northern Ontario Research and Development, 1995

All rights reserved. No part of this publication may be reproduced, stored in a retrieval system, or transmitted in any form or by any means, electronic, mechanical, photocopying, recording, or otherwise (except brief passages for purposes of review), without the prior permission of Dundurn Press Limited. Permission to photocopy should be requested from the Canadian Reprography Collective.

The editors are grateful to Sudbury Mine, Mill and Smelter Workers Local 598/CAW for its generous support in aid of preparing the manuscript for publication.

Copy editor: Robert Clarke
Printer: Best Book Manufacturers

Printed and bound in Canada

The publisher wishes to acknowledge the generous assistance and ongoing support of the **Canada Council,** the **Book Publishing Industry Development Program** of the **Department of Canadian Heritage,** the **Ontario Arts Council,** the **Ontario Publishing Centre** of the **Ministry of Culture, Tourism and Recreation,** and the **Ontario Heritage Foundation.**

Care has been taken to trace the ownership of copyright material used in the text (including the illustrations). The author and publisher welcome any information enabling them to rectify any reference or credit in subsequent editions.

J. Kirk Howard, Publisher

Canadian Cataloguing in Publication Data

Main entry under title:

Hard lessons : the Mine Mill union in the Canadian labour movement

Includes bibliographical references.
ISBN 1-55002-223-7

1. International Union of Mine, Mill and Smelter Workers – History – Congresses. 2. Trade-unions – Miners – Canada – History – Congresses. 3. Trade-unions – Miners – Ontario – Sudbury Region – History – Congresses. 4. Trade-unions – Canada – History – Congresses. I. Steedman, Mercedes, 1943–   . II. Suschnigg, Peter Theobald, 1940–   . III. Buse, D.K., 1941–   . IV. Laurentian University of Sudbury. Institute of Northern Ontario Research and Development.

HD6528.M62I55 1995   331.88'12233'0971   C95-931308-7

Dundurn Press Limited	Dundurn Distribution	Dundurn Press Limited
2181 Queen Street East	73 Lime Walk	1823 Maryland Avenue
Suite 301	Headington, Oxford	P.O. Box 1000
Toronto, Canada	England	Niagara Falls, N.Y.
M4E 1E5	0X3 7AD	U.S.A. 14302-1000

Contents

Acknowledgements	vii
Introduction	1

PART ONE: THE STATE OF THE UNION 11

1 One Hundred Years of Mine Mill 13
   John B. Lang
2 The Decline of Collective Bargaining in the Private Sector 21
   John O'Grady
3 Women and New Issues in Labour Organizing 26
   Laurell Ritchie
4 A Chilly Season for Canadian Labour 30
   Jean-Claude Parrot

PART TWO: UP AGAINST THE MAINSTREAM 37

5 Small Unions and Dissidents in the History of Canadian Trade Unionism 39
   Bryan Palmer
6 Le local 902 du Mine Mill: Les dix premières années (1949–1959) du syndicat des travailleurs de la ville et du district de Sudbury 50
   Donald Dennie
7 Mergers, Organizing, and Collective Identity: The CAW at the Crossroads 68
   Charlotte Yates
8 Women and the Changing Face of Labour in Northeastern Ontario 81
   Mary Powell and Jennifer Keck

PART THREE: SOLIDARITY AND FRAGMENTATION 97

9 Labour Law and Fragmentation before Statutory Collective Bargaining 99
   Eric Tucker
10 Labour Law Reform in Ontario: Moving Forward to Go Back to What Never Was 117
   Harry J. Glasbeek

Part Four: I Remember Mine Mill — 139

11 "We're Still Here" — 141
   A Panel Reviews the Past and Looks to the Future

Part Five: The Expendable Worker — 193

12 "The Name of the Game Is Power": — 195
   Labour's Struggle for Health and Safety Legislation
   Elie Martel

13 Health, Safety, and the Environment in CAIMAW and the CAW — 210
   Cathy Walker

14 "Building Tombstones in Our Lungs": — 221
   Comments on Health and Safety
   Clinton Jencks, Kevin Conley, Elie Martel, and Cathy Walker

Part Six: Technological Change — 227

15 Telework and the Workplace of the Future — 229
   Theresa Johnson

16 A Labour Agenda for Work Design — 235
   Ken Delaney

Part Seven: Creative Responses in Organization and Culture — 243

17 Organizing Part-Time Workers in the Educational Sector — 246
   Mike Groom

18 Working Partners: The Arts and the Labour Movement — 251
   Karl Beveridge

19 Weir Reid and Mine Mill: An Alternative Union's Cultural Endeavours — 269
   Dieter K. Buse

Part Eight: Drawing on the Past for Future Strength — 287

20 Building a People's Movement — 290
   Madeleine Parent

21 It Never Died: How Joe Hill's Ashes Came to Be in the Sudbury Mine Mill Hall One Hundred Years after the Founding of the Western Federation of Miners — 299
   Utah Phillips

Notes — 303
Selected Bibliography — 323
Contributors — 324

ACKNOWLEDGEMENTS

When a few of us began discussions in 1990 about a conference to celebrate the coming centennial of the Mine, Mill and Smelter Workers, we did not anticipate that over two hundred persons would come from across North America to exchange views both on the past and on the problems and challenges facing labour today – and especially to acknowledge that the future may be as difficult as the past. As we soon discovered, Mine Mill's motto "Independence, Education and Organization" offers a strong reminder to academics and labour leaders alike about the ultimate purpose of labour movements.

At the May 1993 centennial conference of Mine Mill, co-sponsored by Laurentian University's Institute of Northern Research and Development (INORD) and Mine Mill and organized by Sudbury unionists and scholars, the interrelationship of the motto's three parts was again demonstrated, and this book is a reminder of the linkage.

The present book grew out of this conference and the issues raised there. However, the book is not simply a record of the conference. Some presentations were omitted; all of those included here were reworked and revised, some in a completely new format. The conference participants included shop stewards, labour activists, various men and women who took part in the formative struggles of Mine Mill, and academics. Their different life experiences are mirrored in the diversity of their contributions. Much of the information contained in chapter 11 has already been published in a different format in the April 1994 issue of *Labour/Le Travail.*

The editors are indebted to many institutions and individuals. Foremost is the union whose history created the basis for what was being celebrated: the Canadian Union of Mine, Mill and Smelter Workers, especially Local 598 of Sudbury. Its present leaders, notably Rolly Gauthier, and its centennial committee co-operated with us in innumerable ways and supplied generous financial support, including funding for labour participants. Rolly demonstrated his sense of humour in dealing with academics and his aplomb in organizing social events such as the Utah Phillips concert. The union made possible the attendance of old-timers and labour participants, as well as providing support for our oral history projects and the banquets.

The advice and counsel of several senior leaders in the Mine Mill movement helped us shape the issues addressed by the conference. We are especially indebted to Jim Tester, Mike Solski, Ruth Reid, Ray Stevenson, and Mike Farrell. They shared their vast experience as leaders in the labour movement and helped us develop a sensitivity to the past struggles and an awareness of the significance of those struggles for the future of labour. Similarly, John Lang – long associated with Mine Mill – offered ideas that proved valuable for shaping the conference.

A conference grant from the Social Sciences and Humanities Research Council covered the expenses of the academic participants and some administration costs. A grant from the Ministry of Northern Development and Mines was used for publicity and initial editing of the manuscript. Both grants were decisive in fostering this collaboration among academics and labour leaders and in making a wider audience aware of labour's past and present. The book's publication was made possible by a Publication Award from the Ontario Heritage Foundation.

Support by Laurentian University took numerous forms. INORD, under director Anne-Marie Mawhiney, helped prepare grant applications and provided expertise for organizing the conference. Nearly all who filled out the conference evaluation forms heaped praise upon the smooth functioning of the workshops, concerts, and discussion sessions. Susan Bisset, Susan Vanstone, Lana Tremblay, Kelly Wilson, Natalie Grguric, Kevin Groulx, and Rick Stow all helped to make the conference a success. Three individuals deserve special mention: Jane Pitblado for her consistent and thorough editorial help, Mick Lowe for his stylistic suggestions, and Robert Clarke for rigorous copy-editing. Guy Gaudreau and Micheline Tremblay edited chapter 6. Paul Cappon, vice-president academic, Geoffrey Tesson, dean of social sciences, and the Office of Graduate Studies and Research at Laurentian provided funds and assistance.

We also greatly appreciate the help of Valerie Pomfret, Stuart Cryer, Joan Kuyek, Marge Reitsma-Street, Brenda Tremblay, and Dorothy Wigmore. And we remain grateful to the participants who made the conference such a valuable experience and the book possible. As always, the editors assume responsibility for errors and omissions.

Fourth INORD Conference

This book is part of series of publications related to themes of conferences sponsored by the Laurentian University's Institute of Northern Ontario Research and Development (INORD). The fourth INORD conference was held from May 13 to May 15, 1993, in Sudbury, Ontario. Entitled "Where the Past Meets the Future – the Place of Alternative Unions in the Canadian Labour Movement," the conference was sponsored jointly by

INORD and Mine Mill Local 598. INORD's previous conferences have addressed issues of particular relevance to Northern Ontario, focusing on the contentious issue of land use in Temagami in 1989, on mines and single-industry towns in 1990, and on political, economic, and social rebirth in First Nations in 1992. In all cases the conferences have fostered healthy dialogue between academics from a variety of disciplines and interested members of the relevant communities (environmentalists, mayors, Aboriginal leaders, and at the present conference, labour leaders and researchers). Each time the meeting of academic theory with practical experience has proved to be both stimulating and rewarding. All conferences to date have been generously supported by the Social Sciences and Humanities Research Council, and the proceedings from all four have been published by Dundurn Press with support from the Ontario Heritage Foundation.

Mercedes Steedman, Peter Suschnigg, Dieter K. Buse
Sudbury, November 1994

INTRODUCTION

This book, in part, emerges from the papers, panels, and discussion of the conference "Where the Past Meets the Future – the Place of Alternative Unions in the Canadian Labour Movement," held to commemorate the first one hundred years of the history of the Mine, Mill and Smelter Workers Union. The union, which began in 1893 as the Western Federation of Miners and grew to a membership of over one hundred thousand in fifty locals throughout Canada during the 1950s, had shrunk to a single local of sixteen hundred members in Sudbury, Ontario, by the 1990s. For its participants the conference provided an opportunity not just of looking back and reflecting on Mine Mill's past, but also of assessing the current state of the Canadian labour movement.

In 1993, when the conference took place, Mine Mill was about to reach another important crossroad in its history. When retired workers, union staff and stewards, academics, and activists gathered from May 13 to 15 in Sudbury, merger talks with the Canadian Auto Workers Union (CAW) formed a constant backdrop, and the topic of mergers was woven into presentations and discussions – continuing right into Madeleine Parent's closing presentation on the final evening. Just three months later, on August 20, 1993, two-thirds of the Mine Mill membership voted to merge with the CAW.

The merger talks took place in a challenging new economic and political environment. The labour movement across Canada is facing a future that no longer ensures opportunities for full-time work at a decent wage. Instead, changes in the nature of work and the increasing globalization of capital have precipitated a crisis that has left all those concerned about the future of work in the "new society" conscious of the need to understand the workings of contemporary social and economic processes. The workforce is under siege as job losses continue to reach proportions scarcely imaginable ten years ago. Trade union membership is dwindling, and as a result unionists from all sectors of the workforce are being forced to come to grips with an uncertain future. At the same time, unions have to service an ever-diminishing and disillusioned membership. If unions want to remain a force to be reckoned with into the twenty-first century, they will have to meet the challenge of rethinking and reshaping the labour movement.

The movement that is encountering these challenges looks different than it did just twenty years ago. For instance:

- Since Mine Mill became an independent Canadian union in 1955, the labour movement has seen continued Canadianization. In the 1990s fewer than 40 percent of the unions in Canada are international, compared to about 65 percent in the 1960s.
- The expansion of unions in the public sector moved ahead rapidly during the 1970s, but slowed in the 1980s.
- North America has seen a marked decline in unionization in the traditional industrial sector. The resource-based sector – which once served as the backbone of Canadian unionism – is in decline, and its unions are under severe pressure.
- The face of labour has changed. More women than ever before are holding jobs outside the home; more minorities are represented in the labour force; and control by white, male industrial workers is slowly lessening.
- There has been a marked increase in part-time work and in the use of contract workers, which poses a special challenge to unionization efforts.
- Labour legislation has served to limit the political activism of the labour movement and has increasingly forced unions to respond to erosions of their rights through legal mechanisms, rather than through rank-and-file mobilization or direct political action.
- Many workers who remain employed have experienced increased hours of work along with an intensification of production.
- With greater commercialization of leisure and recreation, mass culture has undercut the educational and cultural activities of alternative unions.
- Rapid and continuing technological change has reduced the demand for labour and caused permanently high levels of structural unemployment.

The chapters in this book attempt to chart the course of some of these changes. John Lang, Laurell Ritchie, John O'Grady, and Jean-Claude Parrot offer readers a commentary on the "state of the union." John Lang, who has previously written on the history of Mine Mill, reviews the past and demonstrates the generosity of Mine Mill in helping other organizations, listing its community involvements and contributions to unionism. O'Grady notes the decline of collective bargaining in the private sector. He examines the patterns, suggests reasons for the decline, and offers an explanation for this turn of events. Ritchie illustrates how the current economic climate is not conducive to union work and shows that Canadian capital has generally been able to resist unionization in the service sector. She outlines the changing role of women in the economy and within the unions and acknowledges the decline of physically demanding labour, the increase in part-time work, and the challenges of the private service sector. A steady fall in real wages for unionized workers and new legislative measures against the labour movement continue to push trade unions into defensive postures, sometimes forcing serious concessions and layoffs. Parrot emphasizes the need for the labour movement to reach out and forge alliances in its communities. These chapters offer readers a look at the current conditions and give a sense of how to resist and where to draw lessons from the past.

The labour movement will face the next decades in a state of both solidarity and fragmentation. The fragmentation of the movement continues through separation of workers into categories of skilled and unskilled, blue-collar and white-collar, private-sector and public-sector, employed and unemployed, men and women, visible minorities and white – all of which will create potentially divisive tendencies. For instance, as the status of unionized women workers altered, women's voice in the labour movement has strengthened, yet gender issues remain a contentious part of trade union struggles. We have tried to be aware of the representations of sexism that appear in the text, and we have used gender-neutral language where appropriate. At the same time, to avoid rewriting a clearly gender-divided history we have retained some of the gendered language of the past. For example, for the most part the women's trade union auxiliaries remain as they were formally titled, ladies' auxiliaries – although, as we will also see in these pages, there is now a tendency to refer to them as women's auxiliaries. In general, unions must certainly find ways to overcome disunity if they are to have an impact on the next one hundred years of Canadian working-class history, and many of the chapters offer suggestions about how to resolove this problem.

Bryan Palmer provides a history of labour, read from the perspective of small-alternative-dissident unions. This history acknowledges that unionism's experience in recent decades has been one of decline and difficulties, a theme expanded upon by Charlotte Yates. The CAW, it seems, still lacks a new collective identity. Yates's analysis of the last decade reveals how much the union has changed under the pressure of structural adjustments, at first just to survive, then to expand. That story strikes a familiar chord, because survival was an issue for Mine Mill in Sudbury throughout its history. The opposition of the mining companies during the 1940s was matched by opposition from the state during the Cold War. The painful period of raiding by the Steelworkers in the 1950s and 1960s led to the loss of locals and threats to Mine Mill's existence. Earlier, during the 1940s, one strategy of defence developed by Mine Mill was to expand into the service sector – a strategy successfully implemented in the 1950s. Donald Dennie's essay on Local 902 of Mine Mill charts a pattern now being repeated by the CAW – although with the benefit of hindsight we can see that the organization of taxi drivers and hotel workers by Mine Mill hardly touched women workers.

With the increase of women and visible minorities in the ranks of unionized labour, the issues of racism and sexism are no longer peripheral to the labour movement, as Mary Powell and Jennifer Keck's look at women and labour in Northern Ontario makes clear. Trade union feminism has inspired creative responses to the current demands of the social and political climate. Unions are taking up issues such as equal pay, day-care provisions, and sexual harassment as a direct response to unionized women's initiatives. As women have taken their place in the labour movement, their demands for a voice in its future have raised issues around workplace democracy. The problems women identified and presented in the session on women's experiences (introduced by Powell and Keck) are problems common to the entire labour movement. These changes challenge the labour movement to commit itself to a broader agenda.

Trade unions need to exert their power in the political arena rather than in the narrowly defined bread-and-butter issues of wage scales. They also must develop creative solutions that challenge the legitimacy of the legal statutes under which they labour. Eric Tucker and Harry Glasbeek document the present and past legal impediments to greater solidarity. They offer a basis for developing a challenge to the ideology of legalism that hangs over the house of labour. Tucker provides a historical overview of how legalism became established, with Glasbeek showing how legalism functions in the case of the Ontario NDP government's labour-law reforms.

The strong arm of the law not only restrains but also has the potential to protect workers. Health and safety at work have been an enduring challenge for Mine Mill. Throughout its history the union had to address all the greatest fears of hardrock miners – illness, injury, disability, destitution, and death. Much of the current workers' compensation system can be traced back to the struggles waged by the Western Federation of Miners (WFM) and its heir, Mine Mill. In 1940, for instance, Mine Mill submitted an eighty-seven-page brief on working conditions in the Kirkland Lake gold mines.

The chapters by Elie Martel and Cathy Walker show that the struggles for workplace health and safety are far from over. Martel documents government and company collusion, and his thoughtful but spirited critique of a string of commissions to inquire into Ontario's mining health and safety, his unsuccessful attempts to shift the balance of power into the hands of workers, and his pessimistic assessment of current regulatory practices are calls for action. Cathy Walker's chapter can be read as a tribute to Bob Sass, who has done much to give workers the basic tools of empowerment. The right to know about workplace hazards, the right to refuse unsafe work, and the right to participate in health and safety committees in the workplace are the essential first steps towards better workplaces and better working conditions. Walker's discussion of the health and safety work done by the Canadian Association of Industrial, Mechanical, and Allied Workers (CAIMAW) shows the difficulties faced by small, alternative unions. CAIMAW decided to merge with the CAW to gain access to much larger resources. Walker's analysis of the different approaches taken by CAIMAW and the CAW shows how economies of scale enable the CAW to offer education and training programs that are far beyond the ability of a small union.

The 1993 merger of Local 598 with the CAW was foreshadowed in many a conference presentation. Speaker after speaker, starting with Jean-Claude Parrot and concluding with Madeleine Parent, stressed the importance of a united labour movement, calling on Mine Millers to rejoin the house of labour from which they had been evicted. One of the joys of the conference – amidst all the current social and political problems that participants identified – was the presence of so many makers of Mine Mill's history among the delegates. The conference organizers took the opportunity to record and transcribe the sessions at which these articulate activists aired their views on the past and present (see chapter 11).

Regardless of the Mine Mill past, there is no call for a return to the industrial relations of the 1950s. Instead, the current industrial and social climate calls for a reassessment of trade union strategies. The aim of the conference was to provide participants with an opportunity to move into the future better informed and more able to deal with the political and economic struggles that face the labour movement in this new era of global capitalism.

From the globe to the home may seem a long way, but telework represents the future that has become the present. In her chapter, Theresa Johnson relates the visions of working at home through computer technology to the reality of research results. That research contrasts the publicity that offers ideals with a reality that is mundane and malfunctioning. While challenging union practices, telework has failed to provide personal empowerment. Ken Delaney outlines the various responses to the changes he sees in the workplace, from an increasing use of technological changes to eliminate jobs, to growing efforts by workers to make their work sites better places. Workers who are empowered, he says, can turn the fortunes of their workplace to their own advantage. Part of that process of empowerment can come together through educational initiatives, and Mike Groom and Karl Beveridge provide two different perspectives on this sphere of activity – Groom in looking at union organizing among educational workers, and Beveridge in looking at the revival of labour traditions through collaboration between artists and unions. The workers' heritage movement, which Beveridge places in context, recalls Mine Mill's extensive contributions to the cultural life of all the communities it worked in. Dieter K. Buse recounts an example of Mine Mill's contributions through the spectacular and imaginative work of Weir Reid, who worked long and hard with the union leadership to realize the union's social and cultural aspirations.

Drawing the conference together, Madeleine Parent spoke of her personal involvement with Mine Mill. She advocated merger with the CAW, not to reinforce the status quo, but as a way for Mine Mill to regain its rightful place in the Canadian labour movement. She clearly set out the challenges and possibilities facing labour, including Mine Mill. Like Parrot, she asked that unionists learn from the lessons of the past and called for the building of a broadly based people's movement.

These proceedings offer the reader an opportunity to rethink labour's hard lessons. A book cannot recapture the spirit of a conference – especially the experience of hearing Utah Phillips's renditions of labour songs, of witnessing the camaraderie of those who undertook initial organizing efforts and fought off raids or Cold War confrontations, or of seeing the determination of a new generation of activists – but it can pass on a good deal of the experience, information, and analysis presented there. And it can offer the story of how Joe Hill's ashes eventually found their way to the Mine Mill Hall.

A Short History of Mine Mill

Mine Mill can trace its roots back to 1893 and the formation of the Western Federation of Miners in the mining centres of the western United States. In 1905 the WFM joined with the International Workers of the World (IWW) and acted as its mining department for several years. But factional fighting caused the mining section to withdraw. By 1905 the Western Federation had 185 locals, including 20 in British Columbia and one in Colbalt, Ontario. The WFM fought for the eight-hour day, protective legislation, and workers' compensation. By 1916 the union was in decline, and at its convention that year, when its members voted to change the name of the union to International Union of Mine, Mill and Smelter Workers, the current union was born.

For many years Mine Mill continued to struggle with threats from the mining consortiums and with internal conflict aggravated by the dual unionism of the IWW in the United States and One Big Union in Canada. Mine Mill revived again in the 1930s, and its leadership role in the formation of the Congress of Industrial Organizations (CIO) meant that organizational efforts began to bear fruit.

Due in part to the shortage of labour during World War II and to the government's recognition of collective bargaining, Mine Mill achieved certification at many workplaces, including Sudbury. The demand for minerals and metals resulted in an expansion of mines and mills during and after the war so that unions in the resource sector expanded quickly.

By the end of the war Mine Mill in Canada had established a program for organizing, including: "a forty-hour week, $1.10 an hour minimum rate for miners, time and a half after forty hours a week, six paid holidays with double time if worked, shift differential pay, one week paid vacation for two years or less of service, two weeks of vacation for two years or more of service, sick pay for up to two weeks, severance pay equal to one month's wages for every year worked, and guaranteed annual work or wage equivalent."[1]

The Mine Mill efforts ran into several roadblocks. In 1947 the Taft-Hartley Act became law in the United States, and among other things it required all labour unions to guarantee that no members of the Communist Party were working for them. Mine Mill refused and fought the act for many years. In 1949 the Canadian Congress of Labour, responding to a climate of red-baiting, expelled Mine Mill from its ranks. This act opened the door to years of inter-union warfare that resulted in the loss of many Mine Mill locals to the anti-communist United Steelworkers of America.

Mine Mill was certified as the bargaining agent in all Sudbury mines in 1944. In the early 1950s the Steelworkers started raiding Mine Mill, leading to a battle for union membership at Inco[2] and Falconbridge. After a long strike in 1958 and internal feuding that brought a so-called "reform" slate to control of the Local 598 executive – with the "reformers" supported by Catholic priests and educators working for the Steelworkers – the original union solidarity was weakened. In 1962, by a very narrow margin, Steelworkers won the vote to represent Inco workers. A re-vote was called in 1965, and Steel carried the workers at Inco into their union, although Falconbridge workers remained loyal to the Mine Mill union. These years of struggle left a legacy of bad blood between the two unions, and even in the early 1990s, as Mine Mill moved to merge with the Canadian Auto Workers Union, resentment from the past underlay the discussion and decision-making on Mine Mill's future.

In 1955 Mine Mill was the first international union to grant autonomy to its Canadian members. The Canadian union continued the WFM philosophy that union activities must move beyond bread-and-butter issues and take on the broader social and political concerns of the working class. Under the banner of "education, independence and organization," Mine Mill built union halls, sponsored cultural and sports activities, set up libraries, and offered children the opportunity to spend their summers at a camp located at Richard Lake just outside Sudbury. Children of miners and non-miners from all over Canada and the United States were welcome. Many of these activities would not have been possible without the active support of wives and daughters of the Mine Mill men, whether through the Ladies' Auxiliary or as volunteers at the camp.

Mine Mill is unique among trade unions in that it has sought to implement its slogan, "a union without women is only half organized." Auxiliaries were autonomous locals within the Mine Mill family of unions. They had their own chartered locals, sending delegates to national and international conventions. Under the Mine Mill Canadian constitution they had the right to attend all local meetings of the union and to make

First Canadian Constituent Convention, held July 18–23, 1955, Rossland, B.C., in the hall built by Local 38 of the Western Federation of Miners.

Courtesy Mike Farrell

recommendations to that body. In the eastern district of the Canadian section of Mine Mill, auxiliary locals were chartered in Sudbury with groups active in Coniston, Levack, Lively, and Chelmsford, and locals were established in Kirkland Lake, Timmins, Red Lake, Rouyn-Noranda, Marmora, and Port Colborne during the late 1940s and 1950s. The auxiliary mandate moved women's activism well beyond the vision we normally hold of traditional working-class housewives. These women actively lobbied to obtain proper housing, sanitation, and municipal services, to gain improvements in the school systems, and to secure workers' compensation and unemployment and old age benefits. They pushed government bodies to limit increases in the cost of living, improve social services, and generally make elected representatives "work for the welfare of all people, not only for the rich minority."[3] In the rich cultural activities under the imaginative leadership of Weir Reid from 1952 to 1959, women helped run the ballet and drama classes, the libraries, play schools, and film sessions. Before Reid was hired as recreation director, women had initiated many of these activities.

In its heyday Mine Mill was a hundred thousand strong, with fifty locals in Canada; Sudbury alone had twenty-three thousand members, making it the largest local in the International Union of Mine, Mill and Smelter Workers. Today Local 598, the last remaining local of this once-strong union, celebrates that heritage and moves towards the next one hundred years as part of the CAW mining section.

Part 1
THE STATE OF THE UNION

Introduction

These chapters repeat the themes of the Mine Mill centennial conference: Was there a future for Mine Mill and other alternative unions outside the mainstream? Could the mainstream labour movement learn something from alternative unions? We know that Mine Mill's democratic traditions led to its virtual demise and its expulsion from the mainstream of Canadian labour. Have the changes wrought by global economic, political, and social forces made those traditions irrelevant? From the beginning of the conference to its conclusion, all those attending were to grapple with these fundamental questions.

The opening address by John Lang, secretary-treasurer of the Confederation of Canadian Unions (CCU), recalls the first hundred years of Mine Mill and explores its decimation as a national union. Lang wonders whether the time has come for Mine Mill to rejoin the mainstream of Canadian labour. He briefly outlines Mine Mill's position as an alternative union and asks: "If, at this point in the history of our labour movement, there is some convergence between alternative unions and the mainstream of the labour movement, what are the implications for mainstream unions?" Thus the question of a possible merger of Mine Mill was touched on very early in the conference.

John O'Grady, labour consultant, argues strongly for such a strategy. He demonstrates that labour organization in the private sector is destined to decline if the current system of collective bargaining is not replaced by a system that permits broader-based bargaining. These themes are further developed by CAW (Canadian Auto Workers) staff representative Laurell Ritchie. She looks at the increasing labour-force participation of women, the growing proportion of part-time work, and the need for organized labour to go beyond traditional – usually male – sources of membership and to look beyond narrow national boundaries.

Jean-Claude Parrot, Canadian Labour Congress (CLC) vice-president, takes up the themes raised by the previous presenters and calls on labour to become much more inclusive. While many workers will benefit from collective bargaining, labour's voice is muted on issues like free trade, interest rates, tax policy, and deficits. Parrot insists, "Mass unemployment, declining real wages, the polarization of jobs into good jobs and bad jobs, and increasing poverty are the consequences of globalization and the government corporate agenda."

Chapter 1
One Hundred Years of Mine Mill

John B. Lang

We are assembled in what is, for many, the most historic union hall in the country, to mark the one hundredth anniversary of the founding of the Western Federation of Miners, the precursor of the International Union of Mine, Mill and Smelter Workers. We are here to celebrate the accomplishments of Mine Mill in bringing union organization to the hardrock mining industry of North America. We are here as well to pay tribute to the role of Local 598 in representing the mineworkers of the Sudbury basin for the past fifty years.

We are also here tonight – and at the conference in the days to follow – to reflect on the state of the labour movement in Canada and to examine the influence of unions like Mine Mill – sometimes smaller, often more militant, usually outside of the major labour federations – on the direction and philosophy of the mainstream labour movement in Canada.

For me, Mine Mill symbolizes, perhaps more than any other labour organization in North America, what is best in the labour movement. In my opinion the history of the union is characterized by a certain rugged honesty, a fierce dedication to defend and advance the economic interests of its members, a remarkable willingness to challenge not only the corporations it faced in negotiations but also the capitalist economic system as a whole.

Along with these characteristics the union has held a firm commitment to taking a broad view of both its own role and the role of the labour movement. The union has shown a distinct tendency to move beyond the narrow economic struggle between the worker and the boss and to deploy its resources towards achieving programs that would enhance the complete lives of members, their families, and the communities in which they lived.

In the first instance, this understanding of labour's broader social struggle led Mine Mill to achieve comprehensive health and welfare programs for its members and their families. The union's educational programs stretched beyond the immediate needs of stewards' training to embrace a wide range of social and economic issues. From its earliest days, Mine Mill emphasized political action, taking an active part in countless campaigns for legislative reforms and working to elect labour members to legislative office. It gave top priority to organizing campaigns, which in the heyday of Mine Mill ensured that virtually the entire hardrock mining industry in Canada worked under union contracts. In the 1940s and 1950s its cultural and recreational programs quickly became models of their kind for the labour movement. Mine Mill was also one of the first international unions to recognize the need for Canadian autonomy. It granted independence to its Canadian membership in 1955.

Throughout its history Mine Mill recognized the importance of including women in the life of the union. Although the primary structure for this involvement was in the form of ladies' auxiliaries – rightly criticized by feminists today for their paternalistic and patriarchal connotation – still, in most of the strikes fought by Mine Mill, and in much of the union's community activities, women played an important and highly visible role, which was fully credited at all levels of the organization.

The outward-looking social unionism of Mine Mill found particular expression in the Sudbury area. By the mid-1940s, Sudbury's Local 598 represented almost eighteen thousand members at Inco and Falconbridge and had become the flagship local of the union. The local moved quickly to become a force to be reckoned with in provincial and municipal politics. Mine Mill's union halls (which were community gathering places) and its summer camp became the loci for an extensive cultural and recreational program under the imaginative leadership of Weir Reid [see chapter 19]. Mine Mill proceeded to organize a large proportion of the service sector of the Sudbury economy – taxi drivers, waitresses, and clerks in department stores and supermarkets all joined the labour movement under the banner of Mine Mill Local 902 [see chapter 6].

Many of Mine Mill's accomplishments in Sudbury set precedents for the labour movement in Canada, but these accomplishments, unfortunately, are not what has put Sudbury on the labour historian's map. Sudbury continues to be remembered as the primary location for the raids on Mine Mill's membership by the United Steelworkers of America – the biggest and most bitter inter-union confrontation in the history of Canada's labour movement. These raids, motivated by a Cold War, anti-communist hysteria, have become even harder to justify as time goes by. Yet the fact remains that

Sudbury police help members of the pro-Steelworkers faction in Mine Mill Local 598 prevent anti-Steelworker unionists from entering a September 10, 1961, meeting at the Sudbury Arena. The drive to merge Local 598 with the Steelworkers was announced at that meeting.

Mike Solski Collection, Sudbury Public Library

the success of the Steelworkers in gaining the certification at Inco's Sudbury operations led to the death of Mine Mill as a national union.

For the past quarter-century, Local 598 has carried on the struggle, representing its members at Falconbridge Nickel Mines and keeping alive the spirit of Mine Mill. Although its accomplishments in this period may not be as dramatic as those of the earlier era, Mine Mill Local 598 has continued to play an important role in the life of the Sudbury community and the labour movement generally. It has maintained a strong and active union at Falconbridge's operations; it is active in the political and social life of the region; it was a founding member of the Confederation of Canadian Unions (CCU) in 1969; and, more recently, it has expanded its membership to include a number of service industries and social-service agencies in the region.

This aspect of Mine Mill's history – operating primarily as a local union, outside the mainstream of Canada's major labour federations – is to be the starting point for much of the discussion in the hundredth anniversary conference. This is the first instance I know of in which labour activists and academics have come together to discuss questions of this nature. It is a tribute to Mine Mill that, on its one hundredth anniversary, it is yet again providing an occasion for breaking new ground.

I have had the good fortune not only to study and write about Mine Mill in an academic setting, but also, for the past fifteen years, to work with Mine Mill as an officer of the CCU. In preparing for this conference, I reviewed some of what I have written and what others have written on Mine Mill. In this re-examination of Mine Mill research I was struck by the abiding generosity that permeates the union's history. Not enough recognition, I believe, is given to the fact that it was largely because of the dues revenue generated from Local 598's membership that Mine Mill was able to organize miners in virtually every mining camp in Canada during the 1940s and 1950s. In addition, Local 598's membership was well known throughout North America for its generosity in supporting strikes and working-class struggles – no matter where – and most progressive political issues as well. The considerable financial resources of Local 598 were never hoarded; rather, in a continuous manifestation of labour solidarity, they were generously shared with others in greater need.

Unfortunately, this generosity became a major focal point of the attacks levied against Mine Mill by the Steelworkers. Local 598 was vilified for its support of labour struggles. The suggestion was egregiously made that union dues were spent improperly, and Local 598 was portrayed as the milch cow of the labour movement and popular causes. In my view, it is a sad reflection on the labour movement of Canada that such an attack was made – and sadder still that, to a large degree, the attack was successful.

In addition to analysing the history and accomplishments of Mine Mill, this conference plans to examine the role of alternative unions in Canada's labour movement. For the past quarter century the Confederation of Canadian Unions has been at the centre of this controversy. In addition the CCU has, over the last couple of years, engaged in a serious internal debate about the changes taking place within our labour movement and the impact of these changes on CCU affiliates. I want to present my views on the CCU's contribution to the development of Canada's labour movement and to make a few observations about the current choices a number of CCU affiliates are in the process of making.

What is the "difference" that the CCU has offered Canadian trade unionists? In simple terms the alternative presented by the CCU has covered two areas:

1) a commitment to building Canadian unions and liberating our labour movement from the domination of U.S.-based unions; and
2) building and practising an alternative to the philosophy of business unionism, an alternative that must be rooted in a high level of union democracy and control by the rank-and-file union member.

This CCU alternative needs to be understood in the context of the struggles in our labour movement during the 1960s and early 1970s, the period during which most of the breakaways from U.S. unions occurred. These breakaways were usually generated by one of two root causes: the outright rejection by U.S. headquarters of Canadian demands for rudimentary recognition of the particular needs of Canadian workers in either the constitutional structure or the servicing provided by the union; or the poor representation afforded to, or the outright betrayal of, Canadian workers in times of strikes or other struggles with their employers.

Although most of the union breakaways in English-speaking Canada took place in the Western provinces, the impetus for this breakaway movement was supported by events in Sudbury. The prolonged attacks by the Steelworkers against Mine Mill's membership during the 1950s – and especially its raids against Local 598 in the 1960s – reinforced the belief of many unionists in Canada that U.S. unions were more interested in building empires and winning control than they were in fighting for workers on the job.

It is to be expected, at a conference like this, that the impact of the CCU alternative will be scrutinized. I will lead off this discussion by asserting that I believe there is good reason for those of us in the CCU to be proud of what has been achieved.

On the issue of Canadian workers gaining control of their own labour movement, a tremendous transformation has occurred during the lifetime of the CCU. When the CCU was taking shape in the mid-1960s, over 70 percent of unionists in Canada were members of U.S. unions. Today, only 33 percent of unionists in Canada belong to U.S. unions – and this percentage is continuing to decline.

Not only has the presence of U.S. unions declined in the labour movement generally, there has been an equally dramatic change in the composition of the Canadian Labour Congress (CLC) – once considered the mouthpiece for U.S. unions in Canada. When the CLC was established in 1956, U.S. unions accounted for 80 percent of its membership. Today, only 37 percent of the CLC's membership belongs to U.S.-based unions. Some of this transformation is explained by the more rapid growth of public-sector unions during this period. But a long list of U.S.-based unions have "Canadianized" in response, at least in part, to pressures generated by the CCU – beginning with the Canadian Paperworkers Union in the early 1970s and including the Canadian Auto Workers (CAW) in the mid-1980s – which many believe to be the most significant step in the development of an independent Canadian labour movement.

Obviously, this dramatic move towards Canadian unionism has not resulted in a corresponding increase in the ranks of the CCU. Most of the "Canadianization" of U.S. unions has occurred on a relatively friendly basis within the CLC, without the need for breakaways. Nevertheless, I believe it is fair to argue that the CCU has played the role of a catalyst in bringing about these changes. We have demonstrated that Canadian workers can run their own affairs and negotiate top-notch contracts with the largest transnational corporations, and we have also kept the debate over Canadian unions alive within the labour movement.

On the issue of building an alternative to the philosophy of business unionism, an evaluation is more complex. Certainly, the CCU has earned a reputation for being a militant, democratic labour federation. We have had to endure our share of red-baiting, and *The Globe and Mail* regularly refers to the CCU as "left-wing." But a more perceptive assessment of CCU affiliates would have to concede that there is a spectrum of achievement on this issue. We have produced affiliates that are highly politicized, promoting within their membership a critical analysis of our economic system and the world we live in. These affiliates have demonstrated, on many occasions, the resources and the leadership to undertake and win difficult struggles. Still, other affiliates are quite comfortable in not rocking the boat and in going along with the flow. In this respect, the CCU is not dissimilar from unions and labour federations throughout the world.

"Where the Past Meets the Future" is an appropriate title for this conference celebrating the centenary of Mine Mill. Not only does it solicit an appraisal of past endeavours, but it also raises questions about the role and the structure of the labour movement in the decades that lie before us. These are questions that have also received a considerable amount of discussion within the CCU in recent years.

As a leader of the CCU, I have felt that it has been my responsibility to confront affiliates with my belief that the labour movement in Canada has changed – and is continuing to change – in the very areas that the CCU set out to influence. The labour movement is now firmly in the hands of Canadian workers. Although this struggle has not been completely won, we have, you could say, at least pushed the boulder up our side of the mountain and over the top. It will not roll down the other side on gravity alone – there are a number of crevices and plateaus that will stand in its way. But at the same time, it is very unlikely at this point that the boulder will reverse itself and roll back up the hill and down our side.

The politics of the Canadian labour movement – including the CLC – have also changed. Although the mainstream unions might not meet all of the standards that the CCU has set for itself, there is no question in my mind that there have been major changes for the better in the policies and practices of the labour movement as a whole. At the same time, unions in Canada have had to deal with the fallout from the global economic restructuring occurring around us. This restructuring is fuelled by a new generation of technology based on the microchip and the division of the world economy into three major trading blocs. The clearest manifestation, for Canadians, of this new division is the Canada-U.S. Free Trade Agreement and the North American Free Trade Agreement (NAFTA) negotiated under the Progressive Conservative government. These trade agreements constitute a massive rewrite of all national economic and social policies according to the dictates of a handful of transnational corporations.

The impact of these trade agreements on working people and on the labour movement is enormous. Layoffs and plant closures are inevitable as the trade agreements place Canadian workers in direct competition, first, with corporations paying four dollars an hour in the U.S. sunbelt and, next, with these same corporations paying four dollars a day in Mexico. Nobody can escape the repercussions of this insidious corporate plot – as the public-sector workers in Ontario can now attest after weeks of trying to protect themselves against the onslaught of Premier Bob Rae's so-called "social contract."

The impact of this global economic restructuring has stretched the resources of smaller unions to the limit. Within the CCU, this situation has prompted several rounds of discussions over the past several years about restructuring our federation to meet these new realities. We put in considerable effort to try to arrive at a common solution to the problems faced by affiliates. But the differences among the fifteen unions within the CCU – in history, structure, and material conditions – were great, and in the end, after much honest deliberation, the only consensus that could be reached was that it would be up to each affiliate to determine the course of action that would be in the best interests of its members.

Over the past year and a half, several affiliates have left the CCU to merge into larger unions. The Canadian Auto Workers has been the union of choice for these CCU affiliates. It is also the preference of most of the leadership of Mine Mill Local 598 here in Sudbury in their current merger negotiations with the CAW. This is, indeed, a case where the past may be meeting the future.

If, at this point in the history of our labour movement, there is some convergence between alternative unions and the mainstream of the labour movement, what are the implications for mainstream unions? A few weeks ago, while attending the opening of the CAW Local 40 office in Toronto, I could not escape considering this question.[1] Gathered at the opening was a wide selection of activists who have played leading roles in struggles around women's issues, equal pay for work of equal value, human rights, employment equity, immigration, the building of coalitions, and more. The majority of those present had championed these issues from outside the mainstream and spent most of their active lives in alternative unions or movements. As these unions and individuals enter the mainstream of the labour movement, the question confronting me is: where will the issues for the next decade come from? Rapidly expanding unions like the CAW face a crucial challenge to ensure that their structures and organizations will be open enough and confident enough to generate critical issues from within.

Another key issue relates to the fact that Canada does not exist in isolation. In this era of corporate-driven global trading pacts, it is abundantly clear that we need new forms of international solidarity among working people and popular organizations. Because of our unique experiences, the Canadian labour movement may be able to play a leading role in the development of new and solid alliances with working people around the world. We need to recognize, however, that in many Third World countries, the only legitimate labour movement is what we would describe as alternative unions. In Mexico, for example – where the logic of NAFTA demands that Canadian workers become involved in organizing Mexican workers – the official labour movement is bankrupt of ideals and is a corrupt instrument of the government. Alternative unions, many of them operating underground, more truly represent the interests of Mexican workers. The Canadian labour movement must ensure that these alternative unions are included in our international solidarity efforts and recognized in labour's international forums.

For social activists, the past is constantly meeting the future. The colourful history of Mine Mill provides an appropriate backdrop for an examination of the role of unions situated outside the mainstream of Canada's labour movement. Mine Mill stands for progressive, forward-looking unionism with a bold vision on most of the major political and social issues of this century. A combination of these characteristics is needed to equip both academics and union activists in understanding the labour movement today and in charting the direction of Canada's labour movement through the turbulent decades that lie ahead.

Chapter 2
The Decline of Collective Bargaining in the Private Sector

John O'Grady

In Canada it is common to contrast our more or less stable rates of unionization with the falling rates of unionization in the United States. Virtually every Canadian trade unionist knows that overall unionization rates are substantially higher here than they are south of the border. In 1992 the overall rate of unionization among non-agricultural workers in Canada was 37.4 percent. In 1990 – the last year for which I have comparative data for the United States – the rate of unionization there was less than half the Canadian rate – 16.1 percent. Canadian trade unionists have often drawn a measure of comfort from this contrast, but it seems to me that this comfort is misplaced.

On its face, the evidence on unionization provides Canadian trade unionists with reason for satisfaction. In 1971 unionization rates were 32.4 percent and in 1992 they were 37.4 percent. The last twenty years or so have witnessed both an absolute and a relative growth in the number of workers covered by collective bargaining. But this growth in the level of unionization masks a significant decline in the rate of private-sector collective bargaining. Some twenty-five years ago, collective bargaining determined the wages and working conditions of about 31 percent of workers in the private sector. By 1985 that proportion had declined to 21 percent, and by 1990 it had fallen to 18 percent.[1] The growth in unionization in Canada was accounted for entirely by an increase in the rate of public-sector unionization. In the private sector, the Canadian pattern was similar to that of the United States. While the decline in the United States was more severe, there is little in this trend that should provide comfort to Canadian trade unionists.

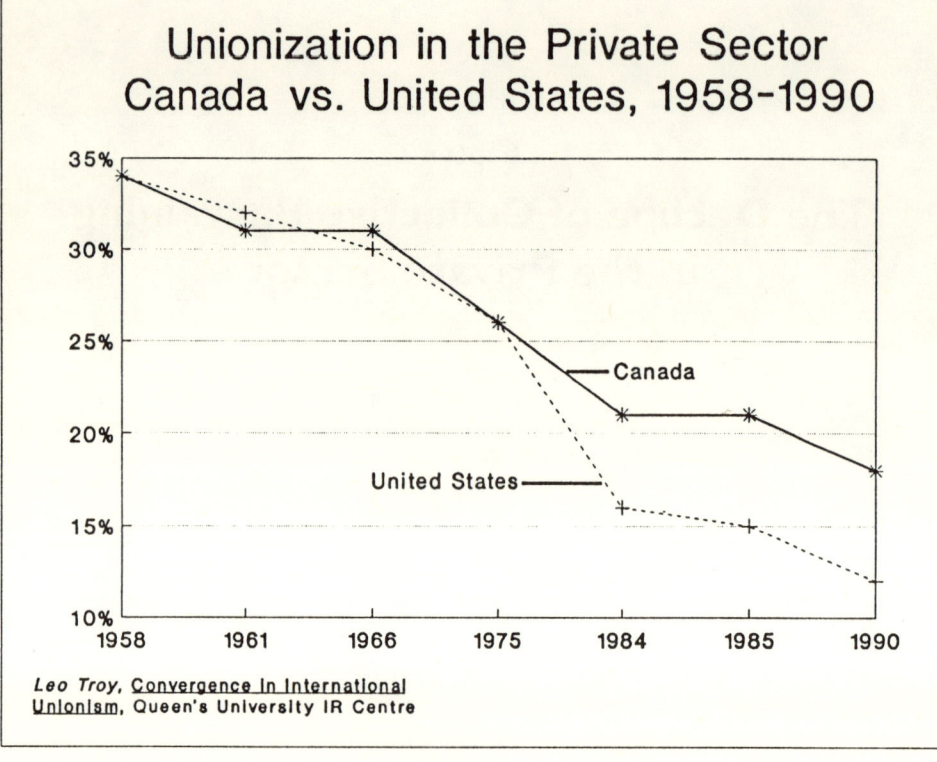

Figure 2.1

Canada's labour market has two segments. The first segment, in which the labour movement has its base, takes in roughly 60 percent of employed workers. It includes manufacturing, the resource industries (principally mining and forestry), the regulated industries (transportation, communications, and utilities, a mix of public and private companies), and the public sector. Its rate of collective bargaining coverage is roughly 57 percent. The second segment is primarily the private service sector – for example, McDonald's and Molly Maid – which includes the other 40 percent of the labour force. Its rate of unionization is around 15 percent.

There are three trends that we need to understand.

First, a secular shift in the economy is seeing labour moved from the first segment to the second. In relative terms, the segment of the economy in which the labour movement has traditionally found its base is getting smaller. The rate of decline is roughly 1 percent every three years. High rates of productivity growth in the manufacturing and resource sectors driven by technological change mean that there are fewer jobs in those industries. Deregulation and privatization in the regulated industries are having a similar effect.

Second, within the segment of the economy that forms the union base, there has been a relative decline in the private sector and a relative increase in the public sector. Ten years ago, just over 43 percent of workers in this segment were in the public sector, while now that proportion is over 50 percent. It would be naive to expect public-sector employment to grow significantly over this decade. Indeed, in the medium term, at least, we are more likely to see a reduction in public-sector employment.

Third, within the first segment of the economy, the union-base segment, there has been a decline in the rate of private-sector unionization, from about 51 percent to around 47.5 percent.

From these three trends, one undeniable conclusion emerges: *the labour-market base of the trade union movement in Canada is being eroded, and that erosion is unlikely to be arrested, let alone reversed.*

As private-sector unionization rates decline, the support for collective bargaining in Canadian society will also decline. We know that about 80 percent of private-sector workers are now outside the ambit of collective bargaining. How much support are public-sector workers likely to draw from these workers as the public-sector unions struggle to preserve collective bargaining in the broader public sector? How much longer before we start hearing significant voices in society arguing that the days of the trade union movement are over and that we need new mechanisms to represent workers and protect their interests?

Clearly, the only course for the labour movement is to shift its focus from its historic base to the segment of the economy in which employment is increasing – the private service sector. There is nothing particularly new in this prescription. People inside and outside the labour movement have been saying that for as long as I can remember; and yet it does not happen. Table 2.1 summarizes the distribution of newly organized workers in Ontario in 1989–90, the last year before the present recession.

Table 2.1
Distribution of Newly Organized Employees, 1989–1990
(excluding construction)

Sector	%
Manufacturing / Resources / Regulated Industries	53
Public Sector	35
Private Service Sector	12

Clearly, union organizing resources are still focused overwhelmingly on the first segment of the labour force and not on the second. In Ontario in 1989–90, about 57 percent of the labour force was employed in the first segment of the economy, while 88 percent of union organizing resources were devoted to that segment.

Some will argue that the obstacles to moving outside the traditional base are related to gender and to gender-biased organizing strategies. I do not dispute that these are factors. However, I do dispute that simply addressing those problems will either arrest or reverse the decline of private-sector collective bargaining.

In Canada our basic labour relations legislation is drawn from the National Labor Relations Act introduced by U.S. President Franklin Delano Roosevelt in 1935. That legislation is usually called the Wagner Act, after the U.S. senator who sponsored the bill. The simple fact is that the Wagner Act was written to deal with collective bargaining in large-scale manufacturing. It was written for the Congress of Industrial Organizations (CIO), and it was written to aid the CIO in organizing U.S. manufacturing. Moreover, the Wagner Act worked – at least for a few decades. However, it was never expected that Wagner Act collective bargaining would be applied to the private service sector.

Our labour relations legislation is based on site-by-site organizing and site-by-site bargaining. Except in the construction industry, multi-site bargaining and multi-employer bargaining only occur when both unions and employers agree. This highly decentralized system of bargaining functions reasonably well in the segment of the economy that forms the union-base segment: manufacturing, resources, regulated industries, and the public sector. But highly decentralized, site-by-site bargaining works badly, if at all, in the private service sector. Here, workplaces tend to be small and the survival rate of employers tends to be much lower – an average of about five years. It is costly to organize and difficult to bargain within this sector, and with the limited life-span of employers it is difficult to consolidate gains. In short, the Wagner Act model of collective bargaining does not work in the private service sector; and because that model does not work, unions have been forced to concentrate their scarce organizing resources in their traditional areas of support.

When you have a labour relations model that fundamentally does not reflect the realities of the private service sector, it should be no surprise that rates of unionization in that sector are low. Obviously, new strategies are required to organize workers in that sector. But new strategies, in the absence of a new legal framework, are unlikely to produce significant results.

In 1989–90, there were 259 certifications granted by the Ontario Labour Relations Board in the private service sector, excluding construction. In other words, in that period the union side was rolling 259 boulders up the hill. But it was losing ground. To stay even with the creation of firms – to score a tie – the union side would have to roll an additional 625 boulders up the hill. It is patently unrealistic to believe that this could happen; the odds are stacked heavily against this degree of collective bargaining. Unless the rules change, the decline will continue, and no organizing strategy, on its own, will prevent that.

The kind of change needed in the private service sector is one that alters the logic of bargaining from site-by-site bargaining to sector-based bargaining. The Ontario government has announced its intention to establish a task force to study the question of broader-based bargaining. In my view, this change is of overriding, strategic importance to the labour movement.

The labour movement still has political and economic leverage, but it must use that leverage strategically to create new social and economic facts. If we achieve a shift to sector-based bargaining in the private service sector, this half of the North American continent will have a different pattern of political social development than its larger partner to the south. If we remain with a labour-law model that essentially reflects the U.S. Wagner Act, we will see the same inexorable pattern of development in Canada as in the U.S. private sector. The stakes are high, and time is running out.

Chapter 3
Women and New Issues in Labour Organizing

Laurell Ritchie

After more than twenty years in the labour movement, I can safely say that a lot has changed, and there is certainly a much larger space, and a much larger voice, for women in the labour movement. I doubt that anybody would say otherwise. There is also a lot that has not yet changed, things that still require a lot more of our attention.

The changes in the workforce and in unionization rates pointed out by John O'Grady [see chapter 2] constitute a revolution in our workplaces. It is not unfair to say that this is akin to the kinds of changes that happened during the Industrial Revolution. Many predicted that incredible changes and disruptions would occur with the full blast of technological change. We talked about this in the 1970s, and I think we were right. During the 1980s, new technologies were certainly being introduced in the structure of our workplaces. Now, in the 1990s, we are really coming to see the restructuring and "lean" workplaces that were anticipated.

There is also a revolution taking place in how capital operates within the world. At the moment there is no doubt as to who has the upper hand. We are going to have to look at very serious changes in the role of unions, and changes in how we organize. The shift is going to have to be at least as dramatic as the one that occurred when unionization moved away from merely organizing within the crafts and trades groups and into industrial-based organizing.

The nature of work is changing, whether in manufacturing or in the service sector. In most jobs the physical component of work is changing, which has implications for the gender of those performing the work. There is also a shift within the overall economy, so that many more jobs are performed within the service sectors – both public and private. There is the shift to more and more part-time work, particularly involuntary part-time work. Unlike the part-time work that most people thought about some ten or fifteen years ago – work that was maybe three or four hours a day, five days a week, leaving people wonderful, predictable quality time with children, family, and other pursuits – what we are finding now is that very often part-time work involves erratic, unreliable, anti-social, and anti-family schedules. It is primarily women doing this type of work.

Some things, of course, also remain constant. They keep many of us active in the labour movement in spite of all the tremendous and difficult changes. One of these constants is the desire for people to be treated as human beings when they are at work – too many people are still treated as something less than a human being after they enter the workplace. A lot of other issues still require our attention. There are certainly going to be women around to remind the forgetful. But I also think that people in the leadership of various unions are going to have to start remembering on their own.

Often these things are small – like turning to the booklet that was put out for this centennial and finding, on its final pages, photographs of the women active in the union's Women's Auxiliary. Unlike the other photographs in the booklet, there are no names identifying any of these women. Women notice these sorts of things, and we hope that others will start paying more attention to them, because it is our history as well. Women want to be able to find themselves within labour history, to know that some of their roots, and the roots of their mothers, aunts, and grandmothers, are within the labour movement. That is part of democratizing the labour movement.

A few things are essential to changing the style and content of the labour movement, to modernize, to democratize it. They are things we can all embrace. They include the new forms of organization now taking place. The organizations in Toronto are the ones I am most familiar with – like Intercede, which is working with domestic workers. These women cannot organize as others can under Ontario labour law, but they have found the most ingenious ways of pulling workers together. They keep them together, and I can tell you that proportionately the numbers they get out at their meetings and events far exceed the numbers that a lot of labour unions can claim.

The same thing is occurring now with the new Home Workers Association, with the support of a number of organizations and unions. Homeworking is an accelerating phenomenon within the industrial sector, even though some will assume it disappeared in the 1930s and 1940s. It is coming back as a form of work, with people working privately in their homes at assembly or sewing machine work. There is also electronic homework, with people doing data processing, for example, in their homes and experiencing the same problems as industrial homeworkers [see chapter 15]. The people organizing around these issues are showing remarkable creativity, and we are going to learn a great deal from them.

Interesting things are happening elsewhere. At a recent conference involving people from Latin American countries, women in the labour movement reported on new labour laws that restrict unions in some countries to workplaces with fifteen or more workers. Lo and behold, even the largest oil companies locating in these countries were suddenly setting up workplaces of fourteen workers. We are going to have to learn from the experiences of others who are outside our borders.

Some of these new forms of organizing and providing representation call for increased attention. John O'Grady mentions the discussion now taking place around broader-based bargaining [see chapter 2]. I believe this proposition requires debate. For example, in the case of the post office, some of us may personally be very glad that it was the Canadian Union of Postal Workers (CUPW) that won the vote, but we have to be leery when votes like this are being initiated by the state. It is all well and good if the unions and organizations you want to see win, do in fact win; but I wonder how it will feel if, in some sectors, we end up with unions that we would rather didn't represent the entire membership of that sector? I certainly feel that this issue arises in the case of the private service sector. Some of the unions that are currently operating in the private service sector are quite corrupt in their practices. We are going to have to have the guts within the labour movement to come to terms with some of the unions that currently represent workers in that sector but do it very badly.

There is also the need both to continue and to extend our work with coalition organizations. Some of the victories we have achieved, always through struggle, are in very serious jeopardy, and it will become more difficult to win new victories and make improvements through bargaining at the table with a single employer.

More and more, employers in a competitive global economy are in the position of blackmailing their own workforce. They are also in the position, through their corporate lobby organizations, of blackmailing society as a whole. So we have to extend our work as unions to coalitions that are also the vehicles for dealing with a whole range of organizations, including women's organizations and unrepresented people, many of them workers, both employed and unemployed. Someone recently suggested that if the unemployed in Canada were to be organized, they would form the largest single union in this country.

The issues that unions are addressing both at the workplace bargaining table and at the broader social bargaining table have to take into account more consciously the issues that concern women, who constitute over half the population and close to half the workforce. Many women, for example, are in workplaces in which a private pension scheme is currently an impossibility. But as pension plans have improved in some workplaces, we have also witnessed a serious deterioration in the fight to improve public pensions. The Canada Pension Plan, Quebec Pension Plan, and even Old Age Security are all now in jeopardy. When we raise issues like Unemployment Insurance (UI) in public, we have to be prepared to talk about the impact of UI restructuring on women, because it often has very particular consequences. What does it mean, for example, to go from 60 percent of earnings now down to 57 percent of earnings, which is a 5 percent loss in income when you're on UI benefits? And what is that going to mean for the expanded maternity and parental benefits we supposedly won just a couple of years ago? I wonder how many women are going to be able to afford to take the full benefit of that leave, and how many men are actually going to undertake the shared parenting that the new provisions allow for? As for the issues of part-time work: the question for women is not only the reduced work week but also what is happening at the other end of the spectrum, where those who have part-time jobs are desperate for more reliable schedules and enough hours to support themselves and their families.

A whole range of similar issues needs to become much more integrated with the proposals being put forth by the labour movement, both at the bargaining table and as part of social bargaining.

Chapter 4
A Chilly Season for Canadian Labour

Jean-Claude Parrot

Globalization, competitiveness, and rapid technological change are causing mass unemployment and growing poverty unlike anything we have seen since the Industrial Revolution. It is not only that the percentages of employed will decline, but also that the quality and meaning of their work will deteriorate as more and more workers become engaged in mindless, meaningless, and monotonous efforts. In a society in which corporate competitiveness makes the final determination, we know the social consequences are far-reaching.

Even Jean-Claude Paye, secretary-general of the Organization for Economic Co-operation and Development (OECD), which has been promoting globalization and what we call the corporate agenda, is starting to worry. He warns:

> Advancing globalization, fiercer competition, and rapid technological progress are posing problems of adjustment, the gravity of which should not be underestimated ... Close to half a century of rapid growth would have yielded a paltry result if deep divides were to appear in our societies between the haves and have nots. There is but a short distance between feelings of injustice and despair, and between despair and revolt.

After more than ten years of the corporate agenda, Canadians are feeling injustice and despair. Many of us would agree that there is a very short distance "between despair and revolt."

Eric Kierans, a former cabinet minister who in his years since leaving cabinet has been teaching about and commenting on corporate power, has also begun to see what the labour movement is concerned about. He asks,

"Is Canada splitting into two parts, one protected under the corporate umbrella, the other vulnerable, weak, and struggling for survival? Is corporate power beyond political control?"[1]

Some see this neoconservative corporate agenda leading to a society based on extreme inequality, a society in which for many the social process of production will have no use except for selling personal services to those who have a comfortable income. This would take us back to the second half of the nineteenth century, when one-sixth of the labour force worked as servants and domestics, creating a kind of South Africanization of society.

If we are not able to implement a people's agenda, Canada's labour force could resemble the one predicted by a German trade union that took a close look at economic and social policies designed for global corporations. There would be a privileged stratum of elite workers, which might eventually comprise one-quarter of the working population. Another quarter would be made up of unskilled or semi-skilled industrial and clerical workers holding stable jobs. Half the working population would be on and off the job continually. This "floating population" would be employed mainly in subcontracting and service industries, either part-time or full-time. In other words, half the population would not have a regular job.

With free trade and the continuing dismantling of social programs, this bleak scenario may already be a reality. Right now half of Canada's entire labour force in any twenty-four-month period experiences a spell of unemployment. Without our social programs, which government seems determined to destroy, this polarization of our society would be even worse. According to the Economic Council of Canada's study *Good Jobs, Bad Jobs* (1990), if we didn't have our redistributive social programs, the income of all households would mirror what has happened to "labour income."[2] There is absolutely no question that in this kind of climate, our society will become torn between a very wealthy minority and masses of desperately poor people. Instead of the Third World joining the industrialized world, this new globalized, competitive-oriented society will reshape our society into that of the Third World.

Those who promote free trade and high interest rates and low or no taxes for the rich have long forgotten that the heart and purpose of an economic system rest in its principle of distribution. Otherwise our economic policy makes production and the pursuit of wealth and power for its own sake an end in themselves, and not a means to serve the needs of people.

For the labour movement the fight against unemployment must, in our system of values, remain the primary goal of economic policy. It is the pivot on which industrial relations and social policy and programs turn.

While the collective bargaining system is at the cutting edge of social change, many of the things won at the bargaining table have later been made available to all through the political system. However, what is gained at the bargaining table is often lost because of government policies that victimize workers and blame them for the economic failures of policy.

Even the Supreme Court of Canada recognized the importance of trade union political action. Mr. Justice La Forest, in writing the unanimous decision of the court in the Lavigne case, summed it up this way: "Many activities, be they concerned with the environment, tax policy, day care, or feminism, can be construed as related to the larger environment in which unions must represent their members."[3] The courts in Canada are very seldom on the side of the workers; it is therefore remarkable when they accurately describe what the Canadian labour movement has been doing and must continue to do if we are to reclaim our future. While the Supreme Court may recognize that the balance of power between management and labour at any given time, or in any particular industry or workplace, is a product of the state of government legislation in the area of labour relations as well as in the areas of social and economic policy, it has not stopped the business and government conspiracy against workers.

The last fifteen years have been difficult ones in the Canadian political arena. It has been a long time since trade unionists and like-minded Canadians have been able to celebrate a truly major social advance initiated by the federal government. What we are undergoing in terms of social change is equal to and as dramatic as the Industrial Revolution. Yet the programs that would help Canadians adjust are under attack or non-existent. Unemployment insurance and federal funding for education, health, and social services have all been cut back. This kind of approach to competitiveness amounts to a fundamental attack on workers' living standards and their basic rights. In effect, the survival of capital or the corporation takes priority over labour, people, and communities.

In this kind of environment, management is the dominant actor in labour/management relations. When the government introduces taxes like the GST and massive tax breaks to corporations and the rich, the balance of power between workers and management is clearly affected. The failure of the federal government to make corporations pay their fair share of taxes, coupled with punishing interest rates, is the source of federal and provincial deficits. Yet governments are pointing fingers at their own workers and social programs.

In the Lavigne case, we know the enormous cost and energy that we invested in getting our message to the learned justices on the Supreme Court. As a labour movement, we must do a much better job of reaching our own members and ordinary Canadians.

Through collective bargaining many workers will achieve job security, and the goals of affirmative action, including pay equity, will be realized for thousands of women. It is at the bargaining table that we continue to fight against overtime and for shorter working hours, better vacations, and a shorter working life, as ways of reducing unemployment and finding jobs. We do this especially for our younger people, many of whom face the possibility of a lifetime without steady employment.

As trade unionists, we are fairly successful in reaching our own membership on our goals and priorities for collective agreements and negotiations. But on issues like free trade, interest rates, tax policy, and deficits, our message does not get through in the way that it should. In other words, we know that mass unemployment, declining real wages, the polarization of jobs into good jobs and bad jobs, and increasing poverty are the consequences of globalization and the government corporate agenda. We also know that the official unemployment rate, combined with the number of discouraged workers and part-timers seeking full-time jobs, means that in Canada well over two million people are being deprived of an adequate family or personal income. We also know that nearly four million Canadians are living on incomes below the poverty line and that a million Canadian children are growing up in poverty. We know that among the Western industrialized countries, only the United States has a higher rate of child poverty.

It is not only the number of jobs we must be worried about. The quality of jobs created is even more important. By the 1990s many jobs were failing to provide a living wage. Since the mid-1970s real wages have declined, and the labour force has become increasingly polarized between good jobs and bad jobs. This polarization has reached obscene and scandalous levels.

In his book *Work of Nations*, Robert Reich – who is now secretary of labour in the United States – notes that at the beginning of the 1980s the typical chief executive officer (CEO) in the United States earned about $190,000, or forty times the wages of the average U.S. factory worker.[4] By the end of the 1980s the average CEO was paid over $2 million per year, or ninety-three times the average production worker's wages. On top of that, the highest tax rate was reduced from 90 to 28 percent. Even after taxes, the CEO takes home seventy times more than the worker on the line. In Canada we do not know the salaries of our corporations' chief executives. But most of the corporations Reich refers to are also among Canada's largest corporations, even though they are U.S. subsidiaries.

The crisis continues, and unemployment continues to increase. Some, however, would have us believe that there is an economic recovery under way. We see a government that tries to blame workers for the problems of the economy, even though workers are the main victims. The hysteria over government deficits and debts is the most recent example. Not only has this made-in-Canada recession caused widespread unemployment, falling living standards, and rising poverty, but also, with federal government leadership, several provinces are also attacking trade unions and basic trade union rights.

At the bargaining table, labour sees attempts in both the public and private sectors to extract concessions, to roll back wages and working conditions, vacations, and employment levels. We see cutbacks in staff through layoffs or attrition, increasing demands for overtime, contracting-out in the public sector, erosion of job security, and the replacement of full-time jobs with part-time and temporary casual jobs at low wages, with low benefits, and without job security.

As new technologies are introduced into the workplace, workers are called upon to adapt, adjust, retrain, and relocate. As competition for global markets increases, workers in Canada are urged to be more competitive by lowering wages and reducing demands on social services.

As a result of the Free Trade Agreement and other federal policies such as high interest rates, a high dollar, and deregulation, plant closures are now a regular occurrence. As we predicted in the 1988 election on the Free Trade Agreement, the attack on social programs and government services has been stepped up, under the guise of fighting government deficits and debt. However, governments determined to deny employees their rights usually justify repressive anti-collective bargaining in terms of essential services. Since the 1960s, when collective bargaining rights were extended to employees in the public service, strikes in the public sector have been halted by back-to-work legislation more than ninety times. This has happened despite the fact that public employees in jobs deemed "essential services" were denied the right to strike.

It isn't simply a case of a few isolated restrictions being imposed on the rights of some individuals in order to protect the general public from a serious threat. In fact, for nearly two decades now anti-labour policies have been an international embarrassment to Canada. Since 1973 the International Labor Organization's Freedom of Association Committee has heard more complaints about this country than about any other member of the G-7. Sadly, the situation is inspired by opportunistic politicians who make it possible to routinely restrict the rights of public employees. In the 1991 Public Service Alliance of Canada strike, the government's initial response to a labour board ruling that the employer was bargaining in bad faith was to table an extremely punitive back-to-work bill.

Some suggest that we place our trust in elected politicians to objectively settle the question of whether a particular strike should be declared illegal.

Governments, of course, are the final arbitrator of what constitutes the "public good." I would argue that successive federal and provincial governments have used that power cynically and with clear political motives to make scapegoats of workers in many so-called "essential service" strikes. We know the same lack of concern has been shown for the public when it comes to funding for essential services in those very same sectors. People suffer – even lives are lost – because of funding cuts.

It has been, and is, a very chilly season for labour.

I have always found it curious that the labour movement, which fights for the things every Canadian cherishes – universal health programs and better incomes and living standards – has such great difficulties in reaching the broad public. Our terrain involves not only what we fight to obtain, but also what we fight to protect and save from destruction. Why then are business and government so successful in whipping up public hostility towards unions? Not that we expect gratitude, but we should expect that our message will be received. We speak for workers and millions of people who are ignored by the power elites. But we know why our message is not heard. The mass media are controlled by corporations that have no interest whatsoever in having us heard. To some extent it is a marvel how successful we are in maintaining solidarity and reaching the broad public with such powerful interests arrayed against us.

I am even more encouraged by our achievements in responding to and advancing the great movements that were born or given impetus over the last forty years. If membership is used as a measure of health, the Canadian labour movement has succeeded where our brothers and sisters in other countries have failed. Some of this success comes from our support of the great movements around social justice issues. The Canadian labour movement has supported and embraced the fight for racial equality, peace, feminism, and the environmental movement. We continue to find common cause with social activists in working towards a people's agenda.

Our alternative strategy is built on full employment and focuses on creating jobs, not on undermining jobs and security. It promotes socially useful investment and not reward for financial speculation. It focuses on increasing real wages and living standards, not undermining them to provide a favourable investment climate. It values and promotes public services built on publicly controlled, democratic, economic planning. Finally, our agenda is built on solidarity among workers, and between workers and others in our community who have also suffered from the failures of the present economic policies.

We know very well what our alternative strategy is. But, because of the conspiracy to isolate and silence people without power, we have no debate in our society. For trade unions, whose strength is through collective action, the conspiracy to silence people must be of concern.

Finding better methods to have our message heard or seen is not the only thing we must be concerned about in reaching our membership and the public. It is much more than finding the best method, such as mailing lists and media relations. The credibility of the messenger is important. In representing workers we must not depart from our principles, even if it means debating with our friends about government priorities. The Canadian labour movement believes unemployment is the number one economic and social issue – not the deficit.

The labour movement will continue the campaign of affirmative action to demand for women their fair share of the economic and social rewards of our society. We will continue to make affirmative action, including pay equity, a high priority in our educational programs, and labour will continue to develop a strong, co-ordinated, and detailed agenda that puts affirmative action at the heart of our collective bargaining strategy. Affirmative action programs for Aboriginal peoples, visible minorities, and the disabled are also central issues for working people. No longer is it tolerable for people in these groups to be deprived of their rights.

We must continue to build coalitions with groups that are not union members, and we must do a much better job of communicating with our own membership. We must find new and more effective ways of reaching the public on government policy and legislation that may not be seen as directly affecting workers. Better communication with our own members is somewhat more in our control than our ability to reach the public – even the part of the public that shares our view. Whether we like it or not, the mass media cannot be ignored. Even before television and radio, the labour movement had to contend with hostile newspapers. Against these and greater forces, trade unionism was able to advance its struggle on behalf of working people.

We must, as a movement and an institution, be the credible voice of all workers. Workers must believe that we represent their interests. The credibility of the labour movement determines our ability to stop the federal government and their corporate friends. Credibility is essential to implement the alternative people's agenda.

Part 2

UP AGAINST THE MAINSTREAM

Introduction

Unionized labour has never been a monolithic block. The character and mix of mainstream and alternative union movements have changed over time, but as historian Bryan Palmer notes: "What is apparent is that small unionism and big unionism, alternative unionism and mainstream unionism, are related phenomena. Neither has existed historically in a vacuum: neither can really be divorced from the other." Charlotte Yates, professor of labour studies, began her research into the Canadian Auto Workers Union (CAW) when it was an international union. While she was in the middle of her work, the Canadian membership decided to break from their international union, which gave her an opportunity to study first-hand the impact of alternative unionism on the Canadian labour movement. She shows how mergers with unions not traditionally associated with the Autoworkers have led the CAW to a crossroad. That union has diversified its membership and decentralized its control, yet it has also increased its bureaucratization.

Mine Mill also took its unionization efforts beyond its traditionally designated mining sector and into the service sector. Université Laurentienne sociologist Donald Dennie's paper on Local 902 of Mine Mill charts a pattern now repeated by the CAW. The organization of taxi drivers and hotel workers by Mine Mill in the Sudbury area is a little known part of Mine Mill's rich history.

Political science professor Mary Powell and social work professor Jennifer Keck document the experiences of women in the labour force of Northern Ontario. Like Palmer's reflections on alternative unionism, the story of organizing efforts by women raises the issue of what constitutes the mainstream of the labour movement. Keck and Powell offer possible responses to the current economic situation experienced by increasing numbers of women working in the unionized and non-unionized sectors. The chapter, which has its origins in a trade union women's workshop held at the centennial conference, draws on the experiences of a diversity of trade union women from the public and private sectors. Together their narratives provide a fresh perspective on the successes and failures of unions to respond to the broader labour-force participation of women in Northern Ontario and in general.

Chapter 5
Small Unions and Dissidents in the History of Canadian Trade Unionism

Bryan Palmer

No union is small. The struggle to create and sustain workers' organizations in the face of staunch resistance from capital and the state is, and always has been, an undertaking requiring large commitments and persistent effort. It is a big job, whatever the size of the rank and file, and the importance of labour organization – measured in considerations of dignity, safety, and human worth – is never a small matter. For these reasons, no union is big enough, at least not as long as labour lacks a truly all-embracing international organization and thoroughgoing solidarity, which has never, historically, come close to realization.

Unions have always been small, inasmuch as they represent minorities of the workforce. For much of the nineteenth century, they were phenomenally small, craft enclaves of handfuls of workers, organized locally and leading highly precarious and unstable existences. But they strove to be bigger, reaching out to amalgamate with workers in other cities and towns, joining or being organized into international brotherhoods, linking up with social upheavals associated with grand international causes – the nine-hour or eight-hour day – and paced by mobilizations with exotic and chivalrously medieval names such as the "Noble and Holy Order of the Knights of Labor."

Whenever workers sought this kind of bigness, they were countered by tangible strengths. Capital and the state often overcame working-class initiatives, and there were always those within the workers' movement willing to constrict labour's struggle in the name of necessity, arguing that the reach for bigness – especially if it called for organizing the unorganized, who were likely to be unskilled, female, non-English-speaking, immigrant – was destined to fail. For labour to succeed, it was claimed, the aims of the workers' movement needed to be small, select, and sectional. Because this agenda kept labour organization contained and constrained, peculiarly adapted to the relatively powerful surviving craftsmen, this form of trade unionism weathered the storms of class struggle relatively better than the larger, more all-inclusive mobilizations of the 1880s and 1890s. It also seemed more conciliatory to capital and the state, with whom it shared certain understandings about what was and what was not possible and legitimate in terms of labour activism.

Ironically enough, this limited unionism, through its capacity to survive tough times and consolidate its strengths in periods of possibility for the workers' movement, had come to be regarded as big unionism by the pre-World War I period. Associated with the small ends of Samuel Gompers's pure-and-simple American Federation of Labor (AFL), this brand of unionism dominated the Canadian workers' movement by 1910, defining the mainstream, separating size from the qualitative ends of class struggle, and collapsing an understanding of what was big and what was small into sheer quantities. AFL unions were big by 1914 because there were more of them than other kinds of unions, and because they had organized more workers within their ranks than opposing unions had.

These AFL unions embraced almost 1,775 locals in 1914, encompassing some 135,000 workers; by 1919 the ranks of the AFL had expanded further, and the Trades and Labour Congress of Canada (TLC) claimed a membership of 175,000 unionists, up almost 100,000 from the previous decade. As a percentage of the workforce they remained small, but in terms of sheer numbers this was large compared to rival bodies such as the nationalistic Canadian Federation of Labour, the largely francophone Federation of Catholic Workers of Canada, the declining voice of east-coast miners, the Provincial Workmen's Association, or the radical Industrial Workers of the World (IWW, also known as the "Wobblies") and One Big Union (OBU) – none of which could claim a Canadian membership approaching forty thousand, and all of them seriously limited in terms of their capacity to organize across the regional expanse of the country or throughout the occupational range of the Canadian working class.

So, from early in the twentieth century, it was apparent that big versus small unionism was to be a constant thread running through labour's development. This was related to the contentious issue of craft versus industrial forms of organizing, just as it also figured in the politics of the workers' movement, with the more militant demand for proletarian political independence often running headlong into the conservatism of Gompers-style voluntarism, which eschewed autonomous political activity in favour of rewarding labour's established Grit or Tory friends and punishing its conventionally affiliated party enemies. Big unionism was small in its program and practice; small unionism was big in what it called for and believed in.

The history of union rivalries and contests in Canada reaches back to at least the 1880s as the Knights of Labor and the craft unions literally came to blows over jurisdictional matters, most of which related to actual organizing and control of dues-paying members but tended to get fought out around the union label. The Knights had their label, and particular unions, such as the cigarmakers, had theirs. Union supporters were asked to patronize only one. In 1902, at the historic Berlin (now Kitchener), Ontario, meeting of the TLC, a Gompers directive to expel all non-affiliated AFL unions from the TLC was implemented, banishing the remaining Local Assemblies of the Knights of Labor and many other rival bodies from the mainstream of Canadian labour.

By the opening decades of the twentieth century, as AFL unions and their bureaucratic leaderships grew and treasuries expanded, jurisdictional disputes within the AFL became serious, but the threat of small alternative unionism, such as that posed by the IWW or the Provincial Workmen's Association, was a more potent statement of divisions within the house of labour.

With the formation of the One Big Union in 1919, an entire regional wing of Canadian labour broke from the conservatism and sectionalism of the AFL-connected TLC. For two years the OBU attempted to make its own small alternative unionism large through appeals to class solidarity, internationalism, and militancy. It failed, but it stoked the fires of a powerful and mobilizing mythology of the potential of class solidarity and proletarian struggle.

It was in the 1920s that this question of big versus small unionism took on added political potency. The lines of demarcation had hardened considerably, a consequence of many factors. First, the employers and the armed, coercive might of the state had come down hard on labour radicals, unleashing waves of vigilante raids, deportations of alien radicals, courtroom assaults on "one big unionism," and open-shop campaigns determined to drive unionism of any sort from North American manufacturing shops, mines, and mills.

Second, the AFL bureaucracy, now thoroughly entrenched, responded to this climate of repression by moving respectfully to the respectable right, deploring radicalism of any sort, championing nativism, and backing away from class struggle. Canadian Labour Congress (CLC) leader Tom Moore deplored the Winnipeg General Strike as "revolutionary madness" that deserved to be crushed by governing authority. Big unionism, not surprisingly, sustained large losses in this context: union membership plummeted from 380,000 in 1919 to 240,000 five years later. Strikes, outside of the coalfields, dropped off equally drastically, and higher and higher percentages of these battles were being won by employers.

Third, however, with the Russian Revolution of 1917 came a certain clarification of radicalism's program, a process furthered by the disintegration of the industrial and political wings of the Canadian left. Various political formations – the Socialist Party of Canada, the Social Democratic Party, the Independent Labour Party – whatever their endurance, fragmented under the pressures to form a Communist Party. Both the IWW and the OBU, moreover, experienced similar internal turmoil, exacerbated by the sharp and relentless blows they received from state power. The big versus small unionism tension at the heart of Canadian labour history took on new meaning as the remnants of retreating radicalism in the socialist-syndicalist tradition of the Wobblies and the OBU hardened their opposition to the reactionary survivalists in the "American Separation of Labor" (as they called the AFL). Canadian Communists, in opposition, turned to Leninist understandings of the need to make the big small, and the small subsequently big, by taking the message of revolution into the heart of mainstream unionism, boring the large AFL/TLC unions from within with the theory and practice of Bolshevism. The ascendant wing of the Canadian left now firmly embraced the notion of working within the established large unions, whatever their leaderships' political views. Dual unionism, or the practice of setting up rival, more radical labour organizations, was shunned as sectarian and counter-productive.

As it came to be enunciated, the Leninist orientation to dual unionism was unduly mechanical and tended towards a rather wooden understanding of the big AFL unions as the site in which communists should be active and of the small, dual, dissident unions as, correspondingly, rival bodies to be shunned. This had the ironic consequence of actually enshrining in conservative AFL craft unionism a sanctity that the Leninist perspective on dual unionism had never intended. The purpose of the Leninist strategy had not been to crown the leaders of the AFL the natural monarchy of the working class, but to dethrone such misleaders and establish a working-class republic.

Dual unionism was understood to be problematic, not because rival unions were set up, but because the masses of workers were not in them. To concentrate communist efforts in setting up such dual unions or in organizing within them when they did exist – thus abandoning the larger mass unions of the working class to business unionist leaders – was seen to be defeatist, a sure-fire way to marginalize communist radicalism, leadership, and ideas. The irony was that the dual unionism dilemma in the early to mid-1920s was more apparent than real. Genuine Leninist strategy dictated working with the workers where the masses of workers were, not endorsing the AFL and repudiating, say, the IWW.

Perhaps the most important North American trade union organizer and working-class theoretician to acknowledge this was James Patrick Cannon, a midwestern socialist whose history spans the prewar Socialist Party of America and the IWW, early leadership in the communist Workers Party, involvement in the famous Minneapolis General Strike of 1934, and leadership of the Trotskyist Socialist Workers Party in the post-1938 years.

Cannon, who knew well the importance of small unionism's militancy from his days as a Wobbly organizer, addressed the issue of trade union principles and practices within the Communist Party in the 1920s. Unlike most commentators on the question he did not paint the issue in stark lines of right and wrong, relegating IWW unionism to the status of a pariah in the workers' movement. He battled the IWW when he felt it committed errors, such as when a Philadelphia Wobbly longshoremen's local loaded arms being sent to crush the Russian Revolution; but he stood firm in his resolve that the ranks of the Wobblies and much of its leadership were committed to class-struggle unionism. Moreover, he understood well that a blunt opposition to any and all involvement in the small unionism of the IWW, and the blanket endorsation of the bigger AFL, was a blind error of abstract theory overriding practical consideration. When Cannon looked at the actual situation of the small IWW and the large AFL in the 1920s he found, not a case of IWW irrelevance and marginality and AFL numerical dominance and centrality, but a more mixed situation that communist activity in the trade unions had to address. He also stressed that the actual conditions of labour organization were such that, in most cases, they did not preclude but rather enhanced the possibilities of unity in the workers' movement.

In the mid-1920s, for instance, the IWW claimed a U.S. membership of thirty-eight thousand. Fully twenty-one thousand of these Wobblies were in the largely migratory sectors of lumber, agriculture, and general construction, and for almost all such memberships, the IWW represented the only trade union organization in the field. Cannon stressed that communist tactics in the trade unions dictated that all working-class activists and militants in these economic areas join the existing IWW unions and work within them. In other areas where larger AFL unions existed, Cannon rejected painting the struggle of large versus small unions as one of "liquidationism." Instead, he laid far more stress on the need to find common ground to unite upon, as in the international labour defence efforts on behalf of victimized and jailed workers and class-struggle prisoners, some of whom, such as Sacco and Vanzetti, were awaiting the death penalty. Even in terms of labour organization, Cannon stressed the need to approach the situation without dogmatism and to conduct open and friendly discussions with an aim of bringing all rank-and-file workers together in one united body.

By the late 1920s communist militants such as Cannon had been silenced by state repression, and the Communist International moved into a period in which it responded to the failures of its increasingly Stalinized international policies of "socialism in one country" with lurches to the left. The call went out to Bolshevize all communist parties and to prepare the working class for revolution. Against the Leninist practice of boring from within mainstream unionism, Stalin's Comintern was calling by 1929 for the formation of separate Red Unionism. In Canada this general movement of the Communist Party into dual unionism had been prefaced by an exit from the TLC and a late-1920s alliance with conservative nationalist railway union leader Aaron Mosher, a move conditioned simultaneously by the drift of Stalinist policy and the increasingly overt anti-communism and fetishization of jurisdictional property rights of the AFL/TLC labour bureaucracy. The result was a short-lived marriage of reactionaries and revolutionaries in the All-Canadian Congress of Labour. But the more forceful communist embrace of dual unionism manifested itself in the establishment of the Workers Unity League (WUL), which represented possibly forty thousand Canadian workers between 1930 and 1935 and challenged the increasingly ossified TLC. This so-called centre of Red Unionism had some strengths among the unemployed, garment workers, and miners, and there is no question that it led a large percentage of the strikes in the relatively quiescent early years of the Great Depression.

But it also marginalized communist militants, cutting them off from the masses of workers involved in the mainstream unions. As Stalinism lurched to the right in 1935 with its wholesale embrace of the popular front, the Workers Unity League was dismantled and communist cadre in the unions were sent back to the Trades and Labour Congress. Fortunately, new mobilizations were in the making, and many ex-WUL organizers ended up leading the struggle for mass-production unionism in the bodies of the emerging Congress of Industrial Organization (CIO), which quickly established themselves as a dynamic rival to the older craft unions of the TLC.

The explosion of class mobilization and militancy associated with World War II and the immediate postwar years, culminating in the arrival of industrial unionism in the auto, steel, rubber, and electrical sectors, injected new rivalries into the trade union movement as the newly established CIO organizations and the old-line AFL bodies battled for the allegiance of workers. Again, much of this internecine struggle was beside the point, for in most cases the craft union sense of jurisdictional property violations neglected to address the blunt reality that AFL unions had seldom ventured into areas where the CIO made its greatest leaps forward.

This period of the mid-1940s also saw capital, labour, and the state seal a postwar settlement in which collective bargaining rights and union recognition were finally legitimized in specific labour codes and a regime of industrial legality. This is correctly seen as a historic victory for the workers' movement, won through class struggle and resistance. But the victory was also sealed by trade unionism's accommodation to an intense anti-communism, and indeed, the recognition of labour's legal right to organize and bargain collectively was twinned to the incorporation of management rights' clauses in contracts binding workers to stable productive relations as well as to the trade union movement's generalized struggle against communism. Specific intra-union battles – such as the United Steelworkers of America versus the Mine, Mill and Smelter Workers Union – predate this moment of class struggle and compromise, but they took on added meaning in the hothouse of contending directions for the workers' movement.

The vicious assaults on Mine Mill represented a new low in the depths to which segments of the labour movement would sink to consolidate the power and authority of big unionism over small; to establish the legitimacy of mainstream labour ideas and practices, defined by the mid-1940s as social democratic and reformist; and to destroy the potency of alternatives,

A 1943 rally on Lisgar Street in Sudbury of the International Union of Mine Mill and Smelter Workers. The gathering is addressed by International President Reid Robinson.

Mike Solski Collection, Sudbury Public Library

which by then were centrally focused in the communist movement, a politics not without its own problems and historic burdens.

No member or advocate of the workers' movement can look with pride on the history of the ugly red-baiting well known in Sudbury. Jack Scott, then a communist and a Mine Mill activist at the Trail Consolidated Mine and Smelting works, recalls how he was fingered while en route to a Mine Mill convention in San Francisco. Thinking that he had been identified to Customs and Immigration officials by the RCMP, Scott was astounded to learn that his own union president – a right-wing CCFer opposed to the Communist Party and perfectly willing to liquidate the Mine Mill union into the Steelworkers were it not for rank-and-file opposition – had written to the border guards and then played up Scott's refusal of entry with the local newspaper, the Trail *Times*. Scott was never again allowed entry to the United States.[1]

Of course, Mine Mill was not without its own flaws. On the west coast, its problems often seemed wrapped up in the authoritarian arrogance of the union's major figure, Harvey Murphy, a bombastic blend of talent and chutzpa. When Murphy appeared drunk before a 1948 Victoria gathering of labour leaders and engaged in a metaphorical attack on class collaboration in which reference was made to kissing the ass of the boss (his barbs directed at the United Steelworkers leaders present), he gave dissident unionism's enemies plenty of ammunition to fire at the International Woodworkers of America and Mine Mill.[2] Both bodies sustained severe attack and considerable difficulty. Like so many other so-called communist-led unions, they were hounded from the house of labour, forced into smaller and smaller corners, or pressured to recant if they wanted to rejoin the big picture of mainstream unionism. Murphy himself helped to orchestrate the liquidationist merger of Mine Mill and the Steelworkers in 1967.

The mantle of small unionism would live on in Sudbury through Mine Mill Local 598, just as it would resurface in a series of breakaway union movements in northern British Columbia and the Yukon in the 1960s and 1970s, when Kitimat workers formed the Canadian Aluminum Smelter and Allied Workers Union and Trail workers experimented with alternatives to the Steelworkers in the Canadian Workers Union. British Columbia was also a pioneer in the attempt to get feminist unionism off the ground with the organization of bank workers in the Service, Office, and Retail Workers Union of Canada. By the last quarter of the twentieth century alternative unionism tended to be concentrated in the nationalist rival of the Canadian Labour Congress, the Confederation of Canadian Unions (CCU). Doubling its membership in the early 1970s, the CCU drew on old strengths such as the mine and metal workers of the Mine Mill constituency, garment workers organized earlier by Kent Rowley and Madeleine Parent, and breakaway movements in the pulp and paper sector.

The hard, differentiated edge of national unionism as alternative unionism was perhaps softened and blunted somewhat in the 1980s, as Bob White and Jack Munro led their respective Canadian automobile and woodworking memberships out of the internationals and into autonomous Canadian sections. It was in Quebec that the national question remained on the agenda as a basis of alternative unions. There Catholic confessional unions underwent a radical secularization in the 1960s resulting in the birth of the Confederation of National Trade Unions (CNTU), the most socially conscious and wide-ranging attempt to wed trade unionism and the project of social transformation in contemporary Canada.

Countless other examples of small and dissident unionism could be marshalled, including forms far from compatible with progressive and left-leaning orientations. What is apparent is that small unionism and big unionism, alternative unionism and mainstream unionism, are related phenomena. Neither has existed historically in a vacuum; neither can really be divorced from the other. The Industrial Workers of the World would have been inconceivable without the American Federation of Labor; Mine Mill, with its roots in the Western Federation of Miners, would have been an unlikely historical actor without the stage set first by the AFL and then later by the CIO. Big unionism, which, surely, we all want, has unfortunately chastised, castigated, and challenged small unionism as the twentieth-century workers' movement has grown more bureaucratized. Big unionism has become more structured with legalistic notions of jurisdictions, such as property-rights enclosing dues-paying memberships.

Big unionism has raided and robbed small unionism of its ranks as well as some of its ideas, but it has in the process increasingly cleansed those ideas of their dissident character. Thus, the historic divide between big and small unionism around the issue of the craft-versus-industrial form of organizing, a telling demarcation of radicalism in earlier epochs, is now virtually irrelevant. Throughout this history workers have gained, as unionism has inched forward; but they have often lost, as chances to advance the cause of labour have been bartered for this jurisdictional piece of organizational pie or that privileged relation to contractual or governmental authority. Without small unionism and its dissident challenge to push the workers' movement in the direction of larger needs and wants, labour's history would be more mundane and less heroic.

But history moves, the stakes change, and the meaning of big and small is constantly in motion towards something different. What are the issues at stake in the big versus small, mainstream versus dissident, themes in the labour movement today?

Put bluntly, they are, for what remains of the left, the same as they have always been, but the context is different. Today it must be recognized that the question of dual unionism is, as it always has been, not a question of bureaucratic property rights, of jurisdictional control, but of what is best for the working class and what will advance the increasingly threatened interests of workers themselves. This means, in general, that big unions are better than small, for large unions are what are most emphatically required to resist ascendant employers and a rapacious state anxious to lay the contemporary fiscal crisis of governing authority at the feet of greedy and irresponsible unions. Moreover, the barriers to entry into big unions are somewhat lessened by the changed status of small unionism's presence in the Canadian workers movement. For the most part small unionism has adapted to big unionism's mainstream character, and there has been a noticeable decline in the ideals, militancy, and alternative essence of much of small unionism.

There are, to be sure, those who will make much ado about nothing. Evidence of this can be found in the curiously fragmented structure of teachers' unions in Ontario, where the existence of five separate unions weakens teachers' capacities to resist boards of education that are routinizing and debasing standards of education in a classic quest to control the workplace and cut costs. In the midst of repeated assaults on teachers and their unions, labour organization in the school system has been kept small by divisions based on religion, grade classification, and, above all, gender: male and female teachers belong to separate organizations, which are currently embroiled in court cases that aim to keep this division paramount. Millions of dollars have been spent, and will continue to be spent, to maintain a division once decreed by the state but with little contemporary meaning, aside from its importance to an entrenched layer of male and female trade union professionals. For all the hue and cry that women need their own organizations, both male and female teachers have essentially the same positions on basic feminist issues, and the elementary call for one big union representing all teachers, with a leadership executive proportional to the sexual composition of the rank and file, would hardly lead to a situation of women's needs being slighted, given the current predominance of female teachers and the experience of their established leadership. But unionism at the current moment is too much about property rights, something that small unionism, in its history, has always shunned.

If the current agenda for the working class demands big unionism, it also demands a revival of the concerns of small, alternative unionism. Big unionism will only grow small, in the worst sense of the word, if it continues to ossify and collapse inward in a Gompers-like program of making more noise about less and less. Small unionism has never been able to sustain such a limited agenda, precisely because its claim on the hearts and minds of the working class was premised on large understandings of what small unionism could become. The dream of what might be, which has historically animated the small alternative unions, which sustained the mobilizations of "one big unionism" from the Knights of Labor to the CNTU, was rooted in working-class solidarity – views that "an injury to one is an injury to all" and "in unity there is strength."

There was a time when the slogan "Picket lines mean 'don't cross'" had a power, rather than being an empty rhetorical sloganeering applicable only to those directly out on strike. Big unionism, if it is to be something more than a mere expression of quantities, needs to look back at the history of small, alternative unionism, the better to project into the future a workers' movement that will reclaim ground that was once won by unionism but that over the course of recent decades has been sacrificed and lost.

Chapter 6
Le local 902 du Mine Mill: Les dix premières années (1949–1959) du syndicat des travailleurs de la ville et du district de Sudbury

Donald Dennie

The Sudbury and District General Workers' Union, Mine Mill Local 902

Although the main concern of this chapter is with the period from 1949 to 1959, a brief overview situates the establishment of Local 902 in the work world and the labour movement of Sudbury between 1900 and 1945. Local 902, called the Sudbury and District General Workers' Union, was established in October 1949 with two objectives: to organize the workers in the city's secondary industry and services, and to enable Mine Mill Local 598 to protect itself against raiding by the Steelworkers and the Canadian Labour Congress.

After briefly describing Local 902's internal structure, Donald Dennie focuses on the campaigns to organize workers and on collective agreement negotiations. Local 902 began by organizing cab drivers and hotel employees, and only a year after its foundation it had one thousand members. At its peak in 1955 its membership numbered two thousand workers from fifty-five establishments – including grocery stores, clothing stores, building supplies stores, hotels, cleaners, and restaurants – and the local negotiated collective agreements with these businesses each year. While the collective agreements varied from one establishment to another, their objective was the improvement of the employees' working conditions and salaries. Dennie details and analyses the tactics used by some employers to prevent employees from joining Local 902 and discusses the union's response.

The chapter also looks at Mine Mill's position in the 1950s with regard to French-Canadians – an important issue for Local 902, given that the majority of its members were French-speaking.

L'histoire du syndicat Mine Mill à Sudbury est surtout identifiée au local 598, bien qu'il ait existé une autre cellule du Mine Mill ayant exercé une certaine influence sur cette ville. Il s'agit du local 902, le Sudbury and District General Workers' Union, dont les activités se sont étendues entre 1949 et 1967.[1]

Ce texte se limite aux dix premières années de l'histoire du local 902, soit de 1949 à 1959, et ce, pour deux raisons. D'une part, ce sont les meilleures années du local et d'autre part, le temps ne nous a pas permis de reconstituer cette histoire jusqu'à 1967 lorsque le 902 du Mine Mill deviendra le Retail, Wholesale and Department Store Union suite à la fusion d'une partie du Mine Mill aux Métallos. On cherche surtout à examiner les antécédents de ce local, sa structure et ses efforts d'organisation des travailleurs[2] dans les principaux établissements de service de la ville de Sudbury.

Les antécédents

Pour comprendre un peu cette histoire, il faut se souvenir que la ville de Sudbury, aujourd'hui reconnue comme une ville minière et fortement syndiquée, fut aussi une ville de services (magasins, hôtels, restaurants, quelques banques) et de transport (Canadien Pacifique, Canadien National). En général, ces établissements embauchaient un nombre limité de travailleurs. Ainsi en 1941, 75 pour cent des établissements de la ville embauchaient moins de cinq travailleurs; et 12 pour cent en embauchaient de 5 à 9; c'est donc dire que près de 90 pour cent des établissements employaient chacun moins de 10 travailleurs.

Cette structure de la main-d'oeuvre locale explique, en partie, le fait que les travailleurs de ces établissements n'étaient pas syndiqués. De plus, les syndicats de l'époque, axés en grande partie sur l'organisation d'ouvriers de métiers, ne portaient pas une grande attention à l'organisation des travailleurs au sein des établissements de services. C'est pourquoi, de 1911 à 1941, on retrouve à Sudbury un très petit nombre de syndicats; en effet, selon la *Gazette du Travail* on y comptait en moyenne au cours de ces 30 années moins de 10 syndicats locaux, la plupart étant des organisations d'ouvriers de métiers ou du transport. Le nombre de syndiqués a fluctué pendant cette période de 15 à 800. En somme, Sudbury n'était pas, avant la Deuxième Guerre mondiale, une ville syndicale à cause du type de travailleurs, du type et de la taille des établissements et aussi à cause de l'esprit anti-syndical qui animait la plupart des hommes d'affaires de la ville.

L'arrivée du Mine Mill et l'organisation réussie des mineurs de l'Inco et de la Falconbridge allaient toutefois changer cette situation. Le local 598 du

Mine Mill, institué pour organiser les mineurs de l'Inco et de la Falconbridge,[3] avait décidé en 1953 de lancer une campagne "to organize all of the workers who are eligible to join a union."[4] Cette campagne avait débuté lorsque le local 598 décida de parrainer le Sudbury Workers Organizing Committee dans le but d'organiser les travailleurs non reliés à l'industrie du nickel au sein de syndicats locaux affiliés au Congrès canadien de travail (CCT). Des organisateurs bénévoles du Mine Mill avaient donc réussi à encourager des centaines de travailleurs à se syndiquer. Par exemple, en 1945, le Mine Mill avait réussi à organiser les employés du CIL et du Sudbury Construction and Machinery.[5] En décembre 1944, le local n° 3 du National Union of Building Workers avait été institué pour organiser tous les travailleurs de la construction de Sudbury. Il avait réussi à signer une entente collective avec la compagnie Evans Lumber, l'une des trois grandes entreprises du genre de Sudbury (les deux autres étant la compagnie Laberge et la compagnie Carrington).

Le Mine Mill a aussi réussi à encourager les travailleurs de travaux publics de la ville de Sudbury à se syndiquer en 1944. Cette campagne d'organisation et surtout les négociations avec le Conseil municipal de Sudbury pour une première convention collective ont été très difficiles et étaient animées, de la part des conseillers de la ville, par un esprit anti-syndical qui régnait parmi les employeurs et les édiles municipaux de la ville de Sudbury peu après la réussite du local 598 face à l'Inco et à la Falconbridge.[6] Les travailleurs municipaux, organisés le 4 février 1944 sous la tutelle du Sudbury Civic Employees Union, un local du CCT, durent attendre jusqu'en juin avant que le conseil de ville adopte un règlement municipal (by-law) pour reconnaître le syndicat. La majorité des membres du conseil ne voulaient pas reconnaître un syndicat affilié au CIO, comme l'était le Sudbury Civic Employees Union, par l'intermédiaire du CCT; ils préféraient plutôt un syndicat indépendant.[7] Cette attitude reflétait une position qui semblait commune chez les leaders d'entreprises de Sudbury à cette époque. A compter de 1935, le conseil municipal, le *Sudbury Star* et le Board of Trade de la ville commençaient à être préoccupés par la présence du Mine Mill et du CIO à Sudbury. Le *Star*, surtout, mena une campagne vigoureuse contre eux en 1943, lors des élections provinciale et municipale.[8]

Les négociations entre le syndicat et le conseil furent si difficiles que l'organisateur national du CCT, Ben Levert, écrivit à M. Conroy: "The negotiations with the Municipal Council of Sudbury on behalf of the Civic Workers has been a nightmare and nerve-breaking ordeal. Not only had we to balk the municipal anti-union members but also the controlling spirit of International Nickel was visible at all times."[9] Une convention collective fut signée plus d'un an après la reconnaissance du syndicat.

Ce syndicat des travailleurs municipaux avait aussi été institué pour tenter d'organiser les ouvriers de la construction, les chauffeurs d'autobus et les employés de restaurants; toutefois, un manque d'organisateurs syndicaux rendit cette tâche impossible. Selon Mike Solski, le CCT se montra aussi indifférent à l'égard de ces groupes de travailleurs: "The Congress did little or nothing to service these groups and in time organization drifted to the point where complete disintegration was imminent."

C'est à ce moment, soit en 1946, que le Mine Mill décida d'organiser un syndicat général de travailleurs (Sudbury General Workers Union) sous l'égide du CCT afin surtout d'organiser les employés de buanderies et des autres petits établissements.[10] Pour des raisons qui demeurent inconnues, cette première tentative de mettre sur pied le local échoua. En 1947, on essaya de nouveau. L'organisateur local du CCT, Harvey Ladd, explique bien la raison d'être d'un tel syndicat dans une lettre au secrétaire du CCT.

> We are making this application for a General Workers Union because it seems to be the only solution to the problems which are confronting small units of workers. I have given the situation a great deal of thought and believe that separate charters for small groups cannot serve either the workers or the Congress as invariably they fall apart or lose the social dynamic to keep them alive and functioning. At the present time I have an organizational committee and members in each of the following industries: laundry and dry cleaning, taxi drivers, warehouse men and truck drivers, building trades, lumber and building supplies, store clerks and the beverage rooms.[11]

Le local fut effectivement établi en 1947 sous l'égide du CCT,[12] tout comme en 1946, mais encore une fois, le manque d'intérêt du Congrès ainsi qu'un manque d'organisateurs locaux firent en sorte qu'il ne fut pas très efficace.

Il fallut attendre en 1949 avant qu'une autre tentative pour relancer un syndicat général de travailleurs ne soit faite. Cette fois, le local tomba sous l'égide du Mine Mill et s'appela Sudbury and District General Workers' Union, local 902. Les motifs entourant son établissement sont bien décrits par Solski.

> Late in 1948, with the start of unconcealed raids on Mine Mill, several Steelworkers' staff people, posing as CCL organizers, appeared on the scene. Since servicing of CCL union members in Sudbury was a rarity, the intention to establish a base from which to attack Mine Mill was obvious. Mine Mill solved both problems by providing Sudbury's general workers with a union that would enhance its members' welfare and at the same time

remove the raiders' base ... In October 1949, Mine Mill General Workers Union Local 902 was chartered.[13]

Dans un article du *Local 598 Mine Mill News*,[14] le nouvel organisateur en chef du local 902 et ancien délégué syndical du local 598, Al Langlois, explique que l'établissement du nouveau local résulte d'une demande de nombreux travailleurs non organisés afin que Mine Mill puisse aider les nombreux ouvriers oeuvrant à l'extérieur du secteur minier.

> Although this is not basically our jurisdiction ... the Canadian Congress of Labour has made many futile efforts to do this job and failed miserably thereby leaving the non-mining Sudbury workers without union protection and subsisting on wage levels far below those of the mining industry. The unorganized workers of Sudbury need unions to come to the assistance of any group of workers who request such assistance.[15]

Ainsi, la naissance du local 902 est due à trois facteurs interreliés.

Premièrement, le désir et sans doute la nécessité de se protéger contre le maraudage des Métallos à une époque où ces derniers menaient une campagne anticommuniste[16] au sein du CCT. On se souviendra que le Mine Mill a été exclu du CCT en 1949 pour des activités soi-disant communistes.

Deuxièmement, le désir bien fondé d'améliorer les salaires, les conditions de travail, et le niveau de vie de nombreux travailleurs qui, dans les petites entreprises de Sudbury, gagnaient des salaires peu élevés, surtout relativement à ceux des mineurs de l'Inco et de la Falconbridge. Et la sincérité du Mine Mill à cet égard ne fait pas de doute. Une lettre du Sudbury Civic Employees Union, rédigée par son secrétaire T. Cooney lors d'une grève déclarée par le local 902 dans un restaurant de la ville (Radio Lunch), en fait foi:

> It was felt that your local certainly deserves commendation for answering the need of a class of labour which seems to have been over-looked and neglected over the past years. It is a well-known fact that their wages and working conditions are such that the establishments in which they work are little better than "sweat shops" and want to be kept in such a category by the hard-headed owners backed by so-called civic-minded groups.[17]

Un article, publié dans le *Local 598 Mine Mill News*, résume aussi cette "mission" du local 902. L'article rappelle d'abord à ses lecteurs que la ville de Sudbury comprend deux classes de travailleurs: les mineurs, qui gagnent en moyenne 83$ par semaine, et les ouvriers de service non syndiqués, qui reçoivent moins de 30$ par semaine. Selon l'auteur, les entreprises de service et de commerce réalisent donc des profits énormes à cause des salaires élevés des mineurs.

> Mine Mill Local 902, Sudbury District General Workers Union, is continuing to make every effort to change this situation and alleviate the starvation conditions under which these service workers are forced to live. They are providing organizational possibilities for these workers and have achieved outstanding success in those instances where they have forced bargaining.
>
> No one should underestimate the high degree of organization prevailing among these establishments through the local Chamber of Commerce, the local press, radio and TV outlets. They are living in a profit paradise and they support each other in their determination to maintain and protect that paradise and to keep their employees at the starvation level.
>
> The organized wage earners of the Sudbury district are determined to bring justice and decent living conditions to the underpaid service workers. This is an objective and an aim that has the full support of all decent people. [18]

Troisièmement, après un demi-siècle de domination patronale, certains leaders syndicaux s'étaient fixés comme objectif de transformer Sudbury en une ville syndicale, et d'organiser les travailleurs afin d'améliorer leurs conditions de vie. C'est du moins ce que l'on peut conclure d'une lettre écrite par le secrétaire du Sudbury Civic Employees' Union au secrétaire du CCT en 1944, suite à la signature de la première convention collective à l'Inco. "From now on our membership should expand considerably as it is our hope to make Sudbury a Union City."[19]

La structure du local

La structure du local 902 n'a guère changé au cours des dix premières années. Cette structure était fondée sur les divers groupes constituants, par exemple les groupes d'employés des compagnies de taxis, des hôtels, des magasins. Chaque groupe nommait ou élisait un président ou une présidente ainsi que des délégués syndicaux. A chaque année, habituellement à l'automne, une assemblée générale des membres élisait un comité exécutif composé des postes suivants: président, vice-président, secrétaire-archiviste, secrétaire financier, gardien, conducteur et conseillers. Le local comprenait aussi un organisateur ou un agent d'affaires. Les réunions des membres avaient lieu à toutes les deux semaines à la salle Mine Mill sur la rue Regent.[20]

Le premier président du local 902 a été Gordon Robinson,[21] qui, pour des raisons de santé, a dû céder sa place à l'été de 1950 à Cliff Mathieu. M.

Mathieu, un Canadien-Français qui avait déjà été délégué syndical au sein du local 598 alors qu'il était mineur à Creighton, a été réélu au poste de président à chaque année au cours de la période étudiée. M. Mathieu avait quitté le travail dans les mines pour devenir un employé de l'hôtel Coulson et ensuite de l'hôtel King Edward. Quant au premier organisateur, Al Langlois, il a été remplacé en 1953 par R.A. LaChance, qui avait déjà servi à titre de représentant international du Mine Mill.[22] En général, les vice-président, secrétaire financier et secrétaire-archiviste ont tous été des hommes; seulement quelques femmes ont été élues comme conseillères. Les femmes étaient mieux représentées au sein des comités de négociations des divers groupes.

Le nombre de membres augmenta rapidement de 1949 à 1951, année où il atteignait les mille membres. Cinq ans plus tard, en 1956, le local comptait déjà plus de 2 000 membres, ce qui constitua un sommet pour le syndicat.[23]

L'organisation et les négociations

De 1949 à 1959, les activités du local 902 se sont centrées sur l'organisation des travailleurs et la négociation de conventions collectives avec les employeurs.[24] En général, le local 902 a tenté d'organiser les travailleurs d'entreprises qui comptaient au moins 10 employés.[25]

Ces activités se divisent en deux périodes: une première, qui dure environ de 1949 à 1953, au cours de laquelle le travail de ce groupement de travailleurs est relativement rapide et facile; une deuxième, de 1954 à 1959, qui s'avère plus difficile à cause, d'un côté, de la situation économique et, de l'autre, de la résistance des patrons.

Au cours de sa première année d'existence, le local 902 a organisé les chauffeurs de taxis, les employés de 16 hôtels,[26] de deux buanderies (Cascade et Lavogue), de la compagnie Laberge, et d'une compagnie de fabrication de bière (Sudbury Brewing and Malting, producteur de la fameuse bière Silver Foam). Après un an, il comptait déjà 1 000 membres. À la fin de 1950, le local avait réussi à signer vingt-deux (22) conventions collectives et à déclencher deux grèves, dont l'une s'est soldée par une victoire (les compagnies de taxis) et l'autre par une défaite (les restaurants Radio Lunch et Maple Leaf Café). L'organisation des chauffeurs de taxis (Empire, Union et Queen's), au début de 1950, s'est concrétisée à la suite d'une grève de 11 jours déclenchée dans le but d'obliger les propriétaires à reconnaître le local 902 et à la suite du congédiement de cinq chauffeurs. Si cette première grève s'est soldée par une victoire, la deuxième a constitué un échec pour le local 902. Lancée contre les restaurants Radio Lunch et Maple Leaf, cette grève, qui a duré plusieurs semaines, a dû être annulée lorsque la Commission des relations du travail de l'Ontario a jugé que le local 902 n'avait pas le droit de commencer une telle grève parce qu'il n'était pas encore accrédité comme agent négociateur.[27]

L'organisation des 150 employés d'hôtels a été assez rapide en partie parce que ces employés étaient déjà organisés dans un local de la CCT et avaient transféré leur allégeance au Mine Mill. C'est du moins la conclusion que l'on tire de la lettre suivante de Cliff Mathieu à la propriétaire de l'hôtel Ramsay, Jeanne Pilon:

> Please be advised that the Sudbury and District General Workers Union Local 902 wish to enter into negotiations with the Hotel Ramsay with a view to negotiate a collective bargaining agreement.
>
> This group at a special membership meeting voted on a secret ballot to disaffiliate from the Sudbury General Workers Union, CCL and affiliate themselves with the S.D. G.W.U. of the I.U.M.M. & S.W.
>
> Kindly advise if you wish to negotiate individually or as a group under the auspices of the Sudbury Hotelmen's Association.[28]

Au cours de l'automne 1950, le local 902 a aussi réussi dans quelques autres établissements à organiser les employés et à négocier des conventions collectives. Ces établissements sont le garage Gardner Motors, le restaurant Kuluttajat (Consumers Cooperative), et le Sudbury Brewing and Malting Company. Dans le cas de cette dernière convention collective, le local 902 a obtenu que les étiquettes des bouteilles de bière Silver Foam contiennent les mots "Union Made" (Fabrication syndicale) et que les bouteilles et les caisses portent le sceau du Mine Mill.

Bien que ces conventions collectives différaient selon les établissements, le Mine Mill tentait toutefois de négocier des ententes standards qui comprenaient des articles au sujet de la reconnaissance du syndicat comme seul agent négociateur, de la reconnaissance des droits du patronat de gérer son entreprise et de diriger sa main-d'oeuvre selon les clauses de l'entente, du principe de la déduction des cotisations syndicales par la compagnie, de la garantie syndicale de ne pas interrompre le travail, des procédures de griefs, de la reconnaissance de l'ancienneté, des heures de travail, de la grille salariale, des vacances et des heures supplémentaires, parfois d'un régime d'assurance (paiements en cas de maladie), de la fourniture de vêtements de travail. En outre, la plupart des conventions collectives signées au cours de cette période étaient d'une durée d'un an.[29] En général, le local 902 a réussi à obtenir des augmentations salariales, de meilleures conditions de travail (périodes de repos, vacances), et surtout le droit de recourir à des procédures de griefs.

Le bilan positif de cette première année du local 902 résulte d'une campagne d'organisation bien menée par les agents du local et appuyée par les officiers du local 598. Dans plusieurs cas, le local 902 a réussi à remplacer des cellules syndicales autrefois affiliées au CCT en promettant aux travailleurs un effort plus concerté pour mieux les desservir et les représenter auprès des patrons des établissements.

De 1951 à 1953, les efforts d'organisation et de négociation du local 902 sont dans l'ensemble couronnés de succès. En plus de renégocier les conventions collectives déjà signées, il a réussi à organiser ou à recruter dans ses rangs les travailleurs et les travailleuses des établissements suivants: les laiteries Standard et Palm, Smith & Travers (entreprise de forage qui effectuait des travaux pour l'Inco), Fraser-Brace (compagnie de construction affiliée à l'Inco), les grossistes National Grocers, Swift et Gamble Robinson, les magasins Dominion, Loblaws et Silverman's, Dominion Tar & Chemical (une filiale de Canada Creosoting), Noront Steel, le restaurant Murray's, les boulangeries Cecutti's, Weston's et Canada Bread, Evans' Lumber, Delongchamp Cartage, et Ed Brown Concrete Products.

Ces efforts d'organisations et d'accréditation n'ont certes pas tous été faciles et même certains n'ont pas réussi comme à l'entreprise Carrington Lumber & Builders, où les employés ont refusé de s'affilier au Mine Mill en 1952.[30] Certaines négociations n'ont abouti qu'à la suite de commissions de conciliation pour régler des différends qui devenaient de plus en plus fréquents (entre le local 902 et Gamble Robinson,[31] l'Association des propriétaires d'hôtels,[32] le restaurant Murray's,[33] National Grocers,[34] et Standard Dairy[35]). Ces différends portaient surtout sur les salaires mais aussi sur la sécurité syndicale. Le local 902 demandait, au cours des négociations, que toute personne employée par un établissement soit obligée de devenir membre du syndicat.[36] En général, les patrons refusaient, mais le rapport de la commission de conciliation recommandait la formule Rand.

À compter de l'automne 1953 mais surtout de l'hiver 1954, les efforts d'organisation et surtout les négociations entre le local 902 et divers établissements devinrent plus difficiles. Dans le *Mine Mill News* du mois de mars 1954, on reconnaît que de plus en plus les négociations aboutissent à des impasses. Un rapport soumis par le local 902 à la Conférence du District 8 du Mine Mill tenue à Sudbury le 15 mai 1954 en fait également foi: "Local 902 has 50 groups under contract and negotiations are in progress for 13 of them. Local 902 is faced with wage cuts but will not accept. Employers are forcing conciliation (four boards have been set up)."[37]

Negociations difficiles

Ces difficiles pourparlers surviennent à une période où le chômage est à la hausse dans la région de Sudbury et où les chômeurs se présentent devant les conseils municipaux de la région pour demander de l'aide financière, du travail et de la nourriture.[38] Selon le *Mine Mill News*, environ 100 membres de l'Association des chômeurs de la ville et du district de Sudbury (Sudbury and District Unemployed Association) se sont présentés aux salles du conseil de Sudbury et de la municipalité de McKim. Ils représentaient plus de 4 600 personnes sans emploi dans la ville.

C'est dans ce contexte de chômage croissant et de négociations difficiles avec certains établissements que les positions patronales envers le local 902 se durcissent. Les négociations traînent en longueur car les patrons refusent d'accorder des augmentations salariales ou de meilleures conditions de travail. Certaines compagnies disent même préférer une grève dans l'espoir que les travailleurs en auront assez de marcher dans la rue et se plieront aux offres patronales.[39] D'autres propriétaires tentent d'intimider leurs employés après avoir appris que le local 902 a fait une demande d'accréditation pour les représenter. En effet, entre 1954 et 1957, des tentatives d'organisation des employés de Loblaws et de Cochrane-Dunlop, des grèves plus fréquentes, et des campagnes de recrutement non réussies illustrent bien que le travail du local 902 devient de plus en plus difficile.

Aux magasins Loblaws et Cochrane-Dunlop, les patrons ont mené des campagnes bien orchestrées pour empêcher que le local 902 ne devienne l'agent négociateur de leurs employés, des campagnes qui consistaient à organiser les employés au sein de syndicats-maison.

À l'entreprise Loblaws, la demande d'accréditation du local 902 pour représenter les employés et les employées des deux magasins de cette chaîne, en décembre 1953, avait été contrée par un syndicat-maison appelé le "Workers' Council" qui disait représenter tous les employés de ces magasins à travers l'Ontario. La Commission des relations du travail de l'Ontario dut organiser un vote auprès des employés des Loblaws de Sudbury, le 16 janvier 1954. Ce scrutin fut remporté par le local 902 car 85 employés se prononcèrent en faveur de ce dernier, tandis que 33 se dirent en faveur du Workers' Council.[40]

Lorsque vint le temps de négocier une deuxième entente, certains employés, organisés sous la bannière du Sudbury and District Loblaws Workers' Union, ont tenté d'intervenir contre le local 902, mais sans succès. Une deuxième tentative de ce genre par l'ancien Workers' Council fut aussi vaine. En effet, en juillet 1955, le Workers' Council demanda l'accréditation pour représenter les employés et les employées des magasins de Sudbury. La Commission des relations du travail convoqua une réunion pour le 27 septembre afin d'entendre la soumission du Workers' Council mais les procureurs de ce dernier retirèrent la demande le 22 septembre.[41]

Malgré ces débuts difficiles au magasin Loblaws, les conventions collectives adoptées au cours des années 1950 entre le local 902 et Loblaws réussirent à améliorer les salaires et les conditions de travail des employés de façon considérable. Par exemple, à la suite du premier contrat, le salaire de base est passé de 65 cents à 80 cents par heure, l'ancienneté est reconnue, les vacances sont améliorées et la formule Rand est mise en vigueur.

Un ancien président du groupe de Loblaws, Maurice Boissonneault, a même reconnu que ces conventions collectives avaient grandement amélioré les conditions de travail et les salaires des employées et des employés de Loblaws et de Dominion dans les années 1950. Le local 902 a également réussi à améliorer sensiblement le plan médical et d'hospitalisation, les congés statutaires et surtout les heures de travail.[42] En effet, au cours des années 1950, le local 902 a fait réduire le nombre d'heures de travail dans la plupart des établissements, celui-ci passant d'environ 48 à 40 heures et ce, tout en augmentant les grilles salariales.

Les efforts d'organisation à Cochrane-Dunlop furent tout aussi difficiles qu'à l'entreprise Loblaws. En novembre 1954, les organisateurs du local 902 commencèrent leur campagne afin d'être reconnu comme unité d'accréditation. Selon le *Mine Mill News*, la compagnie amorça rapidement une campagne d'intimidation contre certains employés et organisa un syndicat-maison (Sudbury and District Hardware Employees Union) pour contrer les efforts du local 902.[43] Selon le *Mine Mill News*:

> À cause de cela, il a fallu attendre plusieurs mois avant d'obtenir la certification et la Commission Ouvrière de l'Ontario a dû faire trois enquêtes.
>
> Au cours de cette période, la compagnie a conduit une des pires campagnes de discrimination et de persécution jamais vues à Sudbury afin d'empêcher les employés d'obtenir la protection d'une véritable Union.
>
> Après les deux premières enquêtes, la Commission Ouvrière a ordonné un vote entre le local 902 et l'autre groupe qui était reconnu comme une Union de compagnie. Le vote a été gagné par le local 902 malgré la pression faite par la compagnie sur les employés pour les intimider et les tromper.[44]
>
> Mais la compagnie n'était pas encore satisfaite. Elle a protesté auprès de la Commission et une autre enquête a eu lieu. A l'audience, les représentants de la compagnie n'ont pas pu prouver leurs accusations contre le local 902 et il y a quelques jours le local 902 a été certifié comme agent négociateur.[45]

La première convention collective de Cochrane-Dunlop a été signée à l'automne 1955 suite au rapport d'une commission de conciliation et en 1957, les deux parties réussirent à s'entendre sur une convention collective d'une durée de deux ans.

A l'été 1955, on voit apparaître une nouvelle stratégie de la part du patronat pour désaccréditer le local 902. Selon le *Mine Mill News*, la compagnie Laberge avait été achetée par de nouveaux propriétaires en 1954, ce qui avait obligé le local 902 à être accrédité de nouveau. Les nouveaux propriétaires ont fait traîner les négociations et ensuite, selon le syndicat, ont refusé d'accepter et de mettre en vigueur les recommandations d'une commission de conciliation. Ces tactiques ont mené à un vote de grève. Mais peu de temps avant son déclenchement, les deux parties sont arrivées à une entente.[46]

Ce changement de propriétaire de la compagnie Laberge allait présager une stratégie patronale qui deviendra plus commune au cours des années 60 et 70: plusieurs établissements allaient changer de nom ou être vendues, provoquant la désaccréditation du syndicat.

Des grèves

En 1954, six employées du magasin Hollywood Shoppe, qui gagnaient en moyenne de 21$ à 27$ par semaine, déclenchèrent une grève à la fin du mois de juin pour protester contre la lenteur des négociations en vue de l'obtention d'une convention collective. Au cours de l'été, les dames auxiliaires du Mine Mill mirent sur pied des mesures de soutien financier pour ces grévistes. La grève se poursuivit à l'automne. (La documentation disponible est silencieuse quant au résultat de ce conflit.)

Une grève lancée en 1956 par une trentaine d'employées du magasin Metropolitan s'avéra longue et difficile. Ces employées déclenchèrent la grève, en septembre, pour protester contre le refus du magasin d'accepter les recommandations d'une commission de conciliation, surtout celle d'une augmentation de 10$ par semaine. Le *Mine Mill News* a rapporté ainsi une partie du rapport de cette commission:

> Selon le syndicat, la compagnie H.L. Green de New York, dont le magasin Metropolitan est une succursale, a refusé d'accorder une augmentation de plus de $3 par semaine. Plusieurs tentatives de négociations ont été en vain. Finalement, après 220 jours de grève, le magasin a fermé ses portes le 24 avril 1957.[47]

Malgré ces négociations difficiles et ces revirements, le local 902 a poursuivi son travail d'organisation des travailleurs des établissements de services dans la ville de Sudbury. Il a ainsi organisé les travailleurs du grossiste J.A. Lapalme, les employés de Hobbs Glass et du magasin A. Earle Hodge de Falconbridge, les employés municipaux de Coniston et de Neelon Garson, ainsi que les employés des hôtels qui s'ajoutaient à l'Association des hôteliers de Sudbury. Il a aussi lancé une campagne d'organisation des employés et des employées de Kresge's, de Woolworth's, de Sudbury Steam et du magasin A & P. Toutefois, ces campagnes d'organisation ne semblent pas avoir réussi.

Discrimination

L'organisation des employés préposés à l'entretien au Sudbury High School et au Sudbury Technical School révèle bien la discrimination contre les femmes à cette époque et son enchâssement dans la loi provinciale. Les employés masculins avaient été regroupés par le local 902, et ce dernier avait négocié, en août, une convention collective avec le conseil scolaire qui accordait aux employés une augmentation salariale de 40 cents l'heure. Or, lorsque le local 902 tenta d'organiser les femmes préposées à l'entretien de ces mêmes écoles, le conseil scolaire utilisa la section 78 de la Loi des relations ouvrières de l'Ontario pour refuser que ces employées soient syndiquées. Selon le *Mine Mill News*,

> Cette décision donne lieu à une étrange situation, vu que les hommes préposés à l'entretien de ces deux écoles sont membres du local 902 et que les femmes ne peuvent pas bénéficier du même privilège. Les contradictions contenues dans la Loi ouvrière de l'Ontario deviennent très évidentes quand elles permettent d'empêcher un petit groupe de personnes employées à l'entretien des classes de s'organiser pour leur protection.[48]

Les activités d'organisation du local 902 semblent ralentir après 1956. En effet, ce syndicat semble avoir atteint son apogée tant au niveau de son efficacité que de sa membriété. Le local comptait alors quelque 2 000 membres répartis dans plus de 50 entreprises diverses. Il avait organisé la plupart des entreprises de services avec un nombre considérable d'employés. C'était l'un des syndicats les plus influents de Sudbury, mis à part le local 598. Ses liens avec ce dernier et le fait qu'il encourageait ses membres et ceux du local 598 à ne magasiner que dans les établissements syndiqués de la ville lui ont donné un pouvoir assez considérable.

Après 1956, le local 902 ne réussit qu'à organiser une poignée d'établissements, comme Scales and Roberts, Champion Fuels, les employés de l'arène de Sudbury. Le ralentissement au niveau de l'organisation de nouveaux groupes est sans aucun doute le résultat du succès et de la complexité du local 902. Car le travail et l'énergie nécessaires pour négocier et administrer un grand nombre de conventions collectives dans des établissements aussi divers laissaient de moins en moins de temps pour l'organisation de nouveaux groupes d'employés.

En 1959, soit dix ans après sa naissance, le local 902 comptait 56 groupes répartis dans une quinzaine de différents types d'industries (voir le tableau 6.1).

En 1959, en raison du travail accru et de la complexité des négociations et de la gestion des différentes conventions collectives, le local 902 embauche un organisateur, William Hall, pour aider l'agent d'affaires, M. LaChance. Un autre changement marquant, cette année-là, c'est le déménagement des locaux du Mine Mill, rue Regent, à de nouveaux bureaux au 76 sur la rue Douglas. Les membres du local avaient approuvé l'achat de cesnouveaux locaux lors d'un référendum. Selon le président Mathieu, il s'agissait là d'un tournant historique pour le local 902 car il lui donnait une demeure permanente qui lui permettrait d'accroître ses services à ses membres.[49] Mais pour l'ancien président du local 598, Mike Solski, ce déménagement constituait une stratégie de la part de la nouvelle administration Gillis pour commencer à défaire les rangs du Mine Mill à Sudbury et ainsi de confirmer les craintes qui avaient mené à la création du local 902 en 1949.[50]

Les femmes et les francophones

Le Mine Mill en général et le local 902 en particulier affichaient un souci assez grand pour l'égalité des genres et des groupes ethniques. Bien que la structure générale du local 902 ait été dominée par des hommes et ce, à tous les niveaux (comité exécutif, délégués syndicaux, responsables de groupes), le local 902 a tout de même procuré à plusieurs femmes une expérience de syndicalisation et, en plusieurs occasions, celle d'être membre de comités de négociations. Selon certains documents, il est même possible de conclure que le local 902 avait aussi le souci d'augmenter les salaires des femmes à un rythme plus accéléré que ceux des hommes.

Le local 902 a aussi procuré à plusieurs francophones l'occasion d'être actifs au sein de ce syndicat: cela était d'ailleurs tout à fait naturel puisque environ 60 pour cent de ses membres étaient de langue française. Plusieurs Canadiens-Français, dont le président Cliff Mathieu, ont servi au sein du comité exécutif, comme délégués syndicaux et comme responsables de groupes. En principe, le Mine Mill était ouvert à la présence des Canadiens-Français en son sein. Deux exemples servent de preuve.

Tableau 6.1
Les entreprises syndiquées par le local 902, 1959

Type d'entreprises	Nom des entreprises
A) Boulangeries	Canada Bread Cecutti's Bakery Weston's Bakeries
B) Buanderies	Cascade Laundry
C) Fonction publique municipale	Coniston Civic Workers Neelon Garson Employees Sudbury High School
D) Grossistes	Canada Packers Gamble Robinson J.A. Lapalme & Sons National Grocers Swift Canadian
E) Hôtels	Belton Belvedere Caswell Coulson Frontenac Frood International King Edward Laurentian Ledo Local 598 (Beverage Room) National New Ontario Nickel City Nickel Range Paris Park Prospect Queens Ramsay

Type d'entreprises	Nom des entreprises
F) Imprimeries	Vapaus Publishing
G) Industries	Canada Creosoting (Dominion Tar) Neelon Steel Noront Steel Construction Rock Iron Plant Sudbury Brewing and Malting
H) Laiteries	Palm Dairies Standard Dairy
I) Magasins d'alimentation	Dominion Stores Loblaws Groceterias
J) Magasins – vente de détail	A. Silverman's Hobbs Glass A. Earle Hodge George Taylor Hardware Cochrane-Dunlop Hardware
K) Magasins – matériaux de construction	Evans Lumber Laberge Lumber
L) Taxis	New Empire Cab Queen's Taxi Union Cab
M) Transport	Delongchamp Cartage Sudbury Cartage
N) Autres	Capitol Theatre Champion Fuels

Dès 1950, soit peu de temps après la parution du *Mine Mill News*, ce journal a commencé à publier de façon régulière une section de langue française qui était rédigée dans un français la plupart du temps impeccable. Ce geste d'ouverture a été bien expliqué par le président du local 598, M. Mike Solski.

> L'exécutif sait qu'un grand nombre des membres de notre union sont Canadiens français. Il sait également que le Canada est un pays bilingue où le français et l'anglais sont les deux langues officielles reconnues.
>
> Comme je le disais, le Canada est officiellement un pays bilingue où le français et l'anglais jouissent de droits égaux. Les traditions, la langue et la culture canadiennes-françaises ont des racines très profondes dans l'histoire du pays. Le français est reconnu non seulement comme langue parlée, mais aussi comme langue qui perpétue au Canada une grande littérature et une grande culture.
>
> Il est donc juste que notre union reconnaisse au français la place qui lui est due.[51]

Cinq ans plus tard, en 1955, ce même journal publie un éditorial intitulé "Mine Mill et les Canadiens-Français" qui reprend essentiellement les propos de Mike Solski. Cet éditorial reconnaît encore une fois la place officielle du français au Canada et parle même des caractéristiques distinctes des Canadiens-Français au sein du pays, des caractéristiques qu'il faut respecter, dit-il.

> Ce qui est encore plus significatif, c'est la participation de nos confrères canadiens-français à la vie de Mine Mill, la réalisation de ses buts et la défense de ses principes et de son programme. Cette participation est devenue de plus en plus importante et significative au cours des dernières années et continuera de se développer à mesure que Mine Mill étendra son organisation.[52]

Conclusion

L'histoire du local 902, de 1949 à 1959, ici trop brièvement décrite, est l'histoire d'un petit syndicat né pour des raisons diverses qui a organisé des groupes de travailleurs souvent laissés pour compte et qui a cherché et réussi à améliorer leurs conditions de travail et de vie dans une communauté rendue prospère par l'industrie du nickel. Parfois il a réussi grâce à la compréhension de certains patrons, mais la plupart du temps malgré la résistance souvent farouche de plusieurs propriétaires.

Le local 902 est toujours demeuré relativement petit en termes d'effectifs (2 000 au maximum), mais il a été important parce qu'il réunissait plusieurs groupes de travailleurs fort différents. Ce type de regroupement a en revanche rendu la tâche d'organisation et d'administration des conventions collectives fort complexe.

Il a subi, lui aussi, les contrecoups du conflit amer entre le Mine Mill et les Métallos et, déjà en 1959, son existence était remise en cause. Mais durant ses dix premières années, il aura rendu des services énormes et aura contribué en partie au rêve de certains syndicalistes de faire de Sudbury une ville syndicale.

Chapter 7
Mergers, Organizing, and Collective Identity: The CAW at the Crossroads[1]

Charlotte Yates

For workers, the past fifteen years have been hard times. Wages have remained stagnant or even dropped as employers have strived to reduce labour costs. In the 1990s, plants and offices are closed or rationalized, increasing numbers of people are losing their jobs, and those left on the job are expected to work harder and longer. Youths face unemployment levels of up to 25 percent, but laid-off middle-aged workers also face a precarious future as age discrimination, inadequate retraining programs, and underfunded or misused pension funds leave them vulnerable and unable to re-enter the active labour force.

Many of these workers look to unions for a way through these times of economic instability and restructuring, while labour organizations are themselves under attack from market forces, managements, and governments. It is said that unions have outlived their usefulness. High levels of unemployment combined with legislative restrictions on union activities have reduced the effectiveness of collective bargaining and strikes. Union resources have been squeezed as memberships, and hence dues, have declined. Scares about declining productivity and unmanageable public debts have led many people to blame unions for the country's economic woes.

The increasing public hostility, when combined with the loss of legitimacy for Keynesian economic solutions, has left unions on the defensive and often incapable of articulating alternatives to the neoconservative agenda. This strategic paralysis has been aggravated by growing internal membership conflict as workers and their communities are pitted one against another in the bid for jobs and investment. For many unions, the combined effect of all these pressures is stagnation or reduced effectiveness. Yet demands for action increase, forcing unions to make difficult choices about streamlining their own functions and services.

Unions and rank-and-file members have searched for new strategies to arrest their organizational atrophy and representational crisis and meet new economic situations. To cope with demands for lower costs and heightened productivity in a more competitive international marketplace, many unions have engaged in co-operation with management. For some workers this has translated into wage freezes and even a loss of jobs. For others it has meant the reorganization of work to allow the introduction of teams and the elimination of waste. Many unions have also expanded their bargaining demands beyond the traditional realm of wages and benefits, moving into collective agreements that provide some form of job security, retraining for displaced workers, and union control over, or input into, contracting-out. When collective bargaining has fallen short in advancing the cause of labour, some unions have returned to the more militant strategies of sit-down strikes and mass demonstrations. In other cases, when businesses teeter on the edge of collapse, unions have pursued worker-ownership schemes.

Tough economic times have also forced many unionists to re-evaluate the organizations themselves. For example, in the face of membership criticism and dissatisfaction, the Teamsters are undergoing a massive reorganization to make the union more democratic and responsive to membership needs. In the belief that union strength lies in greater numbers and internal unity, the Canadian Labour Congress (CLC) is attempting to reunite the building trades and the Teamsters under the CLC umbrella. Mergers and organizing drives have been pursued by big and small unions alike in their drive for strength in numbers and higher dues revenues.[2]

The Canadian Auto Workers Union (CAW) has been especially active in building its membership through mergers and organizing drives. As a result of its rapidly growing and changing membership the union has been confronted with new internal strains and potential conflicts. If these are not addressed, they will undermine the CAW's capacity to engage effectively in collective action. This chapter examines the CAW's merger and organizing activities over the past ten years. It analyses the impact of new members on the union's activities, the changes in the union's organizational structure and culture, and the resultant possibilities for sustaining the union's capacity for united collective action.

Size, Structure, and Strategy

In the absence of legitimate coercive capabilities, unions must rely on their members' willingness to act and abide by union decisions. Indeed, the fundamental basis of union power rests on the ability to mobilize members to take collective action in support of a chosen policy or set of demands. A union's ultimate sanctioning power is the strike or the threat of a strike, and ever since the ascendancy of mass production and the advent of industrial unionism, size has become a critical factor in this power. The larger and more densely concentrated the membership of a particular union, the more powerful the union, because of its potential impact on production or the delivery of a service.

Yet a large membership can also impede a union's strategic capacity if it cannot garner the active and united support of its membership behind a chosen course of action. Moreover, many critics have argued that unions, like other large organizations, become trapped in Robert Michels's "iron law of oligarchy," which states that as organizations grow larger, they tend to bureaucratize. With bureaucratization comes a separation of leadership from the membership and disproportionate control by leaders over organizational resources, resulting in a concentration of power in the hands of the leaders, regardless of the organization's commitment to democracy and membership control. According to this argument, the power gained by unions in expanding their size would be lost through their reduced strategic capacity to mobilize collective membership support for a particular course of action.[3]

Another pressure of growth comes from the growing diversity of expanded union membership. Servicing a greater number of workers with shrinking resources is difficult. This task is further complicated as union populations become more heterogeneous. When unions organize more women, people of colour, and workers from different regional, sectoral, and occupational categories, the interests that must be represented become more diverse and potentially contradictory. Yet unions must still present a united front to managements and governments in order to prevent whipsawing of their members or a possible erosion of their mandate as the legitimate representatives of the employees. The challenge for unions under these conditions is to find a way to articulate a common set of demands for this diverse membership, so that union members will still willingly and actively support union policies and programs of action.

Claus Offe and Helmut Wiesenthal provide a first step towards understanding the process whereby unions define a unity of interest amidst diversity. They argue that for unions to fulfil successfully their dual functions of representing members' interests and of engaging in a concerted program of collective action, they must be able to *express* and *redefine* the interests of members in a way that helps forge a unity of interests among various groups.[4] For example, unions faced with membership demands for employer-sponsored child care are likely to see this demand as a women's issue. In a union with men in the majority, this issue might make little or no headway. The union, therefore, has to find a way to redefine this particular interest so as to build broader and more united membership support for the issue.

Part of this redefinition occurs through the forging of a collective identity within a union. This collective identity must motivate workers to act in the name of the collective good rather than for individual reasons alone. Collective identities filter how union members view the world and understand the place of unions in society. Thus, different collective identities will alter what union members consider to be legitimate activities and interests for their organization.

Organizational structure is the second factor in the dynamic of interest representation. On this question Offe and Wiesenthal are less innovative, accepting the limits to organization proscribed by Michels's iron law of oligarchy. Basically, they too argue that unions that become larger and more diverse tend to bureaucratize, which again separates leaders from the rank and file and erects organizational barriers to membership mobilization. Thus as unions grow larger they gain numerical strength at the expense of their capacity to mobilize their members effectively. Offe and Wiesenthal conclude that there is an optimal size for unions, such that union strength is related to union size by an inverse "U" curve.[5]

While Offe and Wiesenthal's concept of collective identity as a means for creating unity out of diversity is useful, their conclusions about structures of representation need to be readdressed. In essence, their analysis is based on a false categorization of trade unions as classic bureaucracies organized on the principles of rational, hierarchical decision-making. Trade unions, by the very nature of their function as the representative of workers, can never fully conform to standard models of bureaucracies; they are not guided solely by an administrative rationality of efficient decision-making. Rather, trade unions in capitalist societies are characterized by two competing rationalities: an *administrative rationality* involving the drive for efficient use of resources in carrying out decisions; and a *representative rationality* involving the attempt to represent the needs of the membership so that checks and balances and adequate forums for debate and input exist in the process of decision-making. The representative rationality may necessitate duplication of time and resources to ensure adequate representation, which clearly contradicts the administrative rationality.[6] In other words, democracy costs.

Moreover, as individual workers control their labour power – something that cannot be usurped or given over to the union leadership – and as unions rely upon the collective withdrawal or deployment of this labour power for support of their decisions, individual workers always have the capacity to take action into their own hands in the face of weakened union representation. This potential use of labour power against the union leaders limits the capacity of leaders to impose strategies and solutions on members and ultimately engages them in the complex process of interest intermediation inherent to trade unions.[7]

Further, organizational structures are not the inevitable product of growth in the numbers and complexity of decisions being made. Rather, structures of representation are often at the heart of struggles for democracy and rank-and-file input into union decisions. This means that unions will adopt various organizational structures that will most likely have varying impacts on the union, ranging from high degrees of leadership and bureaucratic dominance to structures that facilitate membership mobilization. Moreover, organizational structures are subject to change for a host of different reasons, including, for example, political pressures within the union or the need to accommodate new members within the union decision-making.[8]

This debate over size, organizational structure, and the mobilization capacity of unions cuts to the heart of the issue of a union's changing strategic capacity. Simply stated, as union memberships become larger and/or more diverse, the strategic capacity of a union will probably be altered. To understand these changes and to assess whether a union is more or less able to act effectively as a result of them, we must look at the effect of new members on the collective identity and culture of the union as well as on the structures of representation. Through such analysis, we will be able to assess the capacity of the union to continue to fulfil its role of representing and redefining the diverse interests of its membership into a common set of goals and course of action.

Mergers and Organizing Drives

In 1985 Canadian autoworkers split from their U.S.-based international union, the United Automobile, Aerospace and Agricultural Workers of America (UAW), to form a new independent Canadian union, the CAW. This split was precipitated by strategic differences between the Canadian regional and U.S. parent union over the bargaining of concessions with the major automakers. The international union was determined that concessions were the only way to save jobs and plants in the United States. The Canadian leadership of the union saw concessions as guaranteeing nothing but trouble. They predicted that jobs and plants would continue to be lost even with concessions, and that workers would begin blaming their union for failing to protect their interests in the face of corporate pressure. The formation of the CAW was heralded as the dawning of a new day for national unions in Canada and possibly for the Canadian labour movement as a whole.[9]

Although the CAW was established on the rising crest of an economic recovery following the recession of 1980 to 1982, the union was well aware of the long-term structural change just beginning to hit the auto industry. The biggest challenges to the Canadian industry were offshore competition and imports into Canada, the relocation of parts plants to Mexico to take advantage of cheap Mexican labour, the building of auto plants in Canada by Japanese automakers such as Toyota and Honda, and overcapacity in a saturated market. All of these problems translated into a potential loss of jobs and/or continued company pressure for concessions from unionized Canadian autoworkers. Furthermore, as the industry adjusted to the addition of new automakers, reduced markets, and freer trade, it seemed likely that more plants would close.[10]

The Canadian autoworkers prepared to meet these challenges by restructuring their own union to ensure it a lasting place in the Canadian industry. While they were still a branch of the UAW, the Canadian leaders had proposed the formation of a Canadian metalworkers federation as one strategy to meet corporate challenges. Through such a federation, industrial unions operating in the steel, rubber, and electrical industries, to name a few, would pool resources for research, planning, and possibly even collective bargaining. In this fashion Canadian industrial unions could form a common front of demands and mobilize political influence to gain a say in an integrated restructuring of Canadian industry.[11] Before this idea could get seriously under way, the Canadian autoworkers split from their international parent. The split drove a wedge between Canadian autoworkers and most other international industrial unions, which feared that the CAW's break would foment discontent among their own Canadian membership.

The newly formed CAW then had to change its strategy. While its leadership was still determined to build support for an industrial policy that would give unions some control over restructuring in Canada, they saw that the means to this end had to change. Now that the CAW was on its own, the only way for the union to wield the required political and economic power was to become one of the largest unions in Canada and a truly national union. Since the recession of the early 1980s, membership in the Canadian autoworkers' union had declined precipitously. In 1979 the Canadian region of the UAW had a membership of 130,000. At its lowest point, in 1982, union membership dropped to 98,000. Although union membership rebounded to 135,000 by the end of 1984, when the union divorce proceedings began, auto analysts both inside and outside the union predicted that overcapacity and free trade with the United States would mean fewer auto jobs in Canada.[12] The union thus determined that to sustain its membership and power it must organize new workplaces. Furthermore, if the CAW wanted to speak for Canadian workers, it now had to broaden its membership base beyond the geographically concentrated auto industry.

The CAW put its resources and energy into reaching new workplaces and merging with existing unions. In doing this the union added substantially to its organizing staff and committed an increased amount of money to the organizing department. Between 1986 and 1991 the CAW spent anywhere from 15 to 35 percent of its total departmental expenditures on organizing.[13] The fruits of this effort came in a massive expansion of membership. Between 1985 and 1992 the CAW organized (excluding mergers) thirty-eight thousand workers in 384 workplaces across Canada. From 1985 to 1991 it concentrated its organizing activities in smaller manufacturing plants (seventy-five workers or less) and in sectors in which the CAW had a well-established presence, such as auto parts, aerospace, transportation equipment, and breweries. Most of this membership remained concentrated in Ontario and Quebec. Around 1991 the focus of CAW organizing drives changed, with the union reaching into more diverse workplaces, including offices, fish plants, and hotels. These workplaces were again quite small, but they tended to be scattered across the country.[14]

To continue its thrust into organizing, the CAW initiated major changes. The most radical departure from established practices came in 1992, when the union introduced community-based organizing, which involves training and supporting local union activists to act as volunteer organizers who then co-ordinate and support the activities of full-time organizers during drives. At other times, these people establish community and workplace connections and goodwill. This grassroots approach to organizing reduces the reliance on expert, full-time organizers who are parachuted in from outside the community and is based on people who live, work, and act as goodwill ambassadors for the union within communities. By 1993 the CAW had trained almost 120 community organizers across Canada. These people have played strategic roles in achieving difficult organizing victories, such as the Hayes Dana drive in London, Ontario.[15]

The merger with the Canadian Textile and Chemical Union (CTCU) in 1992 introduced another innovation. The merger agreement stipulated that the CAW would establish and provide financial support for a storefront office in downtown Toronto, which would provide general social and informational assistance to immigrant workers. Although the goal of the office was to provide community support to workers, given the CTCU's established presence among immigrant women workers, it seemed likely that the storefront office would also serve as a basis for organizing new groups of workers into the CAW.[16]

Between 1985 – when the CAW undertook its first merger with the Canadian Airline Employees Association (CALEA) – and June 1994, the CAW concluded eighteen additional mergers, bringing into the union about eighty-four thousand new members, with still more mergers being negotiated.[17] The new members are diverse and include workers from the airline, railway, mining, hotel, and restaurant businesses. They also include a large number of offshore, inshore, and Great Lakes fishers. Not only do workers from merged unions differ from the mainstream CAW membership in terms of the sector in which they work, but they also differ demographically. More of them are women from ethnically and linguistically diverse backgrounds and from scattered regions across Canada. Moreover, many new CAW members have brought along unique union cultures and histories that influence how they see the world and the role of their newly adopted union. For example, when the CAW merged with the Canadian Association of Industrial, Mechanical and Allied Workers (CAIMAW) and CTCU, it was embracing a heterogeneous population of workers with a radical and nationalist background whose commitment to rank-and-file democracy had led to their formation as independent unions in the 1960s.

The combined impact of all of these new members is enormous. Over 100,000 new members have been brought into the union, which had about 120,000 members when it started the mergers. Today the membership stands over 200,000, with some of the anticipated gains in membership lost through another rash of plant closures during the recession of 1990 to 1993.[18] Almost half of the CAW's present membership has joined the union since 1985.

The union has increased in size as well as in membership diversity. Membership from the motor vehicle industry as a percentage of CAW membership dropped from 70 percent in 1979 to 55 percent in 1993. In contrast, the percentage of workers from other parts of the economy has increased. For example, workers in the hospitality and service sector have gone from being unrepresented in the union in 1979 to constituting 7 percent of membership in 1993. Similarly, railworkers, who had no presence in the union before 1990, formed 20 percent of the membership in 1994. The number of women and people from visible minorities has also increased. In 1979, women formed 11 percent of the membership. The number peaked in 1990, when 20 percent of the membership were women, but dropped to 17 percent by 1993, owing possibly to layoffs and more male membership additions through continued organizing and merger activity.[19]

Membership changes also mean that the union must address and reconcile a more widely ranging set of demands. For one thing, it has to deal with workers under different labour codes and provincial political regimes. It also has to reconcile the debate about overtime and the forty-eight-hour week for autoworkers with the miners' determination to gain a much shorter work week. The demands for continued special treatment in collective agreements by well-paid, largely male, skilled tradesworkers must be reconsidered in light of the concerns of immigrant women working for very low pay as cleaning staff. In meeting the challenges of de-industrialization, plant closure, and the loss of its traditional membership through expanding CAW membership, the union has thus confronted itself with a series of new and pressing problems. Can the union continue to be as effective in the workplace and political arena, given the likely difficulty in determining a united plan for collective action and the barriers to mobilizing such a large and diverse membership? These questions can be answered by examining the changing collective identity, culture, and organizational structure of the union.

Culture, Collective Identity, and Organizational Structure: The Key to Strategic Capacity

Coming into the 1990s the CAW's dominant collective identity continued to be determined by auto and other workers from heavy industry. Theirs was a radical, quasi-syndicalist view of the world, in which their union, rather than a particular political party or interest group, was seen as the primary agent of social action and change. Through years of struggle with the international union, including Canadian UAW leaders such as G. Burt and D. McDermott, and because of their particular organizational structure, this syndicalist collective identity also involved a strong commitment to internal union democracy and membership control over union affairs. Unlike their U.S. counterparts in the UAW, who had long internalized the limits of postwar compromise and moderation into their own behaviour, Canadian autoworkers often eschewed the limits to action imposed by Fordist regulatory structures. Such resistance to moderation led to conflict between the rank and file and their leaders throughout much of the 1950s and 1960s. In the early 1980s conflict between the Canadian UAW region and the international UAW executive revitalized the tradition of radicalism and militancy and reopened the possibility for the union to engage in sit-downs, mass demonstrations, and other more militant strategies.[20] CAW radicalism and commitment to internal union democracy have been reinforced more recently with mergers to unions such as CTCU and CAIMAW. Not only did these unions have their own long-standing traditions of militancy and democracy, but their merger agreements reflected their determination to continue this tradition, even if this meant rejecting certain accepted CAW practices. For example, the CAIMAW merger agreement limits the application of those CAW constitutional provisions that give power to the national executive board in negotiations and strike authorization.[21]

The CAW's collective identity has also become increasingly nationalist since the split from the international UAW in 1985. For one thing, the CAW has limited its merger activities to already well-established Canadian unions, including some very staunchly nationalist unions such as CTCU, CAIMAW, and Mine Mill. The addition of union members from across Canada has lent credibility to the CAW's claims that it speaks for Canadian workers in general, but it has also set the union on a collision course with other international unions that perceive the CAW as encroaching upon their jurisdiction and taking liberties in its claims to represent the interests of all workers.

Given its reformulated militant and democratic culture and identity, the CAW has had little difficulty in incorporating the demands and unifying the goals and interests of members around issues pertaining to national politics, relations with other unions, and workers and broad economic issues. The test for the union has come with issues closer to home and issues such as language and race that are not clearly predicated on an ideological basis. For example, on collective bargaining there has been greater conflict between the old guard, who accept the wage practices of across-the-board percentage increases, and new poorly paid workers for whom percentage increases merely perpetuate wage differentials.

The issues of race and gender pose an even greater challenge to the CAW and raise the possibility of a rupture in the union's culture and collective identity. For all its progressiveness, the CAW, like the Canadian UAW before it, has sustained a union culture that is largely male and "white" in its orientation. The style of interaction is aggressive, and the power structures and networks remain dominated by men, with cultural symbols and reference points oriented especially towards the southern Ontario experience. This culture, and the view of the world it structured for CAW members, was jarred by the sudden influx into the union of visible minorities, women, and workers from other regions of Canada. Given the newness and speed of this change, it is uncertain how it has affected union practices and membership relations. An immediate impact has been registered in the CAW's staffing arrangements, where numbers of women and visible minorities have been appointed in areas such as research, organizing, and health and safety.[22]

Beyond the issue of numbers, the changes are more subtle and have been slower to take effect. The greatest problem has come at the level of membership relations. Although the leadership has worked hard to eliminate sexist language and promote non-discriminatory practices, eruptions of racial conflict in British Columbia and Oshawa Local 222's pronouncements blaming employment equity for many current labour-market problems indicate that there is a long way to go before the union culture itself alters and is internalized into membership practices and discourse.

The union's educational system will be critical in helping to work through these problems and build an alternative view of the world more easily incorporating women, visible minorities, and workers from different occupations and regions. For instance, the Paid Education Leave program now incorporates sessions on human rights and equity issues. The union has also begun to hire its more radical members as teachers of education programs, which reinforces a solidaristic view of the world.

The CAW's organizational structure has also undergone massive change in the past ten years. Nonetheless, the greatest potential problems in the near future may confront the union in this area. Two key problems revolving around the issue of interest representation currently face the union. These are the problems of internal organizational drift and of increasing bureaucratic hierarchy with its enhancement of leadership control.

Before the rash of merger activity, in particular the CAW's merger with the fishery unions on the east coast, the CAW's organizational structure combined high degrees of rank-and-file input and opportunities for organized opposition to leadership with the means for centralized control over collective bargaining, strikes, and other strategic areas. The centrepiece of this organization was the District Council, established in 1939 as a constitutionally recognized forum for local delegates to meet, debate, and decide upon policy issues and strategic directions for the union. Within the international union this body was important as the only forum through which Canadian issues could be debated and determined. Moreover, it provided the opportunity for opposition caucuses to co-ordinate their activities and make their opposition to leadership directives more effective. The fact that the council had a source of funding and an elected organizational structure completely independent of the international union executive or the Canadian regional leadership gave this body more power and capacity for independent action.[23]

While it provided the rank and file with opportunities for input and debate over union strategy and policy, the Canadian Council also allowed union leadership to maintain tight control over union affairs and to construct a unity of purpose within the union. The council provided a forum for leadership to monitor local union conformity to policy. This was buttressed by certain constitutional provisions and established practices that gave union leaders a role in all contract negotiations and strike activities. In addition, the council gave the leadership a means of reaching into local unions to mobilize them behind leadership strategies. With its regular meetings of four times a year, the council provided the leadership with a continual means of both communicating with membership and ensuring that they kept their fingers on the pulse of membership concerns. Clearly, these roles were facilitated by the extensive educational network existing in the Canadian region and the relative homogeneity of the membership.

Since the merger with the fishworkers' union, the CAW's organizational structure has become increasingly beset by new structures and practices that reduce the control of the leaders over union affairs, including collective bargaining, strikes, and the spending of moneys. The fishworkers have a greater autonomy over their own affairs compared to other sections of the union, and they also lay claim to large portions of the union's money. For example, on various points the constitution of the Fishermen, Food and Allied Workers (FFAW) prevails over the CAW constitution; the FFAW has control over its own staff; and it alone assumes responsibility for the negotiation and administration of its collective agreements. Other new unions within the CAW, such as the Transportation and Communications Union (TCU) and CTCU, have also carved out distinct places for themselves, which reduces the role of the CAW leadership in collective bargaining and strikes.[24] While this new decentralization can be heralded as increasing democracy by allowing greater local control, it may also be seen as encouraging organizational drift whereby one part of the union works at odds with another section. It can lead to duplication in expenditures of time and money, possibly with contradictory results. While the end result may be collective agreements that better reflect the realities of different economic sectors and localities, the new configuration could also potentially reduce the union's capacity to mobilize support for strategies that are either risky or controversial – such as the no-concessions fight of the early 1980s.

This organizational drift has been aggravated by the CAW's approach in bringing increasing numbers of workers from across Canada into its ranks. The CAW's structure was designed to accommodate a union with a membership concentrated in a small geographical area and in a few large industries. Now the CAW has added workers from many other provinces and diverse industries, from Kentucky Fried Chicken outlets to railworkers. Although the current CAW representational structure – which includes Quebec and Canadian councils, collective bargaining and constitutional conventions, and various sectoral councils (such as the rail council) – provides many opportunities for membership input and debate, it does not facilitate the building of unity or a strong collective identity within the union. Rather the union has just added layer upon layer of representational structure, and some regions have the potential of being set adrift from other parts of the union.

The second organizational problem confronted by the CAW relates to the growth of increasingly bureaucratic structures and opportunities for greater leadership control over the union. Almost as soon as the Canadian region split from its international parent, the CAW was obliged to take over functions previously handled in the United States. The CAW has also attempted to incorporate staff from merged unions. All of this contributed to growth in the central office and the build-up of the union bureaucracy. The gap between leaders and membership increased.

Perhaps the most serious change to the CAW's organizational structure came in its alteration of the Canadian Council. The key to the council's success in the 1960s and 1970s as a body capable of sustaining opposition to the leadership lay in its independence from the union executive. With independence, the executive of the Canadian union was integrated into the council structure, thus reducing the council's capacity to act as an independent source of ideas and hence of opposition to the leadership. This change allowed the leadership much greater control over both the council and policy and strategic deliberations within the union. Debate within the union became limited, and the opposition within the union has been co-opted, squashed, or isolated from the centres of power.

Conclusion

The CAW is at a crossroads. While it has successfully expanded its membership in size and national coverage, it has yet to redefine its collective identity to incorporate all the new groups that have joined the union. This redefinition will no doubt take time and will be the product of struggle between new groups and the older union guard. The mergers with more radical unions such as CAIMAW, CTCU, and Mine Mill suggest that any reformulated collective identity will retain the union's commitment to progressive unionism and sense of class consciousness. The most uncertain aspect of the CAW's transformation lies in its capacity to address the issues of race and gender. Organizationally the union faces a difficult task, primarily because of the possibly harmful impact of organizational drift and bureaucratization.

It is still too early to determine the impact of these changes on the CAW's strategic capacity. If organizational changes continue to move along the same path, the CAW will probably find it increasingly difficult to mobilize workers behind a common course of action. It may also become more difficult to protect members from corporate practices such as whipsawing, practices that the CAW has been remarkably successful in limiting in the past through solidaristic action. What the emergent collective identity undoubtedly needs to do is to forge bonds of solidarity across lines of region, gender, and race, to provide an impetus for the organizational change that could stop short the union's potential immobilization. This is not, of course, the first great challenge ever faced by the union of Canadian autoworkers. In the 1960s and 1970s, when it was organizing a growing number of plants in Quebec, the UAW-Canada was forced to confront the Quebec nationalist and language issue within its own ranks. Whether the union will be as successful at facing its problems now as it was then remains uncertain, but one thing is certain: the CAW of tomorrow will be vastly different from the union of yesterday.

Chapter 8
Women and the Changing Face of Labour in Northeastern Ontario

Mary Powell and Jennifer Keck

One particularly thoughtful and lively session at the Mine Mill Centennial Conference was a roundtable discussion with seven women active in the northeastern Ontario labour movement: Pam Doig (OPSEU), Judy Gilbert (USWA), Gisèle Pageau (LUSA), Betty Rheaume (ONA), Anna Sweet (CUPE), Pat Tobin (USWA), and Lynn Weightman (CUPE). The transcript of that session forms the basis for this chapter.

As a group, these women from Sudbury and North Bay are representative of the changing face of unionized labour in the region. They work in administrative, professional, or clerical positions. Two of them are employed as staff representatives with public-sector unions. They are over the age of thirty, white, and both anglophone and francophone. They were all born and raised in northeastern Ontario, with union experience ranging from two to fifteen years. Three of them have been directly involved in union organizing campaigns at their workplace, and they have all been involved in negotiating collective agreements and been leaders in job actions or strikes. Two of the women are represented by an industrial-sector union. Only one of the women is a member of a male-dominated bargaining unit in the private sector.[1]

The roundtable discussion focused on three sets of questions:

i) *what is it like for women to be organizing in this new workforce?*
ii) *what is the same (or different) about organizing women workers, compared with organizing men workers? and*
iii) *what are some of the predominant issues facing women* as women *within the labour movement?*

The history of the labour movement in northeastern Ontario is rooted in the rise of industrial unions. Unions like the Mine, Mill and Smelter Workers Union organized and bargained for thousands of workers, virtually all male and all concentrated in resource-based industries owned by the large transnational corporations, whose extraction and smelting operations formed the economic bedrock of the region.

Because unionization in northeastern Ontario has traditionally been male dominated, the contribution of women in building these unions is often forgotten or left unacknowledged. Critics have pointed out, for instance, that the Mine Mill centennial booklet, which includes pictures of the ladies' auxiliaries, leaves all of the women nameless, while the photographs of men have captions carefully listing all the individuals' names. Although the role of women was not central to the process of union-building, they did make a contribution in two separate ways. First, women themselves became union members. During World War II, for example, many of the women who worked at industrial-sector jobs to maintain domestic production signed union cards. Second, both before and after the war, trade union wives were active in the ladies' auxiliaries that helped build and maintain the unions.[2] Their role included organizing social and cultural activities that supported the union's importance in the life of the community and contributed to union solidarity. They were also more directly involved in supporting the union during strikes. The ladies' auxiliaries were active in fund-raising and other forms of strike support. During the Kirkland Lake strike of 1941 against the gold mines, union wives took action against strike-breakers.[3] During the 1979 strike against Inco in

Participants at a session of the Mine Mill conference. Left to right: Charlotte Yates, Anne Burgess, Laurell Ritchie, Madeleine Parent, Jennifer Keck, and Barb Cameron.

Courtesy Dorothy Wigmore

Sudbury, a women's committee, Wives Supporting the Strike, launched an overall program of strike defence.[4]

Increasingly, women have become direct participants in both the labour force and the union movement. In northeastern Ontario over the last two decades the face of labour has changed dramatically, as it has in the rest of Canada and other industrialized countries. This shift reflects an increase in the labour-force participation of women and trends in unionization, particularly in the public and broader public sectors.[5] There are simply more women workers, and more women are members of a union. These changes have both been influenced by and had an impact on the union movement in northeastern Ontario and other parts of the country.

Women and Labour in Northeastern Ontario

Many of the factors that have influenced the changing role of women in the labour movement in northeastern Ontario are characteristic of broader changes in the union movement in Canada and other industrialized countries. The enormous increase in women's labour-force participation rate has been a key element in this transformation. In 1950 Canada had the lowest female participation rate among the seven countries of the Organization for Economic Co-operation and Development (26.2 percent compared to the OECD average of 38.2 percent). By 1985 Canada's rate had more than doubled, to 62.4 percent, third highest in the group. By 1991 women constituted 45 percent of the paid labour force in Canada.[6]

The female participation rate in northeastern Ontario is lower than either the national or provincial averages, for a number of reasons. For one thing, the lower the level of economic activity – and northeastern Ontario is less prosperous than other regions – the lower the labour-participation rate for either sex. This general rule is supported by the statistics. In 1986 the northeastern Ontario region had the lowest labour-force participation rate in the province, for the labour force as a whole (62 percent in northeastern Ontario compared to a provincial average of 67 percent), for men (74 percent compared to 78 percent), and for women (51 percent compared to 58 percent). Other factors may also contribute to these slightly lower rates, including the number of Aboriginal people whose traditional activities (such as hunting and gathering, and informal goods exchange) are not included as "economic activity" and the number of "discouraged workers" who, in official statistical terms, are no longer in the labour force.[7]

The industrial structure of northeastern Ontario and the traditional hiring practices of large, resource-based companies also contribute to lower labour-force participation rates for women. In this respect northeastern Ontario is not unlike other regions dependent on resource-based economies. The occupational structure of the region is more highly segregated, and the wage structure is more polarized in terms of the average earnings of male and female workers (relative to the provincial average and to regions with a larger proportion of white-collar occupations).

Although northeastern Ontario is not fully typical of the province or country as a whole, three features stand out in any discussion of the changing face of labour in this region. First, there has been a major increase in the female labour-force participation rate, with more women now in the paid labour force than at any time in the region's history. Second, the main growth in unionized employment, particularly for women, has come from the public and broader public sector. Third, while employment in the traditional resource sectors has declined (which for the most part does away with jobs traditionally held by men), public-sector employment has increased (which adds to jobs traditionally held by women). The expansion of the public sector is in many respects the result of a deliberate effort on the part of the federal and provincial governments to moderate, through decentralization programs, the boom-and-bust cycles that have characterized resource-based regions.[8] It is also a product of expanding social services, including the creation of regional health facilities, some of the community services required by deinstitutionalization, and the expansion of post-secondary educational institutions.

This transformation of the labour force has, in turn, had a major impact on the labour movement in the region. The combined membership of public-sector unions in the Sudbury region, for example, now far exceeds the combined membership of the two leading industrial-sector unions, Mine Mill and the United Steelworkers of America. While Sudbury may not be typical of other major towns in the region, the fact remains that membership in public-sector unions has been expanding in most centres. In this respect, northeastern Ontario does indeed seem to be typical of the larger picture, and especially of what is called "the third wave" of unionization in Canada: the rise of public-sector unions in the period since the 1960s. As Julie White argues, "The third wave of unionization in Canada has meant more women, more public sector and service workers, more national unions and more independent, unaffiliated unions."[9] The women on our panel are clearly part of this third wave and their experiences help illustrate the changes in the labour force and the union movement.

Struggle, Strike, Solidarity

The women on our panel represent unions in North Bay and Sudbury, two of the major population centres in northeastern Ontario. In many respects, their experience is typical of the broader labour movement and provides yet another example of what many unions – and their members – have experienced over the years. One important feature of this experience is how much labour activity remains a struggle. Although union organizing is formally a legal activity, there is still strong resistance to labour rights, and those organizing, particularly in small workplaces, feel the threat. In the panel discussion, Pat Tobin described her experience organizing a union at a small counselling centre in North Bay:

> Within about a year and a half the working conditions were such that a few of us felt that the only option we had was to unionize. I was really afraid, and I was ashamed of myself for being so afraid. I remember thinking that I was so politically incorrect. All I was doing was organizing. It was 1991, after all, and I knew these issues were important. And I remember phoning another friend in Sudbury, who said, "Pat, anytime you pull the lion's tail, it's scary. That's what you're doing here." That conversation was a real turning point for me.

Even in well-established unionized workplaces, like Inco in Sudbury, organizing previously unorganized workers becomes a struggle. In 1992, Local 6600 of the Steelworkers was formed, unionizing the twelve hundred office and technical workers for the first time. The process of organizing a pay-equity complaint led many of the women workers to become involved in a union organizing drive.[10] According to Judy Gilbert, they found out through the pay-equity process just how much better off they would have been if they'd been part of a union and able to have a say in the pay-equity plan:

> In 1990 Inco posted their pay-equity plan. They did a very poor job of it, upsetting a lot of people, both men and women. A group of women got together, organized ourselves, had some meetings, and brought up a labour consultant to help us along. Jennifer Keck kept us organized and on track. Through this whole process we learned more and more about the differences between the unionized groups and the non-unionized groups, and we thought, "We'd better do something about this." A very quiet organizing drive had already begun at Inco, but it was through the pay-equity process that the women kind of got fired up and involved and took a real leadership role in the organizing campaign. It became a long struggle. It was a very close vote, but in the end we did achieve our goal.

When organized workers go out on strike, the struggle moves into a different and often more frightening phase. Partly it is the unfamiliarity of the experience, a "fear of the unknown." For Ontario hospital workers, their 1981 strike took place on unfamiliar ground. To begin with, Lynn Weightman said, it was illegal and "that really scared us." The union leadership recommended that the workers accept the contract negotiated with the Ontario Hospital Association, but many of the members weren't satisfied.

> The next thing I know, we voted against this contract and we ended up on a strike that we really were not very prepared for. I don't think that the union leaders were prepared for it either. It was really the rank and file that pulled everybody out. It was a shock, because it happened so quickly and we had had no experience with this at all; all of a sudden we not only were going out on strike, we were doing something that was against the law. We not only felt that we could possibly lose our jobs, we were afraid we were going to end up in jail. It was quite an experience to be out on a picket line watching the police drive around in paddy wagons taking your picture. And management was looking down from the windows taking pictures.

Many workers in the public sector belong to unions formed since the 1960s. Often, they do not have a strongly developed union culture to draw on in strike situations, and there is a process of acclimatization for those on the picket line. Referring to a bitter six-month strike at Sudbury's public health unit, Betty Rheaume said that as president of Local 87 of the Ontario Nurses' Association she had "walked out with a membership support of approximately a 76 percent strike vote," which was a solid vote. But for the white-collar professionals who don't traditionally pick up a picket sign, "it was kind of intimidating." At first there was a somewhat demoralizing feeling, "a fear of the unknown." The members became more comfortable after the second or third day, especially when the union insisted that 100 percent of the membership be on the picket line. According to Rheaume, it's something everyone on a picket line goes through: "Do I really believe in why I'm out here and can I really get that message across to the people, and if somebody bucks why I'm out here am I going to be able to handle it? Well, we got past that."

When a strike is illegal there are severe consequences for the leadership as well as the members. But at the same time the strike experience brings a strong sense of solidarity and comradeship.

> A lot of union presidents were fired, some were jailed. It took some of them two years, I think, before they finally got their job back. The union was able to get their job back for them. The people that this happened to are all extremely active unionists today, so it really didn't put a damper on things, even though it got kind of wild there for a while. Our commitment became so strong that we made a lot of good changes. (Lynn Weightman)

Our president was fired, yes, along with many other presidents across the province, and our whole executive was suspended for eighteen days. Every union member received from one to three days' suspension, which we grieved. We did win a few things, but the eighteen days for the executive remained. Throughout, the solidarity of the local held firm. I remember the time right after the strike, when we were serving our eighteen-day suspension. The membership kicked us out of a meeting and held their own little caucus. Then they brought us back and told us that they were going to pay us our wages, except for the three days' suspension that everybody else got. The solidarity was just unreal. (Anna Sweet)

Solidarity was a central theme in our panel discussion. In Betty Rheaume's account of the nurses' strike, single parents on the picket line were helped out by strikers with second incomes in their families, people who didn't take their strike pay but put it back into the pot. She explained that, "We paid bills for people who were going to suffer maybe foreclosures, that were not going to be able to pay their car payment or maybe not be able to afford insurance on their car, and it was because of that kind of comradeship that we were able to last five and a half months." The solidarity came as well from other unions in the community:

We're an independent union, so we didn't have a national union we could go to for help. But we did have support just the same. All the groups – CUPE, OPSEU, Steelworkers, Mine Mill, Women's Centre – were just absolutely great to us. I think if there's any message here today, it's that we are all working together to better each other and to advance the cause of women, and it doesn't matter which group you belong to, you should support each other. (Gisèle Pageau)

For some unions, the support had surprising elements, both in who did support the strikers and who did not:

The one thing that I found extremely impressive is that it was the blue-collar workers that supported me and my membership. Support came not so much from the professional people – the teachers, professors, nurses. We had CUPE, OPSEU, Mine Mill, Steelworkers. We had the Women's Centre. We had the people who have had to work all those years and know what it's like to have to battle. We did not have the people who sort of had it easy. (Betty Rheaume)

These themes are common to much of labour history. The "third wave of unionization" has its distinctive features (referred to earlier), but it also shares some important commonalities with union experience from earlier periods and elsewhere in the country and beyond it.

Organizing in Community Services

In other ways, the women on our panel raised issues that have not been part of the common tradition of the labour movement. One of the key elements is that, especially in community services, workplaces are often very small, and "the size of workplaces has a profound impact upon unionization."[11] In 1989 the rate of unionization in small workplaces (fewer than twenty employees) was less than 13 percent. One of the reasons for the low rate of unionization is that the "policy to certify by individual workplace makes the cost of organizing small workplaces prohibitive, particularly when any form of employer opposition drags out the legal delays and expenses."[12] At the same time, over 30 percent of women (and 25 percent of men) work in small workplaces [see chapter 2].

According to Pat Tobin, she and three other fellow workers had great difficulty in trying to "get the ball rolling" to organize their workplace, a social service agency with twenty-two employees. "We phoned two of the larger public-sector unions who normally take social service workers, and were refused because of our size." They finally turned to an industrial union, USWA, to represent them. Pam Doig argued:

> One of the things that unions are going to have to start looking at seriously is the size of workplaces. The unorganized workers of Northern Ontario, particularly women, work in very small workplaces. To refuse to organize workplaces with fewer than a certain magical number of workers is to me unethical. After having organized in some really small workplaces, I understand the difficulties that arise, but as a unionist and as a feminist I couldn't live with myself if I had to tell a group of seven women, "I'm sorry I can't organize you because it's too much trouble, because you're only seven." Unions are going to have to take a really hard look at how this can be done efficiently and effectively, because those workers are really in need.

In the broader public sector, the question of size is related to other characteristics of the workplace. Typically, workplaces in "health, education and directly-operated government facilities and services" are reasonably large, while those that are "Transfer Payment Agencies (TPAs) in the community service sector (agencies that provide social services on a contractual basis with the state)" tend to be small.[13] This raises several problems, apart from the direct question of size. Often the social relations in a small agency can add to the tensions, particularly if there is unexpected conflict about unionization. In addition, members of community-based volunteer boards feel caught between the union-related demands of the workers and their own anxieties about being responsible for overall direction of the agency.

The workers, for their part, may feel that organizing a union is deeply compatible with their professional work. Pat Tobin said that she thought because she worked in a social service delivery agency that it would be relatively easy for her group to organize a union. After all, their everyday work involved advocating for people's rights. On the other hand, some workers may feel a conflict or, at least, may seem to be on unfamiliar (and uncomfortable) ground. "One of the biggest struggles," Pam Doig said, is that people think that "because we're social workers or social service workers, we're in tune with labour issues and know our rights, and in fact we don't. You really have to convince people that they have the right to have rights."

Community-based workers may also believe that the board of their agency will be open to the unionization effort. In Pat Tobin's case, her agency was run by a community board, with many of board members coming from a grassroots background. "Several of them were union members themselves, so I thought that that would make unionizing easier. I was wrong. I was really wrong. So, that was my first lesson."

Even when a union is successfully organized in a transfer payment agency, its relationships with the provincial funders and the community board are full of complexity: "We're funded by nine ministries, which can create quite a nightmare in bargaining. We have a management structure: an executive director, directors of the programs, a business manager, and an executive assistant to the executive director. They're responsible to a community board made up of twelve people" (Pat Tobin).

When unions are operating in community agencies they often have to break new ground in negotiations. Unlike the manufacturing or mining sectors, they do not have examples or models from dozens of previously negotiated collective agreements:

> In the social service sector at CAS [Children's Aid Society] there were a lot of issues around violence in the workplace because of the kind of job it is. Every issue seemed to become an organizing drive. You could never just say, "Well, we've got some serious health and safety problems here and we want them fixed." We had to find out what they were, and how we wanted things to be changed. It's a process of ongoing dialogue, which has resulted in some really different and wonderful things happening. What we have been able to accomplish in our agency is, I think, the first of its kind: a really extensive health and safety policy position that was done by the joint health and safety committee. Our policy position recognizes that workers at Children's Aid Societies are in danger on the job at all times. I think it's the most thorough document of its kind in the province. Again, it came out of that one-on-one talking to people. How many times have you been boinked in the nose by a client? How have you been threatened? How have you been harassed? And so on. It goes beyond just saying you don't have to

do it. It goes beyond the legislation and talks about "Okay, how do we heal? How do we start to heal?" (Pam Doig)

The personal commitment of workers to their jobs is an aspect of work in the public sector, particularly the "caring" professions, that gains little attention. Often, because of the personal contact involved in these jobs, workers *care* about the people they deal with and the work they do for them. Sometimes job action becomes a way of acting on that commitment:

> There were an awful lot of hospital workers at that time who were not interested in unions, and were not interested in organizing. But it was fascinating to watch, because they really felt that the care they gave patients was important for the community. Our numbers had been cut back so badly. We weren't able to provide the kind of patient care that we wanted to. We felt so terrible about that that a lot of us got to the point where we really didn't care whether the illegal strike landed us in jail or not. We were fighting for such an important principle. (Lynn Weightman)

But there is also frustration because, particularly in newly organized sectors, not all workers recognize or acknowledge the role of the union. Traditions of support and solidarity are not strong among many professionals; and for workers who have gone through a long strike, it can be demoralizing to see their work undercut. For instance, the health unit Betty Rheaume worked in was blacklisted during the nurses' strike. "Blacklisting," she said, "is supposed to be the biggest thing, the hardest thing, and the roughest thing a union can do." It "means that you're an agency that is not a good agency to work for." But in this case, "it did nothing." The health unit was able to fill every single vacancy and in the end the union's membership was "not the same membership that walked the picket line, and the issues that were there are not the issues any longer because the people have changed." This means that the union has to get out a different message. "There has to be some form of support. Don't question what it's about. If someone is taking the action, and they've gone to the trouble of getting out there with a picket sign or whatever they're doing, find out why they're doing it instead of deciding you don't like what they're doing."

Issues for Women

Many of the workplaces discussed in the roundtable were female-dominated, so it was difficult to draw comparisons between the union activity of men and women. But at Inco, where women are in a minority even among the office and technical workers, there clearly are male/female differences. For Judy Gilbert, it was perhaps a little more difficult to convince women to join the union. But "once involved, once they signed the card, the commitment from the women was much greater than that from the men. If an extra night's work had to be done that week it was the women that were out there doing it."

If most or all of the workers are women, unions may not be successful with an approach derived from their work with male workers in large industrial corporations.

> I think that organizers, staff reps, executives of locals, particularly the amalgamated locals, will have to start looking at what it means when we're organizing women, at the way that we're organizing, and at what the issues are. It means looking at the workplace through different glasses. It means looking at the context in which women work, the issues that they bring to work. It looks at health and safety, particularly for the industrial-based unions who are moving into social-service areas to organize. Health and safety takes on a whole different perspective. (Pat Tobin)

When unions are not clear about the needs or concerns of a female workforce, the best strategy involves an "ongoing dialogue" with the workers.

> When it came down to bargaining in our workplace, we had to use an internal kind of organizing, as opposed to, say, the service model of unionism where the staff rep comes in and tells you, "Well, you should go for 5 percent more wages." Our stewards, who were almost all women, had to do one-on-one organizing with the women in our local to determine what the issues were, and so we had to go out and talk to all of our members. It was like talking to people over coffee and having a real personal conversation about what this meant to the individual member. We asked what their biggest headache about work was. Well, the answer might be, "I have a hell of a time getting to work at 8:30 in the morning because I've got daycare." (Pam Doig)

For Pam Doig the challenge became one of "moving very personal issues into political issues at the bargaining table with the employer." This approach "met with a lot of resistance, even though some of the people in the higher-ups with our employer were women. It just didn't seem like the traditional kind of bargaining."

The most important issues for women often have to do with their responsibilities outside the workplace, because an increasing number of them have to cope with the "double burden" of paid work and housework, as well as their responsibilities to their families. Gisèle Pageau, who works with the staff association at Laurentian University, reported:

Back when we organized in the early 1970s, the issues surrounding the organization were exactly that: family issues. We had women being fired because their children were ill and they couldn't report to work because they couldn't find a babysitter. We had women being fired because they got pregnant. As we organized and became unionized, some of the benefits that we were able to negotiate included, for instance, emergency leaves, and we had it written in the collective agreement that it's one leave per occasion. So, one morning when you get up, your child is ill, and you can't make arrangements for a sitter, you can stay home with your child and get paid. And one per occasion means it's not one per year, it's as it comes. The university tries at every round of negotiations to take that away because their logic is that if you mass produce children you could be off all year round. This is still being said in the 1990s, okay, so I'm not quite so sure how well we're doing there.

Pam Doig added:

Some of the issues that we came up with throughout that kind of one-on-one discussion with our members were very simple things that recognize the role of women as primary caregivers in families. That meant that we were always having to think about double and triple working days for women. And we had to think about their responsibilities beyond that as well – things like extended bereavement leave, recognizing that women usually have heavy responsibilities when a tragedy happens in a family. It meant thinking differently about maternity leave. It meant thinking about family leave days, flexible work hours, health and safety issues.

There were also issues related more generally to the status of women. Gisèle Pageau recounted several of the episodes that were important to the development of the Laurentian University Staff Association.

We also had one woman disciplined because she didn't pick the right gift for her chair's wife. Such issues really made it very clear for us that we needed to organize. It was worse than that at the university back in the early 1970s. In the cafeteria there was a riser where the men and the professors would sit and have their lunch, whereas the rest of us would have to sit below. As well, a lot of our secretaries were being disciplined because they refused to serve coffee, which turned into a major grievance, which we won.

Understanding the issues that are important for women cannot be done only at the local level. Although some union locals have been very active in promoting women's interests, union centrals also have to show leadership, especially on major economic issues that can have a disproportionate impact on women.

> At the central level of unions, women's issues have to be at the forefront every single day. We always have to be thinking about how this impacts on women's work. For unions to survive, the natural place to be organizing out there is with women. For example, how will the social contract stuff that OPSEU is dealing heavily with right now impact on women? What does that mean to women's work? That's got to be a daily part of union work, and that sometimes means educating our board of directors that these issues are critical to the survival of the union. (Pam Doig)

If unions are to serve women well, women must serve in unions, not just as members of the rank and file but as active participants at every level. In some cases, there is scepticism about women's ability to fulfil these positions. As Pam Doig put it, there is a "whole myth" existing in unions "all across the board" about women not being natural leaders, or not having "the stuff" it takes to be union leaders. "For many women this myth becomes so internalized that it's difficult to combat. In a female-dominated workplace the women are more able to say that they do indeed have the stuff that it takes," Pam Doig said. "Our stuff just looks a little different. It works quite fine."

Anna Sweet said that her experience in a CUPE local had been a positive one: "We've had pretty well equal numbers of male and female presidents, and the membership would consider whether or not candidates had the qualities for the leadership role, not whether or not they were male or female. CUPE has been very active in women's issues. Our two national leaders are currently females, and that's got to speak for something."

Pat Tobin said she had been "pleasantly surprised" by the Steelworkers, who have developed a five-day course called "Women of Steel":

> It's all about assertiveness training, how to work with the press, how to chair a meeting, and so on. Yes, you can empower women and encourage women to become union leaders. Steel has a gender equality committee, and they've passed a national policy on violence against women, which we brought to the international conference. The issue is not just where women work and their day-to-day activities – it's a much broader look at women's lives and how violence against women affects them as workers in their workplace, even though it's something you may not see, or feel, or hear about in the workplace.

Other unions, particularly the newly organized male-dominated local at Inco, have experienced tension about the role of women:

> We did get some real concern from men from the outlying areas, as women seemed to become stronger and stronger in the organizing drive. We would walk into our committee meetings in our circle and hear

> comments such as, "Hope you guys don't think you're going to be running this whole thing once it gets going." In the end we were not running it, but we've maintained our ratio. We're about one-quarter of the membership and we have one-quarter of the executive positions. There's some resistance. I think there probably will be for some time to come. However, we proved that we did the right thing, and there are more women up there on the executive. (Judy Gilbert)

The experience of men and women, particularly on issues of sexism, is different, but the common bond of the union sometimes provides a way to bridge the gap.

> When I first went to a conference, there were 109 people there – seven of us women. It had been a long time since I had been to a conference like that. I noticed that some of the men who were at the conference had a really hard time getting their heads around the sexism – they had no concept of sexism, no concept of oppression. But if you went at it through union politics, I found generally they were much more amenable to discussions about sexism. (Pat Tobin)

Nevertheless, there are major issues about how things are done inside unions. For whatever reason, rules and practices have been put in place that can be used as a way to restrict participation. Pam Doig said that both women and men internalize "the myth that women don't have the skills to be union leaders," and this influences how business is conducted, including everything from the strict use of Roberts' Rules of Order to "the corporate-style hierarchies that are set up in a union."

> I think it's time for unions to take a really serious look at changing the way business is done, both at the local level and at the national and provincial levels. I think that women activists have to be out there hammering away all the time for equality at the board level, the executive board levels, and we have to educate our sisters to say, "Okay, because I hear it, it's that; look you gotta earn your stripes to get to the top." Well, what stripes are we talking about? Let's start to look at what skills really do exist and how women do work together.

Although women have expressed concern about the attitude of some men within unions to their participation and to the issues that concern them, they have also recognized the strong support that many unions have given to women. In this respect, the labour movement is often ahead of the wider society, which perpetuates many discriminatory attitudes and practices. According to Gisèle Pageau, the Laurentian University Staff

Association came up against this problem when the union went to arbitration about its job classification system: "What we have found at the arbitration is no matter how well prepared you are, the arbitrator is still in a male-dominated 1970s, 1980s mode." Pageau said that in their first experience with job classification at the arbitration board, she knew the union was in trouble when the arbitrator said, "Well, how can you compare apples and oranges?" A more recent case before the board concerned a secretarial job. The arbitrator decided that even though the secretary was doing all sorts of work, and particularly highly administrative work, she was working "above and beyond the call of duty." Pageau said, "The first thing I did is I went back to the university and I said, 'Okay, here's a job description. Take out everything that is above and beyond the call of duty so that she's not supposed to do it.' Needless to say there was nothing they could take out."

Conclusion

Clearly, as the experience of the women on this panel illustrates, women are on the move both in the labour force and in the labour movement. While there have always been some women active on the edges of the labour movement, and there have even been those who have played a significant role in key events such as strikes, only in the last two decades have women moved fully into the mainstream of the labour movement. The changing labour force both reflects and contributes to these changes. With the importance of public-sector employment to local economies, the proliferation of small workplaces, the persistent wage gaps not only between men and women but also within the public sector itself (for example, between teachers and day-care workers), and the increasing threat to public services, it is evident that there is still a long way to go. Major structural and attitudinal problems remain to be overcome, and the solidarity long demonstrated by unions like Mine Mill will be an important asset in these future struggles.

Part 3
SOLIDARITY AND FRAGMENTATION

Introduction

During a discussion on labour law at the Mine Mill conference, Brian Switzman, a labour consultant, recounted what he called a "Bill Walsh story." In the 1970s, when giving seminars on stewards' training, Walsh used to ask his largely male audience to explain what a collective agreement was. After their explanations – usually long dissertations about the law – Walsh would say: "Well, I will tell you what it really is." Using the Korean War as his analogy – talking about how years were spent arguing about the truce line – Walsh said that bargaining about a collective agreement was essentially the same situation. A collective agreement is at heart a truce line between competing forces. The question that needs to be asked is whether the agreement advances the interests of one's own side or whether one's side is retreating.

In his presentation, law professor Eric Tucker argues that the development of capitalism created a working class with the potential for solidarity. Capitalism, however, also produces countervailing forces that foster fragmentation. Thus, neither class solidarity nor fragmentation is a natural condition. Both are social constructs, created and shaped in the dialectic relations between labour and capital.

Taking Tucker's arguments a step further, Harry Glasbeek, also a law professor, contends that collective bargaining as established by the Wagner Act was suited to the problems created by the failures of an economy in which mass production was the predominant productive mode during a time when mass consumption was virtually absent. This perpetuation of an industrial relations mechanism so out of step with contemporary workers' needs and lifestyles is simply not acceptable.

Chapter 9
Labour Law and Fragmentation before Statutory Collective Bargaining[1]

Eric Tucker

In capitalist societies the strength of the working class derives from the capacity of its members to act in solidarity. Working-class fragmentation favours capital. But neither class solidarity nor fragmentation is a natural condition. Indeed, workers experience contradictory tendencies, some of them (such as common experiences of subordination) favouring solidarity and others (such as segmented labour markets) favouring fragmentation. Moreover, both workers and employers actively engage in efforts to construct or obstruct working-class solidarity.

Class solidarity is multilevel and multidimensional. For example, in the world of work, solidarity may exist among a group of workers performing similar work for a single employer at the same location (single-site craft solidarity). It might extend to all workers performing similar work employed in a geographical area (craft solidarity), to all workers employed by a single employer at a single location (single-site industrial solidarity), to all workers in an industry in a geographical area (industrial solidarity), or to all workers in a geographical area ("One Big Union").

But working-class identities and class consciousness are not just produced by people's experiences at work, and working-class struggles are not only conducted at the place of employment. Home and community life are also central to working-class experience and can provide important sources of resistance.[2] For example, the political mobilization of working-class families and their communities can put pressure on the state to improve the legal and institutional environment in which future struggles will be conducted. As well, boycotts of "unfair" products are a means by which workers can exercise whatever economic leverage they collectively enjoy as consumers. If workers can achieve high levels of solidarity in the workplace and in the community, and if they can link these efforts together in a coordinated manner, their power will be substantially enhanced.

It is not surprising, therefore, that employers are anxious to maximize the fragmentations of working-class life, and one instrument they have used to achieve this result is the law – although their efforts have been continually contested by workers. Here I define law broadly to include not just decisions of courts, but the whole panoply of rules and rulings generated by courts, legislatures, and the executive. Taken together, these decisions and rules produce a regime of legal regulation.

The existence of a regime does not imply that its various parts fit together perfectly. Indeed, given the diversity of the institutional actors involved in the legal regime, and the contested nature of many of the issues addressed, a degree of inconsistency and uncertainty is almost inevitable. Nevertheless, the legal regime usually contains a reasonably high degree of regularity and coherence that workers and employers understand and react to.

Law also performs different functions. It is said by many to be *facilitative* when it provides the legal infrastructure for a market, for example by defining private property rights and enforcing contracts. However, the legal construction of market regimes is hardly a politically neutral matter, and their legal configuration has an enormous impact on the power of workers and employers. So, although the law may be facilitative in one sense, the market regime it constructs may also be *coercive* to those who are disadvantaged in it. Still, it is useful to distinguish between this legally constructed market coercion and the more directly coercive role that law sometimes plays when it criminalizes certain activities or authorizes the use of force by state officials. (Sometimes "freedom of contract is maintained by the truncheon.")[3] Criminal prosecutions, injunctions, and the use of police and militia in respect of trade union activity are all manifestations of this directly coercive role. Finally, law can also serve a function of legitimation. It can shape workers' values and beliefs and induce acceptance of certain norms and rules that may be antithetical to workers' interests. For example, by projecting an idealized image of the rights of formally equal individual subjects, the legal system may obscure the injustices that inevitably result when unequals are treated as equals.[4]

Law is also not an instrument that employers and state officials can always manipulate freely just as, and when, they please. Indeed, the image of law as a tool can be misleading if it brings to mind a fixed object, there

Panel session "Labour and Labour Law in Ontario" at the Mine Mill conference, May 1993. Left to right: Osgoode Hall professors Harry Glasbeek and Eric Tucker, and moderator Brian Switzman.

Courtesy Dorothy Wigmore

to be used as its owner wishes. Rather, it is more useful to think of law in terms of a dialectical relationship with class struggle, a relationship in which law shapes and is shaped by social forces. For example, workers are not passive victims of the legal system, standing idly by while their employers create and use law against them. They fight back, sometimes successfully, using whatever resources are available. For example, the need of judges to appear autonomous, of legislators to seem sympathetic to the demands of working-class constituents, and of administrators to look like technocrats pursuing a politically endorsed public interest may induce a greater degree of responsiveness to workers' claims than might otherwise be the case. In short, the state can become a site or, more accurately, many sites of struggle, and the ability of labour and capital to advance their goals will be shaped by their power resources and the particular institutional characteristics of different state apparatuses.

The focus of this historical overview, therefore, is on both the struggle over labour law as it relates to collective action by workers and the role of law in restricting that activity and promoting fragmentation within the working class more generally.[5]

The First Industrial Revolution (1837–1895)

The period 1837–95, when industrial capitalism began to take hold in Canada, was a time of very uneven change. In some sectors production was left relatively untransformed, while in others large numbers of workers were brought together into a single workplace and traditional production techniques were significantly altered by the introduction of new technologies, divisions of labour, and management methods. Faced with these changes, workers began to organize to protect themselves. In the early part of the nineteenth century trade unions hardly existed, and combinations of workers tended to be temporary, local, and craft-specific. Although paternalism moderated the experience of class antagonism, by the third quarter of the century conflict had increased, the trade union movement had grown, and legal entanglements were on the rise.[6]

At the outset of this period workers encountered a legal regime that heavily favoured individuals as a starting point and embraced a highly fragmented and atomistic model of the labour market. Workers were expected to bargain and contract individually with their employers over the terms and conditions of work. In legal theory and liberal ideology, this model was defended in the name of voluntarism and freedom, but for workers it was permeated with coercion.

First, there was the coercion of the atomized labour market itself. While its level varied for different groups of workers depending on market conditions, for most workers most of the time the market provided employers with considerable leverage. Second, there was the "extra-market coercion," much of it aimed at constructing and protecting the atomistic vision of market relations. This took two principal forms. Master and servant law held workers criminally liable for breaches of their employment contracts, while their employers could only be held liable in damages. We are only now beginning to appreciate the significance of this body of law, and although we still lack a full picture of the frequency and circumstances of its use by employers, we do know that on at least some occasions they invoked the law to punish workers who struck in breach of their contracts.[7]

The second form, the law of criminal conspiracy, in its most stringent versions prohibited even the most elemental form of worker solidarity – two employees agreeing with each other not to work unless their common demands were met. The law in Canada, however, was unclear for most of the nineteenth century. Older English employment statutes prohibited any combining of workers to raise wages or improve conditions, because these were matters to be fixed by local officials exercising statutory authority. Some common law decisions also held simple worker combinations to be unlawful, even in the absence of a regime of statutory wage-fixing. The value accorded by judges to the protection of individual rights and the promotion of an atomized labour market influenced these judgments. Yet the majority of prosecutions for criminal conspiracy were founded on the use of unlawful means by groups of workers, not the simple act of combination. Unlawful means were broadly defined and included inducing breaches of contract, conspiring to injure, and molestation, coercion, and intimidation. Even peaceful picketing could be readily characterized as unlawful under one of these categories. Thus, at best, simple combinations of workers were barely tolerated in law – provided that only the most benign means were used to achieve their goals – while, at worst, they were prohibited absolutely. In either case, the starting point of labour law was antithetical to collective action by workers.[8]

Because of the low level of industrialization and class conflict in Canada until the 1870s, the law of criminal combinations was not particularly prominent in ordering class relations, but its narrow delimitation of boundaries of lawful concerted activity promoted the image of trade unions as a menace to the community and reminded workers that they could come up against coercive force if they concertedly contested their employers' authority. As the first industrial revolution progressed and conflict increased, so too did the opportunities and incentives for employers to invoke the law of criminal combinations, whatever its uncertainties. Trade union resistance to this aspect of the regime was galvanized when George Brown, a prominent Liberal politician and newspaper publisher, prosecuted Toronto printers during the nine-hour strike of 1872, with Magistrate Denison indicating that the simple act of combination was enough to sustain a conviction. Of course, this most extreme formulation of the law could not have been implemented without resort to massive repression of workers – a strategy that no political party, and few employers, had the will or desire to pursue. As a result, reform legislation was enacted without much opposition, but labour's victory was a narrow one. Immunity from prosecution was granted to workers who did no more than combine for the purpose of improving their conditions. But at the same time there was an elaboration of offences that workers might commit in the course of pursuing the goals of their combinations. For all practical purposes, then, the coercive potential of the law and the taint of illegality surrounding collective action by workers remained largely unchanged.

In the 1870s subsequent amendments to the law were enacted after vigorous lobbying by trade unions aggrieved because the statute singled them out as requiring special attention. But these changes only modified the situation slightly. Indeed, a principal change – the exemption of peaceful picketing from the crime of watching and besetting – was removed when the criminal law was codified in 1892, leaving open the possibility that all picketing in a trade dispute could be characterized as criminal activity. Finally, in 1877, the law was amended so that breach of an employment contract by a worker ceased to be a crime in most circumstances.

It is difficult to gauge the effect of this reformed legal regime on trade union activity. Even during the first great strike wave between 1884 and 1888, few workers were charged with offences arising out of strike-related activity. Nor, for that matter, did the policing of strikes entail much violence. During the 1880s the militia was called out in aid of the civil power infrequently, and at no time were troops ordered to fire. Certainly in comparison to the United States during this period, the law in action was weakly coercive.[9]

The modest role of direct legal repression cannot be fully explained on the basis that trade unionists embraced the legitimacy of the restrictions imposed by law and behaved accordingly, although the desire to be perceived as respectable and law-abiding certainly influenced tactical decisions by trade union leaders. Other factors were more cogent. Firstly, trade unionism was largely the activity of skilled workers who enjoyed a relatively privileged position in the labour market, primarily because they exercised a partial monopoly over key skills. To make their strikes effective, they did not need to resort to mass picketing or other conduct that could be readily characterized as violent or intimidating. Moreover, through custom and dependence, relations between employers and skilled workers were infused with a measure of paternalism that mitigated against the aggressive use of coercive law, even when conflict arose.

A second and related factor was that class conflict in Canada during this period did not threaten the established order in any serious way. Employers were generally confident that market processes of supply and demand would determine the price of labour and that even unionized workers would ultimately be required to accept its outcomes. After all, the unions they encountered were mostly local organizations encompassing only a small portion of the workforce and able to build only limited solidarity. Labour-market conditions were generally not favourable to workers who were widely dispersed in a varied, fluctuating economy. Moreover, labour-market segmentation divided skilled and unskilled workers, men and women – which further impeded the creation of a more broadly based union movement.

In the 1880s the growth of the Knights of Labor – which embraced a more inclusive approach to worker organization than that of the craft unions and advocated an alternative political economy to the emerging industrial capitalist form – created the possibility that a more solidaristic labour movement would emerge. However, the Knights were cautious in their tactics. Strikes were only called when other means failed, and while striking workers might receive monetary and moral support from other workers, sympathy strikes were not in the offing. Consumer boycotts were organized sporadically in an effort to elicit broader community solidarity with workers in dispute with their employers, but their impact was limited. In the end, the level of workers' solidarity, even without direct state coercion, was low. Only on rare occasions, when employers perceived that solidaristic behaviour by workers and communities might successfully interfere with market forces (for example, the Toronto street-railway strike of 1886 and various strikes by building workers in the mid-1880s), did employers resort to the law. By the end of the decade and through the first half of the 1890s, the economic downturn severely weakened the ranks of organized labour and made workers more vulnerable to the coercion of market forces. Extra-market legal coercion was not required.[10]

A third reason for the limited use of directly coercive law during this period was that much of the pre-existing regime of labour law, criminal in nature and rooted in the status relation of master and servant, had been thoroughly discredited. This legacy limited the extent to which the image of law as an expression of community consensus could be invoked and made its active use by employers a dangerous strategy because of the potential for backlash. For example, after Hamilton builders successfully prosecuted members of the Bricklayers and Masons Union for criminal conspiracy arising out of a refusal to work with a non-member, a political campaign resulted in the law being amended to preclude prosecutions for such refusals in the future.[11]

During the first industrial revolution, then, labour law was both weakly coercive in its operation and weakly hegemonic in its effect. But a more direct and active role for labour law was not required, because the capitalist labour market provided employers with ample leverage and the practice of solidarity by workers did not fundamentally challenge the status quo.

The Second Industrial Revolution (1895–1940)

The second industrial revolution was marked by a substantial restructuring of capitalist production. A massive concentration of ownership was brought about by mergers and the influx of U.S. capital and corporations. In many industries large production facilities replaced smaller workshops and factories. In these new enterprises the labour process was also transformed. Wherever possible, skilled workers were eliminated, replaced by semi-skilled operatives. Skill dilution, mechanization, job fragmentation, and greater surveillance by supervisory personnel increased management control. Massive immigration also changed the composition of the workforce. Although the bulk of immigrants were still of British origin, hundreds of thousands came from other parts of Europe and Asia. Often these workers lacked any industrial skills and were concentrated in low-paying industrial jobs or in the construction, transportation and resource sectors.[12]

These changes affected the possibilities for working-class solidarity and fragmentation in contradictory ways. For example, on the one hand, there was a tendency towards the homogenization of labour, which provided a structural basis for greater solidarity.[13] On the other hand, the residuum of craft workers fighting to retain their relatively privileged position, the greater ethnic diversity of the workforce, and the expansion of white-collar work created new, or exacerbated old, lines of fragmentation. These tensions were worked out in a variety of ways, but what is clear is that the second industrial revolution was attended by heightened industrial conflict, beginning with the strike wave of 1899–1903 and followed by the strike waves of 1912–13 and 1917–20.[14]

Faced with these new conditions, employers and state officials looked to the law to play a greater role in industrial conflict, both as an instrument of coercion and legitimation. On the coercive side, direct state intervention in strikes increased dramatically. In part this could be done within the existing legal framework. For example, the criminal law prohibited watching and besetting. Many judges at the turn of the century were prepared to interpret this provision broadly, making it a crime for striking workers to appeal to others to join them. While we do not yet have sufficient data on the extent of its use, it seems clear that even simple appeals to act in solidarity resulted in criminal charges being laid far more frequently after 1900 than before.[15]

When labour radicals were involved, more repressive measures were often taken. Charges of vagrancy, rioting, unlawful assembly, and assault, for example, were laid against some workers and, in the most famous case of the time, the leaders of the Winnipeg General Strike were tried and convicted of seditious conspiracy.[16] Immigration law, too, became a weapon in the war against labour radicals. The Industrial Workers of the World (IWW) was a primary target of the Department of Immigration during the early part of the century, with the department often exceeding its legal authority in pursuing IWW organizers.[17]

The police and militia were also available to maintain "public" order. The historical record on the policing of strikes has been barely scratched, but even when relative neutrality was maintained, it is clear that "the threat of physical repression always existed if the strikers went beyond carefully circumscribed limits."[18] Radical organizations such as the IWW were placed under special surveillance and new intelligence branches were created for this purpose.[19] Military intervention "in aid of the civil power" also became much more common. Between 1897 and 1920, the militia was called out forty-two times because of labour disputes, and on one occasion (Valleyfield, Quebec, 1900) troops were called upon to fire, although no one was killed.[20]

The state could also support employer coercion by not enforcing the law. Acts of violence against trade unionists perpetrated by private security forces hired by employers were not unknown, but prosecutions were rare. Also, on some occasions employers imported scab labour from the United States in violation of the Alien Labour Act, and government officials refused to enforce the law despite the demands of trade unionists.[21]

Clearly, the coercive potential of the existing framework was substantial. Nevertheless, it was found wanting by employers and state officials, and new instruments were created. One of the most important was crafted by the judiciary. Using their jurisdiction in private common law, the courts developed and refined legal doctrines that enabled them to come to the aid of employers seeking damages and injunctions against trade unions.[22] Although the English courts blazed the way, Canadian courts quickly followed in their footsteps. Substantively, the courts developed the torts of inducing breach of contract and civil conspiracy to injure for use in the context of industrial conflict. The former tort limited the right of trade unionists to persuade any worker under contract to join their strike.[23] The latter had even greater ramifications for the legality of collective action. Liability could be imposed whenever the courts found that the purpose of the combination was to injure, and not to protect, legitimate interests, even if no unlawful act had been committed by any of the defendants.[24] This gave the judges enormous power to limit solidaristic behaviour by trade unions. For example, they determined that it was tortious interference for striking workers to call upon other workers not to handle their employer's goods or to ask consumers to boycott them. In addition, the courts also applied the law of defamation and nuisance to labour conflicts. For instance, carrying signs saying that an employer was unfair to labour was held to be tortious in some cases, while in others picketing was considered per se a nuisance.

On the remedial side, injunctions were traditionally only issued to protect property interests. To make injunctions available in trade disputes, it was necessary to expand upon the category of protected interests. This was done. For example, interference with the conduct of business was held to be enjoinable. Interim injunctions would be issued quickly, simply on the basis of employer affidavits, and could be continued for years until the case actually came to trial. Workers who violated an injunction could be cited for contempt and fined or jailed as the judge saw fit. A second remedial issue related to the problem of suing unions. In the past, courts held that trade unions were not suable entities because they did not have a legal personality distinct from that of their members. In 1901 this was reversed when an English court held that a registered trade union could be sued in its own right and that its assets could be seized to satisfy a judgment against it.[25] These remedial changes, in conjunction with the new torts, created opportunities for employers to subject unions to an unprecedented degree of legal coercion.

Canadian employers at the turn of the century were quick to invoke these legal innovations, and Canadian judges rarely disappointed them. The full extent and circumstances of their use cannot yet be determined, but some examples are illustrative. The first published case report of an injunction issued under this new legal regime related to a strike conducted by the Rossland miners against mine owners in the Kootenays in 1901. This was part of a greater conflict that erupted in the late 1890s between the Western Federation of Miners (WFM) – the predecessor of Mine Mill – and western mine operators in both the United States and Canada. The mine operators, faced with declining ore prices and share values, decided to smash the union. They revised customs of work, imposed a contract system of payment, imported surplus workers in violation of the Alien Labour Act, and blacklisted prominent union miners.[26] The workers struck in July 1901. They set up pickets at entrances to the mines and at railway stations to intercept potential replacements. When Prime Minister Laurier refused to call out troops to protect the mine properties and strikebreakers, the mine owners resorted to other forms of compulsion. They hired their own security guards and brought an action for damages and an injunction prohibiting the miners from watching and besetting at railways, the mine property, or residences of strikebreakers.

The statement of claim alleged that the union and its members had combined and conspired together to call out the current employees with the intention of injuring the plaintiffs in their business and had wrongfully and without legal authority watched and beset for the purpose of persuading or otherwise intimidating workers not to work or to leave off working for the plaintiffs. Judge Irving issued a broadly worded injunction in the terms of the order made by Judge Farwell in *Taff Vale*.[27] It was issued late in October and the strike was broken by November. After much litigation, the employers were eventually awarded $12,500 damages.[28]

The use of these legal tactics was not just a western Canadian phenomenon. Indeed, the very first injunctions of this period were obtained by the Massey-Harris Company against its striking moulders in Toronto and Brantford in 1900. Other employers soon followed suit. The Gurney Foundry Company, for example, not only obtained an injunction prohibiting trade union members from interfering with its efforts to hire and retain replacement workers, but also enjoined the *Toiler*, a labour paper, from publishing boycott notices and the St. Catharines Trades and Labor Council from promoting a local boycott. In another, more famous, case the Metallic Roofing Company sued the Amalgamated Sheet Metal Workers for calling out its members to obtain a closed shop and for calling for a boycott of the company's goods. The courts granted an injunction prohibiting interference with the employer's business, including efforts to persuade workers not to become employees. After much legal wrangling over whether the union itself could be sued (resolved by holding that while the union was not a suable entity, its officers could be sued in a representative capacity), the Ontario courts were prepared to characterize the act of striking for a closed shop as tortious interference. The verdict was eventually overturned because of a mis-direction by the trial judge, but the employer had won most of the legal points raised by the case.[29]

In yet another case, the Krug Furniture Company obtained an injunction against the Berlin Union of Amalgamated Woodworkers to prevent them from picketing its premises and watching and besetting at railway stations. When the action came to trial, the court found the union members and its international president, D.D. Mulcahy, liable for a variety of actions, including unlawful watching and besetting, inducing breaches of contract, and secondary boycotting. In passing judgment the court made it clear that the law limited the kinds of actions workers could take in support of a strike, and it admonished, "Every person concerned should be unflinchingly kept within its bounds."[30] These and other cases led the Trades and Labour Congress to begin a campaign to secure anti-injunction legislation.[31] Only in British Columbia was this approach successful.[32] For the rest of the country, common law courts continued to enjoin various strike-related activities by workers at the behest of employers, thereby narrowing considerably the scope for worker solidarity.[33]

While it is important to think about the courts as part of the state, it is equally necessary to recognize their institutional limits. Employers, not state officials, made the decision as to whether, and in what circumstances, to invoke private common law, and the application of the law to the circumstances depended on the decisions of a widely dispersed judiciary that could not be directly controlled by the government. Hence, state officials who were increasingly concerned about the need to manage the "labour problem" in the second industrial revolution saw the need to develop new state apparatuses.

During World War I the expansion of the capacity of the state for coercion was stimulated by the fear of radicalism. Towards the end of the war, the government, exercising emergency powers, issued a number of orders-in-council aimed at the repression of radicals and militant trade unionists. Privy Council (P.C.) Order 2381 prohibited the use of fourteen "alien enemy" languages, P.C. 2384 declared fourteen alien organizations unlawful, and P.C. 2525 forbade the use of strikes or lockouts in industrial disputes.[34] The turmoil of the postwar period, culminating in the Winnipeg General Strike, provided the occasion for an amendment to the Criminal Code proscribing unlawful associations and an amendment to the immigration law expanding the power of the state to deport radicals. Both laws were subsequently used to attack labour radicals and trade union militants.[35] Moreover, the conflation of "enemy alien" with "radical" in many of these measures sought to undermine the legitimacy of the left in Canada, divide workers on ethnic lines, and discourage the development of broad working-class solidarity.[36]

An increase in the level of direct coercion was not the state's only response to the labour conflict that accompanied the second industrial revolution. A coercive strategy, after all, can exacerbate class conflict and undermine the ability of the government to legitimate its policies on the basis that it is acting neutrally in pursuit of a generalizable public interest. More subtle policies and instruments were required that aimed to reduce the level and seriousness of class conflict and to promote agreements that respected the norms of capitalist enterprise, without resort to "extra-market" coercion.[37]

Provincial governments first attempted in the late nineteenth century to create legal mechanisms that could facilitate agreements between employers and workers. For example, Ontario, British Columbia, and Nova Scotia enacted arbitration statutes that the parties could, but were not required to, invoke to resolve their disputes.[38] It was only in the twentieth century that the federal government entered the field, beginning with the enactment of the Conciliation Act in 1900.[39] This legislation established the Department of Labour and empowered it to investigate disputes, arrange for conferences, appoint conciliators, and establish commissions of inquiry under the Inquiries Act. It held out to trade unions the inducement that if they submitted their disputes to conciliation, the state would try to promote a settlement. But in practice the overriding purpose of the legislation was the restoration of production, and labour was encouraged to moderate its demands to make them acceptable to the employer. Not surprisingly, the results of interventions under this regime were not favourable to workers.[40]

Officials also distinguished between legitimate and illegitimate trade unions, modestly supporting the former while attacking the latter. This approach was clearly exhibited in the Rossland miners' strike of 1901. When the miners petitioned the government for a conciliator, Mackenzie King was dispatched. But once King characterized the strike as a sympathetic one organized by the radical Western Federation of Miners as part of a broader attempt to assert control over the labour force and labour process, he did little more than to counsel the miners to accept defeat. In his view, any encouragement of the WFM "might be a disastrous thing for the mining interests of the province."[41] King expressed similar views during his involvement as secretary to a royal commission appointed to inquire into the 1903 strike of Vancouver Island coal miners and other workers on the Canadian Pacific Railway's western lines. In its report, the commission outlined the essential difference between a legitimate and an illegitimate union: "The former realizes that he has a common interest with the employer in the successful conduct of the business; the latter postulates an irreconcilable hostility."[42] In regard to this strike, the commission branded the unions involved, the WFM and the United Brotherhood of Railway Employees (UBRE), as illegitimate because they preached class struggle, forged alliances across industrial boundaries, and engaged in sympathy strikes. This kind of solidarity was not to be tolerated, and the report recommended that such unions should be declared illegal organizations. It also recommended that limitations be placed on the activities of legitimate unions. Clearly, unions were not to be assisted by state intervention under the Conciliation Act or in any other way, unless they agreed to negotiate "within a framework which recognized, at least implicitly, the legitimacy of privately-owned capital."[43]

The voluntaristic foundation of the Conciliation Act was found wanting by state officials concerned about minimizing the number and duration of strikes during a period in which there was a rising tide of industrial militancy in Canada. According to Bob Russell, "As the results of conciliation rolled in, it became increasingly difficult to secure the cooperation of labour in settlement procedures that consistently worked to its own disadvantage."[44] The Lethbridge strike of 1906 provided the immediate impetus to develop a new instrument that no longer depended exclusively on the willingness of both parties to participate.[45] Drafted by King and passed in 1907, the Industrial Disputes Investigation Act (IDIA) became the centrepiece of Canadian industrial relations policy until 1945.[46] The act required workers and employers in the resource, transportation, and utilities industries to postpone strikes and lockouts until ad hoc tripartite boards of conciliation had examined the situation, taken testimony, and made non-binding recommendations. Unilateral alterations of the terms and conditions of employment and strikes to oppose them were unlawful until the conciliation process had been completed. Persons engaging in unlawful action were liable to be prosecuted summarily under the Criminal Code and subject to fines of between $100 and $1,000 for each day that an employer declared or caused an illegal lockout and between $50 and $100 for each day an employee was on an illegal strike. In addition, the code was amended to make it an offence for trade union officials to call their members out on an illegal strike. This approach, which Russell calls "compulsory voluntarism," still maintained the principle of voluntarism in that it did not impose any particular resolution of the dispute, but it did compel the parties to complete a process of conciliation prior to engaging in industrial conflict.

What impact did this new legal regime have on the labour movement and its ability or inclination to act in solidarity? Again, firm conclusions await further research sensitive to conditions varying over time and place and mindful of the other legal and non-legal means through which employers and the state exerted their power. Nevertheless, a few tentative hypotheses might be offered. First, the compulsory aspects of the IDIA were infrequently enforced. State officials rarely prosecuted workers who struck or employers who locked out workers in violation of the act, although illegal industrial action was widespread.[47] Indeed, for workers, illegal strike action that resulted in collective bargaining was the optimal strategy during this period. It was only in the face of employer intransigence that resort to the IDIA yielded any benefits to labour, and these decreased over time during the postwar period.[48] Viewed instrumentally, then, IDIA policy probably did little to inhibit trade union militancy, especially after unions learned from experience that the act did not establish collective bargaining when employers resisted it, and that it provided employers with additional opportunities to prepare for, and resist, strikes. In short, most established craft unions could live without it, while struggling industrial unions could gain little from it.

There was also an ideological dimension to the IDIA and its operations. Jeremy Webber argues that boards under the IDIA constructed and applied a vision of the social order and labour's place in it.[49] On the one hand, the boards recognized the humanity of labour. Workers (men) were entitled to a living (family) wage and recognition of their right to freely associate without retaliation. Employers should be willing to meet with committees of employees to discuss grievances, but were not under any obligation to formally recognize such associations. On the other hand, in the board's view the employer's property rights were to be respected and defended. Workers had no claim on the employer's profits and no right to interfere with management of the enterprise. Trade union demands that challenged these prerogatives, such as the closed shop, were considered illegitimate and not supported.

Whether or how this ideology influenced the labour movement requires further research. Webber suggests that IDIA ideology became hegemonic, but his evidence is inconclusive. Nevertheless, there were significant elements within the labour movement, particularly among the traditional craft unions, that pursued industrial legality and saw unions, quintessentially, as wholesalers of labour power within a capitalist social order. While business unionists may have resisted particular aspects of the legal regime as it applied to them (including restrictions on peaceful picketing) they accepted its basic premises. Laws that offered "legitimate" unions a legally privileged space to "do business" within the social order, even if they provided little by way of substantive reform, would potentially strengthen their belief in accommodation and the plausibility of their strategy. For more radical trade unionists who wanted to build working-class solidarity to the point that it could transform the social order, it is unlikely that the vision of the boards had much appeal.

A legal regime with a high potential for coercion and a lower potential to induce consent had been constructed, but, as with all regimes, its operation varied over time. The labour movement was in a weakened state as a result of the defeats of 1919 and 1920, and there was little need for "extra-market" coercion in the following years. Also, the benefits to labour from the IDIA lessened as employer resistance to collective bargaining increased. The depression at the end of the decade further weakened organized labour and, in general, only well-established craft unions survived this period.

The only significant legal development in the 1920s was the ruling of the Privy Council in the *Snider* decision, which established that jurisdiction over labour relations was primarily a provincial matter. This was a momentous decision, not because of its immediate impact on the IDIA (a patchwork of provincial statutes and a more narrowly drafted federal statute embracing similar principles replaced it), but rather because it precluded the development of a national labour relations system. This promoted more fragmentation within the labour movement, because the multiplicity of legal regimes to which unions were subjected enhanced the difficulty of undertaking co-ordinated action.[50]

As the labour movement began to recover from its defeats in the 1930s, not only did more workers join unions, but also union organization itself changed as industrial unions grew rapidly and embraced a more radical ideology and politics. Communists played a substantial role in this development, initially through the Workers Unity League (WUL) and later during the organizing drives of the Congress of Industrial Organizations (CIO). This militancy was met by a reassertion of the state's coercive authority. The Communist Party was banned in 1931, its leaders were charged, and radicals were deported. The state again attacked ethnic radicals, insinuating that radicalism was alien. Municipal authorities banned radical meetings, and police forces regularly came to the aid of struck employers. These tactics resulted in a bloody confrontation between striking miners and police in Estevan, Saskatchewan, in 1931, which was followed by the arrest and trial of numerous strikers on charges of assault, riot, and unlawful assembly. In 1933 the militia was called out for the last time during a labour dispute in Stratford, Ontario, when furniture and poultry workers led by the WUL went out on strike.[51] Although some attempts were made at the provincial level to develop conciliatory mechanisms (Industrial Standards Acts, proto-Wagner Act legislation), coercion was the primary response to the broader solidarity promoted by industrial unions during these years.[52]

Towards Statutory Collective Bargaining

Despite the regime's flexibility, its inadequacy was becoming increasingly apparent by the end of the 1930s, and especially after the outbreak of the Second World War. During the war years the government's primary objective was labour peace.[53] The enormous growth in trade union strength and militancy from 1939 to 1943 overwhelmed the state's ability to use the existing coercive and mildly conciliatory instruments to achieve this object. As well, the growing political influence of the left, signified by the electoral success of the Co-operative Commonwealth Federation in Ontario in 1943, put pressure on liberal and conservative parties to defuse the conflict over the right of workers to organize and be represented by trade unions. A way had to be found to contain industrial conflict while simultaneously halting the political realignment.

P.C. 1003 provided the solution. It required, for the first time, that employers recognize and bargain in good faith with elected representatives or with a trade union when a majority of the employees had joined the union. In addition, the bill strengthened workers' right to join a union without employer interference. A legal space for collective bargaining had been created, but with a cost. The definition of a group of employees appropriate for collective bargaining was to be left to the Wartime Labour Relations Board, which was also given an express mandate to protect craft units from being absorbed into larger industrial ones. Elements of the prior regime were also absorbed and reproduced in the new one. The property rights and managerial prerogatives of employers still had to be respected by union organizers. Common law restrictions on trade union activity were not repealed, and damage actions and injunctions were just as available as before. Where bargaining failed to produce a collective agreement, an IDIA-type process of conciliation had to be followed before there could be a resort to strikes or lockouts. The bill also added a new restrictive element: when a collective agreement was in force, strikes and lockouts were prohibited. Instead, the law required disputes to be resolved through binding arbitration.

Thus, while P.C. 1003 did not establish the final form of the postwar regime of legally mandated collective bargaining, it did contain many of its basic features. Of particular significance here is the high level of fragmentation promoted by the scheme. Workers were to be divided into discrete bargaining units, not of their own choosing, in accordance with criteria of appropriateness devised by boards that took into account, among other things, employers' decisions about how to organize their workforces. The ban on strikes during the life of a collective agreement put another barrier in the way of solidaristic action. It was an additional legal instrument that could be applied to prevent sympathy strikes and punish those who violated the law.

The order was a temporary measure, a compromise produced at a particular conjuncture. The possibility for more radical change was not foreclosed, but most trade unionists supported some version of this model of industrial legality. What led the labour movement to buy into this regime in a way that it had never bought into any other regimes of legal regulation? Clearly, the regime appealed to conservative trade unionists who had long been prepared to come to such an accommodation. It promised business unions an unprecedented degree of stability and security. It was also introduced at a moment of economic expansion, and it delivered rising living standards to many workers in the mass-production and resource industries, enabling them to participate in the mass-consumption economy. It provided workers with a modicum of dignity on the job as some egregious exercises of management decision-making, particularly when directed at specific individuals, could be challenged through the grievance procedure. Finally, the late 1940s and early 1950s witnessed a massive attack on communists and other radicals within the labour movement, so that many of those who might have resisted industrial legality were too busy fighting, mostly unsuccessfully, to survive.

In short, the statutory collective bargaining regime of labour law was the first strongly hegemonic one, and while it did bring tangible benefits to some workers, it incorporated prior legal restrictions on solidaristic behaviour and entrenched a new series of fragmentations that further limited trade union activity. The law restricted shop-floor solidarity, because workers could not collectively respond to management decisions at the time they were made. It strictly forbade and harshly punished sympathy action in support of striking workers, even by a group of workers employed by the same employer at a different location. Trade unions found that it had now become more difficult to exert whatever economic power they enjoyed in support of larger political goals, and the distance between the organized and the unorganized increased [see chapter 10]. As the historical record suggests, overcoming these fragmentations will not be easy. But history does at least teach us that change will only come about when workers challenge the legitimacy of the legal regime that shapes the conditions under which they live, work, and struggle.

Chapter 10
Labour Law Reform in Ontario: Moving Forward to Go Back to What Never Was[1]

Harry J. Glasbeek

When Ontario's employers faced Bill 40, the Ontario NDP's entry into labour-law reform, they manifested an awesome degree of solidarity. Their attack on the bill was co-ordinated, focused, vehement, and, in the end, successful.

That Bill 40 did become law is not to be seen as a defeat for the employers.[2] They cannot have hoped that they would be able to prevent the passage of some kind of labour-law legislation. During its years in opposition, the NDP had promised to reform collective bargaining law. Its most staunch electoral ally, the Ontario Federation of Labour (OFL), expected the party to deliver when it came to office. This was one promise that could not be abandoned. Employers knew this, and their campaign had other objectives, including:

i) forcing the NDP to spend much of its limited political capital on a rather slight piece of legislation;
ii) making sure the legislation was slight, by having the government itself marginalize it and characterize it as a number of limited modifications to the status quo;
iii) encouraging the government to continue to treat the collective bargaining scheme as if it were something like a free-standing regime, one not clearly articulated to all other aspects of capital-labour regulation and mediation, leaving the private sector relatively free to explore, and to create, opportunities to exploit new labour-market structures and in a position to dictate macroeconomic policy-making.

To a large extent these employer goals were attained.

The NDP, since having brought home some bacon on the collective bargaining legislative front, has been hesitant to introduce any legislation objected to by business. This is not to say that the government became totally inactive, but it did become remarkably slow to honour promises it had made over the years, such as increasing the minimum wage to 60 percent of the average industrial wage, introducing a meaningful publicly run day-care program, enacting and enforcing a sweeping employment-equity regime, or enhancing the right for workers to refuse unsafe work. Of course, politics requires compromises, and there are many reasons for the government's failure to move quickly and decisively on its promised agendas.[3] However, the employers' co-ordinated opposition to Bill 40 turned out to be one of the main reasons for the government's obvious reluctance to make moves that would satisfy the expectations of its constituencies and supporters.

The Soft-Sell of Bill 40

The NDP went out of its way to ensure the employing classes that by enacting Bill 40 it was not about to do anything unusual. It stressed the fact that it was merely modernizing the existing scheme, not changing it structurally or conceptually. To assuage its savage opponents, NDP politicians pointed out that most of the new measures in Bill 40 already prevailed in other jurisdictions.

The easier access to first-contract arbitration was noted to have a Manitoba analogue. It was pointed out that the abolition of petitions after trade unions had filed certification applications would bring Ontario into line with all other jurisdictions. The suggestion that the right to organize should be extended to some segments of agricultural workers was said to be a mere reflection of what existed in all jurisdictions but Alberta. The government noted that the power it advocated the Ontario Labour Relations Board (OLRB) should have to make interim orders existed in several other provinces, as did most of the proposed reforms of the arbitration process. Giving explicit power to arbitrators to interpret all employment-related legislation was, it was indicated, merely to follow the law of Nova Scotia and British Columbia.[4] Similarly, the government was able to say that the proposal to allow a trade union with an overall majority of all the employees to bargain on behalf of part-time and full-time employees and the rather limited proposal to permit the consolidation of bargaining units both had equivalents in other jurisdictions. The new right for domestic workers to organize was presented as a not very effective reform and one which also reflected the law in other jurisdictions. The right to put some limited restrictions on scab labour – a proposal which had been greeted with hatred and venom by the employing classes and the newspapers – was offered as an attenuated version of a decade-old Quebec scheme which had inflicted no hardship on employers.

Inasmuch as the NDP had to acknowledge that it was offering some novel provisions, it sought to minimize their importance. Thus, the government pointed out that, after listening to employers, its proposal to give employees an unconditional right to return to their job after a lengthy strike had been made subject to any seniority provisions which existed and to an employer's need to be able to reach out first for workers who could do the particular work resumed. Similarly, the right of security guards to be part of a general bargaining unit – something for which the Steelworkers had been pressing – was granted, but it was made explicitly subject to an employer's right to raise issues of conflict of interest. The Ministry of Labour, in its discussion paper issued in support of its Bill 40 proposals, noted that the proposed workers' right to the protection of a "just cause" clause during the time lapses between the certification of a trade union and the reaching of a first agreement had excited no employer opposition. But because employers did not want this just-cause protection to apply to probationary employees, the government was not about to impose it in respect of those employees. It left it to the parties to negotiate the safeguards to be afforded these powerless workers.

The government did, however, persist with one of its more controversial proposals, the granting of a right to picketers and labour organizers to conduct activities in shopping malls, euphemistically referred to as "third-party property." This boldness must be seen in context. The demand for this provision arose out of the ill-fated organizing and bargaining efforts at Eaton's, a chain of stores whose businesses are located in shopping malls owned by other people. In Toronto, Cadillac Fairview and the Toronto Transit Commission (whose subway stops give direct access to the shopping mall) had used their legally supported feudal-type property rights to inhibit trade union activity on their premises. The unions and the NDP expressed their outrage at the state of the law that enabled this kind of antediluvian repression. This is why something had to be done about this issue in Bill 40. In the event, little enough was offered.

The access to primary targets in shopping malls remains subject to the condition that the third-party property owner can claim a remedy if it can show that the union activity harms the trading rights of anyone else but the primary target who does business on the site or that it violates the shoppers' right to be left alone. Mall owners can go to the Ontario Labour Relations

Board, as well as to the courts, to protect their residual rights.[5] And, as if to prove that the NDP did not want to be too tough on property owners, the Bill 40 proposals go on to provide that trade unionists and their supporters do not have a legal right of access to a target employer's free-standing property for organizational purposes, a demand strongly pressed by the OFL. Even after Bill 40, then, feudal property rights and the sacrosanct nature of stability of production continue to be privileged over the public policy of enhancing trade unionism.[6]

What the unions hoped for most was that there would be better protection against the employer's general right to contract-out, that they would be able to stop employers from using different divisions of their corporate empires to diminish workers' bargaining leverage, to stop employers from selling their assets to avoid the effect of unionization, and to be able to do something about the adverse impacts of the unilateral introduction of technologies. The NDP disappointed them on all these fronts. Very little was done about enhancing the actual bargaining power of workers and their unions.

Despite a strong argument from the OFL, the NDP merely said that successor rights would apply in respect of a sale of a business, not necessarily in respect of a sale of assets, and the related employer provisions were left unaltered.[7] In respect of new technology introduction and bargaining-unit job losses, consultation rights were provided. As well, the restricted definition of the right to strike was not altered, continuing the inhibition on the use of the economic power given by the strike for political purposes.

The bill left untouched the employer right to contract-out bargaining-unit work, which added to labour's disappointment. The only reform on this front was a contracting-in provision to protect people such as cleaners and maintenance workers employed by sub-contracting employers who can be substituted at the whim of a general employer.[8] Even here the government went out of its way to tell business that it did not want to change the basic rules of the game. It specifically provided that the contracting-in protection is not to apply to construction, production, or manufacturing activities.

One area in which the NDP government did steam ahead was in giving the Ontario Labour Relations Board a much larger arsenal of weapons in respect of unfair labour practices and bad-faith bargaining; it also gave the OLRB the mandate and the necessary machinery to shorten the time for its decision-making. These proposals were offered under the broad rubric of enhancing efficiency and by reliance on the claim that it was necessary to modernize a statute that had not been revised for some fifteen years. These measures may prove to be the most positive aspects of the packet, given the comparatively progressive make-up of the board at the moment and its consciousness that there is a need to protect unions better during a downturn in traditional membership.

However it may sound, the burden of this sketch of the legislation is not that I believe that the reforms do not amount to anything at all. To the contrary: even this incomplete account shows that there were many changes, all supported by labour and all opposed by the employer. Further, even if labour got less than it wanted, many of the measures will improve its position under the Labour Relations Act. None of this is negligible. The point I want to make is that whatever skirmishes may have been won on the ground, they are minor victories when compared to the greater, if less immediate, gains made by business on the larger political stage.

What the employers were able to do was to put the government on the defensive about what was supposed to be one of the jewels in its reform crown. Thus the government went to extraordinary lengths to show that it had given business input into the process. The position of the government was that, though the changes on offer were numerous, they should not be feared. They were intended to help both employers and employees and, above all, they were not intended to alter either the role or the nature of collective bargaining in any basic way. This brings us to the third limb of the success story that the employing classes crafted out of the struggle over Bill 40.

The Limits of Even an Enhanced Collective Bargaining Model

The NDP did not offer the legislative proposals in Bill 40 on the basis that, when in opposition, it had been a critic of the existing scheme. Nor did it say that it was offering the legislation because it wanted to do "Big Labour" a favour. Rather, its justificatory framework was that the world of work had changed dramatically and a new system had to be put into place to deal with this problem. An outline of its proposals states:

> The OLRA [Ontario Labour Relations Act] has not been substantially changed in more than 15 years. But the workplace has undergone profound change. There are more women in the workforce than ever before. There are more part-time employees. And there is a far greater degree of ethnic diversity.
>
> In addition, the nature of work is changing: traditional, skilled and semi-skilled jobs in manufacturing are being replaced for low-skilled, predominantly part-time jobs in the service sector. The OLRA is consequently out of date. And it is essential that legislation reflects the reality of today's workplace if Ontario is to continue successfully to compete against other countries in a global marketplace.[9]

In short, the government was recognizing the existence of a new circumstance demanding a new approach to capital-labour regulation, an approach that would set out to reintegrate the fragmented economy and labour markets. Yet, Bill 40 only tangentially addressed the difficulties the government said it was aiming to resolve.

Some features of Bill 40 will help women and part-time workers to participate more fully in collective bargaining. The streamlining of the processes of the Ontario Labour Relations Board, better and quicker remedies in respect of unfair labour practices, the abolition of petitions after a union certification application has been launched, more easily available first-term contract arbitration, and the enhanced capacity to consolidate bargaining units: all of these should be of some assistance, although it is far from certain that they will have a completely positive effect.[10] John O'Grady [see chapter 2] argues (rightly in my view) that the downward spiral in the level of unionization is unlikely to be much affected by procedural reforms.[11]

Some the proposals in Bill 40, of course, are not just procedural in nature. The contracting-in provisions and the domestic workers' new right to organize are attempts to improve the collective bargaining power of some precarious workers.[12] But Bill 40 does not, in any meaningful way, respond to those aspects of the new economic reality and labour-market structures that the government itself identifies as creating difficulties that have to be addressed.[13]

Inasmuch as the old model worked best when a bargaining unit was large enough to give the union leverage in bargaining, the scheme has been only slightly altered. While the enhanced power of the board to consolidate units may aid the weakest workers who are in gender-segregated and/or small employment settings to organize somewhat more easily, this is not enough. They are still a long way from having been given viable collective bargaining power. Indeed, for some time before Bill 40 became law, the OLRB had been certifying smaller units, trying to establish collective bargaining where it did not exist before. The new economic organization had made it obvious that such expansion in employment as there is going to be will be found in traditionally unorganized sectors in which women, the young, and the racially different are to be disproportionately employed.[14] Yet, despite the board's improved support for employees in small enterprises, the disadvantaged circumstance of these kinds of workers had remained so palpable that the NDP was able to use it as one of its principal justifications for the introduction of Bill 40.

Inasmuch as the prior legislation left it to the market – as mediated by collective bargaining and minimum employment-standard provisions – to deal with closures, contracting-out, the introduction of new technology, and the effect of relocations, this is still to be the case. Bill 40 does nothing to make any of these employer decisions, which so vitally influence employment rights and conditions, more expensive for employers by requiring, say, improved notice and severance pay or by giving workers the right to strike during the life of a collective agreement.[15] For workers, Bill 40's advances are minor, given the obvious needs of labour as explicitly acknowledged by the government. The employers' success – having the role and centrality of collective bargaining left undisturbed by the passage of the bill – is much more significant.

This is not to say that employers are celebrating the retention of a collective bargaining regime they have always liked. They never have liked the scheme. In Canada's turbulent 1960s, as workers flexed their muscles, they were met with employer and judicial repression. While the resulting Woods Task Force stressed the utility of collective bargaining to the political economy, it also acknowledged that it was hard to find a single employer who liked the scheme.[16] Obviously, this is still true. What employers have always wanted is for labour to have no right to defend itself at all. But there is an understanding that the model of collective bargaining that has emerged in North America is not far removed from the state of "nature," given that in a mature, liberal capitalist democracy employers have to accept some unionization.

The point sought to be made is not that our collective bargaining scheme is just a clever device designed to co-opt a bucolic labour movement. This kind of argument relegates the role of workers in capitalist relations of production to that of just being the passive opposition to, or negation of, capital. This is the kind of thinking which suggests that we only have those occupational health and safety regulations we have because individual capitalists are worried that unless they agree to such regulations, capitalism will suffer in the long run because of the lack of availability of able-bodied workers. This is plainly wrong. Capitalists worry about themselves, not capitalism. And workers do not just sit there. They fight the logic of capital, a logic which seeks to make people work for as little as possible for as long as possible.[17]

All schemes that mediate primitive capital-labour relationships represent a political compromise, the reaching of which has involved labour participation. So it is with the statutory collective bargaining regime which first emerged during the Depression in the United States and was adapted by Canada during the Second World War. It legitimated workers' rights to create a relative monopoly over labour power, diminishing competition on wages. Employers were to be forced to bargain with a bargaining agent freely chosen by their employees. Not only that, but they were to bargain in good faith and accept the enforceability of the ensuing agreement. Lockouts and strikes were to be legally permitted under certain circumstances, giving workers an explicitly legally approved (rather than occasionally legally tolerated) power to wage collective economic warfare. And, in due course, the arbitral administration of collective agreements emerged as a logical way to deal with the disputes that would inevitably arise during the life of a collective agreement. The employer was no longer to make unilateral decisions; the union could oppose employer decision-making by the use of arguments based on established criteria. A neutral adjudicator was to choose between rational arguments. The rule of law had come to displace the rule by an employer with overwhelming economic power. In general, a mechanism to blunt the logic of capital had been established.

The scheme that emerged did not only have the virtue of being a self-reliant, voluntaristic one in which the only role for government was that of facilitator, but it could also be characterized as advancing workplace democracy. The proponents of the regime were quick to note that elected trade unions could participate in the governance of workplace conditions and practices, aided by the rule of law (an essential component of democracy, as they defined it). As, notionally, collective bargaining was available to all private-sector (and later, in Canada, most public-sector) workers, it was easy to conceive of it as *the* mechanism by which workers should advance their causes. Collective bargaining was seen as an autonomous and reformist regime, and a central one at that.

This understanding was reinforced in the postwar period. The statutory collective bargaining regime was a crucial component of an entente during a long, continuous period of relatively good economic times. Labour in resource and mass-assembly industries was able to take advantage of the oligopolistic nature of capital in these central sectors and of relatively stable, high levels of demand for their output. Wages seemed to be on a rigid, upwardly slanting slope, and job security and on-the-job dignity were enhanced. Collective bargaining was providing a link between mass production and mass consumption.[18]

In this setting it was easy for labour and its allies to see collective bargaining as a progressive mechanism of adjustment. While no one claimed that capitalism had been transformed, there was a natural tendency to emphasize the symbiotic nature of the relationship between capital and labour engaged in collective bargaining, more than the continued workers' dependence on capital and the conflict that inheres in the wage relationship. Capital and labour were seen to have something like parity now that labour was entitled to exercise legalized, meaningful countervailing power. As capital needed to enter into agreements with workers whose bargaining power had been strengthened, and as those workers continued to have to rely on employers to create job opportunities, it was possible to argue – and it was argued – that capital and labour had a shared interest in making the pie they produced a larger one. There would be inevitable fights over the distribution of the pie, but this did not undermine the idea that the essence of collective bargaining relations was to create a web of rules based on a shared ideology.[19] Indeed, it was argued that these kinds of fights were probably healthy, because capital-labour disputations had to find an outlet and controlled collective bargaining could operate as a catalyst and a catharsis.[20]

As collective bargaining came to be seen as the linchpin in the dominant economic sectors of the economy in which labour had most of its strength, it gained approval as a central institution of a liberal pluralist polity. Its political legitimacy, and the legal possibility that it might be expanded to cover workers in many other sectors of the economy, tended to hide some of the inherent weaknesses of the system. Yet, these were profound. The stage had been set to maintain and perpetuate an economically and politically splintered working class.

Because the core of the system is that employees at one worksite are to bargain with their own employer, each local of a union is a discrete entity. For *legal* purposes, the local is *the* union. Only the local is given the right to strike. Its localized collective agreement is to be enforced by the local bargaining agent. The local union may get financial and administrative support from the union of which it is a branch. The employer, the other party to the collective agreement, may also be part of an integrated enterprise. Its bargaining is enhanced not only by any administrative support it gets from its parent organization, but also by the capacity of the enterprise as a whole to respond to changing production and output requirements at any one site that happens to be buffeted by labour disruptions. The constraints on the ally doctrine – developed by labour boards to help workers offset these obvious kinds of imbalances – and the proscription of secondary boycotts constitute severe limitations on the collective economic power of workers.[21] Given all of this, the failure of Bill 40 to inhibit directly the right of employers to contract-out work becomes very significant.

A second consequence of the local-by-local bargaining model is that the collective power of workers can be used directly only for the narrowest of economic purposes. By definition, demands on single, private employers in respect of the universal needs and aspirations of workers make no sense. Further, the limited nature of the statutory right to strike makes it a difficult weapon to employ politically vis-à-vis the state. This does not mean that workers never use the strike as a political weapon.[22] The Operation Solidarity uprising in British Columbia in 1983, the events of the Quebec Common Front, and the more recent nurses' strike in Alberta are modern examples to the contrary. What it does mean is that trade unions, whose legitimacy depends on their adherence to established collective bargaining rules, are not organized in a way that helps them further widespread political action. Indeed, they feel themselves pressured to dampen this kind of outbreak amongst their members.[23] The fact that the Ontario NDP's Bill 40 did not enlarge the definition of the strike can serve only to strengthen this tendency.

Because of these limitations, trade unions generally make their political stands in non-economic ways. Their officials and members fund and participate in electoral politics; they act as lobbyists in respect of legislative proposals; they support many other social activists and organizations, from injured workers' clinics to immigrant support groups to battered women. They engage in high-profile (and not so high-profile) consultation with government and business. In those meetings they rely on their ability to be rationally persuasive; their counterparts at the table know full well that the unions cannot threaten to engage in economic warfare by withholding their labour in concert, and that they cannot guarantee that they can bind their affiliates and members to any undertaking they give at the table.[24]

The relative political impotence of private-sector trade unions organized around the Canadian model of collective bargaining is replicated in the public sectors. Discrete employers were named so that trade unions could bargain on behalf of groups of workers hived-off on the basis of the government's need to departmentalize its activities. They were not unionized on the basis that government was *the* employer. When there is an impasse, it is immediately obvious that the government is the real employer, and at that point the close connection between the economic and political spheres in the public sector becomes manifest. It is argued that a group given the privilege of looking after its narrow economic self-interest should not be allowed to hamstring a government that has the responsibility of looking after the political, social, and economic welfare of all of society's groupings. Accordingly, many public-sector workers have been granted much more limited rights to negotiate and to strike than have private-sector workers. Further, governments find it much easier to legislate those public-sector workers who do have a full right to strike back to work than they do workers in the private sector.

Despite the appearance of similarity, collective bargaining in the public and private sectors is very different. This strengthens a myth that is most useful to capital, namely that the split between the private and the public is politically logical. This resonates with the historic divide between private- and public-sector workers, with the latter seen by the former as cushioned against competitive forces in a privileged way and as being non-militant, whereas private-sector workers tend to see themselves as insecure front-line soldiers in the war against repressive capital. All of this supports the well-worn argument that the private-economic and the public-political spheres are separate and, to a large degree, antithetical.[25]

Again, because it is a local-by-local model, statutory collective bargaining is not designed to deal with the sharp differences between primary and secondary industrial sectors. Chan F. Aw once calculated that there might be as much as a 40 percent differential in wage rates even between unionized workers.[26] This is merely to say that the collective bargaining scheme acts only indirectly and haphazardly as an incomes policy. There is no mechanism to overcome the pronounced regional differences created by geography, political fragmentations, and the logic of differently situated resource and export-led economies.[27] In the same vein, because collective bargaining, as a matter of constitutional law, falls under provincial jurisdiction, each province has slightly different institutional arrangements, reflecting the different political compromises that flow from their particular economic circumstance. This means that the practical day-to-day organization and preoccupation of provincial branches of national unions differ from one another. This does not aid concerted political activity. More importantly, businesses are likely to have more clout with provincial governments than they would have on the national stage.[28]

An even deeper and more significant fragmentation exists because of the implicit understandings that underpin the collective bargaining model. While the lawyer and the liberal pluralist pretend that collective bargaining is available to anyone who wants to participate, the reality has been that, in effective terms, it applies primarily to large employers in the mass-assembly and resource-extraction sectors. This is so because the machinery makes sense in that context. The oligopolistic nature of these industries and the enhanced stability of production that the unionization of large employment forces can deliver made collective bargaining attractive to government, business, and unions. Collective bargaining in these sectors made it possible for the regime to act as a mechanism to link mass production and mass consumption in the postwar period.

This Realpolitik of the collective bargaining regime dovetails nicely with paternalistic politics that see the heterosexual family, based on a family wage to be earned by the male head of the family, as a core institution. Collective bargaining, as thus envisaged, was intended to have male members of well-placed unions bring home a family wage. Workers in small-employer settings, particularly women in ghettoized occupational streams, could be left to their own devices with such help as the state is occasionally pressured into giving. The statutory collective bargaining scheme gives little, if any, incentive to better-protected workers to use any economic and political powers they derive from the collective bargaining institution to help their disadvantaged sisters in the secondary and tertiary sectors.[29] The importance of Bill 40's lack of response to this issue cannot be exaggerated.

These fragmentations are buttressed by a whole set of pro-employer concepts and biases in the collective bargaining system that are given life and bite by the imperial operation of law. The whole of the scheme presupposes that the statutory regime is a modification of transcendent legal constructs. This modification, therefore, is to be just that: the basic legal constructs are not to be subject to any serious questioning and must not be undermined. Most importantly, private property, as defined and defended by law, is to remain as sacrosanct as ever. The autonomous individual is the key to the legal system, and an individual's personality is inseparable from property ownership. Therefore, there is to be no external intervention with the use individual people wish to make of their properties, just as there is to be no interference with any choice they make about their lifestyles. Any intervention with property rights must be justified by the state. Of course, if employers freely contract to give away to workers authority over some of the uses to which their property is to be put, then they have voluntarily fettered their prerogative and such a contract will be enforced by the law.

As a result of the political compromise that embedded our statutory collective regime, the law has come to accept that collective bargaining is an appropriate way for an employer's prerogative to be fettered. But at the same time, in part because of the law's ideologically powerful starting points, the granting of collective bargaining rights was crafted in a way that would not destroy the quintessential legal principles defending the autonomy of the individual. Further, the law can be relied upon to ensure that, whatever collective bargaining rights have been given, they are not abused by the people using them.

A host of consequences follow. Some of the most significant include:

(i) In Canada, it is tremendously important to the legitimacy of trade union and working-class conduct that strikes be considered legal, that is, that they remain within the confines of the controlled collective bargaining system (as illustrated, for example, in the "Day of Protest" strategy). Ontario's Bill 40 did not alter this condition in any way.

(ii) The right of an employer to trade, being an exercise in individual property deployment, is to be preferred, unless *specifically* bargained or legislated away, to the right of workers to trade *collectively* in their property, their labour power.[30] This is, of course, a restatement and continuation of the law developed by the judiciary in the nineteenth century, when the links between market ideology and legal liberalism were firmly embedded by it. This is why the Supreme Court of Canada was able to hold that, despite the guarantee of freedom of association in the Charter of Rights and Freedoms, there is no such thing as the right to strike known to Canadian law; all there is, it rightly noted, is a narrow statutory permission to withhold labour in certain situations for limited statutory purposes. Ontario's Bill 40 did not alter this condition in any way.

(iii) The same credo signifies that employers do not have to let people organize on their time and on their property. This leads to the absurd spectacle of workers making assignations in tawdry motel rooms to engage in conduct which, supposedly, is an integral part of Canadian public policy, namely, the exercise of their freedom of association in order to form trade unions. Bill 40's only change to this is to give access to workers at the entrances to the property of employers who have their businesses situated in shopping malls. The bill maintains the opt-in system of union formation. An alternative system strongly urged by the OFL, that membership in a union should be considered a citizen-like right similar to the right to vote, was not acceptable to employers, nor to the NDP.[31]

The Effect of the Political Essence of Collective Bargaining on the Social Wage

These understandings, and the operation, of collective bargaining deepen the debilitating split between the economic and the political. The intrinsic belief propagated by this central institution is that the creation of economic welfare is to be left primarily to the decision-making of private-wealth owners in a staple-led growth economy. Collective bargaining justifies itself by its holding out that it promotes voluntary agreement-making between private actors operating in a somewhat modified market setting. It portrays itself as a sophisticated regime that has made it possible for private ordering to work. The state's role is to subvent the operation of a staple-led economy, and beyond that its interventions in labour relations should be limited to the role of a facilitator. With the facility of collective bargaining available, workers are to look after themselves. If workers want governments to do more for them, they should use political processes to attain their goals. Their ability to do so successfully depends on their effectiveness in pluralist politics. But this ability is constrained by the disproportionate influence of private property owners over political decision-making by dint of their virtually unchallenged right to dominate the economic sphere of decision-making.

One of the consequences has been that Keynesianism of the European kind was never whole-heartedly accepted in Canada.[32] Canadian policy-makers have perceived social security solely in terms of income replacement at minimal levels for the victims of a relatively uncontrolled market-based economy. Accordingly, it is like a patchwork quilt: people who are injured at work get quite different sums from the system than do people injured by a fall in their bathrooms; if people lose income as a result of war injuries rather than automobile accidents or mountain-climbing incidents, their needs will be met differently. A social welfare system that provides equally for all those who cannot participate fully in waged work has never been a part of the Canadian political scene.

G. Esping-Andersen presents a useful schematic outline of social systems.[33] He constructs a spectrum of nations running from those whose primary intent is to enhance equity to those whose dominant intent is to provide an efficient economy. He sees the first group as being at the social democratic end of his spectrum, with the other at the liberal end. He places Canada, together with Australia and the United States, at the liberal end.[34] When our governments are pressed into redressing discrimination and oppressions that arise out of the combined impact of unevenly divided economic power, systemic discrimination, and the normal working of capitalism, they tend to do so on the basis that the interventions should leave the operation of the market – which helped create the problems in the first place – as intact as possible.

Obvious examples include the regulation of occupational health and safety and pay equity. Occupational health and safety regulations are based on a mix of external standing-setting (which depends heavily on private-sector input) and an enforcement machinery that emphasizes the voluntary, private settlement of disputations and violations, in which employers have the upper hand. Legislatively imposed and enforceable pay-equity schemes, for the most part, are restricted to the public sector, in which state intervention is logically defensible. When they are imposed on the private sector, as in Ontario, the premise is that the scheme should operate on an employer-by-employer basis, just like collective bargaining. This leaves it subjected to the market as structured by employers, with all their biases reflected in occupational stereotyping and the male-centred evaluation of work. This means that to overcome the resulting inequities the same struggles have to be fought over and over again. The advances made so far, inevitably, are disappointing.[35]

The Freedom of Contemporary Capital Enhanced, in Part, by Old-Style Collective Bargaining

Capital, then, has had a more than solid platform from which it could launch its counter-revolution over the last two decades. The phenomenon referred to as globalization means that capital has been internationalized more than ever. Capital's greater mobility, combined with the availability of radical new technologies, is generating new modes of production that, increasingly, are allowing capital to ignore the boundaries of nation states.

Accumulation, at least in the dominant economic centres of the world, used to be regulated by national governments, but this is now becoming less and less possible.

Capital claims that its dream world – to be free from having to rely on labour in any way whatsoever – is becoming realizable. While this is still a distant goal, employers can show their heightened ability, and willingness, to roam with ease around the world to exploit cheap labour. This potential mobility forces nation states to accommodate capital's demands at the expense of workers and the protections they have won over the years. Acquiescence is the way, they are told, to retain investment within their borders rather than have it go to where capital's need for cheap resources and labour will be more easily satisfied.

The paradox is well understood: the nation state is cutting back on its role of political regulation and mediation to maintain itself as a political being. Depending on the nation's size as an economic and political unit, this tendency is more or less pronounced. Clearly, the impact of these pressures on the United States, Japan, and Germany is different than it is on Canada. Further, the degree of nation state subjugation to capital demands varies with the extent to which the political milieu of a particular country has internalized the ideology of the market.

Market ideology presupposes that the atomized private actions of individuals who are seeking to maximize their resources, abilities, and capacities should be allowed to reign unchecked. This enhances economic efficiency and political freedom, because it leaves individuals alone to make as many decisions for themselves about economic life and lifestyles as it is possible to permit in a complex society. From this perspective, the state is a potential enemy of both efficiency and political freedom, because it might use the power bestowed upon it to facilitate market operations for wrongful ends – in particular, to let collective will override individual preferences.

The more deeply embedded the acceptance of this model, the harder it is for governments to constrain capital mobility and decision-making power. Thus, while Sweden's special form of social democracy is under severe stress, its workers still seem better equipped to resist capital's onslaught than are workers in Canada, where collective bargaining has given pride of place to the market.

It is not only the ideology and practice of collective bargaining which have made it relatively easy for Canadian capital to push its agenda aimed at giving primacy to an unregulated market and unfettered trade:

(i) The politics of the Free Trade Agreement (FTA) and the North American Free Trade Agreement (NAFTA) serve to undermine the sovereignty of nation states. They are not so much trade agreements between states as they are the creation of investment opportunities for corporate actors within designated blocs. The essential plan is to make it easier and more secure for capital to move about, unhindered, within the trading bloc. The agreements seek to prevent present and future national governments from changing investment rules and social responsibility requirements. The resulting inability to favour local investors or to impose costs on foreign ones has the potential of diluting existing social protections and making it increasingly difficult for the working classes in each of the countries to use their electoral and political processes to achieve their goals.

(ii) The visible impetus for the Charlottetown Accord was the failed Meech Lake deal, the pressure on the Quebec government to deal with the sovereignty issue, the electoral needs of Quebec-based federalists, such as Brian Mulroney, and the increased sensitivity to the need to deal with Native peoples' interests more fairly. The ensuing package offered a less powerful central government and an aggrandizement of formal provincial authority. What is more, the package envisaged an extension of this decentralization over time. The power of Canada, as a sovereign state, to deal with mobile national and international capital was to be lessened. This was consonant with the FTA and NAFTA. At the same time, the proposed constitutional deal envisaged that the nominally enhanced political power of the provinces and of Quebec would not be very effective.

The right of the provinces to maintain special programs and trade barriers was to be taken away. The ability of provincial governments to use their legislative mandate to deal with the special needs of their people was to be constrained. Capital and labour were to be able to count on the same conditions throughout this balkanized, new federal political entity.[36] Again, the market ideology was promoted as more important than political democracy. The Charlottetown Accord failed, but the provincial governments' power to impose barriers and provide subsidies within their own borders has been chipped away. This part of constitutional deal-making has not been abandoned.

(iii) Over time governments have obtained less and less of their revenues from the corporations and the wealthy. By contrast, the contribution of middle-income earners to government revenues has increased.[37] Undoubtedly, the pressures generated on Canadian capitalists as a result of the effects of globalization led them to convince our governments that tax imposts should be lightened to create investment incentives here.[38] But, whatever the reasons for these dramatic changes in who contributes taxes to the government, they helped reinforce an anti-government and a pro-market environment. Tax critic Neil Brooks argues: "By cutting taxes ... neo-conservatives contrived a deficit crisis. They then persuaded voters that raising taxes would impair people's freedom and have disastrous economic effects. Consequently, the deficit, which they contended had to be dealt with, could only be controlled by cutting government services."[39]

At the same time, as middle-income earners have had to be taxed more heavily to pay for the maintenance of government services, an atmosphere has been created in which an attack on the public sector – and support for the private sector – flourishes. With increasing resonance the government has launched attacks on the undeserving poor, on the lazy and the malingering unemployed, on the waste of workers' compensation payments, and on the validity of universal health care. In turn this has boosted the idea that social safety-net legislation creates rigidities and has a negative effect on the efficient operation of the market. The privatization of profitable government operations and the deregulation of major industries, such as trucking and airlines, have been pushed with a vehemence, while corporate mergers have been permitted to prosper as never before. To further this end, major corporate actors were able to defang an already weak anti-combines statute. All activities that lead to greater corporate concentration are now decriminalized.[40] As a consequence, the monitoring of corporate mergers now leads to cozy deal-making with the government's regulators. The justification for this dilution of the competition-promotion statute was that, more than ever, Canadian capital needs to be concentrated to be able to compete on a level playing field in the international setting. Implicit in the acceptance of this rationale is the idea that the national economy is increasingly irrelevant to our public policy-making.[41]

(iv) The credo of the individual was also elevated mightily by the selling and the subsequent application of the Charter of Rights and Freedoms. The 1981 entrenchment of the charter assumed that the private actor is always in mortal danger of having her or his choices limited by the coercive action of a majority that can have the state act on its behalf. Further, because the individual and his or her property are indivisible in liberal legal ideology, private property owners who make claims of individual freedom have been able to restrict and inhibit the operation of market regulatory laws. For instance, retailers who believe that they need to be able to sell at any time they would like to do so have been able to make a successful claim that they should be given their wish under the rubric of the abstraction "freedom of religion."[42] Similarly, claims under the abstraction "freedom of speech" can be, and have been, used to support the corporate actors' desire to be able to advertise whatever they like, whenever they like, and, even more importantly, used to support their zeal to manipulate their huge funds to influence public policy-making and control elections (*vide* the 1988 free trade election).[43]

Corporations that want an unregulated market usually want to limit legislation. By contrast, workers and their allies need collective rights, and they need positive enactments from legislatures to get them. They have found, and will continue to find, it extremely difficult to obtain such results by the use of the Charter of Rights and Freedoms. The best they can hope for is that the state will not pass collectivist legislation that discriminates against them. On the whole, the charter favours the individual and the private over democratically determined public intervention. Precisely because of the prestige of this document and of the courts that administer it, the Charter of Rights and Freedoms has played a strong supporting role in the promotion of the unregulated market over other politically structured mechanisms and ideologies.

The Restructured Labour Markets: Coping with Unchained Marketeering

Canadian business has been able to restructure this increasingly market-favouring context without having to overcome many political impediments. Deindustrialization and branch-plant removals have gone along their merry way. Businesses are restructuring by farming out work to smaller enterprises that are legally discrete from, but economically and functionally dependent on, larger ones. This is creating integrated sets of pyramids of producers. In this way business is able to offset the possible impact of collectivized activities by labour. While employment in the core sectors in which collective bargaining works best is decreasing, employment is growing in the sphere in which collective bargaining has been largely irrelevant.

Non-standard employment – which is markedly different from the full-time employment envisaged by the postwar Keynesians and statutory collective bargaining proponents – accounted for half of all the new jobs created between 1981 and 1986. Part-time, short-term, or temporary-agency work and self-employment now represent 30 percent of total employment. Women and the young are disproportionately represented among these precarious workers.[44] Homework, especially among immigrant women, is increasing.[45] As part of this structural shift smaller employment settings are becoming the norm.[46] For instance, the Urban Dimensions Group reports that in 1985 nearly 84 percent of all of Ontario's registered businesses had fewer than ten employees.

These developments were not just caused by the political and ideological manoeuvrings of the past decade. After all, Canada is not unique in suffering from these trends. There are similar alarming movements throughout the advanced industrialized nations of the world.[47] But Canadian capitalism has had to face only minor political opposition to its declared path, claiming that the logic, and the undoubted good, of participating in an unfettered manner in a globalized market is not just the best way to create economic welfare, but the only way. Canadian governments have been either unable or unwilling – or both – to impose costs on employers that decide to de-invest, or that decide to restructure in order to tap the new fragmented and segmented labour markets.[48]

Unions, without any real political clout, have been left to fend for themselves. But, as they have never been given, or been able to win, control over investment or over the employers' ability to contract-out work, they have been virtually helpless in the face of decisions seen to be made outside the scope of their constrained bargaining rights. To make matters worse, the new centres of employment growth are not amenable even to the limited successful collective bargaining that well-placed unions were able to conduct in the past.

Bill 40 as a Bellwether of the Ontario NDP's Limited Vision of Social Democracy

The futility of the kind of labour-law reform offered by the Ontario NDP's Bill 40 is clear. The reform makes a number of assumptions that are not only wrong but also positively dangerous. The starting point is that all that collective bargaining really needs as a mechanism of capital-labour mediation is a change in how the law is framed and works. This position leads to the emphasis on procedural reforms.

Collective bargaining thus continues to be perceived by the NDP – and, perhaps, by many of its union allies – as a mechanism that can improve workers' conditions without costing employers a great deal. The prevailing vision is that well-paid workers mean more consumer power and higher productivity and, therefore, greater profitability for employers.[49] This may have been a more defensible view during the postwar period of relative abundance; the limits of the political and economic liberalism that inheres in the statutory collective bargaining regime were not seen as clearly then. But, given Ontario's social democrats' own statement of contemporary labour-market problems, this kind of approach can no longer be justified. Here, then, is the paradox: social democrats should, perhaps, de-emphasize the values of the old-style collective bargaining, which was once their proudest achievement.

Social democracy stands for a mixed economy of some kind. The nature of that mix is all important. At a time when employers are exploiting their mobility, one approach would be to increase the presence of public-sector enterprise. This could offset the threat posed by capital flight. To be effective, this approach should be accompanied by an emphasis on a growth model based on managed trade between countries, rather than unfettered trade between corporate actors. This would move social democrats towards the democratic socialism end of the political spectrum. Such strategies would be met with fierce opposition, and the government would need to build a political base. Redistribution of income, by different tax structures and social welfare transfers, would have to be undertaken to give workers a common stake in the exercise and to build coalitions. The democratization of capital – primarily by giving workers control over their pensions funds – would have to be put on the agenda. The public sector would have to be expanded.[50] To say that this is a hard row to hoe is to state the obvious. But it is important to recognize that such options do exist.

Social democrats can also deal with the crisis of distribution that capital's gyrations are creating by merely trying to help Canadian capitalists make the most of the opportunities available in a worldwide setting.[51] That is, social democrats can move towards the liberal end of the spectrum. They do so when they accept, as a given, that wealth is created by private property owners and that the government's job is to help make this wealth creation easier. Whereas a dyed-in-the-wool conservative government would approach this task by removing all impediments to capital – by deregulation, privatization, lowering taxes, removing unions, eviscerating the welfare net, and, mostly, by eliminating all barriers to trade – a liberal-tending social democratic government tries to help capital create wealth by positive intervention rather than government withdrawal. The support programs offered by the Ontario NDP – training, labour adjustments, investment capital – are typically of this kind. The government offered Bill 40 on this basis. It said that the bill ought to help capital because it is not intended to diminish its capacity to trade on a global basis. Productivity and aggregate consumer demand will improve if the government enhances collective bargaining and assists localized capital. The Ontario NDP, then, continues to adhere to the Keynesian, social democratic use to which collective bargaining *might* be put. As a consequence, it sees it primarily as an *economic* instrument that can help workers who participate in it and as a mechanism of adjustment that can be part of a national (provincial) entente of the post-war Fordist kind. As part of building that entente, the government has to concede that because of the effects of globalization, it is necessary to improve conditions for employers. Training of the workforce, making investment capital more readily available and cheaper, and subsidizing research and development all become part of an industrial strategy which, together with more civilized collective bargaining, will lead to a more fruitful, new collaborative mode of production.

The hope of social democrats of this stripe is that, as growth occurs, workers in the non-traditional settings can be provided with more protections and a better deal. The difficulty is that this strategy rests on hope. If employers do not co-operate because they do not believe that a renewal of a kind of modified postwar Fordism will suit them, there is no way to make them participate.

In Ontario the political clout of workers has not been improved to enable the would-be social democratic government to impose its will on footloose capital. Precisely because collective bargaining has been endorsed to be a narrow economic instrument by Bill 40, the existing political fragmentations have been left to be exploited by business. More than ever, employing classes can blackmail the government into subsidizing them, increasingly making the government more dependent for its life on the private sector's willingness to invest here, precisely because the vision of politics and economics evinced by the Ontario NDP when it enacted Bill 40 was that it did not disagree fundamentally with capital's position: that capital must be given the capacity to create most of the wealth and thereby to create the welfare for citizens that the NDP would like to see provided.

The government's own logic mandates that it does not intrude too much, lest it spoil its own helpful efforts. The argument that it must not run deficits *merely* to provide services begins to make sense to the administration. After all, deficits require repayment. This can affect tax and interest rates adversely and therefore inhibit private capital's ability to generate wealth. The argument that the public sector's role must be diminished to cut deficits falls on increasingly receptive ears.

The NDP probably did not have these outcomes in mind when it enacted Bill 40, but the results flow from the logic on which the bill is based. Bill 40, by doing nothing about the institutional, political, and economic fragmentations that already existed, has made it very hard to mount a countervailing attack on the more extreme consequences of market-based policies. It would have been very difficult for the NDP to address the problems that it knew labour was facing when it attempted labour-law reform, even if it had grasped the danger of increased reliance on the private sector and the limitations of the collective bargaining regime. But it seems as if the party did not have that appreciation. As a result, the descent on the road to serfdom has been accelerated.

Part 4

I REMEMBER MINE MILL

Introduction

As part of the centennial festivity, Mine Mill contacted retired members now residing in all parts of Canada and the United States and invited them to return to Sudbury for the celebrations. The chapter in this section emerged out of the lively interchange of ideas. Realizing that the gathering of so many Mine Mill veterans from the 1950s and 1960s presented a unique opportunity, the conference organizers asked them to address current political concerns and to reminisce about their rich and varied experiences in the Mine Mill movement. The veterans had a hard task. They were asked to address the following questions – but at the same time they were told to keep their comments to ten minutes.

- How do you see the current global climate, and what do you think are the consequences of this for labour today? Compare this situation to the one you experienced in the 1940s, 1950s, and 1960s.
- What do you feel should be the response of the trade union movement to the global restructuring of labour and capital? What form should the trade union movement take in this struggle?
- What should workers know in order to wage the fight as collective members of a trade union? How has this changed over the years?
- What impact did the Cold War have on Mine Mill? What was the role of the communists in Mine Mill?
- What was Mine Mill's involvement in social, recreational, and cultural activities? What was the significance of Mine Mill's cultural activism?

The resulting statements contain many gems about the past and present of the labour movement. For anyone studying workers' experiences, the nature of work, the difficulties of organizing, and the effects of working conditions and the Cold War on workers' children, the collected anecdotes, lessons, and knowledge about past and present represent a treasure trove of fascinating material. There were two "I Remember Mine Mill" sessions at the centennial conference, and what follows is a condensed combination of both sessions.

Chapter 11
"We're Still Here"

A Panel Reviews the Past and Looks to the Future

The Panelists

Pearl Chytuk was a member of Local 598 when she worked at the smelter in Copper Cliff, Ontario, during World War II. She is a founding member of the Ladies' Auxiliary Local 117 and has remained active in the auxiliary for about thirty years. After retirement from active employment at Inco she worked at several different jobs and has been a leading member of the left-wing Ukrainian movement in Sudbury.

Francis E. "Buddy" DeVito was a legionnaire and Mine Mill organizer and executive member in Trail, British Columbia. He worked in Sudbury in the early 1960s as a national union representative and on public relations during the Steelworker raids. He was also active in municipal politics and was elected mayor of Trail.

Mike Farrell has worked for over forty years in the union movement. He was a Mine Mill staff representative for twelve years, later serving in the same capacity for eighteen years for the Steelworkers after the merger in 1967. Prior to joining the Mine Mill staff, he spent eight years in the mining industry.

Clinton Jencks was active in Mine Mill Locals 557 and 890 in the southwestern United States before becoming an international Mine Mill union representative from 1953 to 1956. He was active in the fight to end discrimination against Mexican-Americans and assisted in the development of the film *Salt of the Earth*. He returned to school in 1959, earning a Ph.D. from the University of California at Berkeley. Retired since 1986, he is now professor emeritus of economics and labour history at San Diego University.

One of the two "I Remember Mine Mill" panels at the Centennial Conference of Mine Mill, May 1993. Left to right: Ray Stevenson, Mike Solski, Ruth Reid, Joan Kuyek (moderator), Clinton Jencks, Barney McGuire, and Mike Farrell.
Courtesy Dorothy Wigmore

Barney McGuire was a union activist beginning in the mid-1930s. He worked as a miner and later held positions in many locals. As an organizer he brought the ideas and protection of Mine Mill to isolated mining camps in Canada's northwest. He began work with the Steelworkers in the early 1960s. He died in 1995.

Ruth Reid came to Sudbury from Hamilton in 1952. With her husband, Weir Reid, she was a volunteer and later co-director of Mine Mill's summer camp during the 1950s and 1960s. She was a leading figure in the Ladies' Auxiliary Local 117 and was secretary-treasurer from 1975 until 1990, when the auxiliary ceased its activities.

Lukin Robinson has worked for the population division of the United Nations, where he helped to organize and unionize workers within the organization. In the 1950s and early 1960s he was research director of Mine Mill, and he now works for OPSEU (the Ontario Public Service Employees Union) in Toronto.

Roy Santa Cruz Jr. is a third-generation Mine Mill organizer and a charter member of Mine Mill Local 938. He has held many different positions in the union and has worked many years with Mexican-Americans. He also worked with the Steelworkers.

Mike Solski was chairman of the Mine Mill organizing committee at the Coniston, Ontario, plant between 1942 and 1944. Since that time he has served Mine Mill in a number of capacities, including as vice-president in 1947, secretary-treasurer in 1951, and president of Local 598 from 1952 to 1959. He also served as eastern Canadian director of District 2 during the Steelworker raids. He was secretary of the first Canadian Mine Mill Council in 1953 and secretary of the constitutional committee that established Canadian autonomy in 1955. He is the co-author, with John Smaller, of a book on the history of Mine Mill. He has also been involved in local politics, including terms as Coniston mayor from 1963 to 1973 and mayor of Nickel Centre from 1973 to 1979.

Ray Stevenson became involved in Mine Mill in 1938 in Kirkland Lake, Ontario, before coming to Sudbury in 1950. He was on the executive of Local 598 and edited the *Mine Mill Herald* for many years. He was elected to the Canadian Mine Mill Council in 1953 and was on the national executive board from 1955 to 1961. He worked for the Steelworkers between 1967 and 1978 in public relations and educational programs. In 1978 he became the first Canadian on the secretariat of the World Peace Council in Helsinki.

Jim Tester was involved in the labour movement for over sixty years. He was in Kirkland Lake during the many important struggles there. Later, in Sudbury, he served as a steward and then as a member of the executive board. He became president of Local 598 in 1969 and served in that capacity until 1974. At the time of the conference, he was secretary-treasurer of Local 598 Falconbridge pensioners' organization; he had been active in that organization since its inception in 1987. He was also a columnist for the local Sudbury paper *Northern Life*. His analysis of conditions in the workplace and critiques of political events won him provincial journalism awards. He died in late 1994.

The sessions, held 14 May 1993, were moderated by Marge Reitsma-Street, School of Social Work, Laurentian University, and Joan Kuyek, a Sudbury activist and author.

The Participants Speak

Clinton Jencks: I really can't sit down and talk about stuff that's so important to me, and I want to start in a kind of unusual way [stands and sings]:

I dreamed last night I saw Joe Hill just alive as you and me
Says I, but Joe, you're 10 years dead [the audience joined in at this point]
I never died says he, I never died says he
From San Diego through all of Canada in every mine and mill
Where workers strike and organize
That's where you'll find Joe Hill
That's where you'll find Joe Hill

That's what I think this is all about. The thing that makes this union important, like the thing that made the farmworkers' union important, was that the old Western Federation and Mine Mill made the rank-and-file member feel that he and she were important. They weren't depending upon the union to deliver the goods; they knew that the union could only deliver what they were willing to fight and to suffer for. Now I learned this the hard way.

You know my name is Clinton Jencks, and I was nicknamed "Palomino" by the Mexican-American people, with and for whom I worked in the southwest during the 1930s, 1940s, and 1950s. One of the reasons that I have such a strong bond with the Canadian section of this union is that I was working in the colony of the south – the southwest of the United States – and you were working in the colony of the United States of the north. I found that we could depend on you when we got in trouble, and you could depend on us when you got in trouble. I think that is what this conference is all about.

Clinton Jencks, Utah Phillips, and Ray Stevenson at the Mine Mill Hall, May 1993.
Courtesy Susan Vanstone

The big thing that has changed is the fact that we now have a global economy, and now we've got to look beyond our national borders and support our sisters and brothers wherever they live.

Well, let's get down to looking at the past. What was the impact of the Cold War on Mine Mill? Well, in a few words, it was devastating. Why? Because Mine Mill was a democratic rank-and-file-controlled union with direct election of union officers and direct membership referendum on constitutional changes. The Cold War and its associated anti-communist hysteria was used by the major corporations that Mine Mill bargained with as a direct weapon to weaken solidarity between workers, between local unions, and between national unions. In addition, the government's ability to harass the unions was in direct relationship to the power of the corporations.

Picture specifically the following scenario: Mine Mill officers, staff, and representatives sitting in hearing rooms all week long, defending the right of the union to do its job – representing its members – and then flying out to all corners of Canada and the United States to participate in bargaining conferences, wage-policy negotiations, and dealing with the raids of people who wanted the dues but not the responsibilities. In my opinion – and it's only my opinion – ultimately, the impact of the Cold War and the anti-communist hysteria was to force the Mine Mill merger with Steel. It destroyed Mine Mill as an international union, but it can never destroy the spirit of Mine Mill any more than you can destroy Joe Hill.

Now, on a more delightful, upbeat note, I would like to relay a personal experience of mine. The giant Kennecott Copper Corporation decided in 1948 that they would no longer bargain with my local union, Local 890, until our officers, local and international, signed the non-communist affidavit. They claimed the union just wasn't "patriotic." Patriotic, bullshit – Mine Mill was a threat to their profits. A lot of our members got scared: "They're not going to negotiate a contract with us, what will we do?" I had done a little reading about the early history of Mine Mill, and I'd done a little reading about another organization that the Western Federation started, the Industrial Workers of the World.

I didn't talk about that history. Instead I said, "Look guys. Look what's been going on for years. We fought hard and we won national bargaining, didn't we?" "Yeah," they responded. "And that made us stronger, didn't it?" "Yeah."

And I said, "Look what the companies are doing. They've got us tied down to contracts, they hold out for months, drag on negotiations, they wear us down, and eventually what do they do? They try to buy us off with a little wage increase. And some of the most vital things that affect the men and women on their jobs – their working conditions, the way they get treated, the right to promotion, and the right to grieve – well, we can't get that this year." And the list of unsettled things began to pile up. So I said, "Look, we're free now, we don't need to negotiate once a year, we can negotiate every day. We're not tied down. We don't have to wait for the company ..." And we did that; we organized our committees. Every day we were in the company's offices with something that hadn't been settled for years. And the guys understood they weren't going to get anything unless they backed it up. So we had a few quiet shutdowns – they couldn't be called wildcats, because we didn't have a contract.

The end of this story was that after six months nobody had signed the affidavits yet, but Kennecott Copper came and begged us to sign a contract so they could get us tied down for one, two, or three years. So that's the other side of the story. When we're not divided by political beliefs but we do our job, then the Cold War can't destroy us.

Now, I got two minutes to deal with probably what's been the most debated question in our union: what was the contribution of the communists in Mine Mill? Well, I'm going to say some not-so-surprising things. In all my years – and that's a lot of years – in Mine Mill, I never knew who was a communist and who was not. We never judged each other according to political beliefs or affiliation, but rather we judged one another by what we were willing to do or not to do to carry out the union policies democratically determined by the rank and file.

I never, and nobody else that I knew of, ever supported or opposed any person running for union office on the basis of political affiliation, communists or otherwise. Instead I offered my support based upon how effective I thought that person would be in serving our membership. Never in all of my years in the union did any communist or Communist Party representative try to tell me what position to take, what to do, or influence me on union matters. Sure, I talked to members of the Communist Party during that period, because they were people that I could depend on to help us when we needed help. Those communists I did know outside of the union were generally strong supporters of the union idea, of working-class solidarity, non-discrimination, and national autonomy. And I generally thought of them as people we could depend upon for support in the community when we got into a struggle and we needed and asked for their support. That's my experience, and all of the rest was a means of the company taking our eyes off the ball and confusing people about what we were doing. It was all a lot of fluff signifying nothing except that very thing – to confuse us, to divide us, to weaken us. When we refused to be weakened or divided we were strong ... and that doesn't mean we walked out on every issue, it just meant we sought compromises but we were not hampered or tied down by somebody else's rules, except the ones that we made up.

Mike Farrell: I'm going to relate briefly a history of the union as I remember it, a bit of Mike Farrell, and tell a couple of stories you might find interesting.

I joined the Mine, Mill and Smelter Workers Local 240 in Kirkland Lake in 1950 at the age of nineteen. In those days in Ontario, for those who are old enough to remember, the province was tied up tighter than a drum on Sundays. There was no television of course, there was no bowling, there was no pool. There were bootleggers – but you know, miners didn't frequent those places.

At that time the union used to have its meetings on Sunday evening. Somebody whose name is lost to history dragged a young fellow out to the membership meeting and, lo and behold, I became involved. Within a few months I was on the executive board and entertainment committee of Local 240. Incidentally, that local was the oldest active local union in the Mine, Mill and Smelter Workers in Canada.

That was about the same time that the split developed within the Canadian Congress of Labour, the predecessor of the Canadian Labour Congress, and a number of unions were ostracized or kicked out, whichever phraseology you want to use. The two most prominent ones were the Mine, Mill and Smelter Workers and United Electrical Workers of America (UE). So the raids had started. Basically they started here in Sudbury – and as Mike Solski will probably tell you, they couldn't get to first base in Sudbury at that time. But in Timmins and Kirkland Lake, they were successful to a degree.[1]

So at a tender age I found myself passing out leaflets at five-thirty in the morning at the plant gates and fighting for a principle that I felt was correct – and nothing has ever changed my mind about that, I want you to know. There was a group of us at that time – I suppose we were young Mine Mill lions, idealists, packsack miners – who went from mine to mine. We really didn't know too much about the union, but we knew that the boss hated the union. I'm not sure if that's logical, but since the boss hated the union, the union had to be a damn good thing for the workers. That was the early thinking. So wherever we went we tried to organize the union, and we were reasonably successful in places like Cobalt, Temagami, Elliot Lake, and Bancroft. I ended up at the Faraday Mine in Bancroft in the fall of 1956. It was a lot of years ago when two gentlemen by the names of Ray Stevenson and the late Nels Thibault came to me and said, "Farrell, you're doing a pretty good job organizing, you're signing people up, do you want to go on the staff?" I said, "What the hell does that mean?" "Just keep on doing what you're doing." So I tried it for three months, and three months became a full-time vocation for over thirty years. And organize we did, to the best of our ability.

It was an extremely difficult era. I talk to a number of young people about this period of history, and when I start to talk about the McCarthy era they ask, "What was that, Mike?" Then I realized how old I am getting. As Brother Jencks pointed out – and I know it was not as bad in Canada as it was in the States, but it certainly overflowed into this country – if you had a progressive bone in your body, you were labelled a communist. The heat was on, the battle was on all over North America.

I had the good fortune – perhaps that is not the proper term – but I had a friend of a friend who called me up in Kirkland Lake when I was up visiting my relatives probably about twenty years ago. He was a cop at one of the mines which was closing down, and even now I won't say which mine it was because it wouldn't make any difference or mean anything to you. He had a twinge of conscience. He had been given the blacklist, the black book, and told to burn it. He called me up on a Sunday afternoon, and he said, "I hear you're in town, Mike, I got something you might want to see." And I said, "What's that?" He said, "I got the blacklist on one of the bigger mines in Kirkland Lake which has been running for approximately forty years. Would you like to come and have a look at it before I burn it?" Well, I looked at it and I tried everything to take it out of his hands, without success, but I spent two or three hours over three or four drinks, or maybe it was five or six, perusing the book, and my God, it was a who's who of the labour movement.

Everybody who was involved in the labour movement, whether in the Mine, Mill and Smelter Workers, the Steelworkers, the UAW, the UE, were in that book. And they were labelled. Oh, Stevenson was there, Solski was there, Thibault was there, I could go on. Farrell was there, Larry Sefton was there, and other names that would mean something to you if I went back thirty to forty years. They had, I guess, meticulously recorded any name that appeared in a union publication written by an activist. You may recall that the old *Mine Mill Herald* listed the names of men who stood for local union election. You could tell from the way it was written in the book that they had somebody subscribing to the miners' union paper. So the guy who was on the executive board, his name went into the little book. Incidentally, the book wasn't very little either. So I saw it. I'm probably the only union staff rep that I know of who ever saw a company's blacklist. And I tell you, it was a pretty sobering experience. A pretty sobering experience.

When I became involved in Kirkland Lake, the first contract I worked under had four things. Obviously, we had wages. You never forget your first job in the mine – $9.17 a shift for a runner, $8.72 for a helper on a machine, the liner machine. We had five paid holidays a year, time and a half if you worked overtime – not double time and a half, not triple time – time and a half. We had $2,000 life insurance. And lo and behold, we had two weeks of vacation after five years. After one year we had one week, after five years, we had two weeks. It didn't matter if you were there thirty-five years, you still had two weeks of vacation. Some of the things that we have today – optical plans, drug plans, dental plans, floating holidays, extra vacation leave – God, we never even thought of those things. We were so happy to get the forty-hour week (you had the forty-hour week here in Sudbury long before we had it in the gold mines in Timmins and Kirkland Lake), but we had to pay dearly for it, believe me. Struggle and strife, the old story. When we got the forty-hour week, we thought we were on cloud nine. So I guess as I got older, I learned to have little patience with some of our younger brothers who really didn't want to work Friday night any more ...

Being a union rep was a rewarding experience. I travelled to most of the major mining camps in Canada. I missed the Labrador iron-ore range, and from what I've been told about that, I don't suppose I missed very much. But I met a lot of good people, I met some characters, and I saw and dealt with people in negotiations, arbitrations, and all the things a staff rep has to do which I probably would not have done otherwise.

Barney McGuire: What I would like to talk about is the importance of unions being involved in community affairs. And the example that I want to give is the Cumberland Historical Society, their annual Miners' Memorial Days, and how they have been connected with Mine Mill 598.

About eight years ago, the Cumberland Historical Society decided to embark upon a historical restoration program. As a historical society they have always had as their fundamental policy to document *anything* that happened in the area as *history*. If I had to stop speaking right now, those are the words that I would repeat. I think that says volumes.

I went into Cumberland, British Columbia, promoting the Mine Mill book about eight years ago, and as a result of our conversations, they embarked upon a historical restoration program.[2] Cumberland was where Ginger Goodwin was murdered; he was a member of the Mine, Mill and Smelter Workers' Union. One of the events that they sponsor is an annual Miners' Memorial Day. It is patterned after the ground that you people in Sudbury broke for us. We pay respect to all workers who lost their lives in industrial accidents and, most importantly, pledge to work for safe working conditions for all workers for the future. In sponsoring their Miners' Memorial Days, they absolutely insist and will not sponsor it unless there is representation from all union bodies – the Confederation of Canadian Unions, the Canadian Labour Congress, and the B.C.-Yukon Building Trades. The city council and the mayor are actively involved.

One of the things we have done in the past several years is erect a cairn honouring the members of the Chinese and Japanese communities, and one honouring the black community. We have placed a storyboard plaque on Comox Lake, and on one side of it is "The Ballad of Ginger Goodwin," and on the other side a map of the area. This plaque was consecrated by Bishop Remi De Roo from Victoria, British Columbia. We were successful in getting the mountain on which Ginger Goodwin was murdered named Mount Ginger Goodwin, which was the result of over two years of work. We have placed the plaque at the foot of the mountain. It reads: "Mount Ginger Goodwin was officially named by Cumberland mayor Bronco Moncrief on Miners' Memorial Day, June 24, 1989. Albert Ginger Goodwin, pacifist, socialist, and trade unionist, was shot by Dominion police just above this site. One of B.C.'s labour martyrs, a worker's friend, Goodwin lies buried in the Cumberland cemetery." His headstone was erected by the Canadian Association of Industrial, Mechanical and Allied Workers' Mining Council and by the Sudbury Mine, Mill and Smelter Workers' Union Local 598. A replica of a coal mine has been built in the basement of the museum. We placed a plaque sponsored by the B.C. Federation of Labour at the site of number four mine. That mine had a very unusual history. One of the important points to remember was that sixty-four men were murdered in that mine.

Another year we sponsored a book, *The History of Ginger Goodwin*. I want to say that I think this is a part of our trade union history and that we should make the book available to as many trade unionists as we can. The people of Cumberland, at one of our annual events, erected a plaque at the entrance to town. This plaque is twelve feet by eight feet and it states, "In honour of our miners." It's a magnificent document. No picture does this

Mine Mill Local 598 President Rick Briggs and former Mine Mill organizer Barney McGuire at the Mine Mill stewards' banquet at the centennial celebrations, May 1993.

Mine Mill Local 598 (CAW)

plaque justice, because a picture does not show the flame on the miner's lamp and other details. Last year we erected a plaque at number five mine site.

This coming Miners' Memorial Day we are going to show a film made by high school students in Vancouver after they read the book on Ginger Goodwin. And, another highlight of this year's events, the Cumberland Historical Society is working on a project to tell the history of all the women who worked in Cumberland, how they lived after their husbands were murdered in the mines, and so on. Also this year, our guest speaker is going to be Nancy Riche, vice-president of the Canadian Labour Congress, and our guest of honour is going to be June Roberts; you know her well.[3] During the strike in Yellowknife, when the authorities came to remove her trailer and her car, she said, "I would sooner lose it all than have my husband cross that picket line."

Ruth Reid: I'm going to talk about the wonderful women of Mine Mill, especially the Ladies' Auxiliary. I was a little upset at the booklet that was put out by someone associated with Mine Mill.[4] It had pictures of our twenty-fifth anniversary celebration, and it said, "Goodnight Ladies." Well, it'll never be *goodnight ladies* to the Ladies' Auxiliary, because the work they have done in this community is very important and I think everybody here is aware of it. So I would like to just say that we were very unhappy about those pictures. I think they came from Mike Solski's collection, and he has given me the names of some of the people who were in those pictures.

When I say "the wonderful women of Mine Mill," you know, I think that the women were the heart of the union. Mine Mill says, "A union is only half organized if it doesn't have the women." Now the auxiliary was organized in 1943, and when I came to Sudbury in 1952 many of the cultural activities were being run by the women – there were play schools and movie shows, and there was a day camp out at Richard Lake. As more cultural programs were developed by my husband Weir when he became recreational director, more women became involved in these activities. When you think of the women who helped in the dance school and how popular it was, they not only took part in the dance school, but they helped plan the programs, they made costumes, they did the publicity.

The same with the drama group – they were not only acting, but they were behind the scenes promoting it. And at the children's camp the women were there as mothers, cooks, and at the beginning of the summer the parents and Ladies' Auxiliary always helped get the camp cleaned up for the new season. And really, Mine Mill was the heart of the community. It's kind of nice that here today we do have a few of our charter members – Anne Macks is here, and another charter member, Pearl Chytuk.

When I think of all the variety of things that the ladies' auxiliaries did!

Do you know, when the halls were built there were ladies' auxiliaries formed in each of the halls, and they had a central committee that would meet once a month with representatives from all the various auxiliaries, and I remember Pearl Moir was chairman of that committee. Remember the Murdochville strike in 1957? We put on a supper to support them. In 1961, of course, we had to meet down in the 902 hall.[5] There again, the women were catering, putting on their favourite suppers, always raising money for things in the community. They supported so many causes through these efforts. Someone once referred to the Ladies' Auxiliary as social workers because they supported so many things in the community. The auxiliary was active in the Red Feather campaign, raising support for the people in the sanatorium, the plastic surgery ward at Sunnybrook Hospital, the Vietnam civilians, and also the welfare of our own members.

During the strike in 1958 at Inco, our wonderful women looked after the clothing store downstairs in the union hall, and we also went out and visited people, seeing that no one went without during that time. Do you remember in 1954 when the Mine Mill theatre troupe put on the Joe Hill presentation? In going through some papers with Dieter Buse, I came across a letter from Barrie Stavis,[6] and also a letter from Paul Robeson saying how happy he was that we were going to present the Joe Hill play. And I mustn't forget to say that when all these exciting things were happening in the community, Mike Solski was the president of Local 598, and that made quite a difference. Some other things too that my husband was interested in – remember the low-rental programs? A lot of the women were interested in that program. Women were also active in the efforts to extend the public library system. As soon as we had the halls in the outlying areas we were able to get libraries out there.

Of course, after the merger in 1967 it was rather difficult, but I remember the women – I notice Lillian Mason here – how they struggled and worked and catered to earn money because there were still many things that we wanted to support in the community. I mustn't forget to mention the Christmas parties. Remember the Mine Mill Christmas parties? There were thousands of youngsters, weren't there? There were always the women there who were helping. In 1966 the auxiliary made its views known to the Select Committee on Mining, Taxation and Youth, and they also opposed the sales tax when it was first put in.

There were so many things that they did, and these are just some of the things that I can remember. Now, I hope I haven't left out anything, but here again I'm going to go back to the wonderful women of Mine Mill. I remember their concern for the children. A lot of the programs that the people participated in then were sponsored by the auxiliary and the women were always around to help at these events. I think too that it was fortunate for us that we were able to go to union meetings. We had a voice, we could always express our views, even if we couldn't always vote. I think that was very important.

Mike Solski: I have a couple of words to say. Last night, the lady that spoke to us by the name of Laurell Ritchie was critical of the omissions in the one hundredth anniversary brochure. [See chapter 3.] Ruth has expressed similar feelings, and all I want to say to anyone in the future is that if you're looking for pictures, there's plenty of them. There are three thousand at the public library, the reference library here in Sudbury, and 95 percent of them have names and dates on them. So no more goofs like you've committed this time. Now can I start?

We've been asked to review the past. I have some difficulty selecting what to talk about in the past. There are so many good things and so many things that are not so good. I guess I can feel fortunate that I've had the opportunity to record some of that past, and I was very happy to see here last night both Liz and Harry Smaller, Jack's children – Jack helped me to put the history of Mine Mill together. I know there's a lot of detail in that book that I could refer to in speaking here this evening, but as much as there is in that book, there is still a lot more that could and should be written. I hope that with all the interviews being done by all these young people at the university, that you're not wasting our time, that you put the information into book form so that there will be more said about the history of this very important union, a union that has done so much for working people not only in this community, but throughout the United States and Canada.[7]

Throughout this conference a number of people have referred to the subject of political action, independent political action. This union of the Mine, Mill and Smelter Workers was a pioneer in that field. Many, many years ago we took independent political actions, or our predecessors did, and as a result of those actions we were able to establish legislation setting out the eight-hour day and compensation legislation. We elected people of all political stripes, as long as they were committed to doing a job for the miners and the smeltermen. How ironic it is, at least to me, to see those big badges that some of you people are carrying around.[8] We were criticized for our independent stand. Well, my God, those of you that tied yourself to the tail of one party have sure been getting a whacking from that tail in the last couple of months. There are lessons to be learned, even at this late stage.

This union was a pioneer in many fields. We look around here, we've been spoiled in the Sudbury area, we had so much working-class culture.

Half of it has disappeared. But you go back to the early days, both in the United States and Canada, we pioneered in those fields. We looked after our own sick, we looked after our own widows, and some of that even rubbed off at Mine Mill in Falconbridge. Not too long ago, Jim Tester and his group of pensioners took on the cause of fighting for the widows in Falconbridge. And they attained, I think, a pension of $150 a month for women who before weren't getting a cent. Unfortunately, that didn't happen in the company I worked for; at Inco, all they got was $125 in one lump sum, and nothing else since that time.

A lot of new information surfaced when we were completing the manuscript for the book. We were not able to include very much of it, but for the benefit of the future generation, I hope somebody

Mike Solski, past president of Local 598. He was elected vice-president of the local in 1947, became secretary-treasurer in 1951, and was local president from 1951 to 1959. He served as eastern Canadian director (district 2) of Mine Mill during the Steel raids. From 1962 to 1978 he was active in civic politics, serving as mayor of Coniston and Nickel Centre.

Courtesy Dorothy Wigmore

else will. We accidentally came across the Professor Boudreau files at the Sudbury university. There were only seven files at the university, but they sure exposed some of the dirty work that went on in the early 1960s. Another booklet that some of you in academic fields have no doubt seen was put out by Father Hogan. He revealed the connections that went on in the clerical society to help do us in. You can even learn something from *The Unfinished Journey*, the story that was written about the Lewis family.[9] It may not be in all the stories, but look into the references and you'll find a lot of material there. I recall one at this time: Oliver Hodges [organizational director of the CCF trade union committee] admitted how they were boring from within to do this union in. So, despite all the good things that we did – we had established the highest wages and best conditions anywhere in Canada – that wasn't enough. The mining companies were out to get us, at least they wanted to weaken us, the other unions wanted our membership, the politicians wanted to control us, and the church certainly wanted to influence us. So it's no wonder we had difficulty in surviving. But the things that this union did, as Clint said in his comments, will never die.

When we look to the future – I've heard a lot today and yesterday about globalization. You want everything to be big – unions to be big, and the bigger you are, the bigger the match you're going to be for the employers. Well, I think it's a lot of hogwash because all I've got to do is look back at some of those radio programs, and the literature – that's the story they gave us all the time.[10] Be big and you're going to get everything. Well, we didn't get too damn much. Because after the raid here was finished and the smoke cleared, it took three or four years and about seven strikes to get back on your feet. So be very careful of the moves that you make. You're better off to be small and have the membership understand what the heck you're doing and what you're fighting for, instead of being big and somebody on top dictating the terms that you're going to work under.

Ray Stevenson: If Clint Jencks can start off by singing "Joe Hill," by golly, I'm going to go right along with him and I'm going to read the contract miner's poem I wrote for the one hundredth anniversary Sullivan celebration in Kimberley, British Columbia. I'm not going to read it all, it's too long. But this is the way the contract miner starts his day:

> *We'll all go below when they ring the shaft bells;*
> *And stumble along to the company hells.*
> *Hard hats on top and our feet in wet boots,*
> *Rock dust and smoke invading our snoots.*
> *We're more sick than healthy, but it can be said*
> *We're strong and quite virile and only half dead.*

I'll leave it at that. If you get the Mine Mill anniversary magazine you'll see the whole thing in there, if you want to read it.[11] I want to disassociate myself from the production of this magazine. I had something to say in it, I'm even listed as a contributing writer or something, but I'll be gall-darned if I'm going to accept responsibility for the fact that the names of the Ladies' Auxiliary members were not there. That's not my fault. Neither am I going to accept responsibility for the errata we had to insert which got those cutlines back in their proper place.

I would like to discuss the character of the problems that confront the metal-mining workers of Sudbury, of Canada, of North America, of the world. And I may find myself in disagreement with my old president here, Brother Solski, but that's not a new thing. We had a couple before, Mike; not serious, but some. I believe that we now confront a situation nationally, internationally, on a world scale that goes like this: 3,500 workers were laid off at a van plant in Scarborough, Ontario, last week. In the meantime General Motors, Ford, and I don't know who else are setting up consortiums of capital to invest in Russia, under a capitalist regime, to produce what? Quality motor cars. Who's competing with whom? If you want to turn to the question of metal production of nickel, in the Kola peninsula in Russia today they are producing primary nickel at an unprecedented rate, sneaking it onto the international metals market at scrap-rate prices, undercutting the price of nickel generally. This is happening in the whole world metals market. What the downfall of the Soviet Union has created is some of the biggest appetites that ever came down the pipe, and they are looking for new areas of investment to make more money under Mr. Yeltsin. That's why they gave him all the money to run his Tammany Hall campaign over there and make sure that he stayed there to look after American capital interests. That's what it was all about. Don't let the media kid you.

This situation confronts the working people with a new necessity. It's not new, exactly, but it's even more urgent now than it was in my day. The fact of the matter is, unless the workers of Russia who are working for this new capitalist bunch over there, whoever they may be, and unless the nickel workers of Canada working for Inco, Falconbridge, and so on can begin to discuss with each other, "How are you going to meet the see-saw whiplash that they're going to put upon you?" then the strength of your organized labour movement will go down. And I think it's vitally important at this stage of history to understand that, because it's across the board. I'm not here trying to rejuvenate the Soviet Union or anything of that nature; that's a little bit beyond even my powers. But I will say that the organization of contact between workers of Canada, the United States, and Mexico and so on, to deal with the new world order of the United States and their capitalist friends, is something that you must now understand and undertake.

I want all of us to understand, when we're talking about the Mine, Mill and Smelter Workers' Union or the Western Federation and the one hundredth anniversary, we're not talking about some little peanut outfit. Precisely because we were the workers involved in the production of the metals that made capitalism work in North America, it gave us power. They fought us from day one, it goes back to 1863, not just '93, when the workers, the gold miners of Gold Hill and Virginia City in Nevada, had this notion that they would find a way, as we did here in Sudbury and all over the place in the metal-mining industry, through collective action to be able to put a price on the only thing we have to sell: our ability to work. And if the companies didn't buy our ability to work, we were down the chute. So the history of this union is a struggle for that collective strength. Last night we heard someone talking about all the terrible things that are happening in the bargaining field. [See chapter 2.] I'm not here to tell you how to do things – I'm too old for that – but I am here to say this: when the ideology and the understanding of the production of wealth, values, commodities, that can be put into the marketplace depend only on entrepreneurship, the new religion of entrepreneurship, then they have switched attention from the fact that people still work to produce goods that you can eat, that you can sleep in, that you can live in, and so on.

Entrepreneurship is what the new religion is, and you'll get it from every angle. The media claim that only entrepreneurship produces anything in this world any more, while the sweat that you people who worked underground or in the smelter put into this thing doesn't amount to a hill of beans. That's all bloody nonsense, and it is designed to take you away from the notion of collective action to achieve the minimum programs of agreement amongst workers.

You know unions weren't established to decide what church you went to or what you did on your spare Sundays, or where you were born, or your colour or creed, or anything else. None of this was part of the union mandate. The unions were designed to define and establish minimum programs, if you please, upon which people could agree. And I say that as an old organizer. And Mike will agree with me and all the people will. When you went in to organize a plant, what did you do? You found the thing that everybody could agree with, not what they could disagree about, not some alternative program that would cause them to divide and split. You found the thing they could agree upon. When you got that, you had that place organized, and there is no place, no place, where a boss, a corporation, can beat workers who are united, organized, know their union program, and know where they stand.

Let me conclude with one thing. I read some of the press here and I see it is doing nothing new. I can recall how over fifty years *The Sudbury Star* and Bill Mason, who founded *The Sudbury Star* and was the most fearless publisher that the world ever saw, would fight anybody at the drop of a hat over any issue, except one. Never in those fifty years did there ever appear a critical note about International Nickel. That's the truth.[12] At the same time as they were not criticizing Inco, they were finding ways and means to split Mine Mill unionists like Tom Taylor away from me and Mike Solski and to split the women and so on – to create the divisions amongst us that made it impossible for us to act collectively. That's what the Steel raids were about, that's what all this nonsense of the Cold War was about, because they feared like the devil feared holy water the notion that the nickel miners of North America would stand shoulder to shoulder, understanding their own programs, carrying out union activities, because that reality was going to cost them money. That was going to cost the boss money.

Finally, when we talk about Mine Mill and the formation of the CIO [Congress of Industrial Organizations], please understand I'm not doing this out of any great notion that I'm going to run for office or something like that; at my age it's too late. Fifty years ago, in the proceedings of the fortieth convention of the International Union of Mine Mill held in Butte, Montana, what do I see? Let me read it:

> Dear Mr. Robinson [Reid Robinson, the union's president]: American miners are doing their full share in the all-out effort of the American people and their allies to overthrow the Axis power and to overcome all the evil for which they stand. The metal miners and their associates, like patriotic Americans in all walks of life, will continue to give their best in the months ahead, and thus speed up the ultimate victory which every day draws nearer. Yours very sincerely, with hearty greetings to all of your members, Franklin Delano Roosevelt. [dated August 30, 1943]

My God, how respectable we were, eh? But we were in the game, we were in the game and they bloody well knew it. And they had to pay attention to us. And the Cold War, which was instituted over international politics, political problems, came down on our union, on Mine Mill, because we were the target union that said regardless of what you say, we are going to stand for a world at peace, and the production of goods and things for a decent future for all humanity. That was our program and we preached it from the treetops, and we went into the field and organized on that basis. And we won support and by God, I'm proud of it, and I'm proud of you, and I'm proud of all of us here.

Pearl Chytuk: It's nice to see some of my old friends that I hadn't seen for so many years – I'm getting emotional about it. I came to Sudbury in 1941 from Regina, Saskatchewan, and I had never lived in a company town before arriving here. I found it so very different, people were always whispering, even your friends. The war was already on and Inco was hiring people. The reason we came out here was that my late husband came to get a job. The conditions were very bad so I got a job as well, worked with people, and I was a bit surprised because out west we were talking unions for beauty salons and restaurant workers, but in Sudbury, people were reluctant to talk about it. One lady took me aside – we were working in the Red Cross at some lady's home – and the woman said to me, "You be careful. Don't talk union, because in Sudbury if you talk union and if your husband is working for Inco he isn't going to be there very long."

I couldn't believe it, that things were happening like that, but apparently they were. And by 1942 I got a call from Inco. Inco was declared a war industry; they were producing nickel for armaments and the women got to work in the smelter. Some got to work in the mines; I was lucky, I got a job at Copper Cliff smelter. I worked at the nickel reverberator. At that time I weighed 116 pounds, and when I went on the job my instructor give me a bar. I don't know what you'd call a bar, it's not your fireplace stick – it was about four times as long and it weighed fourteen pounds. And he says, "You want to keep your job, with this you tap the arms as the nickel turns around in the roaster so it doesn't pile up and break the machinery."

I learned fast and it was very interesting to work as a manual labourer because you have something in common with others and you become very close with the other people there. It didn't matter whether you were a man or a woman. You had this respect for each other because we were there to do a job and before very long we used to meet in little groups. Different people were talking. There was talk about the unions. I also heard it from my husband. He used to go to some meetings at night. At first they were meeting in houses, then when the meetings got too big, they would rent some place. They were very secretive about it. But by then it was getting big and people were less afraid to talk about the union. It was really getting great, it got so great that they rented a place on Lisgar Street, a pretty big building. The first time I attended a meeting the whole building was full. They explained to us how to organize, but we still had to be very careful. We had a piece of paper and a pencil, and then you got your friend's name. He gave you a dollar, you got his name and address, and once a month when we went to the union meeting you turned these slips in, and your friend got a union book with a stamp, initiation stamps, and they got called to the meeting and got sworn in as members. Those were the days when your dues were not deducted from the company. When I think back on it now, how dedicated these union people were – every month each one brought a dollar to the Mine Mill Hall. I think that was a terrific union, because there's a difference in trade union commitment when the workers are so dedicated that they voluntarily pay their union dues each month. Years after that when I worked under a different union and the dues were deducted from their paycheques, the workers said, "You know, just deduct it. I'm doing my thing for the union. Why do you want me to go to the meeting?"

So it was a great experience for somebody coming from out west and thrown into this great big dirty smelter. It's clean now, you wouldn't know it's the same place it was in '42. I worked at the smelter until '53. The war had ended, that is, the actual war ended, and then the Cold War began. So we were all laid off.

In the meantime there was a Ladies' Auxiliary being organized. I knew that when I was no longer in the labour force, the best thing I could do was to be with the women. Because we had a terrific Mine Mill, Local 598, they wanted us to be there. Mine Mill husbands and sons wanted their mothers, their wives, or their girlfriends to know where they worked, to know what conditions were like where they worked. So Local 117, the Ladies' Auxiliary, was a very nice organization to belong to. When we applied for a charter for our local, the constitution required that we have twenty-five women members to be able to get our charter. The first night we went to sign up women, I am sure we must have had over sixty-eight women, never mind the twenty-five required. Women just lined up to join up, and that was a great feeling. Since then I have worked in other jobs, but no matter what other jobs I did, I tried to see that we had a union in the place, but some big companies were rather difficult to organize. So I stayed in the Ladies' Auxiliary for many years, twenty-five years. I got a pin from the union, and after that I think I stayed on another few years – you'll not know my age. But it was a very informative, very good organization. We worked hand in hand with our brothers in the locals and we had the right to sit in Local 598 membership meetings. We had a voice. We had no vote, but we had autonomous power as the Ladies' Auxiliary, and our requests were never refused by Mine Mill. We attended their conventions. We had a voice at Mine Mill conventions, no matter where they were held and that was great.

So you get older and you think you're not needed any more. Then we have this conference today. Even last night, when I met some of the people here again, it started coming back to me. My goodness, it's not over. We're still here. One thing I want to say is that people should always be organized no matter what job they work at, because without being in a union organization you're going to be divided, no matter who you work for. Your management, they are very clever. Remember, we are the working people who've taught them a lot of things. They didn't know too many things, but now we're getting clever and they're learning from us, so they monopolize us.

You might work in a place where they sort of make you a head of department or you're the head of this, or you're the head of that, and they are working you to your bones. They just give you a name, there's nothing else, you still have no say in the corporation or whatever it might be. But they just make you feel you're somebody a little bit better and that the guy who's behind you, he isn't as good as you are. This is put up to divide the working people. All I have to say to the future generation, wherever they are, is that you must organize and work together, because if you don't work together you will always be divided and it's very hard to come to a correct decision when you're only one person.

Francis "Buddy" DeVito: I can't boast of any record of working in the industry. I was born in Trail, British Columbia, lived there most of my life, and therefore I am very familiar with the mining and smelting industry. As you know, Trail is the centre of that activity in British Columbia, and in fact at one time the Trail smelter was the largest non-ferrous smelter in the world and employed close to five thousand people. My trade is as a shoemaker, but I am also a student of history and I've been involved in community activities on every level, including provincial politics, so I'm well aware of the kinds of things that help develop a community and hold us together.

I'd like to just outline briefly the history of Mine Mill from our point of view in the west, and that history is a little more extensive than it is in the east. At one time Trail was the centre of an organizing effort by the Western Federation of Miners, and in 1895 ten local unions around Trail were organized by the Western Federation of Miners. Many of the communities no longer exist. However, the record is very clear, if you read Mike Solski's book, about the involvement of the Western Federation of Miners in those communities. At that time the Western Federation of Miners were also organizing coal miners on Vancouver Island and in the Crow's Nest Pass. Of course I don't imagine there were any jurisdictional regulations at that time. The miners in Rossland were successful in electing an MLA to the legislature, and in 1899 the B.C. legislature passed the first eight-hour-day legislation in Canada on behalf of those miners. The Western Federation of Miners was active until 1910, and then it petered out.

At the same time the One Big Union, the OBU, and the Industrial Workers of the World, the IWW, were also active. In 1917 there was a strike in Trail led by Ginger Goodwin. At that time the war was going rather badly for the Allies and the strike – which of course affected very much the supply of lead and zinc for the war effort – caused considerable consternation amongst the generals of the Allies and their governments. Ginger Goodwin, who left Trail to escape being inducted in the army – after being previously classified unfit [because of tuberculosis] to serve in the services – was then hounded down on Vancouver Island and subsequently shot by a hired policeman. To this day that event is hotly controversial, because there seems to be no question with the evidence that's accumulating that there was an order placed against Ginger Goodwin's life.

Following the 1917 strike – for any number of reasons the strike only lasted one month – there was very little union activity in Trail until the 1930s. Then a workers' committee was formed. It was largely a company union – I think you had something similar to that in Sudbury, it was called the Nickel Rash, wasn't it? Until that time there had been no success in organizing a union. In 1938 Art Evans came to Trail working for the Mine Mill union and tried to organize a union, but he was run out of town. It wasn't until 1944, during the war, when the government relaxed the regulations regarding union organizing that Local 480 was organized. It held the certification from then until 1964, when Mine Mill merged with Steel. You know, of course, the famous Harvey Murphy, or some say infamous Harvey Murphy, who spent a lot of time in Sudbury during that period. He was very active in the organizing of not only Local 480 in Trail, but also Local 951 in Kimberley.[13] Mines all over the province were under the certification of Mine Mill. It was the best period for Mine Mill, and I think that was the best period for smelter workers and miners right up until 1950 when the union raids started.

In 1950 Steel raided Trail, and I became involved in the union. I had served in the services for four years, had been radicalized because of the experience that I had both in our own community and during the war. I came out of the war very much an admirer of the Soviet Union and therefore considerably attracted to communism. My admiration for the Soviet Union, which I still have today, is based upon my knowledge that it was the sacrifice of the people of the Soviet Union that saved my life as a serviceman. If the Soviet people hadn't undertaken the sacrifice and the casualties that they had during the war, I'm sure that the Allies would have lost the war. Of course that might be debated, but that's how I feel about it. Following the war, in 1950 – or was it 1947? – I was the first young veteran of the Second World War to be elected president of the Canadian Legion in that community, a position I held for two years. In 1950 I was charged with being a communist, because I was a member of the Canadian Peace Movement and we were objecting to the war in Korea and Truman's threat to drop the atomic bomb on China. However, I turned up at the trial and the chap that charged me didn't turn up. Just a few months ago I received a life membership in the Canadian Legion in Trail. Some of what I stood for seems to have been vindicated.

Then, following the 1950 raid in Trail after Steel lost the final vote, I left the union and went into municipal politics. I stayed as an alderman on the city council until 1960, until the raids started in Sudbury. Al King and Harvey Murphy and other friends of mine asked if I'd like to go to Sudbury, and I said, "Well, why not?" And so I left my job and came here to work for the union for three years. I left in 1963 after Steel won the vote at Inco. I came back in 1965 for a couple of weeks for the second ballot and they lost the vote again there, and the merger of Mine Mill and Steel took place.

So I've always had a very close tie with the Mine Mill union, and I view my time in it with a great deal of satisfaction. I see nothing to apologize for in that period of our history. Certainly the three years in Sudbury were amongst the happiest years of my life, because in many ways Sudbury is just Trail with the same kind of cosmopolitan community, with the same kind of social, economic, and ethnic tensions, and so I felt very much at home here. However, I must say to the people who have driven through Trail and through Sudbury – and there are a lot of Canadians who seem to have driven through Sudbury and Trail – and they say, "My God! You lived in two of the worst cities in Canada." Well, I admit that sometimes these communities were very blighted, but I am certainly very happy to be back here today.

Following my return to Trail, I ran for city council again and was eventually elected to the council as mayor and held that position for six years, from 1967 to 1973, something like that. I was a great mayor – I just couldn't add, that's all. I retained my interest in politics. I haven't recanted very much or very little and I haven't changed very much, except some of my feelings about the trends in our country are stronger now than they were in those early years. After leaving the city council – I quit after six years, I felt that was long enough for people to listen to me and I also felt that I was wearing out, that my energy was diminishing – I decided to try something else. At the beginning of the Vietnam war I had become involved in the peace movement, and I was instrumental in forming a peace group which was active until two or three years ago, when apparently or supposedly the Cold War ended. Since then I have become active in the mental health field and I'm now president of the local Canadian Mental Health Association and I serve on the provincial board of that group.

Rosa Luxemburg is reported to have said – you know she was the German Social Democrat who was murdered in 1919 – that the German people at that time had a choice between barbarism or socialism. Now I know there are a lot of arguments about what's socialism or what isn't, but there seem to be fewer and fewer arguments about barbarism, and we're living in a time of barbarism if I've ever seen it in my seventy-three years. You've heard a great deal about this today, and so I won't pursue that. There are some better able to speak about that than I am, but I think that as Pearl has said, and as will be said by others here today at this table again, and for the next two days of this conference, that the future depends on us learning to live together, to band together in unions, and I prefer to see the unions band together. The form that the unions will take, as we've heard, will probably be dictated by circumstances, but there is no question about the importance of unity amongst the working people. I believe there is a class struggle in this country. I believe there always has been one, and we see some manifestation of that when even the politicians and the newspapers are talking about the middle class in this country disappearing. Well, I guess there *was* a middle class, but I'm certainly sure that there *is* a ruling class. I think I made my choice early in my life to join Mine Mill and chose that way to join the class struggle, and I see that the struggle continues. When I was in my business as a shoe repairman one of the things I learned to do very well is save soles and nail heels, and I'm still doing that.

Lukin Robinson: I want to say something about what seems to me the significance of the left unions, since one of the themes of the conference is the role of the left unions in the 1940s and 1950s. The first thing that I think should be said is that in the rising period of the trade union movement in Canada and North America, all unions were left in one way or another, because they were all against not having a union. All the unions in the mass industries were built largely by the efforts of communists and left-leaning people. For me the past goes back, as far as Mine Mill is concerned, to 1952 when I joined here, but I was a left-winger before that. Mine Mill and other unions in Canada won bargaining rights during World War II, the war against the Axis powers, and the recognition of unions and plans for the postwar world were all parts of the same historic struggle. They weren't separate, and when the war ended – as those of you who remember that will recall – there was a tremendous upsurge of hope and determination that we were going to build a better world and that we would be able to build a better world. A better world in those days meant that the capitalism of the 1920s and the 1930s had to be radically altered and the power of capital had to be radically reduced, and the claws and fangs of capitalism had to be either pulled out or filed down or clipped, and people had to have more power than they had before the war.

Now, the capitalists obviously had different ideas, and they decided that the unity and the hope with which people came out of the war had to be broken. And at the same time the unity of the big powers of the time, of the United Nations, with the Soviet Union on the one side and America and

Lukin Robinson, former researcher at the national office of Mine Mill, looks at memorabilia on display during the Mine Mill conference, May 1993.

Courtesy Dorothy Wigmore

England on the other, had to be broken. And all of a sudden after the war the Soviet Union became the great enemy, and if you read the literature of that time, the Soviet Union was the imperialist power. The Soviet Union was the insatiable aggressor, the evil empire, an ogre worse than Hitler had been, and that was part of the anti-communist religion and the anti-communist crusade which helped to break the unity of people at the end of the war.

The split in the labour movement was precipitated by the left-led unions' refusal to accept that change in the view of the Soviet Union, and they refused to join in the anti-communist crusade. And for that they paid a price, but the significance of the left unions is precisely that refusal and the struggle they made against the Cold War; to carry on as best they could the vision with which the war was won and which many people held – millions of people in the world held – at the end of the war. This struggle began in the late 1940s and continued throughout the 1950s and eventually most of the left unions went under. But some of them survived and now they are merging back into what is called the mainstream of labour. In my judgement you have to understand the significance of the left unions in that sense, and I think they played a very important part of history.

Everywhere in the world today, everywhere without exception, capital is on the offensive and the gains that working people have made in the past are under attack. In the countries of the former Soviet Union, that's obvious. There has been a disastrous fall in the standards of living of the people there, and the budding capitalists and the so-called reformers and the liberals are saying quite clearly that the people have to give up the gains they made and their attachment to collective property, job security, and social welfare. In the Third World, under different and even worse circumstances, it's the same thing. Because capital has been so successful in defeating popular movements in the Third World and making a sham and a delusion of the struggle for national independence where national independence has been achieved, they are now attacking working people in the fortress countries of capitalism, which means here in Canada, in the United States, in England, in France, in Germany, in Italy, and in Spain. That's why the struggle today is so important and why it's so difficult.

We've had a recession for three years and we've had restructuring for a good many more years, and we've had free trade and we've had the Bank of Canada's John Crow, and we've had the GST, and all those are aspects of the offensive of capital against the conditions and the gains of working people. These events have to be understood, in my judgement, in that sense. For example, concession bargaining – ten years ago nobody had ever heard of concession bargaining – is now necessary in the sacred name of being competitive. In government policy it means that the deficit as we know it has become the main issue.

The significance of the deficit is not that it's big or small or that interest rates are high or low, but that it's used as a means of attack by the capitalist class against the gains of working people in the form of medicare, education, health, social programs, and welfare. That's why the deficit has taken the leading position in public debate that it has.

Right here in Ontario, public-sector workers have been offered – I should say, threatened with – a social contract. A social contract, as the president of OPSEU (the Ontario Public Service Employees Union) said, "is a choice between cyanide and the chopping block." The sentence of execution has been passed and is not on the table for discussion. The only question is the method of execution, and if that can be agreed to it's a social contract, and if it's not agreed to then it's not a social contract. One of the significant results of this is that the public-sector unions, twenty-eight or thirty of them, have come together in a common front, called the Public Services Coalition, never before seen. Some of the people didn't even know each other three months ago, and they're now sitting in the same room working out strategy together. And I can tell you no government of Ontario in the last fifty years, not even Colonel Drew, if you remember who he was, has attacked the public service the way this government has.

The conclusion I draw from all of this, and which I hope you will draw from all of this, is that capitalism is as bad as it's always been, and today, boasting that it has won the Cold War and freed itself from the enemy, it's now on the rampage. We have to fight it. And the job of the trade union movement is to make working people understand this, and to organize them, to help them win allies, and to give them confidence that they are not going to be beaten – that in the long run, if not tomorrow, they can still build a better world than we have now. A better world means a socialist world of one kind or another. There's a lot of debate about what that means, but in the long run I think socialism grows, you might say organically, out of the struggle of working people, and the struggle of working people certainly grows inevitably out of the existence and attacks of the capitalist class against working people. That struggle is as necessary and inevitable today as it was a hundred years ago when the Western Federation of Miners was organized.

Comments and Questions

Dieter Buse: I want to make a remark regarding what Mike Solski spoke about, and that is the delicate relationship between the university and this union. That history, in 1959, was the beginning of a tragedy. Some of us at the university feel a responsibility to history about that, and we want to emphasize that we know you have something to offer us. Some of our students are here collecting your history. We intend to take up this torch, to make your history come alive again. But we want you also to realize that we have something to offer you, some expertise that will help you, the union movement, and I hope that's seen in the sessions. It's in that way that I want to suggest how we see this conference, that we see this conference not as an end of a hundred years, but the beginning of another hundred of Mine Mill.

Andy Flesch: I have this question for Buddy DeVito. You were telling us some of the past history. You mentioned the 1917 strike in Trail, B.C., that lasted one month. You didn't elaborate on that. I just want to ask you, was it successful or not?

Francis "Buddy" DeVito: I'd say it wasn't successful. The workers there had no experience and there was, because of the war, great pressure put on them to resume work. And after Ginger Goodwin left, and after he was executed, the trade union movement in the community collapsed for a number of years.

Unidentified Speaker: I want to ask Pearl a couple of questions. I had the sense when you were talking that you were reluctant to go out of the industry at the end of the war, and I wanted to know what had happened to the women who had been working. What was your experience in that period? Did women want to continue working in industry and weren't able to, or exactly how did things happen? I also wondered if you could say something about what the Women's Auxiliary did, the kind of work you did, and what kind of priorities the Women's Auxiliary had?

Pearl Chytuk: I think all the women liked to be recognized as human beings, and when they went to work in industry they had freedom, like it's the first time you have your own paycheque and you don't have to say, "Honey, leave me seven dollars for groceries" or something. We all felt that way. We got stronger, but there were no jobs for us to go to from there, outside of clerking jobs, that is.

Speaker: You skip over a lot when you say that. You weren't able to continue in the industry – you weren't allowed to?

Pearl Chytuk: The government let the women go because the war finished, and the soldiers who returned had the priority to get a job. That was the reason why the women were let go. And to answer your second question about the auxiliary, it felt pretty good working together and it gave women something to do and allowed them to help their fellow men, because we must understand that with great big corporations, not only the husband went to work. His wife or mother was tied to the corporation, too. She had to do the shopping. She had to prepare his lunch. We're the world's biggest lunch-bucket-carrying district here. There was no refrigeration on the job. So I always said Inco and Falconbridge should be honouring the wives of the miners, because the whole family works for them.

Yes, when the war finished, prices were going up and women took initiative in an organized way – writing letters to their member of parliament, meeting with local and federal MPs. Then when the Cold War started, the auxiliary was very good about belonging to peace groups and being active in peace work. They were active in protests that there should be no more war, because the Cold War was really advancing pretty fast. And there were other things that the auxiliary did. You know, it's so long ago that I keep on forgetting it. I suppose I'll go home and then I'll remember and kick myself for not being able to say it now.

Kathy Brankley: For the past couple of years I've been fortunate enough to work with Mercedes Steedman researching the Women's Auxiliary, and I would like to address the question that was asked about the other activities of the auxiliary. Two things come to mind. Pearl, you probably took so much for granted the fundraising that you did, and this is part of the generosity that I think John Lang mentioned. [See chapter 1.] The fundraising was done on an international level – you were sending money, raising funds on your own as the women's auxiliaries, and sending them to labour communities around the world and supporting strikes in small communities in many different countries. You also did fundraising on the local level – certainly the strike funds that you contributed to, and the sustaining work that you did during the strikes, through all manner of fundraising – and also the work to help needy families within the community and within the labour movement, which you did in an ongoing way, which you probably don't think of very much because it was second nature.

The other point I want to make is about the nature of the convention resolutions that were passed by the local groups, and then went nationally, and to the North American level. These resolutions that were coming out of the women's auxiliaries in the 1950s dealt with issues such as day care, preventative women's health, housing, and peace, political issues – a very wide spectrum of resolutions, things that were achieved twenty, sometimes thirty years later. So I do want you to take the credit you deserve on those points.

Richard Marcotte: I'm a chief steward with Local 598 of Mine Mill. I was formerly a steward and I've also been elected as a trustee to the board of

Mine Mill, and it gives me a great honour to be here. I feel moved inside to be so close to labour activists with such insurmountable experience and knowledge.

As a young activist, I felt that I took advantage of a system that was given to me – where everything was running so smoothly that I didn't play a more extensive role – and now I feel a little bit sorry about that, but I can't correct it. I can only correct what is here, now. When I heard you speaking about the future, the situation you describe is one that also confuses the young people I have on the job. We have young people working, and my job as a steward is to try to police the collective agreement and try to keep unity in the union. What I would like to know is, from your knowledge of the future, how do we hold the union together? Do we need strength from a bigger union, or do we need to bring the old knowledge back? I'm confused – it seems to me that we're drifting apart rather than coming together. We're getting big in magnitude and we're getting lost in a whole chain of democracies, and we're not getting united enough within or working with the same common denominator.

Jim Tester: I'm going to give a partial answer. I think it has to be understood that it would be a miracle if the younger generation were able to pick up from where we older ones left off, because they didn't come through the same experiences. They didn't come from the same place, they didn't come through the thirties, they didn't come through all the tough days. There were virtually thirty years of prosperity after the Second World War, as far as Inco and Falconbridge were concerned. To expect the younger workers to have the same understanding and knowledge of that early experience would be almost to expect a miracle. I feel rather deficient myself, inasmuch as I wasn't able to pass on as much as I would have liked to the younger workers. But certainly a large part of education is experiencing life itself and drawing conclusions from life itself. I was raised in the 1920s, and my father, who had been very much influenced by the Western Federation of Miners and had heard Big Bill Haywood speak many times, used to talk about him in such admiring terms. But I really didn't know what my father was talking about until the Depression began in 1929, and then the lessons began to come home. It was much easier for me to draw conclusions than it was for the average person, because I had that kind of a labour background. It wasn't until my actual experiences required answers to many of the problems that I discovered there really is a class struggle going on out there. So I wouldn't feel too badly about that as long as you are prepared to pick up the banner now and understand the struggles that we are currently faced with – and they are considerable – and take it on from there. There are no easy answers.

Jim and Doris Tester at the Mine Mill conference. Jim was a past president of Local 598.

Courtesy Dorothy Wigmore

It's a tough road, but I'm sure that if you have confidence in yourself and your fellow workers, you can achieve what we achieved in the years gone by.

Lukin Robinson: You'll never be successful at teaching how to struggle, for you cannot teach it. You cannot help younger workers to struggle by telling them that they have to read about the past and learn from the past. Once you realize from your experience that struggle is necessary, history may help you deal with today's problems, but they are never the same in detail in each individual's life. You have to understand capitalism or what the boss is up to, not in terms of what the boss may have done in 1930 or in 1950, but what the son of a bitch is doing today. If you can understand that, maybe you can make your fellow worker draw the conclusion from experience that *capitalism* is in fact what is happening. That is how the unions grew in the 1930s, that is how Jim and I came to struggle, and how all of us up here on the panel came to struggle. Your experience is different from our experience, and our experience is different from our parents' experience. So don't start telling them, "Yes, there were great heroes of labour in the past and we have to imitate them," because that's the wrong way to do things. It's not only putting the cart before the horse, but it's shooting the horse and letting the cart run downhill.

Roy Santa Cruz: Like Lukin says, today when you're confronted with a worker, don't tell him, "Here, you know, this is the way we did it in the 1930s and 1940s and 1950s." But I have a different observation. My observation about the labour movement here in Canada and the United States is that you have too many unions, and too many guys thinking all kinds of things. I always said, and Mine Mill said it in the 1940s, "You need one big union in the labour movement." In the 150 international unions down in the United States, they all go in different directions. How in the hell are they going to pull you together? Do you tell a worker that this is the union, this is the way we're supposed to do it, and this is the way we did it in the thirties, forties, and fifties? Amalgamation is one of the biggest challenges that I think the labour movement in Canada and in America has to face, to see if they can get five big unions – and that's all you need. You don't need anybody else. You got so many little groups going here and there. This is one of the biggest things. If you put that together, then you become political activists like we were in the early forties and fifties and sixties. We were activists, in all of the mining community. I know this because I have been through it, and I have service as an international union representative, and I am a miner. We used to elect the mayor, the councilmen, and the sheriff of that particular community. That's the way you start to change things around. It's very true, we've gone through recessions, we've gone through all kinds of things, and I'm very, very interested in what Lukin said with regard to capitalism versus socialism, and that we have to fight back. It's not easy. You just have to get out there and do it ... I think the biggest task you should have, in my own opinion, is to get

Roy Santa Cruz, international representative of Mine Mill, speaking at the Mine Mill conference, May 1993. He is a charter member of Local 938 of IUMMSW, son and grandson of members of the Western Federation of Miners, and an elder statesman of the labour movement in the United States. Before retirement he was a subdistrict director of the United Steelworkers of America.
Courtesy Dorothy Wigmore

five big unions here in Canada and start from there, and start taking on the capitalists. You can't do it in separate little sections. Unite – unite into two, three, or maybe five big unions in Canada.

Lukin Robinson: One of the figures that you'll certainly hear a lot about and should hear a lot about in connection with the history of Mine Mill in Sudbury is Weir Reid. Weir Reid was the cultural personification of the struggle of the working class to gain their own culture. When culture is under the domination of the capitalist class, it weakens the working class, and Weir's role was to try to give the working class a little bit of their own culture. A worker who is a militant worker on the job – whether it's a woman or a man makes no difference – and then goes home and watches three or four hours of TV is exposed to one of the most insidious and powerful instruments for the dissemination of capitalist culture. It's not didactic or overt, it's not explicit, but it's there.

Let me put a different question to you: how many kids ever learn anything about trade unionism in school? Why is it that there is no course of trade unionism in the schools, where the majority of children are children of working people? Who dictates the contents of what is taught at school? The working class? Hell, no. So, if you're an active unionist and especially if you're involved in some struggle which takes you away from your family, from your kids – that's rough on the kids, and you have to explain to the kids what the significance for them is of why you're not there. If Sudbury, a union town, could organize to have a school board composed entirely of workers, and if the workers said, "We want the curriculum to be this and the hell with that," that would be a tremendous advance. Then you wouldn't have to read it in the Sudbury "Dirty" *Star*, as we used to call it, or listen to the CBC news in the evening.

Jim Tester: I hate to do this, but I think Lukin oversimplified the question of history. There's an old saying, the lessons of history unlearned are doomed to be repeated. That's a truism, and the fact is that we do want to know where our own roots are. We do want to know where we're coming from, and we do want to draw inspiration and courage from what our fathers did and from the battles they engaged in, to give us assurance that we can cope with the enemy in the same way. You do have to deal with each experience on the basis of its merits, that's true, but you nevertheless use the knowledge that you have learned about other experiences in order to cope with this new one. And if you don't do that, then you're flying blind. I don't know any tactic, not a single tactic, that's used by the bosses today that wasn't used fifty years ago. The only thing was, fifty years ago they never smiled. Today they're always smiling.

Unidentified Speaker: That's right ... that's a tactic.

Jim Tester: That's a tactic, that's right. They're always your buddy. They're always your friend. They always want to co-operate today, and that's the big transition, but the tricks are all the same. Every trick they pull off, every deal they pull off, is exactly the same as it was before. Now, in reading the history of the miners' union, for example, I read from the United Mineworkers' history that a coal miner never strikes against the stockpile. I learned that forty, fifty years ago, until it was ground into my consciousness. Never strike against a stockpile. If you have to get laid off, get laid off. Don't take up your grievances, don't take up any causes. Wait until that stockpile's gone. Wait until you get back on the job, and then if you have to strike, strike because there's no stockpile left and the boss needs you. You don't strike when he doesn't need you, and that's a basic rule. Now, is that out of date, is that old fashioned? Maybe it is, but I think it still holds. I learned from my friend Bill Walsh that it's a question of who is the more uncomfortable, you or the boss.[14] It's a battle of being uncomfortable. No worker ever feels comfortable in times of a strike. He's suffering, and if the boss is not suffering, you're in trouble. So what I'm saying is that yes, Lukin's rhetoric is great stuff and it's important, but it's a part of the theatrics of organization. While it's great to listen to, nevertheless we have to know our history because it sheds light on the future. It doesn't solve the problems, but it lights up what lies before us and gives us encouragement to be able to tackle it.

Lukin Robinson: I have to defend myself against that one. I have never thought that you shouldn't learn from history. The point I want to make is that when you're talking to someone you're trying to organize and who is not yet a union man, if you start by telling him the history, you turn him off. Once he's with you, then you can tell him about the history and he'll be interested. You have to know about the history to help him understand what he's going through and what's happening today. So it's a question of whether A comes before B or B comes before A, but they're both necessary. You have to walk on two legs, but you have to start putting the right foot forward, or the left foot forward, if you prefer it.

Roy Santa Cruz: In the Mine Mill unions I come from we were taught how to lecture in the high schools. In any school we could possibly get into or lecture to, we would get on the pedestal and start talking about the union, our history. That's one thing I would like to ask. Is that going on here? If not, start it. Ask the schools, tell them that you want to get a little history of your organization or of the labour movement in the schools. We did it back as far as the early forties, going to high schools and universities and lecturing about the labour movement, and how the labour movement started. We were taught by people who knew this history, and that's when we started, as young teenagers, talking about this in school. It's not too late to do it now, and that's one of the things that you must do. Rather than trying to sell the union to a guy beginning with the history, start telling him that history when he's a young guy in high school or in grammar school.

Rolly Gauthier: I'm a staff rep for Mine Mill. In my humble opinion, a lot of unions are somewhat introverted with regards to their actions. In other words, they're satisfied and content with just servicing the members, and their full and only goal is to service the members. I would like to ask the panelists how important it is for unions to look at external forces or be an extrovert in their actions to be effective for their members.

Francis "Buddy" DeVito: It was mentioned here today about moving out into the community. I know what happens with trade unions – and that is that the officers usually have plenty to do and the activists have plenty to do, and there are large numbers of the membership who do not participate in union activity, even though they may be active in other areas in the community. But I think moving out into the community is absolutely vital, and I don't know what the experience here has been, but I was a bit of a political fluke in Trail in being elected to council and then being elected to mayor. Considering my involvement in the union and my political reputation, I guess I was in the right place at the right time. Right now in Trail we have no elected union members on the city council and only one recognized trade unionist on the school board. The hospital board is appointed by the government, and even during that period when I was mayor, when I had the authority to appoint people to various boards, it was difficult to get the active people in the union to take positions on these local boards.

That's the route that has to be taken, because it does two things. First of all, it places in the community people who have a direct and distinct orientation. Don't let people bullshit you, saying you can't sit on the city council if you're a trade unionist because you're a one-issue member or something. Well, of course, the businessmen sit in the council, and they don't make apologies for being one-issue representatives. The second thing it does, and this is really important in anything we do, is that the power that trade unionists have through electing people to certain parts of the community reinforces their feelings and their philosophies. They gain strength from that kind of activity and that kind of success. Of course there's a third thing that happens, which I see is happening in British Columbia and Saskatchewan and Ontario now: the difficulty is to tie some of these scoundrels down after they get to Queen's Park or Victoria or Saskatoon.

But then, even out of this activity one has to have some kind of way of getting at these representatives and insisting that they do what they promise to do, if nothing else.

Jim Tester: I think that from the very beginning of Mine Mill as a union, and even prior to the Western Federation of Miners, the local unions in the mid-west United States discovered that you couldn't separate the union from political action, that political action was as much tied to a union as economic action was, and that political action flowed out of economic action. There's no way you could avoid political questions. The problem was, how do you unite the membership around political questions with the realization that you have a membership that's composed of people with all kinds of ideologies? The union members understood this from the very earliest days, and the constitution of Mine Mill talks about no discrimination because of race, colour, creed, or politics. The members have understood that you have to be prepared to accept everyone on the basis of working in the same place that you happen to be working in, and what you have to do is unite people on the basis of their common needs. You have to be able to go into a political action based on the politics that they all have in common, not on the basis of any particular political party or political group.

Essentially, this is what Mine Mill discovered: to make progress there should not be any partisan politics within the union structure itself. What the union had to do was have its own political agenda that it was prepared to present to any political party and in that way influence the political process. I also think it has to be said that the basic purpose of the union is serving the members on the job, and to do that properly you have to enter into political action of one kind or another, and you have to see that the two are tied together.

Roy Santa Cruz: The first thing, as you say, is servicing the local union, but there's a lot of things that you can service and help. I remember when I was a full-time business agent, the membership thought I had to just sit there and service. But I said, "Look, I gotta go out there and move into political action. I gotta move into many things in the community that would benefit you, not just service you."

Well, I just gotta tell you some history of my three generations of being miners; we go back as far as my grandfather. I married a Bisbee[15] girl, and my father-in-law was one of the deportees in the deportation of the Wobblies. My grandfather was with the Western Federation. I think they had a strike in 1917, as he told me.[16] My mother was in the picket line with my grandfather.

I got involved with the Mine, Mill and Smelter Workers in the 1930s and 1940s, before the war. I worked as a teenager and in the summers I worked in the smelter where they had an extra board list that you could work, like an unknown worker. The first experience I had with one of the local unions, with the Mine, Mill and Smelter Workers, was Local 586 in the Globe-Miami area, a local that no longer exists. The Morenci area, which is part of the Bisbee group, was also organized in the late 1930s, and it took about two, three years to get a contract negotiated with the Phelps Dodge company. That local also no longer exists. It was one of the locals that were on strike against Phelps Dodge, and all the workers were replaced. We had a big struggle in that area, and all of the Phelps Dodge local unions went under. In that particular strike, I was the sub-district director of the states of New Mexico and Arizona.

There are no local unions in the Phelps Dodge copper industry. That company has been the most arrogant adversary that we've had in negotiating collective bargaining agreements. I negotiated as a chairperson with the Dumont Copper Corporation, now Magma Copper, one of the biggest producers in Arizona. I negotiated agreements until 1987, prior to my retirement. I was one of the staff representatives from the Mine, Mill and Smelter Workers to go to Winnipeg in 1967 to try to get all the workers in Canada to merge with the United Steelworkers of America. We also took a vote in some of the local unions that I serviced in Arizona and New Mexico. But most of the voters were very reluctant to say that we have to get into the mainstream of labour. I know that this local remained to carry the name of the Mine, Mill and Smelter Workers, and I have to say that you should be commended. I know that some of the delegates you sent to the convention in Winnipeg at that time were very adamantly against the merger.

A problem of raiding is that we become a target for every company and we are used as tools, and they try to use us one against the other. It's like the raids we had by the United Steelworkers of America. We were trying to protect our local union at the same time as we tried to negotiate with the copper companies to get a contract. But we were so busy watching and seeing that we were not being raided that we couldn't actually do the job we were supposed to do, which was to get better wages and benefits for the working members of our organization.

I still believe very strongly that the unions should develop a bigger group with only a few unions. I can remember a vice-president of this Mine, Mill and Smelter Workers, Charlie Wilson, who was out of Bessemer, Alabama. Charlie passed away about four years ago in Tennessee, but he used to tell me all the time that we have too many unions and we should have no more than five so that we can really develop a united front against management. And I still believe that very strongly. That's one of the reasons why I felt that we should get into the mainstream, and we should merge with the United Steelworkers of America. I think that we ought to set our differences aside because we need to get together.

Look at what's happened to labour in the United States. The United Steelworkers of America came from a million and a half members down to about five hundred thousand. The other unions, it's the same thing. In the mining district that I used to represent, I had over twenty thousand miners in Arizona, and we had another eight thousand in the New Mexico area. We have dwindled to approximately half of that amount. You can see that they have been able to lay off a lot of miners, and so the thing we must do is start organizing. The industry has changed very much from the smelting and milling process. I don't know how to explain it to you, but you have to go and see it yourself. They can make copper by pumping out water from underground into different sections, and with electrodes they make copper bars, pure copper balls, and all that. There are only twenty-four people working in that process alone. So they have automated – they have really done some work in trying to get as much money out as possible.

The Mine, Mill and Smelter Workers was the only union that really helped the struggle that Cesar Chavez had. Cesar Chavez organized the farm workers. He just passed away here about two and a half weeks ago. We, as Mine Millers, were the first union to recognize his movement, and we helped him financially.

Jim Tester: There was a booklet put out on the hundredth anniversary of Mine Mill, and for some reason the last thirty years in Mine Mill's history were missing in it. In other words, only the first seventy years were dealt with. The last thirty years in the history of Mine Mill are just as important, perhaps more important than the first seventy, in telling us who we are, what we are, and where we're going. So I'd like to present some of the highlights of the last thirty years to give an indication of how Mine Mill has functioned as a union and virtually just as a local union.

That history starts with the wildcat strike in 1960 at Falconbridge. In my view, and in the view of most labour analysts, it was provoked by the company and assisted by the union's "reform" executive, led by Don Gillis. [See also chapter 19.] The wildcat resulted in the firing of twelve of our brothers, who were very ably defended by Lukin Robinson. But, unfortunately, when you read the evidence and read the testimony, all these men were guilty of was of *not doing something* – and what they didn't do was to advise the workers to go back to work. For that they were discharged, and that discharge was upheld. And I would state categorically that somehow the chairman of that board was influenced to make such a decision, because in subsequent years that kind of a premise has been overruled and been changed, and no such liability exists on shop stewards at the risk of losing their jobs. In any event, I believe it was Lukin who had a conversation with the general manager of Falconbridge when they happened to be travelling together by train to Sudbury, and the general manager said to Lukin something to the effect, "Are these guys going to behave themselves now?" The idea was to destroy the militancy and the determination of the stewards' body at Falconbridge.

What I'm indicating is that the Gillis executive, which we accused at that time of laying the groundwork for the Steelworkers' raid, proved to be very much the fact of life. Before the Steel raid, we at Falconbridge had attempted to separate ourselves from Local 598 by setting up an independent union at Falconbridge, a separate union for the Falconbridge workers under the banner of Local 1025 in 1961, and we were denied a separation by the Ontario Labour Board. That has to be one of the greatest ironies of history, because the Gillis executive strongly opposed us, the management opposed us, everyone opposed us, and we were defeated. And if we hadn't been defeated we would have never have fallen into Local 598, and that is one of the twists of history, that sometimes when you are defeated you actually win.

The Steel raids began in 1962. A vote took place at Inco, and our union was declared defeated by fifteen votes more than the required majority. At Falconbridge it was proven before the labour board that there were a number of forged cards among the Steelworkers' applications, and it became so embarrassing for the Steelworkers when the numbers dropped down to less than 40 percent that they withdrew their application. Following that, Local 598 carried on negotiations with Falconbridge in 1963, and it was precisely at that time – I guess it was the year before the negotiations – that the contract with the American government for nickel had ended. Falconbridge was enjoying a premium price for nickel in order to build up the American strategic stockpile, and they had done that for ten years and they were able to expand their smelter and build their operations out at Onaping on the basis of that American finance, and that's the only money that I have ever known that came as a gift from the United States to Canada. I don't know of any other such occasion. But the financing of the expansion of Falconbridge was paid for essentially by the American taxpayers through the premium price that they paid for nickel. Thank you, Uncle Sam.

Negotiations were extremely difficult that year, and Ken Smith, the national president of Mine Mill, was negotiating on behalf of our local union at Falconbridge. The strategy was to call for a strike mandate in order to force the company to give concessions. An 85 percent strike mandate was given, but the company refused to make any further concessions and at a union meeting that followed – which was largely packed by the

Steelworker dissidents within our local – the members were insisting that the strike mandate be put into force. The national executive officers believed at that time that they had no alternative, but it so happened that Buddy DeVito was there as the public relations officer for Mine Mill, and he and I had a serious discussion about the question. He said to me, "Jim, what do you think about a strike at Falconbridge?" We discussed the ramifications of it and I said, in essence, "Buddy, we'll be chopped to pieces. There is a stockpile waiting there and they'll kill us."

Buddy went back to a meeting of the national officers and convinced them that a strike should not take place, regardless of the strike mandate, and Ken Smith then ordered a vote of the membership on the last company offer. The number of people was very small who were prepared to stand up at the union meeting and advocate accepting the contract, because it was a poor one, but in fact the contract was accepted by a half of 1 percent majority. Some 50 and a half percent voted to accept the contract, and it was accepted. And I can say with some degree of pride that among all of the officers of the union, I was the only one prepared to stand at the gate and hand out the contract proposition. Anyway, there was a great deal of discontent on the job because of having accepted this inferior agreement, but only for a month. A month later one-third of the workforce was laid off, back to ten years' seniority in virtually all the mines, mills, and smelters, and then it was clear to the membership that if they had gone on strike they would have been walking into a trap. I think that the respect of the membership for the leadership that they were given then helped to solidify their support for Mine Mill.

We attempted to convince the company to accept a plan of sharing the work, which they refused to do, and we had even got an agreement with the Unemployment Insurance Commission to allow workers to work for three weeks and go one week on unemployment insurance, but the company refused to accept that too. We pointed out to them that they would have maintained their whole workforce. The result was that they lost their best young miners and their best young smeltermen. It was only six weeks to two months after the layoff, instead of the expected year, that they were trying to get the workers back, but they had lost them irretrievably. They had gone elsewhere to get work. And the company never liked to be reminded of the mistake that they had made when they refused to listen to the union's proposition about sharing the work.

In 1965 we attempted a comeback at Inco. We had a sign-up campaign and we actually signed up something like 50 percent of the Inco workers, and the main recruiting force for Inco workers consisted of Falconbridge stewards and Falconbridge captains. We as a team were the greatest assistants that the Inco workers had in their sign-up campaign. We went from door to door assisting them, while at the same time taking on a raid by the Steelworkers at Falconbridge. The Steel raid at Falconbridge was just as dismal in 1965 as it was in 1962, with them not being able to get 45 percent of the vote. When it came before the labour board, their vote was somewhere around the 40 percent mark, 40 percent of the sign-up. As well, we were not able to win the vote at Inco for a large number of reasons, the main one being that the workers wanted things to settle down. They were not prepared for another raiding campaign, because they figured that if Mine Mill were to come back at Inco, the Steelworkers had pledged that they would not give up, that they would continue to harass us. I think the majority of workers at Inco accepted that.

By 1967 the merger agreement was on the agenda, and the majority of Falconbridge workers were opposed to the merger. At the merger convention in Winnipeg we voted strongly against it and spoke against it. I know I spoke against it, and said that as far as I was concerned, and as far as the Falconbridge members were concerned, this was not a merger agreement that was a victory for the trade union movement as they were claiming, that this merger with the Steelworkers was a treaty – or, if you like, the terms of surrender of Mine Mill. I think if they had characterized it in that way, I might have accepted it, but by trying to characterize it as a victory, I certainly wouldn't accept it. I said as terms of surrender they were generous terms, but as terms of victory they were not acceptable.

In 1969 we got an opinion from the court that legally justified our continuing existence as Mine Mill. Up until then it was questionable whether or not we were Mine Mill, but in Justice King's decision it was declared that we hadn't gone anywhere, that we were like the continuing Presbyterians who were entitled to their church even though the United Church combined the Presbyterians and Methodists and Congregationalists. But we were staying where we were, and the others had moved out, so we were entitled to all the properties and everything that belonged to Mine Mill and the Mine Mill legacy, and that's how we happened to remain here as an independent union. So if you want to say that we chose to remain an independent union, that's how we chose it. The others left us. It's like a man whose wife has left him, and you say he chose to be a single man.

I think this is a very important point, and it does point to the future. In 1969 the Steelworkers were on strike at Inco. When they were on strike for about a month and a half, the question came up, "What are the Falconbridge workers going to do? They are now going into negotiations." The company offered us twenty-five cents an hour down payment on our wages, which in those days was a fair amount of money, plus whatever the Steelworkers get, if we continued working. Now, what did we decide to do?

As Bill Walsh says, we did the honourable thing. We did the completely unexpected thing. Nobody would have anticipated we would have done what we did. Over 80 percent of the workers voted to go on strike in support of the battle against the two nickel giants, and to strike shoulder to shoulder with the Inco workers. And in 1969, for the first and last time, we engaged in a joint Labour Day parade down the streets of Sudbury.

Clinton Jencks: I'd like to address myself to Ruth Reid's remarks in a very positive way. I'm very grateful to the committee for having her on the panel. I'm very grateful for her courage in expressing on behalf of all women and all men the need for greater participation in the union movement. Actually that is what this conference is all about, it's what Mine Mill has always been about. But I remember in New Mexico when we were struggling to involve the women in the union – this is long before the film *Salt of the Earth* – I wondered why the Canadian women were so courageous and making the international officers so uncomfortable and demanding the right to attend international union conventions and demanding the right to say something on the floor and not just to be the auxiliary that serves the coffee and the cookies. Lil Greene and Ray Stevenson gave me a little bit of an answer to that question.

"Well," they said, "it didn't happen by accident." There were many women and there were a few men who realized that we were fighting with one hand tied behind our backs. Because for many women, the union was an enemy – they had to provide for the kids, and they didn't know what was going on in the mines. All they heard about the union was when the men came home full of fire, piss, and vinegar and a little bit of beer, saying, "We're not going to go to work tomorrow." And here's this woman wondering, "How am I going to take care of these kids?"

We ran into the same thing in New Mexico. The first time I brought it up that we should invite the women to the union hall to hear what our plans were, I got voted down by a bunch of men who were scared of giving up some of their power and privilege. So like my friend Barney McGuire said about his community work, if you can't go in the front door, go in the back door. We got into the union hall by making the hall a community centre, where all the family had a right to be, where we could have fun together and where we could learn together too.

Back in those days, and it's something we've got to re-create again, we had this thing called Brandon Films. It used to have 16-millimetre documentaries on other unions and other countries. So I'm very grateful for having been pushed by the women. I'm very grateful that I was one of the ones that saw that we wouldn't be the losers, that we'd all be a whole lot stronger when we had all of our allies. Thanks, Ruth.

Barney McGuire: Brothers and sisters, I want to say something that in my haste I didn't say when I was speaking about our Miners' Memorial Days in Cumberland. I'm sure you all realize that if we didn't have the support of the membership of Mine Mill 598, all that happened in Cumberland just wouldn't have happened. And I want to tell you that the people of Cumberland are very grateful to you, the membership of Local 598. You have no bigger booster than the people of Cumberland.

Now on the question of the eight-hour day, I think we have a lesson placed before us. I would like to comment upon the fact that back in the early 1900s, it was the Western Federation of Miners that won the eight-hour day upon the basis from collar-to-collar or portal-to-portal, which is very important.[17] The struggle for an eight-hour day tells us what to do. If we don't get together as workers, as unions in the mining industry, our conditions are going to be eroded and there's going to be a continuation of some things that have recently happened in western Canada. And that is this: the employers, by devious means, got employees to sign petitions for permission to work ten hours a day, and they have sent them to the appropriate government body. The government granted their request. This was also done in isolated unionized camps where the representatives couldn't get to them. And just recently the scabs in Yellowknife signed a petition to get the ten-hour day, and my understanding is that underground workers got it. Now I think this is something that we all have to guard against in the future.

Ruth Reid: There is some talk now of a monument to the miners being built in Bell Park. I want to remind you that in 1967 the Ladies' Auxiliary decided to put a monument in Bell Park. We were going to have a mother and child sculpture done by Paul Affetio of Toronto, but then the men got going and they wanted to get involved in it, and they decided it should be something like this. Now remember this was in 1967, and the sculpture was to be called "Man and His Work." But you know what happened in 1967 – we didn't have any money, and despite all our efforts we couldn't raise enough money to build it. So I just wanted to inform you that now it's finally going to be built.[18]

Mike Solski: I have a few disjointed cracks that I'd like to make. First of all, this one is directed to the militant trade union women and men in the professional and white-collar groups. I say to you, you owe our organization a vote of thanks. The reason I say that is because I sat through a session – a bilingual session, and my French is not too great – where we reviewed what the Local 902 had organized. [See chapter 6.] I recall the days when you people were ashamed to walk on the same street as myself and Ray and other officers of this union for fear of being seen by your employer or getting contaminated by what we were doing. So I ask you to thank us, and we certainly will thank you, because you finally grew up and are militant and standing up and doing a job.

Another point I would like to make: I'm a little puzzled – you know, pensioners have a lot of time to think and sometimes we talk out loud – about all the union negotiations that have gone on for a number of years now. It's happening with the small unions and it's happening with the big unions. All I can see is you keep negotiating for severance pay to put more and more people out of work. Somebody else said this morning – when are you going to start fighting to stop plant closures in this province and this country? There are enough big unions here, and if the small ones can't do it, the big ones should do it. And Ray, you say they're sneaking nickel from the Soviet Union to Europe. Well, I don't think they're sneaking anything, they're doing it wide open.

Ray Stevenson: I haven't said they were sneaking, I said they were dumping it.

Mike Solski: Well, I apologize if I'm not using the right word. But they're not only sneaking nickel from over there, they're sneaking technology from here. The government gave grants to the International Nickel Company to do research, and what are they doing now? They're taking that research and they're moving it down to the southern states. I mean, it's our government and it's our taxpayers' money, it's the research of our resources here in these mines, so why are they moving down to Tennessee, or wherever else they're talking about going, to put up a plant there instead of here? So I say to the trade unions big or small and to the local politicians who seem to concentrate on getting money out of the taxpayers instead of the mining companies, you had better do something about that. And then maybe we will get somewhere.

Ray Stevenson: I want to tell you a little story that happened to me. One of the great experiences of my life was being involved in the Kirkland Lake strike of 1941 and 1942. It was the first mass action of working people that I had been involved in. I was a pretty young fellow at that time, but I learned a great many things, and one of the things I learned I was taught by the Ladies' Auxiliary. During that strike, the women and the wives of the miners upholding that strike were running the clothing shop, patching pants, looking after food vouchers, making sure that we guys were out in the bush cutting wood to get to the people in the houses so that you'd be able to heat the house, making sure that people got the wood.

That strike went on from November until mid-February in 1942, and

Mine Mill and Smelter Workers Union Eastern Staff Conference held at the Coulson Hotel, Sudbury, between Christmas and New Year's, 1956. Seated, left to right: Harvey Murphy, Nels Thibault, Bill Longridge, Bill Kennedy, and Ray Stevenson. Standing: Pete Mongeon, Mike Ellis, Floyd Gates, Bob Carlin, Mike Farrell, Joe Kaminiski, John Smaller, and Gilles Huneault.

Courtesy Mike Farrell

finally about ten days before the end of the strike, the issue that was at risk or that had to be resolved was with the federal government, because Mackenzie King would not utter a statement to the effect that gold was either essential or non-essential for the war effort. Mackenzie King, in his usual style, rode right down the middle and he wouldn't say anything. We repeatedly sent delegations to Ottawa, usually led by Bill Simpson, who was the president of the local at that time, to get King to make a declaration about whether or not he wanted gold produced for the war effort. Because we said as miners, "If you need the damn stuff, make the company bargain with us, and by God, we'll give you enough gold it'll bury you. If you don't want it, get us the hell out of here, put us in base metals or wherever it should be, and we will produce base metals for the war effort. (That did happen eventually wherever it was necessary.) We're not unpatriotic, and we want to support the war effort against fascism."

So the delegation went down to Ottawa. They sent a wire back: "King has refused to meet us." By God, the strike was over. We had to go into this big theatre, all of us, and we went in there, and we stood up there, and they said, "Guys, this is the situation." And we cried, literally. We went out of that meeting; another wire came from Ottawa: "King has agreed to meet us." By God, the strike was on still. You know what happened? The Ladies' Auxiliary – and I get emotional talking about it even yet – you know what they did? They went out on the street and they snake-danced up and down Government Road and Duncan Avenue, and I don't know where they got it because there was no money around, but bottles of wine, a little beer, and whisky were passed around and we had a hell of a celebration. The Ladies' Auxiliary taught us a lesson. They taught all us young guys. They were there, not just in our minds, but their hearts were in that fight, and it was a real fight for the miners of this country.

The final thing I have to say is related to this question Mike has raised, and certainly I'm in agreement with him. What the devil is wrong when we have a situation in Ontario where Bob Rae, an avowed socialist leading a government of the left, is compelled into the positions he's taking at the present time? I feel sorry for him because I know who's doing it. It's just like you and your mortgage. If you don't pay your mortgage, the bank will foreclose. And you remember a few weeks ago, when the Standard and Poor's, or the bank ratings in Montreal, said that Ontario's ratings were down. You're not triple A, you're double A plus. What did that mean for our government? It meant that they had taken out loans and loans and loans. The people who were chiefly responsible were the previous governments who spent money like it was going out of style. So now we have a national debt of $500 billion. The banks are calling in those debts. That is why we now confront the near crisis that we do in the province of Ontario and nationally. Unless the people are mobilized and get to understand this and begin to move collectively, the banks may well have their way, and our governments will be reduced to the level of a Second or Third World country operating in a vacuum where they have no credit with the financial institutions. That's what we face.

Mike Farrell: You know, sometimes we forget that if Inco or Falconbridge could take that ore body out of the ground and move it someplace else where the wages are much, much lower, I think we all know, or should know, they would do it. Fortunately, they haven't found a way to do that yet. Never will.

Trudy Upchan: I'm one of your born-and-bred-and-weaned-and-fed Mine Mill union babies. I was raised in a home where I can remember the trauma, I can remember the tears of the men that died in that war. To me, the inter-union fighting was a war. I was just a child, but I knew that there was a war. I heard the men in my home talking with my father, Nick Upchan, one of your founders, and all I remember is the terror. And I remember being screamed at that I was a communist; so yes, we were affected, very much affected. I just wanted to say that some of us children were, and some of us are, still fighting. I'm a political activist.

But on another issue, I'm sick and tired of the company putting the men out to work at starvation wages for six and seven months for seventeen cents an hour, and there's no compensation for the industrial diseases. I'm born with brain damage from sulphuric acid from the shit that my father sucked in. He lives with the disease, and there's never any compensation for that. What we have is this wonderful multitrillion-dollar sick-care system that was paid for off your backs, and the women sat behind and paid for, and the children are inheriting, but it's not getting any better.

Personally, I just want to say that I hope to hell you do not join with any major global union. I worked in the executive offices in Falconbridge in 1970, and I watched them take a $60 million loss when they shut down their pollution-free plant in Falconbridge. Inco, thanks to Trudeau, was allowed to put up that goddamned superstack that just increased the sulphuric acid throughout the world, and everybody is sitting back and nobody cares about what is going on. Even Greenpeace and David Suzuki and all the rest of them, nobody's looking at what's happening to the children of these men and to these men themselves.

Ron Mrochek: I'm an executive board member of Mine Mill, I'm very proud to be a member. And I want to thank these older people that gave us what we have today. And I'm a confirmed believer in Mine Mill – that Mine Mill will stay here forever.

Tom Taylor: If I wax a little sentimental, it is because some of the statements that were made really hit home.[19] And to be in this hall on a day like today brings back a lot of memories. It's a fibre, it's a movement, it's a feeling, it's an electricity that no one can understand unless they've found it too. It's a strange, strange thing, a union, and when we have it and lose it, it is only then we understand how important it is. I stood in this union hall with my hand up when Mike Solski was our chairman, and in those days there was a crater down the middle of this hall. There was a left side and a right side, and I, through my inexperience, was on the right side. And all these magic people who were doing things for people, their actions were twisted out of shape, and I, as a young influenceable person, was misguided. I make no apology for that. But it's the kind of poison that can be fed to young people to lead them to misunderstand the ambitions of the unity idea. When I see my good friend from Toronto, Ray Stevenson, and Mike Farrell, it brings back ideas of a 1948 picture, in which these laminated beams above us now were set up in a scouted-up form when that picture was taken.[20]

This was the largest union hall built on an old sand hole. McLeods had a great garage here, a ramshackle thing made out of lumber that looked like a great big stable. This was almost the boundary of the city of Sudbury. The hall started as a basement, Nick Skakoon was looking after the bar. What a joy it was. And the Ladies' Auxiliary made the meals – dinners where the plates were overloaded. I remember the gladness and tears. Oh my God, what people! I remember Jack Wendall during the 1958 strike, when the hydro would go and cut off the power, and he was up the pole two minutes later hooking the guy up.

That picture that stands at the back of the hall demonstrates so realistically what people are all about.[21] In the Sudbury situation, where the Finnish guy lived in Lockerby, and the Italian guy lived behind the brewery, and the French guy lived in the Flour Mill, and the ethnic groups were up in the Donovan, it wasn't by chance that they were divided. It was better for the company; they liked it that way. The company had offensive terminologies for all those people – they called an Italian a "dago," a Hungarian fellow a "honky," a Finnlander a "swimliner."

But God bless the Frood miners. I couldn't go another day past the one hundredth birthday without recognizing those beautiful, wonderful, wonderful men. Along with the help of the leaders, they made this union and the city of Sudbury. And if Joe Smallwood was the boss, they said Smallwood was a p-r-i-c-k, and it was on the wall. And that's the way they did the job – they did the job on the boss. Forty-nine guys sitting in the cage, or standing in the cage, and Mr. Brown at the front of the cage checking that nobody gets on the cage before their time. And somebody's in the back of the cage and saying to the fellow three guys from him, "What colour is your asshole, George?" "Brown!" he says. And that's the way they built the union.

But I'm so very happy that these men and women have come and said their piece so that you, the young people, can understand what our union is all about and where it came from. I'm old enough to remember the freight trains travelling across this country with fellows on the top of them travelling from one coast to the other looking for work. Don't look too far away, young people. The freight trains are going to be calling men and women looking for work again. It is amazing, the apathy of this country, when they stand back and look at it, young people and old as well. What happiness is there when young people accept somebody reaching into their pocket and taking seventy cents of every dollar they earn? My God, you must get angry. Politicians have to be made accountable, and they're only being made accountable by men and women like you. You only get what you're prepared to fight for.

Anne Macks: I'm a charter member of the Ladies' Auxiliary 117. I'm very proud to be here today, and I'm happy I am still alive. I would like to pay tribute to Ray Stevenson, because when my late husband Rhodie Macks died, Ray sent me the most beautiful letter, which I didn't know would come to me. But Rhodie Macks was a very big union builder for Mine Mill, and although we were in business, he really knew what the term "working man" meant. He worked in Frood Mine, and then he got into business with his mother and opened the store.[22]

But when the union was first going to be building – and I was one that they called a peasant and a good worker – I knew what the union and the Ladies' Auxiliary would mean to Mine Mill. And they said you can't join the union unless you have a relative in the union, because if you're in business you can't belong to a union. But I have a brother that was a union man, so that is how I came to join the Ladies' Auxiliary with the strength of all these years I've given to it.

But getting back to Ray. Ray wrote a letter and said that no one would give him any credit. When he came into our store, Rhodie of course knew Ray, and Rhodie said, "Just come downstairs and take what you want. We have miners' clothes." So Ray went downstairs, picked what he wanted, and he says, "Well, Rhodie, I can't pay you." And Rhodie says, "That's okay, Ray, whenever you have it, you can pay me. It doesn't matter." He trusted all the workers and he really supported the Mine Mill.

I worked from the bottom of my heart building the Ladies' Auxiliary and helping them in different situations. So I greet the panel, thank you very much for having me here today, and I'm sure I'll enjoy all the people tonight and tomorrow at the banquets.

Lil Greene: I'm proud that Ray Stevenson is my husband, and I think that I've been his support all the way along. I was his secretary, and Bill Longridge's secretary, and Ken Smith's secretary in the national office of the Mine Mill in Toronto for thirteen years until the merger with Steel. I'm also proud, talking about unions, that I was a secretary in the dressmakers' union in the 1930s, together with Esther Walsh, who's right here – Bill Walsh's wife. During those days, and in all real working-class unions, you not only did the typing and the cleaning of the desks, but you went out on the picket lines, and you got up early and you helped to distribute the leaflets to organize the workers. Then I had the privilege of being the secretary in the Workers Unity League, and that goes back a long, long time. I was Tom McEwen's secretary. I was Annie Buller's secretary. I was Charlie Sims's secretary, all in the office. There, too, we went out and helped organize. I also had the privilege of going on the great unemployed trek in Ottawa. It's true I didn't walk, but I sat in the old boxcar trains and went as the secretary of the Workers Unity League, and I sat at the desk of R.B. Bennett taking notes. So

I guess when you get old, you have a lot of memories. I also had the privilege of working for the Workers Educational Association that maybe some of you were associated with, and I was Drummond Wren's secretary.

I guess you can say, and Ray will agree, I still try to help him in being his secretary. And when he gets tired of banging away at his little old typewriter downstairs, I go upstairs to my old Mine Mill union typewriter. When the union merged, I bought the typewriter, I bought the Mine Mill desk, I bought some of the office furniture. I paid for it. Ray has, in our home, the original desk belonging to Nels Thibault, who was president of Local 598 at one time. He has Nels Thibault's swinging armchair, which we recently had renovated so he could invite people, as they came to interview him about this conference, to sit in Nels Thibault's old chair. So I just felt I had to say something. I am absolutely delighted to be here. It's made my year of 1993, it's been just wonderful, and I'm sure that as long as there's unity amongst the workers, that we'll gain in our lives.

Ray Stevenson: Since Lil took the microphone and told you all those things, now you understand why I stand straight and narrow. You understand also, I hope, that she's the person in the family who really has the seniority. Because I never was a member of the Workers Unity League. But I have here a lot of material from the Workers Unity League that I'll show to anyone who's interested in it. And I want to make this point: the Workers Unity League was organized as part of the Red International of Labour Unions in 1929, led and organized by people like Harvey Murphy, Tom McEwen, Becky Buhay, Annie Buller, Sam Scarlett, and on and on in a long period where they were organizing in the teeth of the Depression. I think it's important to make that point, because after the Mine Mill was revived in the United States in 1933, they chartered Local 239 Sudbury, 240 Kirkland Lake, and 241 Timmins in 1936.

I might also tell you that in Noranda in 1934, there was a strike led by Jeanne Corbin, a French-Canadian woman who went in there as a communist organizer in the Workers Unity League to establish and lead a strike. That was the basis upon which Mine Mill came into being in eastern Canada. Because the instructions and the decisions of the Workers Unity League were that in every instance where they had managed to organize locals – whether they were bargaining or whether they conducted strikes or whatever – the Workers Unity League locals would become and adhere to the Committee for Industrial Organizations (CIO) in the United States led by John L. Lewis. I think it's important to know this because, whether you like or hate communists, the fact is that the Workers Unity League was one of the building blocks of the modern labour movement.

One short story now. You see all these beautiful beams that have been referred to up here? [Points to the ceiling in the main hall.] I remember poor Mike here, I shouldn't say poor Mike, but he was sweating in those days because those darn things were late in delivery, you remember that? And there was the whole business that went on about whether we were going to have this hall open on time or not. Eventually we got it open and we brought from the United States a black, stately man of immense integrity by the name of Asbury Howard, who was the elected vice-president of the International Union of Mine Mill, and he spoke in this hall – though this part of the hall wasn't quite open and we had the meeting for him downstairs. But he walked around here and we took him on a grand tour, and as Mike Solski was showing him all this beautiful stuff, Asbury didn't say very much. He kept looking and looking and looking with his hands behind his back. Finally Mike kind of poked him a bit, and said, "Well, what do you think of it?" And in that southern drawl Asbury said, "Well, it's sure a beautiful building, I've got to say that. It's a beautiful building. I just hope it don't take your mind off the union." I never forgot that.

Ruth Reid: Asbury Howard sent his daughter to the Mine Mill Camp.

Ray Stevenson: Yes, he did. We had very close relationships. Weir and Ruth Reid looked after her when she was here for a whole summer at the Mine Mill Camp. And I have to tell you with great regret that Asbury passed on not too long ago. But before he died, after he retired from all union activity, he was elected a councilman, I think, in Alabama to the state legislature. That was a tremendous victory, because when he came here he'd just finished doing six months on the chain gang for registering black voters in Alabama.

Jan Longridge: I'm the son of Bill Longridge, former secretary-treasurer of the union. I'm a former camper at the Mine Mill children's camp, former counsellor in training, and presently a branch president in the OSSTF, Ontario Secondary Schools Teachers' Federation. Now, my memories of Mine Mill are among my oldest memories. The thing that really stuck out in the earliest years, when I was a child growing up, was the camaraderie of everyone, how everyone pulled together. I remember at the children's camp when we had people up from the Buffalo area, from the Mine Mill in the States, there wasn't an anti-U.S. feeling towards those people. They were all part of the union, they were all children of workers. And that's what's important: the unity of the working class. That is why a conference like this that reminds people of the history of the union is important, because when people see the history, they can see there's a continuation of the strength, and it can be built upon.

Nothing scares employers more than seeing workers unified. One of the things that is scaring the provincial government right now is they want to break everybody into little sectors so the unions can pick on each other, and say, "No, no, don't cut us, cut them." Well, the unions aren't going for it, and the government doesn't know how to handle it any more than the employers – Inco and Falconbridge – know how to handle it when the workers are united. And that's why things like this conference are important.

Clinton Jencks: We've been talking so much about memory, and I think memories are important because they're our treasure, our precious stuff, and they contain the lessons of our hurts and our wounds, and they contain the mistakes we've made and the achievements that we've gained. But memories can be a prison unless they challenge us to build an even better future. One of the very challenging requests that the organizers of this conference gave to us to do was to address the present and the future.

What are the issues that are the key ones now and for the future of trade unionism and political activists? This is a pretty important question when everybody is moaning and groaning about the sad condition of the labour movement, and when those islands of democracy are sinking. Mike Solski gave voice to the fears we have that if we grow bigger, we're going to lose the personal touch. And I'm reminded of the gift to us from the environmentalists and from the civil rights movement – and a lot of people are picking it up now – that I think contains an answer for us, and these are the words: "think globally, act locally."

In a few words I want to say for the future: I think that we will not survive unless we reach out to every natural ally we have in every country in the world. We will not survive if we turn our power as men and women locally over to some giant labour cabal sitting in Geneva or anywhere else. We will not survive unless we value and respect one another – really value and listen to each other; like Barney has been talking about, taking the issues that people understand and building monuments to those, and then telling other people about them and connecting them up with their issues. There are many ways that we tried to do that in New Mexico, and there's not time to go into it, but what I'm saying is I think the whole key to the future is extending the hand of friendship and support to workers of whatever industry, whatever colour, whatever gender, whatever nation, retaining local responsibility for what we do here, not surrendering our power to anybody, but not denying our responsibilities so that we have work and you have none. I'm tired of hearing about workers scabbing on my sisters and brothers, of producing copper in New Mexico when the workers in Chile are on strike. And what I say about copper is true of everything else, isn't it?

So those are my words, and they contain a lot of meaning for me of practical day-to-day work like Barney's been talking about, and Ray, and everyone else here. Think globally, but act locally.

Mike Solski: Well, Brother Clinton Jencks represented us old folks in the Mine Mill union by singing "Joe Hill," and I think it's time that you young people got up and let us know if you can sing "Solidarity Forever" so that we can close this session off. I'm waiting for you young people. [Audience rises and sings.]

Solidarity Forever
Solidarity Forever
Solidarity Forever
For the union makes us strong

When the union's inspiration through the workers' blood shall run
There can be no power greater anywhere beneath the sun
Yet what force on earth is weaker than the feeble strengths of one
For the union makes us strong

[chorus]

They have taken untold millions that they've never toiled to earn
But without our brain and muscle not a single wheel can turn
We can break their haughty power gain our freedom when we learn
That the union makes us strong

[chorus]

A chorus of "Solidarity Forever" at the Mine Mill conference banquet, May 1993.

Courtesy Dorothy Wigmore

Part 5
THE EXPENDABLE WORKER

Introduction

These chapters include contributions by Elie Martel, a former Sudbury East MPP whose long legislative struggles on behalf of Ontario workers have become legend; Cathy Walker, national health and safety director for the CAW, who has worked for the health and safety of workers in British Columbia and Ontario; and a number of "old-timers" and health and safety activists.

The focus of Martel's presentation is the history of neglect and collusion between companies and the Ontario Ministry of Mines that was punctured by the 1973–74 strike in Elliot Lake. These struggles, and others that followed, ultimately led to the bipartite system we have today. While it seems that there has been some improvement in workplace health and safety, much remains to be done. The bipartite system, Martel asserts, is in a state of paralysis.

Walker argues that the CCU (at the time of the conference Mine Mill Local 598 was an affiliate) has played a role in occupational health and safety, workers' compensation, and the environment that is far greater than its size would suggest. She further asserts that the CCU and its affiliates, particularly in western Canada, were in the forefront of resistance to retrogressive changes in workers' health and safety and workers' compensation legislation.

Chapter 14 consists of various comments made at the health and safety session of the conference. Its title encapsulates the grim reality of miners' working lives and is borrowed from a remark made by Clinton Jencks during a roundtable discussion on health and safety.

Chapter 12
"The Name of the Game Is Power": Labour's Struggle for Health and Safety Legislation

Elie Martel

Mine Mill has long been in the fight to improve the quality of life for working people. We have made some headway, but I am afraid the one ingredient that will change it all is not within our grasp, and that is power; because without power, we have nothing.

In my experience there have been many issues that have exposed the collusion between the government and the various mining companies in the Sudbury basin.

The first question I raised as a member of the provincial legislature at Queen's Park concerned health and safety. I was elected in the fall of 1967, and I asked that question during the first session in February 1968. We had set the stage about two months previously. There had been an explosion in the coal plant at Copper Cliff. Soon after that, Mickey McGuire – who later became president of USWA Local 6500 at Inco (1972–76) – called me on a Sunday morning to indicate that on that day the workers were working around the clock to clean up the results of the explosion, and the feeling was that there would be an inspection of the coal plant by ministry staff the next day. I asked Mickey to send me a telegram, dated Sunday the 17th of December, so that I could eventually use it at Queen's Park to prove that there was advance knowledge of the inspection, and a preparation for it.

The minister of mines of the day was Allan Lawrence, who would later nearly become the Conservative premier. His reaction was unbelievable.

When I raised my question about safety at the plant he was very irritated. When I suggested to him that I had a telegram that forewarned the inspection was coming, he replied that I was not interested in having a healthy and a safe workplace, which is in fact what the inspectors found. I suggested no, I wanted the inspectors to find the real conditions the workers worked under every day. There was no sense having an inspection that found everything okay – and after the inspectors walked out the door the mining companies could go their merry way for the next six months until there was another explosion, and you'd get another warning of an inspection. Then you could clean up again, the Ministry of Mines would come in again, and you would get another good report.

Another time, there was a serious situation at the roaster plant at Inco, where a bunch of fellows got into trouble because the conditions were so bad they sat down on the job. They were ultimately sent home. I co-ordinated the attack with my friend, Paul Falkowski.[1] For about three or four months we wrote a series of letters to the minister indicating there were problems with this particular plant. After we got to a certain point, Paul said, "Okay, now set up a meeting for me with the minister and all his staff." Which I did.

I have in my possession two letters pertinent to that situation [reproduced on pages 197–201]. One, dated July 31, 1970, is marked confidential; it was sent by Charlie Hews of Inco to E.B. Wright, district engineer for the Department of Mines and Northern Affairs. Inco's letter says, "The source is located and all practical preventive measures are taken as quickly as possible." The other letter, dated September 17, 1970, is from Minister of Mines Allan Lawrence. It reads: "The source is located and all practical preventive measures are taken." On the second page it says, "It would appear therefore that the conditions are highly exaggerated and that the complaints are not justified." Both letters bear exactly these exact same words.

In fact, what the Ministry of Mines did was take a report from Inco, rewrite it as though it were their own, and chastise us for suggesting there might be collusion. The last paragraph of the letter from the minister of mines reads: "In respect of the latest reference in your letter concerning my commitments with the Company, the accusation is so ridiculous no comment is necessary." Now you talk about gall!

Paul Falkowski and I went to the meeting, with about sixteen or seventeen staff and the new minister, Leo Bernier, sitting around a large table. Paul very systematically and slowly went through this procedure: he would lay a letter down and say, "Now I want to draw your attention to this," and he would pass seventeen copies out. We did this for about half an hour, and Paul finally said, "I'm going to come to the last two letters, I'm going to

CONFIDENTIAL

THE INTERNATIONAL NICKEL COMPANY
OF CANADA LIMITED

ONTARIO DIVISION

AUG 12 1970

COPPER CLIFF
ONTARIO

July 31, 1970

Mr. E.B. Wright, P. Eng.,
District Engineer of Mines,
1349 Lasalle Blvd.,
Sudbury, Ontario

Dear Sir:

Relative to the union complaints regarding gas and dust conditions in the Roaster Building of our Copper Cliff Smelter contained in their letters of May 28th and July 8, 1970 we reply as follows:

Due to the nature of roasting and smelting operations and despite thorough and continuing maintenance procedures, conditions involving high SO_2 readings do occur from time to time in areas of our Roaster Building. As the process is continuous and is not amenable to frequent starting and stopping without the danger of damage to installations, it is necessary to keep equipment operating despite these conditions. The occurrence of these conditions is not continuous however, despite claims to the contrary and we feel that this will be evident when the readings obtained by the Department monitor become available.

Company policy is that none of its employees is required or permitted to work in an atmosphere which might be dangerous to his health without adequate protection. In keeping with this policy the following action is taken when a high SO_2 condition occurs.

1. The source is located and all practical preventative measures are taken as quickly as possible to stop the escape of SO_2 or provide extra ventilation to disperse it.

2. Every man is provided with the best procurable approved respirator and encouraged to use it. These respirators give adequate protection to the respiratory system in any concentrations of SO_2 which might be encountered in our operations.

3. When an SO_2 condition is severe or prolonged the men are given adequate relief to enable them to get out of the uncomfortable condition to fresh air.

-2-

All the employees mentioned in the complaints were interviewed in your presence. Most of these complainants appeared satisfied with their treatment. With one or two exceptions the following general opinions emerged.

1. There has been a notable improvement in SO_2 conditions in the area concerned and this is continuing due to repairs and renovations to the building and installations which have been and are being made. Steps are taken to remedy uncomfortable conditions promptly as they arise.

2. The respirators provided give satisfactory protection and no trouble is encountered in obtaining adjustments or changes to suit the comfort of individual employee. (It was noted that several of the employees interviewed did not have their respirators with them.)

3. Adequate relief is provided and at no time within recent memory had any of the complainants been compelled to work in conditions which caused them undue discomfort.

It would appear therefore that the conditions are highly exaggerated and that the complaints are not justified.

The company is continuing its efforts to improve conditions in the Roaster Building. The extensive capital program including the new stack and electrostatic precipitators due for completion late next year is expected to largely overcome the problem.

Yours very truly,

C.F. Hews,
Superintendent of Safety.

JGR/zd

```
AREA CODE 416                                              WHITNEY BLOCK,
TELEPHONE 365-1301                                         QUEEN'S PARK,
                              ONTARIO                      TORONTO 182, ONT.

                DEPARTMENT OF MINES AND NORTHERN AFFAIRS
                         OFFICE OF THE MINISTER
```

September 17, 1970.

Mr. Paul Falkowski, Chairman
Safety and Health, Local 6500
United Steelworkers of America,
92 Frood Road,
SUDBURY, Ontario.

Dear Sir:

     RE: Roaster Department - Copper Cliff
       Smelter Plant - Inco.

  Your letter dated August 25, 1970 has been received pursuant to my reply dated July 14, 1970.

  Due to the nature of roasting and smelting operations and despite thorough and continuing maintenance procedures, conditions involving high SO_2 readings do occur from time to time in areas of the Roaster Building. As the process is continuous and is not amenable to frequent starting and stopping without the danger of damage to installations, it is necessary to keep equipment operating despite these conditions. The occurrence of these conditions is not continuous, however, despite claims to the contrary and this is indicated in readings obtained to date by our SO_2 monitor.

  This Company's policy as previously stated is that none of its employees is required or permitted to work in an atmosphere which might be dangerous to his health without adequate protection. In keeping with this policy the following action is taken when a high SO_2 condition occurs.

  1. The source is located and all practical preventative measures are taken as quickly as possible to stop the escape of SO_2 or provide extra ventilation to disperse it.

  2. Every man is provided with the best procurable approved respirator and encouraged to use it. These respirators give adequate protection to the respiratory system in any concentrations of SO_2 which might be encountered in the operations.

- 2 -

3. When an SO_2 condition is severe or prolonged the men are given adequate relief to enable them to get out of the uncomfortable condition to fresh air.

All the employees mentioned in the complaints were interviewed. Most of these complainants appeared satisfied with their treatment. With one or two exceptions the following consensus emerged.

1. There has been a notable improvement in SO_2 conditions in the area concerned and this is continuing due to repairs and renovations to the building and installations which have been and are being made. Steps are taken to remedy uncomfortable conditions promptly as they arise.

2. The respirators provided give satisfactory protection and no trouble is encountered in obtaining adjustments or changes to suit the comfort of individual employee. It was noted that several of the employees interviewed did not have their respirators with them.

3. Adequate relief is provided and at no time within recent memory had any of the complainants been compelled to work in conditions which caused them undue discomfort.

It would appear therefore that the conditions are highly exaggerated and that the complaints are not justified.

The Company is continuing its efforts to improve conditions in the Roaster Building. The extensive capital program including the new stack and electrostatic precipitators due for completion late next year is expected to largely overcome the problem. This was detailed in my letter of July 14, 1970.

In connection with your misstatements or inferences that Inco is being forewarned of inspections by my Department, this has been explained previously and specifically on September 2, 1970 covering the Roaster Kiln Building, I.O.R.P. with which you have taken issue.

Regarding the complaints of gas and dust conditions in the Roaster Building of the Copper Cliff Smelter contained in your letter dated July 8, 1970, I reply as follows:

The Company was not forewarned by my Department; in fact, the investigation of the complaint was instituted immediately after the matter was drawn to the attention of the Superintendent of Safety and the Manager of Reduction at Copper Cliff. This is factual but because of the number of complainants whom you wished interviewed, the investigation was necessarily spread over the time required to get the facts from each. We were not concerned

- 3 -

as our continuous SO_2 monitor was in the area.

Further, and relating specifically to the last paragraph on page 2 of your letter dated August 25, the implementation to alter the environment from the normal working conditions or to make temporary adjustments to improve SO_2 conditions during the engineer's investigations is not a simple one, but very complex. Your inferences therefore lack validity in this instance for the reasons I shall explain.

The roasters in the Copper Cliff Plant operate at drafts varying between 0.85 and 1.0 inches of water. This draft is controlled by means of dampers operated from the No. 1 Cottrell Plant and changes are made infrequently since they directly affect the process. Two adjustments were made in August and five in July.

These temporary adjustments are made in order to help to alleviate occasional severe SO_2 conditions in certain areas where maintenance or operating crews are working. Adjustments must be authorized by the General Foreman. A record is kept of the time they are made and the name of the authorizing person. We would point out that the Cottrell Operators who make these adjustments on instructions from supervision are hourly rated personnel who belong to the bargaining unit. Should any attempt be made to change conditions through draft adjustments preparatory to a visit by an engineer, a check with these men would soon reveal it.

In respect of the latest reference in your letter concerning my commitments with the Company, the accusation is so ridiculous no comment is necessary. I explained my reasons why investigations under my direction with the Union and other members of Parliament are open to question in my letter to you dated July 14, 1970.

Yours very truly,

Allan F. Lawrence,
Minister

cc: Hon. Dalton Bales, Minister of Labour
John Dowling, USWA - Toronto
Gaston Demers, M.P.P.
Elie W. Martel, M.P.P.
Elmer W. Sopha, M.P.P.
Dr. V.L. Tidey, Director Environmental Health Services
Chris Braithwaite - Globe & Mail
Chester Morong - Sudbury Star
Mary Thomas - CHNO News Room
Allan Thain - CKSO News Room

cc: Dadly Morgan
Gordon Hogden
R.J. Vanderwyst
Teo J. Nadeau
A. J. Comeau
Raymond Pomerleau
R. J. Smith
E. B. Wright, P. Eng.

give them to you at the same time." So he gave them the two letters, and he said, "Now let's start to read together, from either letter." And I want to tell you it was a delight to watch them squirm. Those people shrank to about a foot high. I couldn't find the minister, he was under the table; I swear to God he was!

For me, those two incidents – the first question I ever raised in the legislature and this second example – convinced me early there were no bounds to the collusion between the corporate sector and the Tory government of Ontario of the day, and that there would be no limits to which they would go to put the workers down. I could go through chapter and verse of the events that went on over the years of these put-downs.

In Sudbury about two hundred people who had worked in the sintering plant at Inco are ill or have died from cancer. As the problem developed, Paul Falkowski, John Gagnon, Floyd Laughren, Bud Germa, and I got together and decided we had to find out what was the root cause of this situation. People were being operated on in Sudbury, lungs removed – cancer was prominent, rampant almost. The doctors in Sudbury, of course, were not telling us anything. Apparently, workers did not have a right to know that they were going to die from cancer if they worked in the sintering plant.

After months of searching, of flying by the seat of our pants, the only break was when Paul Falkowski contacted a doctor in Hamilton, Dr. Cecilioni, who drew a connection between the cancer and the workplace exposure. His medical colleagues made fun of him, denying the connection, but we ultimately won that terrible battle. Two hundred workers! We ultimately got benefits, but benefits are no help to you personally if you are dead. And this type of problem continues today.

The real battle that led to Bill 70 took shape in Elliot Lake. It actually started out as a five-and-ten-cent strike, if the world only knew. Through the work of Paul Falkowski again, we turned it into a health and safety battle. We spent a lot of time in Elliot Lake, Stephen Lewis and I, and Floyd Laughren, and a young researcher named Linda Jolley. We met with the men and their families. I was at meetings where there were four or five hundred people, and they were telling us about their experience, how they would go home at night exhausted, and they would just collapse after the shift.

Ultimately, Stephen Lewis made probably the finest speech I've ever heard in the Ontario legislature. As we sat down at our places after we'd gone to dinner, the minister of mines, Leo Bernier, said, "I'm going to tell you right now that we're going to have a Royal Commission" (which turned out to be the Ham Royal Commission). Stephen Lewis whispered to me, "What the hell do I say now?" I said, "Well, we've got him, we'll see where it goes."

It went a lot of places, I want to tell you. What we learned is mind-boggling. Management knew, the Ministry of Health knew, and the Workmen's Compensation Board knew that workers in Elliot Lake were dying from exposure to the radioactivity of the uranium. It should not have been any secret. We knew people were dying from uranium as early as 1959. In fact a 1961 report by the Ministry of Mines itself warned that we had better be careful in Elliot Lake – and everybody forgot to be careful. Within ten years of the opening of the mines, sixteen out of twenty deaths from cancer were from exposure to radon daughters.

The only people who did not know about this were the workers. No one from the Workmen's Compensation Board bothered to say, "You know, sixteen of twenty deaths are from cancer." None other than the director of occupational health in Ontario, Dr. Ernie Mastromatteo, in a report called "An Unusual Pneumoconiosis in Ontario Uranium Mining Industry," documented the first forty cases of silicosis. And guess where it was first presented? San Francisco! Not in Elliot Lake with the miners, not in Ontario. San Francisco! No one told the workers. I mean, they are expendable – always the workers are expendable.

Following that there were several international conferences, several industrial conferences, and a presentation made to the Ontario Mining Association. Again, the only people not advised were the workers. Hell, you could always find another strong back and a weak mind somewhere; you could go and get those a dime a dozen. None in Canada? Then bring in some immigrants and let them work there too. Workers are expendable.

Out of the Ham Commission came two significant changes that I think captured the essence of what we needed.[2] Getting rid of having four or five different agencies responsible for health and safety prevented the bureaucrats from paper-shuffling. Matters used to go from one agency to another and you could never pin down who the hell was responsible. It was a great way of not accepting any of the responsibility for what was happening.

The other change was the establishment of an internal responsibilities system, which at least in theory said that the workers and management would get together and identify issues. They could work to prevent the condition from deteriorating further. They could go back and improve conditions and eliminate the thing that was causing the accidents or the deaths. Well, that is great in theory, but it really did not get very far.

There has been tremendous resistance to Bill 70 from every source. Management went crazy. The government introduced the bill, and management said, "Well, that's it. We've lost control of the workplace. They're going to shut the province down." We finally had the right to say no. It did not happen! Labour is much more responsible than that, too responsible at times, in fact. If they would get a little radical once in a while and shut a few joints down, then we might get some meaningful health and safety. But it did not happen.

Employers have done everything in their power to impede the resolution of health and safety problems. If you were in a non-union shop, you never got fired for trying to bring in health and safety, they just found another way of getting rid of you. In fact, if you are in an unorganized shop, they don't have to give a reason for firing you. So if you were involved in occupational health and safety, you were gone. In union shops, any union members involved in occupational health and safety went through hell. They were intimidated, they were demoted, they were never allowed to work overtime, nothing. Employers just got you slowly, surely, subtly, every inch of the way a fight until most of the people on occupational health teams quit. The pressure was too great.

What did management do? A few examples only! They would not give you pay for the health and safety meetings you attended. The minutes were all taken by management, and management buggered up the meetings. No one was in a position to ensure that the proper wording was taken down, and the worker reps had to fight constantly about the wording in the minutes of previous meetings.

What did the government do? It was every bit as bad. If there was a charge laid by an inspector, it would go to court, and then the government lawyer would not show up for the hearing. Case after case was thrown out – when the Ministry of Mines or Ministry of Labour lawyer did not show up at the hearing, the judge had no choice but to throw it out. To make matters worse the overwhelming majority of health and safety inspectors were hired from management – retired managers, in fact, made up the preponderance of health and safety inspectors in the province of Ontario. The few who came from the trade union movement ended up with too many plants to inspect – one had fourteen hundred plants to inspect in a year. Total and absolute disaster for health and safety!

I recall getting a brown envelope in 1986 – one of the loveliest things at Queen's Park is the brown envelope. In it was a confidential report prepared by the minister's own advisory committee on occupational health and safety. It was drafted by representatives from labour, management, and universities, who were heavily involved in a lot of the research and health and safety work. It said that after ten years the workers were no better off than they had been prior to the introduction of Bill 70.

I raised this issue in the legislature, and we put forward a motion for an emergency debate the first week the house was back into session. The newspapers yawned and said, "Aw this is a slow day." And the content of the report by the minister's own advisory committee, that health and safety was going nowhere after ten years, was not even carried by the media. The media, I have to tell the working class, are not your friends.

Conditions continued to worsen. During the early 1980s labour started to encounter a series of problems. For example, Bob DeMatteo of the Ontario Public Service Employees Union (OPSEU) found that at Surrey Place, a centre for disturbed children, repairs to the building caused chunks of asbestos to get mixed in with the kids' toys and dolls. When DeMatteo raised the issue, the government threatened him. They were hard on him. They did not want him in the building. Worse, no charges were laid!

We saw case after case after case of government neglect. In Ottawa they were changing the telephone system in a hospital two days before the asbestos regulation came into effect. They did not even take the patients out of the beds, and the asbestos was falling from the ceiling. But because the asbestos regulation had not been set in place, the Ministry of Labour would not lay charges. The fact is, they could have charged the management under Bill 70 as it was, but no charges were laid.

Asbestos became a serious problem. We had several commissions, among them the Royal Commission on Matters Arising from the Use of Asbestos in Ontario. At Johns-Manville, 68 workers out of 714 died of cancer. What did the commission say? They reported in 1984 that some of these conditions would improve; but their underlying philosophy was the philosophy of acceptable risk.

The acceptability of a risk depends upon a social value judgement made by the injured party or the legislature or society as a whole. Who the hell believes that? Numerous significant risks have been judged acceptable by individuals who face them. Certainly, a worker knows what to do: if you have to go to work and conditions are bad, and if it is a choice between having a job or walking the street, you stay and work. But to suggest that this is acceptable! To whom? Management? Do the workers have a choice?

The Burkett Commission was established when mining accidents proliferated in 1980.[3] Burkett concluded the mining unions were too confrontational and that the union members of the joint committees on health and safety should not be members of the union executive or involved in collective bargaining. You know what they were saying? Take the experienced leadership out of the committees. In many cases, the best leadership is in the executive; that is not to say there aren't good people in occupational health and safety, but most of them will not stay and fight the battle because they get discouraged. Burkett did not want workers on the health and safety committees who might be full-time and could really put some crunch into the proceedings. Get rid of them – that was one of Burkett's major recommendations.

In the early 1980s I did two task force reports, one called "Not Yet Healthy, Not Yet Safe," and the second one "Still Not Healthy, Still Not

Safe." With the help of the trade union movement we went to ten cities and gathered stories, the likes of which would make you cringe. In Ottawa, for example, we found that workers in the hospital were carrying the waste from surgical operations in the back of a Volkswagen down to the incinerator to be burned. On the way back they were buying lunch, pizza and food like that, throwing it in the back seat and bringing it back to the hospital. This is fact, not fiction.

Also in Ottawa we went to the Public Service Alliance of Canada (PSAC) building for our hearing, and the day we got there there was an overhead crane at the entrance lifting material as people walked in and out of the building. I got on the phone and called the Ministry of Labour and said, "Elie Martel here; I tried to walk into a building and there's a crane overhead. It's got a load, it's right over the entrance, and there's no barrier." Well, within thirty seconds they just nearly went bananas. They cleaned it up, but it's the sort of thing that happens every day.

With the two task forces, we met people from plants, hospitals, and mines. Adverse conditions are everywhere, not just in mines. For example, there was a two-hundred-page report on the problems at Carleton University. In schools kids were handling stuff like formaldehyde – they were dissecting frogs and whatnot with these materials on them. Students were exposed to asbestos in the schools.

We had the minister on the run, because I had developed a network of some fifteen hundred people who would phone me before something even got in the newspaper. Somewhere in the province something would occur, and before the minister could prepare an answer we had the questions for him – and it hadn't even been in the newspaper yet. Usually the government looks in the newspaper every day, finds all the stories, and has its staff prepare the answers to any issues that might be contentious. But when issues are not in the newspaper, the government cannot get prepared. I sometimes managed to get in trouble with the trade union movement because callers from health and safety committees were bypassing their own local or their own international. They just said, "To hell with it, we're going directly to Martel and he can put it on the floor of the legislature."

In our second task force the minister of labour asked us if we would accept his people following us to the hearings. We agreed, saying, "Look, we have nothing to hide. We just want conditions improved." Out of that tour came Bill 208, which legislated the bipartite system.

The McKenzie-Laskin Commission was nicer and quieter.[4] One of the commissioners was a consultant, the other a lawyer. They did a little in-house inquiry. There was no cross-examination, it was private, and it cost $450,000. They came to my office, and each of them spent three hours with me. They borrowed all my files, and after listening to them I said, "My

God, we finally have it made. These two guys know what's going on." Well, their report came down, and you know what the conclusion was? They claimed they had found a conspiracy: that the trade union movement and the NDP were trying to find a way to get control of the workplace, and that they were going to use occupational health to do it. Now can you imagine? We spent $456,000 on this pair of birds, and they came out with this report! None of it could be verified. It was all done *in camera*, in hiding.

Two days before the end of my term at Queen's Park, I managed to get a private member's bill, which had gone through first and second reading in the house, into committee. I did not think it would succeed. Management went absolutely crazy, and the bill was such a hot commodity that there were no copies left at the printer. My bill had only eight items in it. One was that you could shut a plant down dead until a problem was fixed. More importantly, the health and safety committee would always have an uneven number of members and management was to always get the smaller number of representatives: I said that if it was a five-member committee, management should get two, and labour three. That drove them absolutely crazy because for the first time, the workers would have had power. And the name of the game is power.

After I left the legislature, the Liberals brought in the bipartite system and the Workplace Health and Safety Agency with Bill 208. This has created a state of inertia. After two and a half years, at a cost of about $60 million a year, they have now managed to agree on a training program, a one-week program, a two-week program, and a three-week program. It is bipartite – management on one side of the agency, labour on the other side, with nobody to break a tie. If they disagree, they just go on fighting. Four of the management representatives walked out and resigned because of the training program. They've been replaced by four other people, but none of them represent large management groups, which causes me to worry. What kind of trade-off are you going to have to make to get an agreement? We can work on it and water it down till hell freezes over, but someone has to make tough decisions based on need – not on compromise.

In the training programs, I don't mind training with management for a while, but there has to be a labour-oriented session as well. Workers' interests do not always match management's interests. And I know people are going to really be uptight when they hear that I think the system can't work.

In fact, they forced out the chairman, Vic Pathe, who didn't have a vote. He quit because of the abuse he took from both sides. And it has been in a stalemate. When I meet people from the network I had and from management, they just tell me the whole thing is dead.

After twenty-five years of this work, I'm absolutely convinced we're going down the wrong path. We can't deal with workers' well-being in piecemeal fashion. Ham was closer to reality than he thought when he said, "We've got to get rid of all of the groups out there because you can pass the buck."

Presently education rests with the bipartite system, the agency, it is called. The agency is separated from everybody else; they can contact the ministry and the Workers' Compensation Board (WCB) for information, but who are the only people who know all of the employers in Ontario? The WCB – who are not friends of mine, by the way. They keep the records, they have the names of the companies that exist. If you go back some years to Dr. Ted Harvey's report, you will find that at least 38 or 40 percent of the workplaces in the province did not have a health and safety committee, particularly the unorganized workplaces. WCB has that information, or should. So we are going to leave education at the Workers' Health and Safety Agency. But who will ensure that workers in all shops are known and trained?

Who does the inspection? The Ministry of Labour. Who knows who the bad actors in Ontario are? Again, the WCB. They're the only ones that have the reports on accidents, illnesses, and what is going on in the workplace. The Workplace Health and Safety Agency has the ability to phone the WCB and find out who's bad and who's good and who isn't doing anything. The Ministry of Labour has to phone over and find out which companies to inspect. They used to have what they call a code 66, which meant that if a company got into serious trouble, an inspection was needed. Some of the inspectors have to attend to fourteen hundred workplaces, so without a code 66, they don't know where to go.

Who delivers if you do get injured or you do get sick? The WCB! We have made this process so confusing that it is a disgrace. In fact, the new Ron Ellis system has the WCB in a real dilemma. You can't get a hearing for an injured worker in under a year, even if your life depends on it. There are really only three things involved in compensation: if you get hurt, you get income; you have to get better so you go to the hospital or get whatever type of assistance you need; and if you can't go back to your job, somebody should retrain you. We've made workers' compensation a minefield.

The WCB looks after workers' health, income, and retraining; the Workplace Health and Safety Agency, the bipartite system, looks after education; and the Ministry of Labour does inspections. The left hand doesn't know what the right hand is doing, and this package is supposed to protect workers. The whole system must come together, so we deliver a total package that is effective. It must be co-ordinated, so that when the WCB sees statistics that say Company A has too many accidents, then an inspector is sent to that plant, and this inspector, in turn, can insist by legislation (if need be) that a health and safety committee be appointed when management and labour cannot agree. This is particularly important for non-union shops, and the WCB must insist on compliance, saying, "The inspection shows things are bad, there is no health and safety committee, we're putting in an inspector and an educational program." I'm not advocating doing away with the bipartite system; it would just be too radical for some. But put everything under one delivery system.

Until the whole system comes together, the safety of workers is at great risk. Statistics show that in 1968, there were 105,000 lost-time accidents in Ontario. At the height of the recession in 1991, there were 153,000. We've made a hell of a lot of headway, haven't we? We must stop this carnage. You can have all the meetings you want, but until you have some power, this mayhem is going to continue.

Mine Mill staff representative Rolly Gauthier, Ray Stevenson (past Mine Mill executive board member), Clinton Jencks, and Roy Santa Cruz (the latter two both international representatives of Mine Mill) converse at the Mine Mill conference, May 1993.

Courtesy Dorothy Wigmore

Chapter 13
Health, Safety, and the Environment in CAIMAW and the CAW

Cathy Walker

In 1964 a group of Winnipeg trade unionists became frustrated with the bureaucratic interference of the U.S. headquarters of their union, the Moulders. They set up an independent Canadian union called the Canadian Association of Industrial, Mechanical and Allied Workers (CAIMAW). Similar struggles were taking place elsewhere in Canada. In 1966 a group of workers, mostly women, engaged in a wildcat strike at Lenkurt Electronics in a suburb of Vancouver. The issue was a desire by the company to institute compulsory overtime. The workers' U.S. union, the International Brotherhood of Electrical Workers (IBEW), sent union bosses up from Washington to sign a deal with the company behind the backs of the workers. The number of workers fired was 257. The U.S. union signed up the scabs.

Outraged, the workers decided to form their own democratic Canadian union, and the Canadian Electrical Workers (CEW) union was founded the following year. With a relatively small electrical industry in British Columbia, growth was steady but slow. A meeting with the CAIMAW Winnipeg leadership in 1969 convinced the CEW to merge to expand the jurisdiction of the union. Everything was not as it seemed, however, and it took a stormy 1971 Convention led by the B.C. activists and supported by rank-and-file Winnipeg workers to transform CAIMAW into a democratic organization.

Growth was rapid during the early 1970s, as Canadian workers in British Columbia and Manitoba left U.S.-based unions – the Steelworkers, the Machinists, the Sheet Metal Workers, the Operating Engineers, to name but a few – to join a union controlled in Canada by Canadian workers. Workers in many mines, especially, were eager to leave U.S.-based unions, and none were more eager to leave than those in the Steelworkers. Many were former Mine Mill activists, fed up with the deal that gave their membership to Steel. Many others were young workers who could not see any purpose in allowing U.S. bureaucrats to control their destiny. Silver miners in Manibridge, Manitoba, and B.C. miners at Bethlehem Copper, Endako (molybdenum), Gibraltar (copper), Similkameen (copper), Bell Copper, and Western Resources all led successful battles to leave their U.S. unions, usually Steel, and join CAIMAW.

The 1982 recession, however, led to a number of mine closures and massive layoffs in the mining industry. The recovery took several years, but the mines of the 1980s never returned to the employment levels of the 1970s. The B.C. manufacturing industry also never returned to its pre-1982 levels. Unlike Ontario, there was no boom in western Canada during the 1980s. Organizing was tough, therefore, and CAIMAW began to expand in the service industry, especially in hotels and restaurants where jobs, though low paid, were plentiful. Events elsewhere in Canada were to allow the western Canadian trade union activists to re-establish the industrial base in, for the first time, a coast-to-coast organization.

In 1985 a very significant event occurred in Ontario. The Canadian Auto Workers (CAW) was formed out of the United Auto Workers (UAW). Canadian workers had successfully fought the "Big Three" (General Motors, Ford, and Chrysler) automobile manufacturers' drive for concessions, but the UAW leadership had not, and expected the Canadian membership to fall in line. The Canadian union leadership had responded to the resistance of the rank and file to the U.S. directive and taken the initiative to set up an independent union, the CAW, free of U.S. control.

Since then, Canadian workers, organized and unorganized, have flocked to join the CAW. Mergers were concluded with airline unions, rail unions, and fishworkers. In 1991 and 1992, mergers were concluded with two unions that were formerly part of the Confederation of Canadian Unions (CCU) to which Mine Mill is affiliated: CAIMAW, and Kent Rowley's and Madeleine Parent's union, the Canadian Textile and Chemical Union. In 1993 another progressive union, United Electrical Workers (UE), joined the CAW.

In addition to the mergers, the CAW has done an outstanding job of organizing the unorganized. Significantly, while many CAW plants have closed as a result of free trade, high interest rates, and the rest of the corporate agenda, the membership of the CAW has remained constant through organizing and mergers. The CAW is now the biggest progressive private-sector Canadian union in the country.

Health and Safety in CAIMAW

In 1975, as CAIMAW expanded in British Columbia, the staff decided it would be wise to specialize in areas beyond collective bargaining. The regional vice-president, Peter Cameron, had already become an expert on the new Labour Code introduced by the NDP government. Next on the seniority list, with two workers' compensation appeal victories freshly under my belt, I volunteered to look after the Workers' Compensation Board (WCB) issues. (British Columbia, like Quebec, has a combined jurisdiction of workers' compensation and occupational health and safety.)

As a person new to the workers' compensation system, and with a new WCB system introduced under the NDP (an independent appeal mechanism, the first in Canada, was a major feature), the time was ripe for learning and change. The founding meeting of the B.C. Council of the CCU in November 1975 in Prince George saw a resolution calling on the appeal board to reduce its backlog of appeals to ensure that disabled workers did not have lengthy delays in their attempts to achieve justice. Although the delays seemed long at the time, little did we realize that our members would have to wait much longer once the Social Credit government returned to power.

December 11, 1975, was a fateful day in British Columbia history, with the "socialist hordes" replaced by the Socreds. One of the first actions of the new minister of labour was to rescind the appointment of the chairman of the Workers' Compensation Board, Terry Ison. Professor Ison is one of the world's experts in workers' compensation.

Things began to go downhill rapidly in British Columbia. Financial penalties against employers who violated health and safety regulations had been controversial under Ison's leadership, with employers lobbying heavily against them. Ison was replaced by a board composed of: John Berry, former board counsel and long-time "grey eminence" at the board as vice or acting chairman; Terry Watt, employer commissioner; and George Kowbel, labour commissioner. With the new board, the employers succeeded in slowing the rate and amount of penalties. The independence of the workers' compensation claims appeal board was threatened when the caretaker administrators decided not to implement successful appeals. A number of other retrogressive policy changes began to be made in secret (Ison's board had been the first in Canada to make its decisions public). CAIMAW issued a news release in April 1976 alerting the public to the problems at the WCB. Although we had almost daily contact with the press thereafter, explaining every new outrage, nothing ran in the newspapers until November, when the secretary to the board, Connie Munro (now chief WCB appeals commissioner), got the boot for refusing to rescind workers' successful WCB appeals. After that, almost daily stories ran in the *Sun* and the *Province*. Reporters Rod Mickleburgh (then with the Vancouver *Sun* and now at *The Globe and Mail*) and Jan O'Brien (now with the Newspaper Guild) did a sterling job, keeping the pressure on the board and the government.

Earlier in the year, the government had commissioned a management consultant's report to respond to the concerns of the employers. Attempting to avoid public scrutiny, the government released the report on December 22, 1976. The media ran a lengthy summary as a front-page story. We worked over the Christmas period and rapidly produced a lengthy response which received excellent media attention. Ison, as well, wrote a critique that was also well documented in the news.

We kept the pressure up, and this pressure, as well as the mistakes of the arrogant board – for one thing, deliberately passing inaccurate information along to the minister of labour – led to the demise of Berry, Watt, and Kowbel by the end of January, to the glee of those of us who had worked so hard over the previous year to get rid of them. The efforts of our small union had been the primary reason that the WCB leadership fell. Honing our skills with the media in that battle ensured that later fights were equally successful. In 1985, for example, we were able to get rid of the chairman of the WCB, the head of the appeal board, and the assistant deputy minister of labour. It took an enormous amount of effort, but as the Social Credit government moved ever more to the right with appointments of bureaucrats who were increasingly more reactionary, our efforts to unseat them were critical to ensuring that our members received a fair shake from the WCB claims adjudicators and health and safety inspectors.

Some issues have taken us years of work. The lead regulation, for example, was controversial. At the May 1976 hearings into the WCB's health and safety regulations, CAIMAW argued long and hard for a reduction in the amount of lead workers were allowed to be exposed to, from 0.150 mg/m^3 to 0.050 mg/m^3. The lower level was the standard proposed the year before by the U.S. Occupational Safety and Health Administration (OSHA). Cominco, the company that owned B.C.'s largest lead/zinc smelter at Trail, took over the public hearings to argue against a reduction. Their presentation included slide shows, and a physician from England alleged to be an expert on lead poisoning was flown in especially for the occasion. By contrast, the Steelworkers had planned to give no presentation – at least until they heard the CAIMAW presentation. At the last minute they scrambled to bring in their health and safety representative from Toronto and another health and safety representative from Pittsburgh. Much of both of their contributions consisted of apologizing for not being better prepared and explaining that they had only heard about the hearings at the last minute.

All of our hard work has finally paid off, though it has taken years of lobbying with the board, health and safety inspectors, and employers to bring about this change. Finally, in public hearings in May 1993, the B.C. WCB was set to propose a reduction in the allowable exposure limit for lead from 0.150 mg/m^3 to 0.050 mg/m^3. All of our members exposed to lead will be much better protected by this more stringent regulation.

Collective Bargaining

The collective agreements CAIMAW inherited as a result of workers leaving U.S.-based unions were bereft of health and safety language. In these agreements and in new agreements, it was incumbent on us to negotiate health and safety protection for our members.

Surprisingly, perhaps, the wage-control period helped us focus our attention in this area. The Anti-Inflation Board prohibited the wage increases we had been successful in bargaining for before October 14, 1975, but exempted safety-related items. We were able to bargain successfully for excellent safety boot allowances, prescription safety glasses, and the like, but we also used this opportunity to bargain for improved excellent health and safety language. The members supported our attempts because they knew we could not get much in the wage area (although today 6 and 5 percent look pretty good), and the employers bought our arguments that they had to give way in the health and safety area if they were to conclude a collective agreement with a workforce that was not embittered and hostile. In the economic climate of the 1990s, I think that a similar opportunity presents itself.

During this period, our model health and safety language was developed. It provided for extensive worker rights: to participate in joint health and safety committees, to inspect the workplace, to conduct accident investigations, to know about workplace hazards, and to refuse hazardous work. A number of these rights were guaranteed in health and safety regulations, but we knew laws could change – and we were right: in the late 1970s, the board tried to limit workers' rights to refuse hazardous work. We also knew that to guarantee these rights for our members we needed effective language in our collective agreements. As well, we found that the large membership meetings around contract time ensured that these health and safety issues were discussed by everyone. Once we bargained for the language, members had ready access to these rights, because the rights were contained in the contract and every union member got a copy of the contract.

The model language changed over the years, with the most recent revision occurring in 1989, when environmental issues were included in the collective agreement for the first time and the role of the health and safety committee expanded to include this important issue. Thus health, safety, and environment committees began to be negotiated.

The CAW, by contrast, has extensive health and safety language within its contracts with the Big Three (Ford, Chrysler, General Motors). As well as workers' rights, the language includes extensive training provisions. By virtue of the scale of production in Ontario as well as a deliberate CAW strategy, nearly all Big Three workplaces have at least one full-time (and in a number of cases, several) health and safety representatives chosen by the union and paid for by the employer. Not all of these achievements in the Big Three have been necessarily emulated in all CAW collective agreements, but most large workplaces have good language.

Mining

Although there are four other unions in B.C. mines, there is no question that CAIMAW was, and now the CAW is, the leading B.C. mining union in health, safety, and the environment. Prior to the merger with Steel, there is also no question that Mine Mill was the leading mining union in this area in western Canada.

Some of the labour disputes in the mid-1970s in CAIMAW had health and safety as part of the demands. An outmoded separate health and safety statute and regulations for mining in British Columbia meant that bargaining rights such as joint committees were extremely important. Another ongoing problem was the common practice of supervisors asking workers to perform hazardous work after there had been a work refusal. The classic case occurred when a haulage truck operator would shut his or her unsafe truck down, be assigned another job, and a second operator would be asked to drive the same truck without being advised of the first refusal.

By 1977 the government announced a review of the Mines Regulation Act. We met several times with the leadership of all of our mining locals, sent out detailed questionnaires, and used all of the information to develop a detailed set of proposals for a massive overhaul of the mining health and safety law. Lawyer Craig Paterson was hired to write the submission. Craig had been hired as research associate at the WCB to write their health and safety regulations when Terry Ison was chair. He did a first-rate job on our brief, capturing the issues of concern to the membership and, together with the CAIMAW Mining Council (now the CAW Mining Council), developed a strategy for improving health and safety in the mining industry that we have relied upon ever since. Our union has taken the same position as Ontario unions did before and after the Ham Commission: we lobbied for omnibus legislation so that workers in all industries would be afforded the same protections, and we insisted that miners not be treated as second-class citizens.

Under the Social Credit government and given a weak bureaucracy in the Mines Inspection Branch of the mines ministry, we made progress, but it was extremely slow. Fortunately, ten years later the appointment of a new chief inspector of mines made all our work worthwhile.

In 1987 the soon-to-be-appointed chief inspector (then regional manager) invited the five mining unions in British Columbia along with the mining companies to participate in a committee to review the statute. CAIMAW attended the first few meetings, with the four U.S.-based mining unions conspicuous by their absence. An unfortunate fatality at the Afton mine near Kamloops led to an attack by the Steelworkers on the front page of the Kamloops newspaper about the inadequacy of the mines regulations. A public counterattack by the Mining Association suggesting Steel should put its money where its mouth was led to the Steelworkers showing up at the next meeting of the review committee. On issues of health and safety, CAIMAW always put aside any differences within the labour movement. We worked closely with Steel on the review committee and subcommittees to develop labour positions.

Our efforts to amend the law were undoubtedly assisted by the job actions of our membership. On several occasions miners at the Westmin Resources mine on Vancouver Island had refused to go underground because of the bad air. Production had begun in the new HW mine before the proper development work had concluded. Ventilation raises not all completed, a bad mine design, and new trackless diesel equipment replacing the locomotive system in the old mine all contributed to bad air. Reasoned argument with management and with the mines inspectorate produced no improvement.

Our thirteen years of hard work at the face and in the mills as well as the work at public hearings and on the review committee paid off with a new Mines Act and Mine Health, Safety and Reclamation Code becoming law in 1990.

We have been lobbying the New Democratic Party government to fulfil the promises of every NDP mining critic we have met with since 1977 (including the present minister of energy, mines and petroleum resources) to transfer the jurisdiction of mining health and safety away from the production-oriented mines ministry to the WCB, which has health and safety as its exclusive concern. As well, the B.C. WCB has tough enforcement powers enabling them to levy large financial penalties on employers that violate health and safety regulations. With the recent appointment of the chief inspector of mines as vice-president, Prevention, at the WCB, we hope that this will lay the groundwork for the transfer of jurisdiction.

Work Refusals and WHMIS

The influence of a small western Canadian union is, almost by definition, regionalized. By contrast, the influence of the CAW has been much more national. One example involves work refusals.

The mass work refusals of the aerospace workers at de Havilland and McDonnell Douglas in 1986 and 1987 resulted in health and safety improvements in workplaces well beyond those plants. The issue was the right to know about workplace hazards. The CAW members in both plants refused to work until they were fully informed of the nature of the chemicals they were working with and the hazards of those chemicals. These mass refusals, involving hundreds of workers for weeks on end, resulted in information on the chemicals finally being provided by the companies and suppliers, training by the union based on the information provided, and the clean-up of the workplaces themselves. All workers who participated in the refusals were paid for all of the time they were off the job.

More importantly, for the rest of the workers in Canada, the de Havilland and McDonnell Douglas CAW members showed that the "right to know" about workplace hazards was important enough to workers to shut down production. Agreement was soon reached on the right of all Canadian workers to know about workplace chemical hazards. WHMIS (Workplace Hazardous Materials Information System) legislation was agreed to by federal and provincial authorities and became law in all health and safety jurisdictions soon after the CAW work refusals.

Environment and the Mining Locals

Our mining locals have been very active on environmental issues. Our first major public presentation in British Columbia took place at the 1978 public hearings on Pollution in the Mining, Mine-Milling, and Smelting Industries, when we worked closely with our then-affiliate Canadian Association of Smelter and Allied Workers (CASAW) to expose the tragedy of the devastation to the environment caused by Alcan's Kitimat aluminum smelter. The fluoride emissions from the Kitimat smelter have damaged the forests downwind from the smelter and contributed to a lessening of forest stocks used by the sawmills and pulp mills in the area.

Our mining locals have been very concerned about the damage to the environment by the mines they work in. Our members have often chosen mining as a way of life to allow them to hunt and fish in their spare time. They have rejected the congestion of cities and enjoy living in an environment free of pollution. They have therefore often been very active in attempting to reduce harm to the environment caused by their workplaces.

Our members at the Gibraltar copper mine near Williams Lake, British Columbia, have worked with ranchers and farmers in the area to expose the ground-water contamination from acid mine drainage. Our Similco members have fought against spillage in the mill, which poses not just a health and safety problem in the mill itself but can harm the Similkameen River if the spillage runs down the hillside into the river. They have tried to work closely with the Ministry of the Environment to contain these problems. Our Westmin miners have been concerned about damage to Buttle Lake from the tailings waste from the mine. These Westmin miners live in Campbell River for the salmon fishing. They do not want to see a water system adjacent to their workplace damaged by tailings from their workplace, because this water system could potentially contaminate the ocean.

Education and Training

CAIMAW ran annual health and safety seminars for our health and safety committee activists since the mid-1970s. At first the lost time for these seminars was paid for by the locals, but through bargaining we began to get all or part of the lost time paid for by the employer. These meetings were always run as union seminars with union participants.

In Manitoba participation in our annual seminars picked up when the New Democratic Party government legislated an annual two-day training period for health and safety committee members, following the lead of Saskatchewan in 1972. This enabled the union to run two-day seminars for all CAIMAW health and safety committee members, with the employer paying the lost time.

It is in this area of education and training that there has been the biggest difference in approach between CAIMAW and the CAW. The CAW education and training programs have been far more extensive than CAIMAW's, not just in health and safety but in all areas. There are some things that, by virtue of the economies of scale, simply cannot be done by a small union.

Health and safety training programs were first developed in the mid-1970s by the Ontario Federation of Labour (OFL), by such people as Linda Jolley (now senior vice-president, Strategic Policy and Analysis, WCB), Gary Cwitco (then health and safety director, Communication Workers of Canada), Jennifer Penney (technical advisor to the labour caucus, Joint Steering Committee on Hazardous Substances in the Workplace), and Jim Gill (then health and safety director of the UAW in Canada).

By western Canadian standards, a staggering amount of government money was provided for this project. And this is another significant difference between CAIMAW and the CAW. The CAIMAW position was never to take government money. By contrast, the CAW never hesitates to seek, and indeed demand, government money for a wide variety of useful projects. This money has been put to good use. Project money has often been used as "seed money," with the union itself carrying on with the initiative after the government funding has run out. In CAIMAW we were always worried about "tainted" money, that the money would have strings attached. There is no question that this is a danger, but the CAW has always approached this issue more pragmatically than CAIMAW did, weighing the pros and cons of available funds. Many useful CAW projects – health and safety, new technology, or disability rights, to name but a few – would either not have happened at all or would have occurred in greatly reduced form were it not for the use of government money. CAW members have benefited greatly from these projects.

The OFL training course set the standard for health and safety training in Ontario and throughout the country. It has been the basis for health and safety education through the Workers' Health and Safety Centre (WHSC) and for the new certification training developed by the Workplace Health and Safety Agency. The centre, of course, is union run with the agency bipartite. The agency's course is thus not as union-oriented as we would like it to be. In the CAW, we are therefore developing a one-week CAW health and safety course, and we will do our best to ensure that all our health and safety representatives and committee members take this course so they understand their duties as union representatives. We will begin running the course through our Paid Education Leave (PEL) program, which we have bargained for in nearly all of our collective agreements (except, of course, for the newly merged bargaining units).

The CAW has bargained an enormous amount of training for health and safety reps by CAIMAW standards. We have a group of some eight hundred health and safety instructors who have taken the WHSC one-week Level I training and the two-week instructor training. These instructors return to their workplace to teach their fellow workers and, in many cases, management as well, in bargained training programs. They run weekend health and safety schools and evening classes. This depth in the organization is truly remarkable.

The health and safety training programs at the workplace often involve everyone, not simply health and safety activists. Among many examples are two-day training for a broad-based Workplace Hazardous Materials Information System (WHMIS) program, one-day lockout training for skilled trades and operators, a one-day course on ergonomics for auto-assembly plant workers, and a one-day PCB course for railway workers who are exposed to PCB-laced paints.

Another distinction between CAIMAW and CAW is in the area of joint training. In CAIMAW we never engaged in joint training with the employer. In CAW such training is common. Being familiar with both, I can say there are pros and cons in each approach. It is often much easier to bargain a large amount of training time if the union agrees to involve the supervisors. Certainly, training programs developed in whole, or even in part, by the union are preferable to training programs developed exclusively by management. There is also a great deal of satisfaction to be gained when both workers and managers are participants in courses instructed by workers who, by definition, will give a worker's perspective to the course material.

But there is also a downside to joint training. There can be compromises on content, as there have been with the agency certification course. Union instructors sometimes temper their comments if there are supervisors in the room. Worker participants may not speak out or ask the same kinds of questions if their supervisors are in the room. There is a fundamental assumption that health and safety is a technical question, rather than a political or class question.

There are strengths and weaknesses to both joint training and union training, so that we have to judge in each circumstance what we stand to gain by the particular approach. One concrete example is with respect to the new agency certification course. The CAW position is to propose joint training in every workplace in the province and to insist on training conducted under the auspices of the union-run Workers' Health and Safety Centre. If management disagrees with this position, we will conduct separate training, and management can use the IAPA (Industrial Accident Prevention Association) instructors or anyone else they like. This sensible, pragmatic approach was put forward by CAW President Buzz Hargrove at the December 1992 CAW Council meeting and endorsed by the delegates. He reasoned that we have more to gain by having union instructors conduct joint training than we have to lose in not having an exclusive union forum for workers training only workers. This will therefore be our initial proposal to employers, and we hope they will agree.

In the end the influence of CAIMAW in British Columbia from 1975 to 1992 in issues related to health, safety, and the environment far outweighed its size. We chose to concentrate in this area and were unable to make the same contribution in other areas because of our small size. The resources of the CAW enable those in the former CAIMAW bargaining units not simply to maintain health, safety, and environmental activities, but also to expand and improve upon them to the benefit of not just the CAW membership, but to the benefit of the Canadian union movement as a whole.

Chapter 14
"Building Tombstones in Our Lungs": Comments on Health and Safety

Clinton Jencks, Kevin Conley, Elie Martel, and Cathy Walker

Clinton Jencks: In my earlier work with the old Mine Mill I found that the union only resorted to work on health and safety issues as a kind of a last resort, when there wasn't something more dramatic to do. But my experience with my sisters and brothers on the ground was that they cared a whole lot more about whether they were going to come home at all than whether they got another nickel an hour. We used to have a saying in New Mexico about going to work every day and building our own tombstones in our lungs from silicosis, from pneumoconiosis, from all the fancy medical names, and all the other stuff.

I used to work in an acid recovery plant in a Denver smelter, where they furnished us with army surplus woollens to wear on the job. The clothes would only last for three shifts. We didn't have any respirators. Later on I thought, "What was that doing to my lungs?"

Like the experience of CAIMAW as related by Cathy Walker [see chapter 13], the time when we made the most headway in New Mexico was also during that wage-freeze time when the companies couldn't divert us to talking about cents per hour because they couldn't buy us off that way. We had the same experience as well of how hard it was to get our own membership to serve on health and safety committees because they knew that they were really going to get the heat as individual workers. It was costly, but we found that we got something done when we had the kind of health and safety guy who was willing to go to the rank and file and say, "We're not going to go underground until this is fixed."

My question is: is it your experience that if we were to have the courage to raise these less dramatic issues, we would get that kind of backing and response from the rank and file to go to the wall if necessary? And how in CAW, for instance, have you been able to get support for the health and safety – I don't know what you call them – of stewards or reps, so that they don't take the heat individually and they can't be squeezed off or given the worst workplaces? I'd just like to know: how do you ensure that these guys are protected on a day-to-day basis?

Cathy Walker: I realize that I've sort of glossed over the McDonnell Douglas and de Havilland cases, and those might not be issues familiar to people who are not from Ontario [see chapter 13]. These involved two very large aerospace plants in the Toronto area, where the workers became concerned about the wide variety – the chemical soup – of substances they were exposed to. They dealt with every kind of solvent you can imagine; the working conditions were really terrible. People suffered acute asthma and a wide range of problems as a result of the isocyanates. They organized from the ground up, with the plant workers saying, "We're simply, absolutely not going to take this any more; we have a right to know about what we're working with." The companies had not even bothered to inform the workers of what they were being exposed to. The workers initiated mass work refusals, saying, "We're not going to go to work any more until you tell us what it is."

This was a tremendous mobilization of people. I remember reading about it in the paper in British Columbia, where I was living. I thought these guys were nuts. They had hundreds of workers refusing work, and then I read they expected to be paid for it because of their right to refuse hazardous work. I thought they would not be able to pull this off, that all their leadership would get fired and they would lose big, but they did pull it off. They had their courage and their convictions, and they had leadership at the plant level.

If you look at the CAW approach to health and safety, a lot of it involves training, and it is a more technical and much less political approach than what I think is needed in our union. This is a big debate in the union right now. I don't mind telling you that coming from a relatively small base in western Canada, where we've done things rather differently, I could use some help. I think I've got some good support certainly in the aerospace locals, but in the Big Three auto companies – Ford, Chrysler, General Motors – there has been a fairly conservative approach to health and safety, and the companies are very sophisticated. The auto companies have this team-concept approach down to an art – they love this "jointness" perspective in the joint health and safety committee – and they see this as a method to co-opt workers.

Because we haven't done enough education in terms of seeing health and safety reps as union activists, as union stewards, as union fighters for health and safety, the health and safety reps in a number of workplaces are no threat to the boss, and we don't have the problem of having to protect them. They think their job is to go around and tell their fellow workers they ought to be wearing their safety glasses. So we've got a lot of work to do. But I know the direction we need to head in the CAW, and I know there is a lot of good rank-and-file support there, and for those people who are good union fighters, there is no question the boss is often after them.

At one of our aerospace plants, our health and safety rep got suspended for a couple of weeks – the real issue was health and safety, but they used a different excuse. The leadership of that local went in there, defended the worker, and said they would defend him to the death because they knew this was a bogus charge.

It's tough, but the ultimate answer, of course, is that we must raise the profile within the union as a whole, following the ideas that Elie Martel introduced of power for the health and safety committees, of worker majorities for the health and safety committees. Some people in the union movement are terrified of the idea. Oh my God, rank-and-file workers, you're going to let them have power at the workplace? Everybody knows it ought to be the bureaucrats in positions like mine who should be running this. But if we trust them, if we fight for this kind of position, that will change the attitude of the union as a whole towards the rank-and-file people, I think, to ensure that this is a much more important issue than it's been in the past. I think that there's enormous scope for change and improvement, as long as we keep in mind the direction in which we need to be headed.

Elie Martel: I was involved with Jim Gill of the CAW at the time of the de Havilland struggle. It was, and is, very difficult to move on health and safety issues because the rank and file really aren't behind you on them. It's much easier to get a group out to a trade union meeting if it's about contract, where the guys are going to come out and worry about the pay, with some justification. But the difficulty is that people aren't as willing to go to the wall for occupational health and safety, and the unions know it.

I spent a lot of time in the union halls in Sudbury, and the biggest meetings were votes for contracts and discussions around contracts, but occupational health and safety took about fourteenth spot despite tremendous effort to move it up. Currently the mining companies play games and give awards for safety and for no-lost-time accidents, with the result that the workers say, "God, we'll lose our jacket or our tool or our toy if we report accidents."

I'm being quite blunt with you that we're having difficulty getting the rank and file to realize that the most important thing they've got is their lives, and nothing matters a hell of a lot beyond one's health. We haven't recognized it, and that's still the Achilles heel I think. I know that in the McDonnell Douglas case, the union made presentations to the task force I led because of the difficulties they had encountered, and it was an atrocious situation, hard to mobilize.

One of my concerns about negotiating health and safety is that the basics shouldn't be negotiable. We have to have laws that take out of the hands of a powerful corporation the opportunity to decide what they're going to give. I think we have to have standards that protect people, and we shouldn't have to worry about arguing on a plant-by-plant basis, because we'll never live long enough to get all the plants properly organized and we'll never live long enough to get the workplace cleaned up if we do it on a plant-by-plant, negotiation-by-negotiation basis. There's got to be a bottom line at least, and if you can get further protection beyond that, fine. Health and safety still doesn't rank where it should – it should be number one.

Kevin Conley (USWA): I have a comment on Elie Martel's presentation about accountability, and accountability to the Workers' Compensation Board.

For years we've been fighting industrial disease claims, and it's a shame that today we still have to go to appeals on sintering plant claims. Gary Hyrtsak and I both sit on the nickel consulting process for industrial disease, and I was amazed to find out through those processes that the WCB had actual film footage of the sintering plant process. For years we were going to appeals, and it just seemed like we were beating our heads against the wall because we couldn't describe the conditions in the plant. Lo and behold, they already knew!

Today we consider the question, "Was work a significant contributing factor?" Well, they bring up the issue of cigarettes. You'll have to excuse me, I get a little emotional when we face widows and children who've watched their husbands and their fathers die. When the board has awarded an injured worker a 35 percent impairment award for respiratory disease and that worker eventually dies, and then they deny the spouse benefits by claiming work wasn't a significant factor, I get very upset. Something's got to change. Where's the accountability? It's just amazing the things that have been hidden throughout the WCB over the years. Elie Martel and Mine Mill and the Steelworkers have presented papers to the board and, even with actual footage, the board still denies claims. It's pretty difficult to say to a worker, "You smoked, so you're going to be denied benefits, but your partner that worked beside you never smoked a day in his life and he has the same disease as you have." Where's the justice?

Recently we had some guests from a Washington airplane factory tour Inco. The president of their corporation had told them that employers are going to have to close their plants if industrial disease, especially lung cancers, are allowed as compensable diseases by the board. He described the people who sit on those consulting processes, myself included, as irresponsible, and said we'd have to take the responsibility of major shutdowns throughout the province. That's totally ludicrous. As Elie said, Bill 70 didn't close plants – just as the right to organize hasn't closed plants. It's incredible. The president of our company turned around and said, "Well, we pay more money out in industrial disease than anything else within the board." If you look at the actual figures, out of two hundred industrial disease claims, only about two or three are paid, if that. And you have to go through the appeal process. So, as Elie says, we have to step forward and make the board more accountable.

Elie Martel: First, I can't see why a case out of the sintering plant has to be appealed any more. I don't need the footage, I was there. I worked three shifts there, and in the middle of the third one I decided to hell with this, I'm not working in this place, and I punched out and went home. Maybe that was the best move I ever made. But my understanding of the Ellis appeal system of the WCB is that once you establish a precedent, you don't have to appeal every case. But now it is so mixed up that it takes a year, or even a year and a half, to get a decision. But those decisions should be automatic. If you have three days' work in the sintering plant – I think we eventually got it down to three days – you're entitled to benefits.

Second, let me tell you why I argue that you must have power in the workplace. I put forward an eight-point bill, of which one of the items called for all new processes and all new chemicals introduced in the workplace to be approved by the workers. There is simply no way that people should be guinea pigs today. Profits notwithstanding, you shouldn't be allowed to introduce into the workplace a substance, a process, that hasn't been proved to be safe. And the onus should not be on the guinea pigs, the workers, to show up dead. It should be tested on the employers or on those selling those products to ensure that they're safe and properly tested before they're introduced in the workplace at all. I used to say that in committee, where I was critical of the Occupational Safety and Health Administration (OSHA) in the States and all the academics who said it was okay, that it was good for the workers. But they never had to prove through testing that the stuff was safe. There are more people dying today from occupational disease than from injury, but there's no compensation because it can't be proven. Weiler's second report said that there would be more people dying from industrial disease than occupational accidents on the job.[1] And that is probably what's happening, but we just don't have a handle on it.

It's not a new game when they talk about cigarettes and lifestyle. That's the *bête noire* they hang everything on to make sure they don't pay the workers.

Third, workers have to have power. If you don't have power, you've got nothing. The fact is that we have no more power now than we had ten or fifteen years ago, and until we get some, we're in trouble.

Gary Hrytsak: The problem with the Ontario Workers' Compensation Appeals Tribunal (WCAT), chaired by Ron Ellis, is they are not consistent in any of their decisions. When you bring case studies or tribunal decisions to a tribunal and you argue the case the same way, and you argue that the decision has already been made, that you shouldn't be there again, they turn around and say, "Well, we judge each case on its own merit. It doesn't matter if they were co-workers or not; two fellows working side by side, we judge the claim on its own merits."

Another thing with WCAT these days is that the employer-side people have made a radical change. When you go through the appeal process, you argue only the issue at hand that's been presented to the board and then to WCAT. Unfortunately, the employer-side people are now saying, "We want to look at the whole thing." I've got files this high. Are we going to spend weeks and weeks going through the whole thing to find out if the entitlement should have been granted in the first place?

Elie Martel: The whole appeal procedure is a farce. In my last year in the legislature, I went after Ellis in committee. I said to him, "With your process, you've created a lawyer's nirvana." It has become so complex, so deliberately complicated that people who don't have tremendous expertise and lots of time can no longer go and represent an injured worker. My comments in committee really angered them. A hearing used to take two hours; now it can stretch as long as six or seven days. It's become so complicated and legalistic that it's very difficult for trade union people to represent workers – and the lawyers want it that way. In fact, in 1986, the bar association wrote the minister of the day and said that non-lawyers should not represent women at the Social Assistance Review Board, or represent somebody before the appeal tribunal of the Workers' Compensation Board, or do an unemployment insurance case. These are make-work projects for an oversupply of lawyers.

Part 6
TECHNOLOGICAL CHANGE

Introduction

It is now common knowledge that technological changes in the workplace are not neutral, and that the introduction of new technologies into the workplace serves to restructure work in a manner that may well meet the needs of capital but may not be so "user friendly" towards workers. These chapters attest that labour strategies in the current economic climate must draw upon the expertise of workers themselves.

Theresa Johnson, a researcher with the Public Service Alliance of Canada (PSAC), portrays the reality of working at home with computer technology. Based on evidence coming from her work in the Technology Adjustment Research Program, she describes telework conditions in the public sector and reminds us that the sweatshop is not a thing of the past. She warns us that the employers' strategy of introducing telework demands collective action that may force unions to abandon their traditional relationship with their members. Unions must begin to explore new ways of communicating with a membership that will be dispersed in their homes for much of their work week. The effect of telework on the organizing ability of unions and its influence on union struggles around health and safety will be far-reaching.

Ken Delaney brings to this discussion a wealth of experience as a research director in the United Steelworkers of America (USWA) and, prior to that, as a researcher with the Autoworkers. His look at the Steelworkers' response to changes in the workplace includes the increased use of technological changes to eliminate jobs; the development of new work systems that offer workers consultative roles in the management of the workplace, but leave the structure of power untouched; the continued globalization of the economy; and the increased efforts by workers to humanize their place of work. He argues that these trends in the workplace offer opportunities to build a new agenda for the labour movement.

Using the experience of the USWA at Algoma Steel in Sault Ste. Marie, Delaney shows how empowered workers can turn the fortunes of a failing steel mill to their advantage. Workers' majority shareholding has created management-labour relations that give workers a real voice in the workplace. It is too soon to know whether that experiment will succeed, but it demonstrates that greater worker control is not inimical to production and reminds us once again that workers can be the authority in their own workplaces.

Chapter 15
Telework and the Workplace of the Future

Theresa Johnson

The whole question of telework has become what might be called the "darling of the media." Many people now work at home with computers, away from factories and offices and schools and stores, and know what that is like. It is portrayed in popular media as a very *avant garde* way to work, but some of the media hype around this creates a challenge for trade unionists.

In late 1992 *The Globe and Mail* published a series of articles that included a front-page story that read, "Oh, give me a home where I work all

Mine Mill Women's Auxiliary activists Pearl Chytuk and Ruth Reid, Liz and Harry Smaller, son and daughter of Mine Mill activist and author John Smaller, and D'Arcy Martin, staff representative of the Communications, Energy and Paperworkers Union, listen to a session at the 1993 Mine Mill conference.
Courtesy Dorothy Wigmore

alone, and the boss is a long way away." On the second page there was a picture of a parent, a father, with a practically newborn infant on his lap, and the father was toiling away at his home computer. Well, this picture caused a great deal of laughter and rather dark humour around the union office. We all speculated that there were at least two caregivers, probably off camera, who were ready to take the child the minute the child caused a fuss.

Most of us are not naive, and we know what the reality is out there for union members. The media are presenting telework as glamorous and a way to integrate work and family life, to reduce child-care costs, to cut down on commuting, and basically to save the planet. That is really far removed from the world in which our members work and live. In my research over the past two years I have done some detailed case-study work, and the reality is quite different from what the media are presenting. I think we have to remember that the push of the media and the business community for telework is clearly related to selling a lot of the equipment for home use, to increase profit margins, to cut employer costs for plants and overheads, and to increase worker productivity. This agenda has not changed for a long time: it has always been the agenda around work reorganization.

Recently *The Globe and Mail* carried a whole insert about the home office: how to set up your home office, how wonderful it is, the kids can play video games, you can work, do your taxes, whatever. It should have been an advertisement for the industry instead of an insert in the paper. The president of our union wrote a letter to the *Globe*, saying that the Public Service Alliance of Canada (PSAC) was involved in a major two-year study of technology and telework and that he hoped when the results of our surveys became available in a few weeks, we would receive as much coverage in the *Globe* as the insert had. It was worth a shot, but that is unlikely to happen.

For research purposes, we talk about telework as basically work away from the central office. You work away from your main office and you use the technology – home computers, laptop computers, and modems – to do the work and communicate with your central office. But working at home is not new.

The critical issue is the use of the technology to facilitate work at home, mostly with home computers and laptops. Telework happens during the day for some people who work from home for a couple of days a week instead of going in to the office; but it also occurs in overtime situations, and I found a lot of overtime resulting from the introduction of laptop computers. Among the PSAC membership, people are also doing work in transit, travelling around with a laptop to gather information and conduct interviews – tax auditors, veterans' affairs counsellors, people who go to hearings. A third kind of telework is satellite office telework. We will see more of this in the future – setting up an office away from the central core of a major urban centre, usually to accommodate people who live away from the city centre.

We surveyed all of our Ontario locals and found that there are not yet large numbers of people teleworking. It is just starting to take off in the public sector. When we asked people what they liked most about working at home, the answers were quite interesting. They mentioned efficiency and expediency and getting more work done in a shorter period of time. This says something important about resources available for doing work in the federal public sector, and it says something about what the employer expects people to get done. In the federal public sector we are working with the same number of workers now as we had in 1973, despite a 20 percent increase in the population. Also, as the unemployment rolls swell, so does the demand on public-sector workers who deal with the unemployed. There is clearly more work being done, and we are seeing that the employer is not investing in people, but rather in technology.

The private sector is doing this and off-loading employer costs and responsibilities onto homeworkers. As a result there are some disturbing trends in that area. Our employer, the government of Canada, developed a telework policy that gave a very clear indication of the direction it was heading in. The employer invited us to consultation meetings about the policy, and we spent our time talking about how we wanted this new way to work placed in collective agreements. The employer made it clear that this was not on offer. We have been trying, without success just yet, to get bargaining language to cover teleworkers.

The telework policy states that the employer is going to provide teleworkers with supplies and equipment (note the absence of furniture). The employees are responsible for the costs of maintaining the teleworkplace, such as insurance, heat, hydro. In the private sector these costs are dumped onto the individual worker, and the same trend is beginning to be imposed on the public sector. The employer's policy says the worker shall ensure that the telework place is adequately equipped from a safety and health point of view. We have continually pointed out the Canada Labour Code to the employer, and we are involved in a major education campaign with our membership to say to them, "You, brother or sister, are not responsible for health and safety in terms of maintaining your workplace. That is your employer's responsibility."

The government's policy also says that the environment of the teleworkplace must be such that the employee will be able to respect the terms and conditions of employment, relevant collective agreements, legislation, and policies. This would involve teleworkers in a major research effort to find out what their responsibilities are. It also indicates the employer's agenda in a clear way. Taking this document out to our membership and talking about what is in the policy really assist us in getting out our message – namely, that we need bargaining and protection for teleworkers in collective agreements.

In the private sector telework has been used as a low-wage strategy, and the same ideology is at work in the public sector. There is absolutely no question about that. We find that telework reaches into every aspect of our work as trade unionists trying to represent our members. It touches health and safety issues, hours of work, and equity issues. Our members with disabilities are asking, "Does this mean that the employer is not going to make the workplace accessible to us and that we're going to have to work at home?" There is a move in that direction. Telework takes away the pressure on the employer to make the workplace accessible.

Telework also raises serious issues around workers' compensation. We have had to fight to get workers' compensation benefits, particularly in the office sector. How are you going to deal with it when you're at home working and you're injured on the job? Can you imagine the battles we're going to have with the Workers' Compensation Board? "Well, were you working or doing the laundry?" Right now, the issue of workers' compensation is a blank slate, and we do not know where it is headed.

Child-care issues are central to the question of telework. In the *Globe and Mail* article showing Dad working away at the computer with the child on his lap, the employer is quoted as saying, "The telework model of work is not meant to be a replacement for child care." The article says that one of the advantages of telework for employees is that telework will reduce child-care costs. That seems to be a contradiction.

The employer's policy includes a package of questions and answers. One of the questions asks about telework for parents of small children. The answer given is that studies in the United States have shown that parents (I read "women") with small children at home should not do telework for more than thirty hours a week. They should, in fact, go to a reduced schedule of work hours, which amounts to working part-time.

The women in our union are not pleased about this. We struggle to maintain full-time jobs and decent wages for women, and the employer comes out with a policy document that says: go part-time because of your children. The Conservative government did not put a national child-care policy in place, as they had promised, and there is speculation that they are using this federal telework policy as a substitute for putting a national child-care policy in place.

We have concerns about the disappearance of after-four programs, if mothers are expected to be at home. There are a whole lot of issues around this, and women are telling us: "We're not going back home because of the employer's policy. We struggled long and hard to get into the workplace to work collectively, and we won't be individualized again."

We have real concerns about the lengthening workday. Linda Duxbury, a professor at Carleton University, surveyed six thousand public-sector workers in the Ottawa area and found that people who had technology in the home worked an average of 2.5 hours a day more than those who did not have technology in the home.[1] This indicates that our eight-hour or seven-and-a-half-hour workday is being lengthened. Our members are saying, "Oh, yes. I'm working longer hours. There's no question about it." They're saying things like, "What I do is, I work my day and then I bring the laptop home, and I do dinner and time with the family" – this is men and women alike – "and then when the kids go to bed and the house is quiet, I fire up the laptop at about 9 o'clock and I work for a couple of hours." There is a trend here towards a split day: you work your eight hours, you do some family things, and then you work again, fitting it around the children. Once workers begin to adopt this method of work, there are implications for the type of health and safety problems created by shiftwork. We may find office work moving toward a split-shift model – something we have not had to deal with much in the public sector.

The employer talks about telework as a positive thing. We can see why they say that: it increases productivity. The members I interviewed said, "We don't really see that we have a choice in the matter." A lot of the deadlines that our members have to meet are contained in regulations and policies that flow from legislation. So, if a report is due, they have to do it, and they take it home and do it; and they said that what they found positive about telework was that it allowed them to do the overtime at home rather than at the office. Now, the employer tells us, "Your members like telework." But I say people do not want to work longer hours. What they like is a decent workday, but if they have to do the overtime, they will do it at home as opposed to in the office.

Employers do not easily grasp some of those subtleties. Is portability of work part of the problem here? Members have said to me: "The fact is that the eight-hour day, as we have come to know it, is gone, because when five o'clock came and you hadn't finished, it would wait until tomorrow because you go home at five o'clock. Now the employer says, 'Take the laptop and finish it at home.' So we have really no choice." We have worked hard to make sure that we have hours of work that people can live with, and now those hours of work are being altered.

Parents who work at home during the day said, "It's unreasonable to pretend I could work at home and care for a child." Yet some people who have not tried it are saying, "Oh, I can work at home and I'll be able to look after my kids." There is this big difference between what the speculators are saying about telework and what the teleworkers are saying, and that is a message that we have been getting out to our members through our education program.

We have gathered from our members not only what their concerns are, but also what they would like to see the union do about this issue.

We will see with telework the individualization and fragmentation of workers, just as Harry Glasbeek argued [see chapter 10]. People go off into their homes and work individually, so that our ability to work together to effect change is going to be seriously undermined by this new work design. The underpinnings of telework, from the employer's perspective, are higher productivity and lower costs. But we have some problems in terms of people trying to cope individually, and using telework as a way to do it. Sometimes working at home is not related to a particular love of telework, but rather to a lack of other choices being offered to those working longer hours.

Existing power relationships and gender relationships are being superimposed on this new way to work, and there are some big differences between, say, what support staff/clerical workers do with telework and what administrative and officer-type workers do. Ursula Franklin came to a Technology Adjustment Research Program (TARP) meeting some months ago and said, "Things are not personal. They are political and structural." When I think about telework, I think about how our members are trying to cope individually with a growing workload and higher expectations, with the employer providing only this one option. So for workers, the possibility and the attraction of telework become quite personal.

We are in the process, through our education and our outreach with locals, of making this a political and structural issue so that we can put in place bargaining language that truly protects people. Our members want an escape clause. They have said that telework must be absolutely voluntary. Our members do not want to feel locked into the home. Most of them do not want to do telework on a full-time basis. Some are talking about a one-day-a-week minimum (preferably more) in the office to interact with colleagues, to try to deal with some of the isolation, and to run our union committees.

The implications for our organizing, solidarity, and union subcommittees are quite amazing, and the issue needs to be discussed in the trade union movement. As a movement, we do not have our act together about telework. There are a number of unions and workplaces affected by this. There is no question but that electronic highways and virtual offices are the wave of the future. I would like to see the trade union movement come to grips with this whole issue and develop a clear position that we can take to employers – because employers do have their act together. They are meeting with consultants and figuring out how to get more for less, and that is a major threat to how we operate as a union movement.

Chapter 16
A Labour Agenda for Work Design

Ken Delaney

Workers face a vast number of changes in the workplace today. Technology in particular is having a profound impact on the nature of work. It has eliminated jobs, increased the incidence of repetitive strain injury, reduced the amount of control that workers have over their work, and has certainly increased management's control over the way that work gets done.

However, technology can improve the workplace as well. It can reduce the volume of work and decrease the pace of work, it can eliminate unsafe work, and it can create the opportunity for new skills and better jobs. Unfortunately, very little work has been done on designing technologies that address the human side of work, the so-called human factor. A recent U.S. study showed that almost no engineering schools teach ergonomics or examine the impact of technology on stress levels of workers. Clearly, the human side of work is neglected by those who design our workplaces.

Workers are confronted with a workplace environment in which little attention has been paid to human factors in designing and implementing technology. We have health and safety committees that try to respond to workplace design problems after technologies are in place, but as a labour movement in North America, we haven't been successful at gaining control over workplace design and over how technologies are introduced. My own union, the United Steelworkers of America, identified four major trends that led us to develop policies and strategies for dealing with new technologies and work designs.

The first and most obvious trend is the effect on employment of the explosion of new technologies over the last ten to fifteen years. In the late

1970s Algoma Steel in Sault Ste. Marie, Ontario, had 12,500 members. There are now fewer than 5,000, but the company produces the same amount of steel it did fifteen years ago. In Sudbury, Inco produces roughly the same amount of nickel with about a third of the workforce that used to work there.

The second trend is an increased reliance on new systems, such as Total Quality Management (TQM) and teamwork.

The third trend, and actually one of the more interesting, is the work that is being done by some Western European unions. A friend of mine from the large German industrial union IG Metall – who is an industrial sociologist and a mechanic, and has become an expert on ergonomics and work design – told me that his union has done a lot of work on design issues. I said to him, "It would be great to be able to do all those things, but how do you get people motivated? How do you get your own members excited about this? You're not going to go on strike over whether or not a chair at some machine is the proper height, are you?" He replied that they have dramatically strengthened the union by focusing on "humanizing" work. In a workplace such as the Mercedes-Benz plant in Bremen, members see what the union has done for them every minute they are at work, not just every two weeks when they get their paycheques, and not just when they get disciplined by the employer. They see that the union has made the nature of work better and the workplace more comfortable.

The fourth trend is one that faces all unionists, and that is increased globalization of our economy and the resulting increased competitive pressures and responses of employers. Because of high unemployment and severe economic restructuring, our members are now often sympathetic to what employers are saying about new work systems. There is no union in the country that is not affected by that. You only have to pick up *The Globe and Mail* and turn to the "Change Page" to read about some local union talking about the virtues of Total Quality Management and teamwork.

In this environment, it is critical to develop a worker-oriented agenda for workplace change. When we started our Technology Adjustment Research Program (TARP), we set out to learn more about what was happening in our own workplaces – not only what was happening to the nature of work, but also what was happening to the union. From there we developed our agenda for workplace change. We have identified four bases of power which must be addressed during negotiations. All forms of technology, including the allocation of tasks and the nature of the workplace, must be considered. The four issues, or bases of power, are:

i) *The power to define the issues.* When the workplace is changed, we must have the ability to define the criteria for choosing new technologies. Typically, work teams are set up through TQM, with the objective of identifying ways to improve productivity and quality and to lower costs. A worker's agenda is never part of that.
ii) *The power of information.* We must have access to information, and know what the company's plans are with respect to capital expenditure programs, and so on. Obviously, if we do not have this information, we cannot respond effectively.
iii) *The power to make decisions.* This is the most difficult power to obtain. It seems that only when we negotiate our collective agreements do we have power. Once we sign the collective agreement, we lose a lot of that power until we enter into negotiations for the next agreement. Because technologies are introduced on a continuing basis, we must find a way to exert pressure continually and to influence decision-making on an ongoing basis.
iv) *The power of knowledge and resources.* Employers have engineers, engineering schools, business schools, and so on. Because trade unions cannot possibly compete with those resources, we must find ways through public policy initiatives and through collective bargaining to give comparable resources to workers. When trying to advance a worker-oriented design agenda, we do not want merely to have input; we want to be able to shape decisions and to have the resources to make informed decisions.

The story of Algoma Steel provides a compelling example of what unions and their members can accomplish when given the resources and the power to make decisions. In 1991 Algoma Steel was pushed into insolvency. The economic situation was such that we had no choice but to accept lower wages and develop a proposal for worker ownership. Our primary objective was to restructure the company in a way that maximized the number of jobs possible within the context of an economically viable entity. But we also knew this was an opportunity. Since creditors and government traditionally support the right of capital of decide what happens inside a corporation, we wondered whether we could as major stakeholders actually try to do something to improve the work lives of our Algoma Steel members. This was an opportunity to develop and implement a worker-oriented design agenda.

One of the first issues we raised when we were bargaining the restructuring package with Algoma management was levels of supervision. While our bargaining unit had gone from 12,500 members down to fewer than 4,000, there had not been a corresponding decline in levels of supervision.

This had led to a very top-heavy operation. One way to improve economic viability of an enterprise is to reduce its indirect labour costs by eliminating a lot of the unnecessary supervisors, thus giving workers more control in the workplace.

We said this at the bargaining table, and the company replied, "Wait a minute, you can't be serious! We don't have time for this kind of posturing and bargaining. What are you really talking about?" When we told them we were serious, they replied: "We have a moral obligation to those people." This is obviously an obligation that stands in stark contrast to whatever obligation they felt they had to their bargaining-unit employees.

Once we had addressed the issue of excessive supervision, we turned our attention to identifying other issues which could improve the workplace. We felt that after identifying worker-oriented design objectives, we could then identify a process to achieve those objectives.

I'll deal first with the question of stress in the workplace. Research coming out of Western Europe indicates that the three most critical determinants of stress in the workplace are: the amount of control you have over your job; the psychological demands on you (the number of decisions you have to make in a short period of time, and the complexity of those decisions); and the opportunity to communicate with other people and have access to social support within the workplace.

Many individuals think of psychological demands as the primary source of stress. There is a tendency among lawyers and doctors to think that they are under the most stress. But lawyers and doctors also have tremendous control over their work, and they certainly have the opportunity to interact with other people.

The research shows that the most stressful jobs are the ones over which you do not have control and the ones that do not allow for interaction. Miners working alone, telephone operators, and assembly-line workers have very stressful jobs. These jobs have the greatest incidence of depression or substance abuse. Redesigning workplaces to give workers more control and the opportunity to interact with other people is an integral part of a worker-oriented agenda.

Second on my list is ergonomics, the physical design of the workplace. Is the workplace comfortable? Some of this is actually quite simple. You can reduce repetitive strain injuries in your hand by using drills and instruments with longer triggers that you squeeze with your whole hand instead of just your finger. Injuries can be reduced by using buttons that you press with the palm of your hand instead of your finger.

Other problems are obviously more complicated, but the fact is that when new technology is introduced, these issues are rarely considered and workers are expected to respond after the fact. So finding ways to reduce the amount of force that workers need to use and making sure that posture is correct and giving workers an opportunity to rest are important considerations when designing new technologies for the workplace. Reduction in toxic substance use also needs to be considered.

In many cases gaining control means dealing with the amount of supervision that you have, which is always a tough nut to crack. Adequate representation – making sure the union has a strong voice in the workplace – gives workers more comfort. Another trend that has occurred with the introduction of new technologies, particularly with statistical process control, is the creation of a new class of workers: technicians and technologists. They are often very difficult to organize outside the bargaining union, and they often perform the work that tradespeople or operators were doing before. We rarely get to make the decisions about whether this kind of work belongs to the bargaining unit or not.

Finally, if technology is going to march forward – and it is difficult to imagine bringing it to a complete stop – we need to consider a shorter work week. This is something that the labour movement has been very slow to address in this country. The decreased numbers at Algoma and Inco speak for themselves. We must respond by reducing the work week; otherwise, the situation leads to chronic unemployment.

So if this is our agenda – less stress, higher skill content, better ergonomics, more control, better representation, and reduced work time – our next challenge will be to put all issues relating to the workplace on the collective bargaining table. If we are to negotiate an effective way of redesigning the workplace and responding to technological change, it is vital that we identify the criteria for making decisions about what kind of technology gets introduced. Because the ability to identify and shape criteria and agendas ultimately rests on access to sound information, we must be provided with appropriate information, including the company's capital expenditure program. All these things are difficult to negotiate, but unless you know what the company investment plans are, it is nearly impossible to influence workplace design.

As well, because we lose so much of the power of collective bargaining after we sign a collective agreement, we need to find a way to facilitate ongoing collective bargaining. The terms of the agreement must provide an inducement to the employer to negotiate with us on an ongoing basis.

At Algoma Steel we prohibited the employer from performing certain acts without the agreement of the union: training is one example. The company and the union are obliged to negotiate a comprehensive training plan, and in fact only training that is agreed to by both the company and the union can be performed. This creates an inducement to the employer to negotiate because, since people have to be trained, there's a price to pay for not agreeing. We have also tried to implement the same principle with respect to work design: new technologies above a certain value can't be introduced without the agreement of the union. We are in the early stages of working on this, and I do not know how effective it will be over the term of the agreement, but we have reason to be optimistic.

The final base of power which we must try to obtain is knowledge and resources. People who have sat on joint technology or TQM committees will know that workers are typically called out of the plant or out of the office to come and sit down with management people who have prepared background material and have spent a lot of time thinking about what they want to get accomplished in a particular meeting. As long as that continues to be the case, it will be hard for workers to advance their own agenda. At Algoma we negotiated a substantial amount of company-paid, union-designed, and union-delivered training. All members receive some training, stewards and executives are given more. Those that get the most are those who are going to be negotiating some of these issues on an ongoing basis.

We also negotiated full-time positions paid for by the company to co-ordinate the union's workplace design activities. I think the element of the program that probably frustrates the company most is the budget that we negotiated. The company actually gives the local union some resources, so that it can, for example, send members to an off-site training course or hire advisors with expertise in training or engineering.

No doubt we were able to put those kinds of things in place because of the unique circumstances surrounding Algoma Steel;[1] now we must push it in other workplaces. Certainly, we have been able to make some progress in other workplaces in negotiating full-time co-ordinators and union-designed and union-delivered training. We have not yet been able to get anybody else to give us money so that we can be more effective in negotiating with management, but it is certainly something we pursue.

The people in Sault Ste. Marie say that these financial resources and training are absolutely critical. Being able to come to the bargaining table prepared and being able to caucus separately to discuss the union's position has been of paramount importance, and in fact union members think that they have been able to gain an edge on some committees because they come to meetings more prepared than management.

So those are the four basic sources of power: resources, the ability to decide, the ability to frame the questions and the criteria by which to make the judgments, and access to information. Generally speaking, we have been slow in the labour movement to exploit existing structures within our unions in pushing this agenda. People from some of our health and safety committees say, "We've been trying to do this for years, mobilize for better work design and safer workplaces. We have a network in place." Trying to mobilize people through existing networks, like health and safety committees, is something that unions have not been able to exploit effectively.

On the public policy side, we must deal with another group of issues. First, we need changes in labour law. We need new bargaining mechanisms to force this process of ongoing bargaining with respect to workplace design. One cannot deal with all these issues through the traditional collective bargaining environment.

Labour law needs to be changed in response to other trends as well. The nature of the workplace is going to change further, with more and more people working at home [see chapter 15]. Workplaces themselves are also getting smaller. In terms of labour law, we're still using a model that was designed to organize large industrial facilities in the 1940s. If we are to respond effectively to technological revolution and structural changes in the economy, we must examine the impact of sectoral bargaining and find new ways to organize people who do not work in large industrial settings.

We must also do a better job of arguing the case for publicly supported trade union research. The Technology Adjustment Research Program was a great achievement: for the first time we have a government paying for union-oriented research. Since business and engineering schools completely ignore workers' needs, there is a tremendous institutional bias in research and teaching. We need to develop alternative models which consider the impact on workers. Providing resources directly to unions themselves is the best way to ensure that necessary research on the impact of workplace design gets done.

Although technology has had a profound impact on working people, workers have not benefited. Throughout the 1980s, productivity in the industrial sector actually increased by 1.5 percent a year, measured by the traditional method of units of output per hour worked. Despite that, wages in the industrial sector declined in real terms throughout the 1980s. In the late 1970s, we moved above 7 percent unemployment for the first time since World War II. Since then, we have not been below 7 percent unemployment.

While we have huge productivity gains, workers' real wages have fallen and their working conditions have not improved. Technology has not been used to create better jobs and unions in Canada. Nor has it made the workplace better; in many cases, technology is making the workplace worse. Somebody always benefits from new technology – and now it is up to the labour movement to ensure that working people are the beneficiaries.

Part 7

CREATIVE RESPONSES IN ORGANIZATION AND CULTURE

Introduction

The labour movement today has a different character than the one faced by the Mine Mill organizers of the 1940s and 1950s. Global restructuring of the economy has shifted Canadian workers out of the traditional industrial and manufacturing sector into the service sector. In the process the character of work has changed, creating more part-time workers and more white-collar homeworkers. As a result, employers' demands for a flexible workforce place increased pressure on those remaining in full-time work. Unions are searching for more creative ways to address these changes. These chapters show that we can use the expertise of union activists and the lessons of the past to address the challenges of the 1990s and move beyond the traditional concepts of labour's tasks.

Among the few growing sectors of the economy is the lower rung of educational workers. Mike Groom, a national organizer for the Canadian Union of Educational Workers (CUEW), describes the difficulties of organizing this geographically dispersed group. These individuals are reluctant to see themselves as workers with common problems. Unionization in this sector has been a real challenge, and Groom details how the CUEW has found new ways of responding to the fiscal crisis in the educational sector.

Education of a different type is examined in Karl Beveridge's résumé of developments on the cultural front. Karl is a photographer and artist who, along with his partner Carole Condé, was one of the founders of the Independent Artists' Union. He has been working in the area of labour and the arts for many years and now serves on the Ontario Federation of Labour's Arts Committee. In his chapter, Beveridge describes the attempts to revive labour traditions through collaboration between artists and unions. He cautions union activists not to ignore the cultural dimensions of work in the labour movement. Mainstream cultural production reinforces individualism at the expense of collective expression of creativity, and as Beveridge suggests, it "strikes right at the heart of trade unionism and the trade union ideal of collectivity and collective action." Cultural work in the labour movement offers us one way to challenge the changes in the new social and economic order on yet another front.

The final chapter in Part 7 returns readers to the past, as Dieter K. Buse, a Laurentian University historian, looks at how Mine Mill contributed to cultural work through the work of Weir Reid. As director of recreation for Mine Mill in Sudbury during the 1950s, Reid initiated dance and theatre groups, fostered cinema, reading, and sports, and developed a comprehensive summer camp program for children. Buse shows how Weir

Reid's life trajectory parallels the building and destruction of workers' culture during the 1950s and early 1960s. Mine Mill's efforts to reinforce workers' culture in the communities in which it worked remind us that trade union struggles on the cultural front add an important dimension to union battles overall.

Retired union activist Tom Taylor speaking at the stewards' banquet at Mine Mill Hall, 1993. Seated on the left is Jack Gignac, past president of Local 598.

Courtesy Dorothy Wigmore

Chapter 17
Organizing Part-time Workers in the Educational Sector

Mike Groom

The Canadian Union of Educational Workers (CUEW) currently has nine locals in Ontario, Alberta, and Manitoba, all in postsecondary institutions. We have about ten thousand members: part-timers, sessional instructors, sessional faculty, teaching assistants, graduate assistants, and sometimes research assistants, such as those at the Ontario Institute for Studies in Education. Our locals are in places like the University of Toronto, York University, or McMaster – very Toronto-centric – but we are also at the University of Manitoba and Athabasca University, and we have recently applied for certification for eight hundred workers at Dalhousie University. More than 50 percent of our current members are women and about 30 percent are international students.

CUEW has existed since about 1974. It began at Victoria College at the University of Toronto, when eight teaching assistants decided they needed to become organized in order to take on the administration. Since then, we have increased to ten thousand members, and we are still growing.

One of the reasons for this growth in membership lies in the nature of postsecondary education today. Cutbacks in federal funding have squeezed out a lot of staff – we lost $22 billion in that sector during the Mulroney years. The provinces are tightening the screws, and the universities are all crying poverty, which means that there will be more and more part-timers being employed, to the detriment of full-time faculty and faculty associations. The teaching assistants have always been considered as people who are not really working – they are gaining an education, learning teaching skills, how to mark papers, how to grade, and how to lecture. They have always had to deal with this collegial atmosphere.

One of the earlier labour board hearings pointed out that a university could not function without teaching assistants. They are definitely educational workers. Otherwise, classes would be left to "a handful of bearded scholars lecturing to thousands of people at a time." These educational workers are working for a living. University administrations do not like to see it that way; they still like to believe in the "collegiality" aspect. So there is a conflict, because teaching assistants not only work, but also want to get paid for it, and the administration does not want to pay them well, arguing that their teaching is part of their education.

The structure of CUEW is very similar to that of traditional trade unions, in that the annual convention is the highest decision-making body of the union. The national executive board, which meets four times a year, is our second level of administrative structure. It consists of vice-presidents, who are the chairs from all the locals. When the board is not meeting to carry out convention policy, the national executive officers do the work. The locals are at the bottom end of that four-part hierarchical system. However, the locals have incredible power in our union. Local autonomy has always been a major part of CUEW, much to the detriment of the national office.

CUEW is a rank-and-file-based democratic union, where delegations for a convention are based on the number of workers in each local. Officers are elected at conventions. The only thing we have in our constitution that is inconsistent with this policy is that at least one of the two chairs of our union – a chair of local affairs and a chair of national affairs – must be a woman. This progressive policy came about as part of some changes we made about ten years ago. We have two other officers – the national financial officer and the national communications officer.

The problems that educational workers face are very similar to those of other workers – low wages, issues of overwork, harassment (whether gender, sexual, or racial), arbitrary job allocations, class sizes, no postings, arbitrary evaluations, and no benefits such as sick leave, bereavement leave, dental, eye care, maternity, paternity, and parental leave.

Educational workers organize because they want to overcome these objective conditions. There is also a twisted relationship with the administration, the bosses. The theory in the universities is that a person has to suffer and struggle before eventually becoming a tenured professor, after which life is great. We are finding that very few people are becoming tenured faculty; more and more people are becoming part-time and sessional instructors with ghettoized positions.

So what solutions are these part-time and sessional instructors looking for? They want better pay, of course, and contract language on all of the other problems they face. They are looking for grievance procedures, stewards' networks, vacation pay, pensions, dental plans, appointment language, and fair postings using seniority. Issues of academic freedom are key, as are questions of office space, proper safety and health procedures, campus security, thesis allowances, tuition waivers, and child care. The list can go on and on. For example, our local at York University has a bridge in its collective agreement that transfers "x" number of part-time jobs into tenure-stream jobs. In addition, there are penalties for cancellations of classes and for oversized classes. There are agreed-upon performance notations and files, with members being notified when things go into their file.

CUEW's collective agreements have some of the best discrimination and harassment language I have ever seen in collective agreements. That language deals with issues such as discrimination, interference, restriction, harassment or coercion, and it allows no mandatory blood or urine tests. Nor does it allow urine tests or blood tests related to AIDS, AIDS-related illnesses, AIDS-related complex, or positive immune deficiency tests. This contract language goes on for two-and-a-half pages in small print. It addresses sexual and gender harassment and racial and ethnic harassment. The contract points out that undergraduates can be problematic for teaching assistants and part-timers.

The agreements include this language because these are the conditions that educational workers face in their work. It is a subtle form of the boss exercising power – and not just the boss, but people they have to deal with every day. People are telling me that a university is no different from anywhere else in society, because it is a segment of society. (At least that is what was said at St. Mary's University when the Klan decided to organize a student club, and the president of the university said, "It's just like society out there.")

When it comes to organizing workers in the educational field, the one thing that is very difficult is getting them to understand that they are workers in the first place. A lot of them feel that if you keep your nose to the grindstone and you put up with the bosses, your immediate supervisor, or whomever, then a tenure-track position is going to become available to you. At least, the hope is always there. But we are finding that more and more people who are in part-time work finally understand that they are not going to get any kind of appointments unless something major happens, or they do more work, or something else comes along and they will be teaching three or four courses, catch as catch can, when they can do it.

The same "collegiality" problem makes the teaching assistants difficult to organize. Once you explain to them that they are educational workers, that they're selling a product – the product happens to be their labour, whether it's brain labour or sweat labour – and you can get over that hurdle of convincing them, then they can start discussing issues of what is rightfully theirs.

One of the problems is that universities are not in the business to make a profit, or so people think. When I explain to workers about corporate involvement in the postsecondary sector, they can see what kinds of profits are really being made in the university system. When people identify with the university, they automatically identify with their supervisors or with the bosses. It is very difficult to break that conception.

Educational workers tend to think that problems occur in isolation. If it happens to someone else, it cannot really happen to me. We have had cases, when we were organizing, of women being fired because they were the victims of sexual harassment and all of a sudden they are portrayed as incompetent or their work as not good enough. We point out the pattern to their own department representatives, and they say, "Oh, she was doing great, but she's having personal problems and it just won't happen to me." At universities, there is always an issue of individuality rather than any kind of collectivity, and I do not know if it is because of the competitive nature of trying to get work afterwards, or if it is because society has engendered that in the first place.

One of the fun parts about organizing educational workers is watching what the bosses do when you catch them at something that is not legitimate. For example, while we were organizing at the University of Guelph in 1993, the university decided to have a special president's advisory commission on graduate teaching assistants, in order to circumvent our unionization drive among the teaching assistants. The commission took the old so-called agreement, eliminated all references to graduate service assistants, who were basically doing the faculty association's work, and because the service assistants are students, the commission was able to do that. In this way, they eliminated 150 positions.

Then they took the wages of the teaching assistants and subjected them to a 70–30 split; they kept the 70 percent as wage and called the other 30 percent a bursary. When you call something a bursary instead of a wage, the employer does not have to pay Workers' Compensation Board contributions, employer health taxes, Canada Pension Plan, or Unemployment Insurance Commission benefits. The money they saved from calling this piece of the wage a bursary they rolled back into the bursary portion; the 70 percent, which was down to $2,500, they raised by 1.5 per cent because of inflation so that the official wage was now $2,537.50. The bursary went up by 16 percent. Altogether, the university claimed that they were giving the teaching assistants a wage increase of almost 5 percent – it was 4.65 percent – although they had used 2.2 percent real money.

We decided we could not let this happen. If we achieved a collective agreement in there, starting already 30 percent below what they were really earning, it would take us ten years to catch up. So what could we do? Should we go to the Labour Board and file a complaint, and if so, what would the university do? They would just turn around and say, "Hey, your union just lost you 5 percent," and rip up the agreement.

I decided we should call the government, and we contacted Revenue Canada. After I explained what was happening, and after the woman's jaw came back up off the table, I said, "Can they do that?" She replied, "Of course not, it's illegal to call a wage something that it isn't, in order not to pay taxes."

That was all we needed to start a public relations propaganda war. So we published pieces in the Guelph *Mercury*, in student papers, and in leaflets, and wrote letters to the deans, the chairs, and the president. We wrote to the president because when the president's advisory commission report had come out, he had said that it was a wonderful thing. He could see no problems with it on the surface, it was brilliant, it was innovative, and he was very happy that the proposal was going to be tried through all the universities across the country because it would be a great cost-saver.

Revenue Canada got into the act. The investigator decided that this was far too big for their Guelph or Kitchener office, and sent it up to Ottawa. Otto Jelinek, minister of revenue, handled it, and Guelph was caught. It is strange that even though the Guelph *Mercury* picked up the story, the Canadian Press wires did not, and it was not reported anywhere else. This issue arose at a time when workers in this country were being blamed for defrauding the system, whether by the Unemployment Insurance Commission or by employers or by the Ontario Hospital Insurance Plan, and here was an employer who was defrauding the system on purpose to save money and to shaft people (because lower premiums mean lower benefits). When we explained all of this, it made a lot of sense to some people, especially the president of the university.

The next thing we knew, the university cancelled the plan – it was supposed to be implemented May 1, 1993, but they postponed it. The bottom line is that the 4.65 percent wage increase has been maintained. Somehow, they found the money to pay these people, and now we are saying to the membership, "The union got you your first pay increase. Now it's time to sign a card." It's great when the employer helps you get a union started!

In the educational sector, such cases raise awareness as to why organizing is a necessity.

Chapter 18
Working Partners:
The Arts and the Labour Movement[1]

Karl Beveridge

Culture is a broad term, and can mean many different things depending on how the term is used. I want to make a broad distinction between what I call an "informal" culture – which in the labour movement is primarily oral – and a "formal" culture – which is a conscious kind of production of artistic products. Examples of these artistic products are the mural at the back of the Mine Mill Hall or the production of plays or music.

I will consider two aspects of formal culture here: the relationship between professional artists like myself and trade unions, and the situation of trade union members who themselves produce art works. The history of formal culture or the arts has been erratic in the labour movement, because most of the relationships between artists and unions have been voluntary. A union or an artist sought out each other and developed a project, which was often short-term. Because a lot of the artists, as well the unions that generally supported culture, were left-wing, they were often vulnerable to political pressure.

As a union, Mine Mill has been in the forefront of supporting culture, from the legacy of the Industrial Workers of the World (IWW) and the traditions of Joe Hill to being one of the first unions in Canada to commission an artist to produce a mural. That was a work by Henry Orenstein, who painted the mural that is at the back of the Mine Mill Hall in 1955. He was a member of the International Fur and Leather Workers (IFL), which along with Mine Mill and other unions was hit by McCarthyism in the 1950s. (See Orenstein's self-portrait, Illus. 1.) Unions initiated the production of two murals at that time. The IFL commissioned the other, by Fred Taylor.

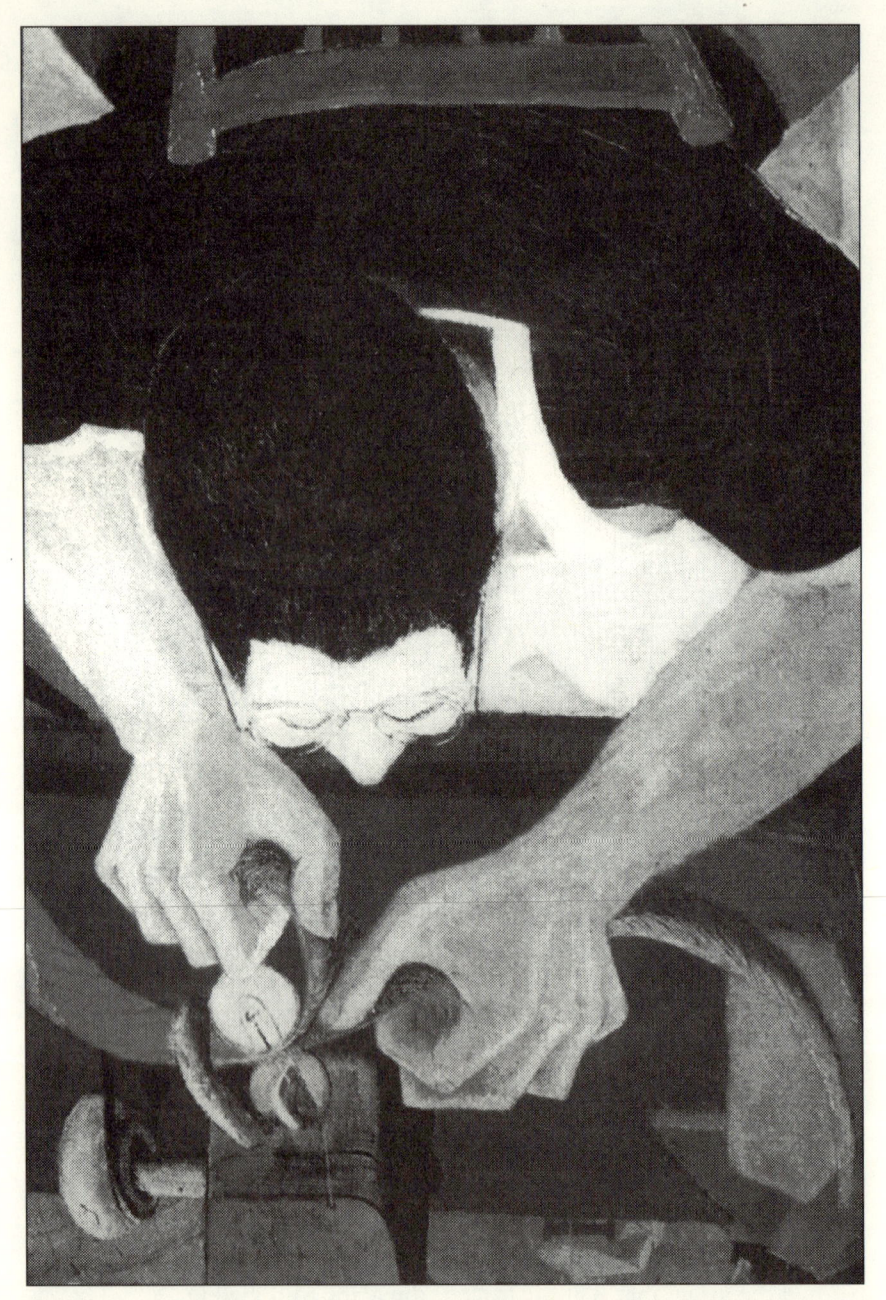

Illus. 1. Henry Orenstein (the artist who painted the Mine Mill mural), *Self-portrait as fur worker,* 1949, oil on canvas, 98 x 70 cm.

Mine Mill has continued that tradition with the mural at the front of its hall (Illus. 2).

About ten years ago an initiative was undertaken to establish an ongoing relationship between culture and trade unions and to establish as well a structural base within the trade union movement so that new projects could be developed. The initiative was the result of a conference co-sponsored by the Canadian Labour Congress and the Ontario Arts Council, the arm's-length government agency that funds various cultural enterprises from the Art Gallery of Ontario through to independent artists. The conference included a Swedish delegation illustrating community culture in Sweden. As a result of that conference and the example of community arts practised in Sweden, a number of trade unionists and artists at the conference organized to develop a relationship between arts and labour and to develop arts projects within the labour movement.

That meeting gave birth to a committee under the Canadian Labour Congress and then, because it was primarily focused in Toronto, a committee under the Labour Council of Metro Toronto. In 1986 the members of the Metro Labour Council committee managed to convince the Ontario Arts Council to co-sponsor the Mayworks Festival. The funding for the Mayworks Festival, which is now in its eighth year in Toronto, is about two-thirds from the Ontario Arts Council and one-third from union donations and other support. A similar festival started about five years ago in

Illus. 2. Irvine Marshall, Ellen Lagrandeur, and Christine Burtch, mural outside Mine Mill Hall, Sudbury, 1987.

254 / KARL BEVERIDGE

Vancouver with the support of the British Columbia Federation of Labour, and there have been sporadic Mayworks festivals in places such as Cobourg, Windsor, London, and Ottawa.

The Mayworks Festival is multidisciplinary, involving music, theatre, visual art, film, and video (see Illus. 3). Mayworks has sponsored posters by Barbara Klunder (Illus. 4) and music by Arlene Mantle, a well-known singer in the labour movement (Illus. 5).

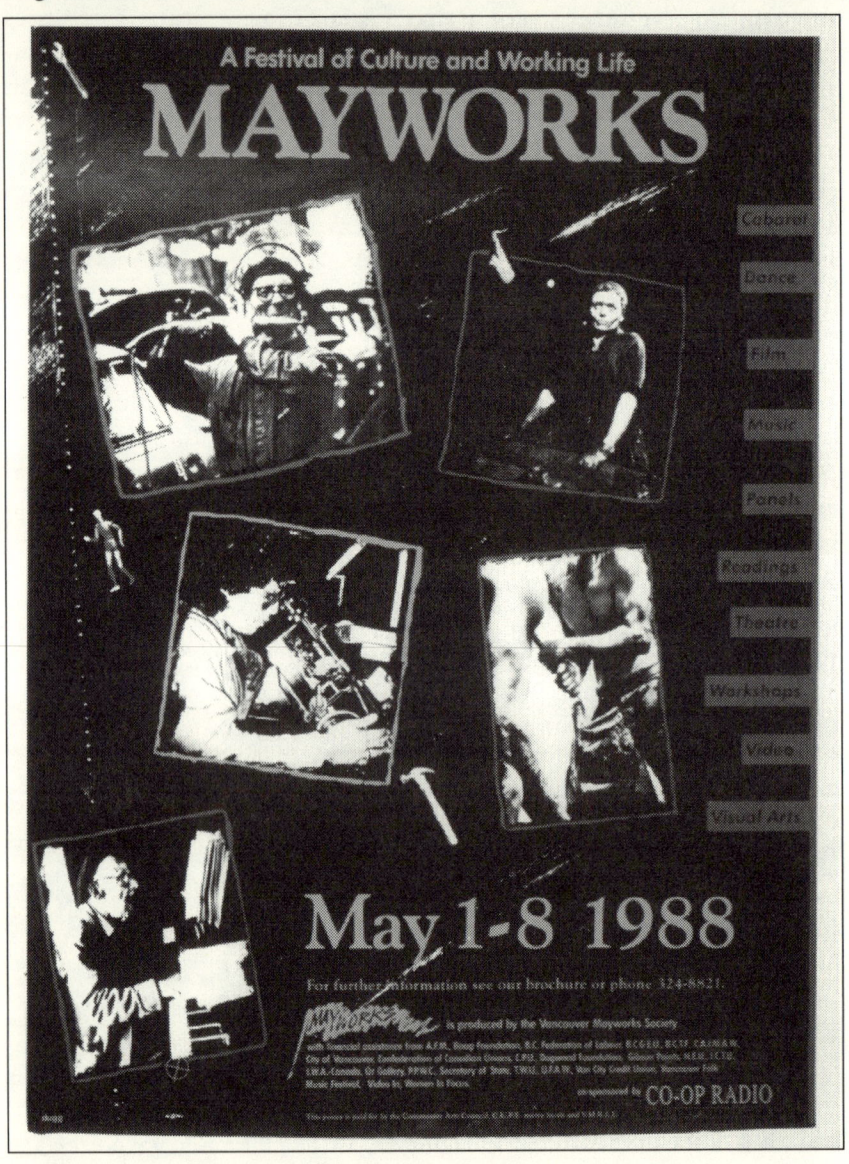

Illus. 3. Poster, Mayworks Festival, Vancouver, 1988.

Illus. 4. Barbara Klunder, poster for Mayworks Festival, Toronto, 1987.

Mayworks developed a unique project in 1992: we commissioned four artists and four trade union members – among them, artist Grace Channer of Toronto and CUPE member Wes Jean – to decorate or design lunch pails. These pails were then auctioned off at the end of the Mayworks Festival to help raise money (Illus. 6, 7, and 8).

In 1989 members of the committee approached the Ontario Arts Council to develop an "artists and the workplace" program. The idea for that came originally from Australia, where an extensive program is funded by the trade unions and the Arts Council of Australia to have artists work

Illus. 5. Arlene Mantle and band, playing at Mayworks Festival, Toronto, 1987.

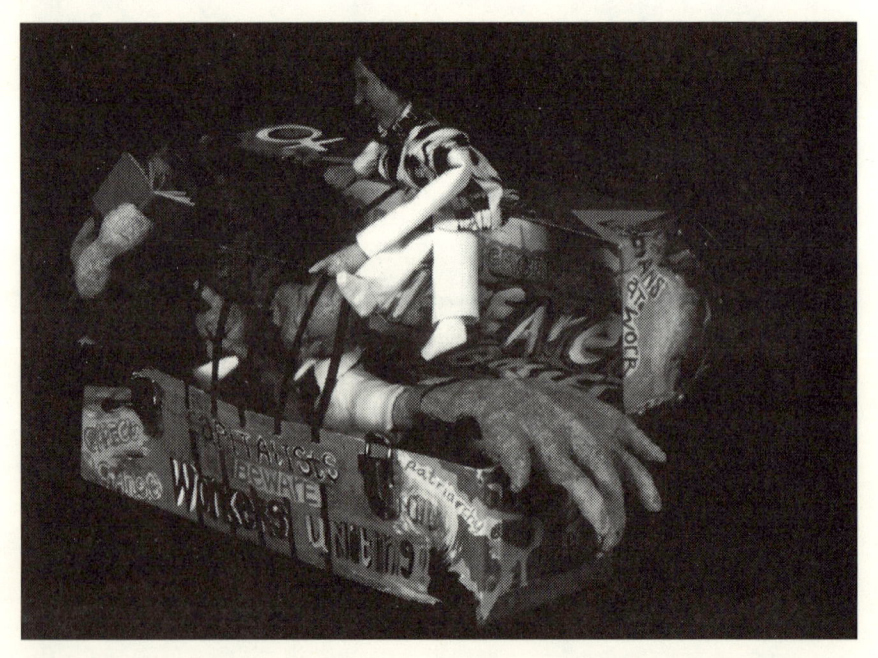

Illus. 6. Grace Channer, lunch bucket, commissioned by Mayworks, Toronto, 1991.

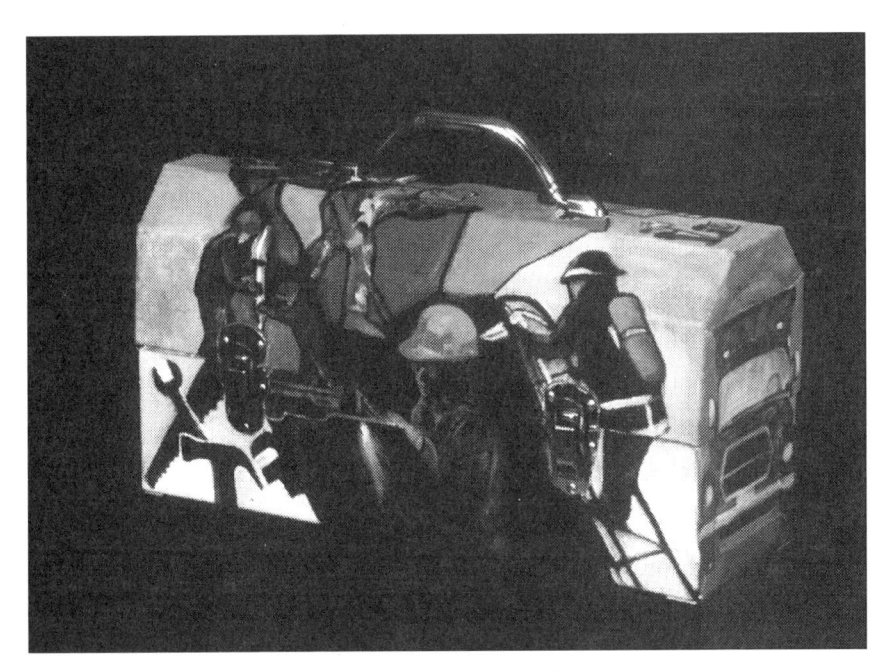

Illus. 7. Wes Jean, lunch bucket, commissioned by Mayworks, Toronto, 1991.

Illus. 8. Wes Jean, lunch bucket, commissioned by Mayworks, Toronto, 1991.

in residence with trade unions. We negotiated with the Ontario Arts Council to develop a similar program through which artists can work in residence with trade union locals throughout the province. The sticky point in the negotiations came when the Ontario Arts Council wanted to allow companies as well to be able to apply to have an artist come and work in a workplace. We responded that if that were the case, the unions would not be involved in the program. We suggested that the Labour Relations Act, which defines unions in Ontario law, be used as the defining principle of who can apply, and they accepted that. So, any union or organization that is recognized under the Labour Relations Act can apply to have an artist work with their organization or local. The artist-in-residence program is in its fourth year now and a number of really exciting projects have developed out of it. Every union local in the province is eligible for programs, and the Ontario Arts Council pays 75 percent of the cost of the project and the union has to kick in 25 percent. An example of an artist in the workplace is Charlie Stimac, who lives outside of Cobourg. He worked with the Northumberland Labour Council to do a series of paintings of various workplaces in the area, including a plastics moulding plant in Cobourg (Illus. 9).

Another project in this program was by Bob Moir and Sally Lawrence, two artists who live in Kirkland Lake; this was a sculpture for the Steelworkers Hall in Kirkland Lake, a miners' memorial. It's quite an interesting work – a multipiece sculpture depicting a miner coming out of the

Illus. 9. Charlie Stimac, Complax plant, Cobourg, 1989.

ground, with the rail cars in the background. This is an example of installation sculpture. (Illus. 10 and 11 are photographs taken before installation, when the sculpture was still sitting outside the rail station in Cobalt.)

Illus. 10 and 11. Bob Moir and Sally Lawrence, miners' monument, Kirkland Lake, 1989–91 (Artists and the Workplace project).

Yet another project had a photographer work with members of the Ontario Public Service Employees Union (OPSEU) to develop photographic skills as well as to photograph members' home and family life, because often in a workplace people have no idea of their fellow workers' lives outside of or after work. (See Illus. 12 and 13, from OPSEU's magazine.) At a Canadian Auto Workers (CAW) project, well-known writer Rick Salutin came to work with editors of local newspapers to do a creative writing course. The resulting booklet, published by the CAW, has a number of poems and writings by the workers who took the course. The illustration is by Gail Geltner (Illus. 14).

A different project resulted in a play, *Postscript*, about the trials and tribulations of a letter carrier (Illus. 15). It was done in collaboration with a theatre group in Peterborough and with the Canadian Union of Postal Workers (CUPW) local.

One other item of this type is a project that Carole Condé and I did in the summer of 1992 through the Metro Labour Council with the Ontario Coalition Against Poverty. We worked with various unemployed groups and

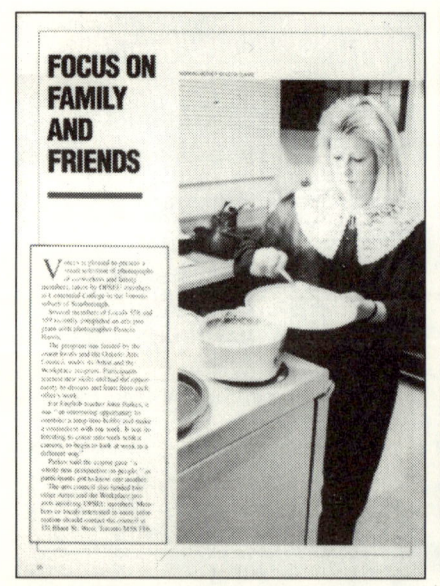

Illus. 12. Pam Harris/OPSEU, photography workshop, 1989 (Artists and the Workplace project). Used with the permission of OPSEU.

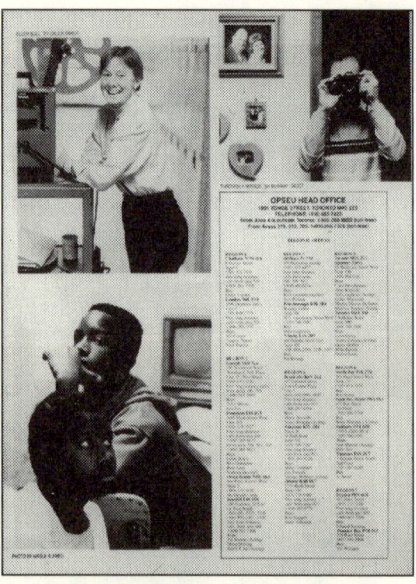

Illus. 13. Pam Harris/OPSEU, photography workshop, 1989 (Artists and the Workplace project). Used with the permission of OPSEU.

Illus. 14. Rick Salutin/CAW, writers' workshop, 1989 (Artists and the Workplace project); illustrations: Gail Geltner.

unemployed people to produce an image that was then used as a poster by the Ontario Coalition Against Poverty (Illus. 16).

Another project undertaken by the committee, now under the Ontario Federation of Labour (OFL), is a banner contest, started in 1991 and based on the Australian and English tradition of trade union banners. Given Canada's connections to the British labour movement, there were banners early on here, but as we became more Americanized, banners were lost as a tradition. The OFL put together the competition in order to encourage a resurrection of that tradition in Canada. An example is a banner that Carole and I did for the OFL itself. These banners measure roughly about five by seven feet. On this one the lettering is painted on the back, the hands are done with fabric, and the lettering is raised (Illus. 17).

An earlier banner was done under the Artists and the Workplace project for the International Ladies' Garment Workers Union (ILGWU). Artist Phillipa Majdu worked with members of the union to design and produce the banner (Illus. 18). Another Artists and the Workplace banner project done by the Canadian Union of Public Employees (CUPE) Local 79 in Toronto represents the municipal workers for the City of Toronto. Again, the artist worked with members who produced each of the small patches,

Illus. 15. Rehearsal in Progress theatre collective/CUPW, *Postscript*, 1989 (Artists and the Workplace project).

Illus. 16. Carole Condé and Karl Beveridge/Labour Council of Metro Toronto, anti-poverty poster, 1992 (Artists and the Workplace project).

Illus. 17. Carole Condé and Karl Beveridge, OFL banner, 1991.

and then their work was assembled together into a large banner (Illus. 19). CUPE 79 commissioned the artist again in 1993 to produce another banner for them.

Finally, Carole and I did a banner for the Communication Workers of Canada (CWC), now the Communications, Energy and Paperworkers Union (CEP). As part of the project we had to make a detachable logo so they could switch from the CWC to the CEP (Illus. 20). The workers in this banner are painted, and the rest of the banner is sewn material, so that the computer chip in the background is actually sewn strips and dots. The cable that loops around the workers moves from an electrical cable to a fibre-optic cable, because the CWC represents both workers at Bell and industrial workers in the electrical sector of the industry.

Another initiative that has emerged is the Ontario Workers' Arts and Heritage Centre. It came from a discussion on the need for a museum that would represent workers' history and workers' culture in the province, because those are not being preserved. Often, when museums deal with work and the workplace, they focus on technology and machinery. After lengthy discussion involving many people from both the arts and the labour movement, a board for the centre was established. The OFL has three nominees to the board, which also includes labour historians and educators in

Illus. 18. Phillipa Majdu/ILGWU, banner, 1989 (Artists and the Workplace project).

Illus. 19. Judith Tinkel/CUPE Local 79, banner, 1992
(Artists and the Workplace project).

Illus. 20. Carole Condé and Karl Beveridge, CWC banner, 1992.

developing the project. In late 1992 we received funding from the Ontario Ministry of Culture and Communications to undertake a feasibility study. This is the first step on the way to obtaining buildings and to qualifying to apply for funding to operate a museum. We are in the middle of the feasibility study, which will guide us to choose a location as well as exploring exhibition and programming concepts.

A major concept behind the museum is to make it more a "living" museum, which is why we call it a centre, not a museum; that is, we do not want only glass cases and exhibits hung on walls. We want to have it more decentralized, with various regions of the province involved. It would be a resource centre that could have displays in it, but also, more importantly, it could mount displays that could be circulated around the province. The centre would have connections with a group in Sudbury, and with people in Thunder Bay and other centres, and would be able to both exchange and circulate resources.

The Workers' Arts and Heritage Centre is planning a conference on arts and heritage for November 1993, just prior to the OFL convention. By scheduling it just before the convention, we hope that a number of trade union people who will be coming to the OFL will also be able to participate in the conference. By that time, the feasibility study will have been completed and serious decisions will have to be made about where exactly the centre will be and what it will do.[2] We see the conference as bringing that all together and launching what will become the Workers' Arts and Heritage Centre.

There have been numerous other arts activities, and there are now arts committees in many unions: the Autoworkers have a number of arts committees in locals. I think the Steelworkers are the only union in Canada that actually has an arts policy, and they also have mounted a number of shows and exhibitions of their members' work. The OFL will be developing an arts policy for the next convention, which will probably be the first time in North America that an arts policy will actually appear in front of a trade union federation.

A final question emerges concerning the importance of trade unions and culture. William Thorsell, editor-in-chief of *The Globe and Mail*, recently wrote an editorial connecting culture and authority. He argued that if you have a breakdown of cultural values, you'll have a breakdown of the systems of authority within our society. He is quite right about that, but the question is: whose authority?

I think that one of the values strongly perpetrated by mainstream cultural production in North America is that of individualism, and it is one of the values that people like Thorsell want to maintain. This is an individualism at the expense of collectivity. Often the arts are talked about as a form of self-expression, but I think they are a form of social expression. There may be part of a self within any given art work, but ultimately it is a social language and it is about social life. Yet most of the culture that is produced in this society is about the individual and often about how the individual can do nothing in the face of social forces. That emphasis on individualism strikes right at the heart of trade unionism and the trade union ideal of collectivity and collective action. Of course, that is what our culture lacks – our expressions of our collectivity and how our collectivity has actually shaped the society.

When we talk about the future of unionism, culture is going to be very important, in two specific ways. One is the development of the formal culture, which I have been talking about. The other is that the trade unions need to develop a political position around the democratization of culture. It is my estimation that 99 percent of cultural production comes out of the private sector, with only 1 percent out of public funding. If education were that way we would rebel, but culture is that way, and this situation has to be changed. It must change to a community-based culture, with communities gaining access to resources and artists being able to work within those communities to produce expressions of the values and beliefs of those communities.

Chapter 19

Weir Reid and Mine Mill: An Alternative Union's Cultural Endeavours[1]

Dieter K. Buse

When Weir Reid died in August 1971, *The Sudbury Star* wrote that given his talents and background he might have become a member of society's elite.[2] An obituary editorial noted Reid's wonderful way with words, his artistic bent, and his personal charm, but commented that these traits were wrongly employed in the cause of dissent and socialism. Earlier, *Time* magazine had branded Reid the "last angry socialist."[3]

Why had this individual achieved such notoriety? Reid helped to develop an organized workers' culture in the Mine Mill union during the 1950s. He became the focus for a major part of the Steelworkers' concerted attack on Mine Mill, bearing the brunt of Cold War character assassinations about being a communist and recruiting for that cause through Mine Mill, in particular at its summer camp at Richard Lake near Sudbury. In addition, through a series of long, costly libel and slander cases, Reid went to the edge of bankruptcy to defend his and Mine Mill's honour and property.

If the historian's gaze is lifted beyond the details of a fascinating individual life, the larger implications of Weir Reid's case become clear. Reid's personal trajectory illustrates the creation of an organized workers' culture plus organized labour's disengagement from it. Many studies have shown a similar pattern for Europe where, during the 1920s, the cultural endeavours by unions and leftist parties reached their height and then were destroyed by fascism, Cold War, and the commercialization of culture.[4]

Intrigue played an important role in the Reid and recreation story. In 1955, James Kidd, a member of the so-called White Block – a group that schemed for years on how to get Sudbury union members out of Mine Mill and into the United Steelworkers – wrote his brother about the way to undermine the local leadership, in particular 598 President Nels Thibault:

> In any event between now [and] Dec[ember] when the decision will be made re [union] elections we must fight him to beat hell. To do that we will attack on three points. The summer camp is one. Therefore I would like a run down on the director Weir Reid. I have heard that he came from Hamilton. Then we will attack the Local 598 newspaper. On that we would like information on [Mine Mill newspaper editor John] Smaller ... When I say information I mean a breakdown of his past political connections and jobs. The last and most vulnerable point of attack will be the way they conduct Union elections.[5]

Kidd also advised the Steelworkers on how to use the influence of local Catholic priests. He noted: "In the prov[incial] election [CCF candidate Bob] Carlin had the Nickel Belt riding sewed up. On the last Sunday on orders from Father Regimbal all the priests blasted [Carlin]. They said ... a vote for Bob was a vote for the communist party. That fixed him good." Kidd knew that to identify an individual with communism made defence almost impossible during the height of the Cold War, and Reid's early associations made him vulnerable to the charge.

The Making of a Recreation Director

Alexander Weir Reid's early life influenced numerous aspects of his later work. He was born on March 18, 1918, to a farm family in Georgetown, Ontario. As a youth he loved reading and gardening, and he attended Norval Public School from 1926 to 1933. Lucy Maude Montgomery, the author of *Anne of Green Gables*, came to Norval in 1926 and established a theatre guild and organized plays with young people. Reid's brother remembered this as Weir's first contact with theatre, which Weir later loved as actor and director.[6]

Although he failed a number of subjects at Georgetown High School, which he attended from 1933 to 1938, Reid collected enough credits to start towards his stated "plans – medical college."[7] At the same time the young man's religious views were reinforced by the local minister, Norman MacMillan, with whom Reid stayed in contact for some time after leaving Norval-Georgetown. "I must reach a decision soon on what I'm going 'to do with Christ,'" the young man agonized in his diary during 1939. "Norman's sermon on Sunday morning disturbed me ... If I can find in

Christ something to give me poise and direction."[8]

Reid's religious convictions combined with a powerful social conscience. One of his formative early insights into social injustice came following the cave-in of the Port Stanley cofferdam. Weir had worked on the site himself, and when eight men were killed after the collapse of the retaining walls in December 1939 he was shocked by the deaths and a subsequent inquest finding that the company was without blame in the tragedy.[9] In another diary entry he referred to a discussion about girls hitch-hiking during the Depression: "The girls were generally decent kids trudging to anywhere seeking a job – a home, denied them thro' the selfishness and blindness of a few ... Ah! This land of democracy."[10]

Reid's character developed under stress and self-reflection. Illness, in the form of diphtheria at age ten and later circulatory problems, plagued Reid and may have inspired his interest in medicine. Dizzy spells interfered with his university studies. He attended McMaster University in Hamilton from 1938 to 1940 and the University of Toronto in 1941–42, not doing very well and petitioning to take correspondence courses.[11] Illness may have resulted in an early discharge from military service in 1942.

Those who knew the flamboyant, confident Reid of later public debates and daily performances would be surprised at the hesitant young man who confided to his diary in 1938, with words reminiscent of the young William Gladstone:

> I so admire the fine, courageous in life, yet faced with reality I am a traitor to myself approving all the pettiness of this inert society, too timid to assert myself ... I have never been a friend, too shallow and empty to build with those who have met with me. I am disappointed in so many, they seem to have no "ideals." (Christ's ideals of service and the brotherhood of man).[12]

Reid's searching led him to read religious and biological studies, novels, and poetry. He copied into his diaries passages that he found important. By January 1940 he was writing speeches for his aunt to read at the Hamilton Women's Institute. Reflecting on one such speech about education he noted, "I should like to dispel the idea, popularly held, that education is a product of our school exclusively, rather than a development stimulated or inhibited by our environment."[13] His own life could be seen as confirmation of that view, since he responded to stimulation and provided an environment to stimulate others. Those who knew him well identified an important trait allied to his wide-ranging interests: his desire to share his knowledge, to share his joys, to share his ideas, and to share material goods.[14]

A deep but wavering religious faith, illness, and sexual desire led to Reid's serious reflections on life, warfare, and society in the early 1940s. Exactly where those reflections led him as a twenty-five-year-old remains vague. But the "ideals of service and brotherhood of man" would remain even when he had trouble holding jobs in the late 1940s.[15]

Gaps remain in his biography. He worked at the Cockshutt farm implement company in 1942, where he apparently helped organize a union while in the personnel department. As a volunteer with the YMCA at Brantford in 1944, Reid dealt with community development and welfare issues. He tried his hand at editing *American Hi News* in New York before taking a job as program director with the West Toronto YMCA.

Marriage in September 1944 to Ruth May, who also worked in the Christian youth movement and had experience in recreation, seemed to have little impact on Reid's varied and colourful work history. His interest in housing led to a job with the Normanhurst Community Centre in Hamilton. There he also ran a flooring tile business that ended in bankruptcy before he turned to real estate in the early 1950s to support a quickly growing family.[16]

Reid's social and political views remain sketchy, but by the end of the Second World War he had become interested in co-operatives, helping people, and exchanging ideas in the process of developing himself. He searched – reflected almost in a frantic fashion in his diaries – for a purpose to life. Typical of many talented people in their youth, he lacked direction and went through many crises. Yet by the early 1950s, he had met union and leftist leaders such as Paddy Bell. Those postwar contacts may have led him to a six-month flirtation with the Hamilton branch of the Communist Party.[17]

Reid had finally found his calling in the field of recreation. He had discovered a place to serve his ideals by his work with Wartime Recreation at the Hamilton Normanhurst Community Centre and the Toronto YMCA. His emerging strength of character influenced those about him. A friend with whom he took a weekly woodworking class wrote Reid in 1971: "You were then a rather large influence on me."[18] Reid himself later explained how his commitment grew, though muddling the order of events:

> I had had several years' experience with both public and private agencies, principally with the Central Y.M.C.A. in Toronto, and further experience of a year in New York with a youth project under the New York City University, and subsequently I was in charge of the war-time housing community centres in Hamilton ... I had three years university, followed by a number of seminars and short courses in services training at the Y.M. and various other places.[19]

Through his involvements with recreational and community work, Reid had gathered organizational skills, public-speaking abilities, and experience in arts and crafts programs. He may already have had that special skill with people which later observers commented upon as "the ability to draw the best out of various individuals."[20]

Reid's abilities in the recreational field were illustrated a decade later in a revealing manner. In March 1959 a new firm called Recreation Consultants of Ontario sought to recruit him. By April he and the president were corresponding about possible park developments in Sudbury and Ontario Hydro's plans for an employees' recreation program. In May 1959, just after Reid had been wrongly fired from his post as recreation director by the new leadership of Mine Mill, the same consultancy president informed him: "While discussing business with potential customers, I was amazed to find that in four distinct cases, the customer stated flatly that due to your presence in our group, they could not do business with us. Their reasons were manifold, but essentially political." The firm's president explicitly acknowledged Reid's "ability and experience in the recreation field."[21] Reid would not have been thrilled to receive this glowing report card, because it meant that in a short time his livelihood had twice been cut out from under him; first with the union and then as a consultant in recreation. The exchange does, however, raise the questions of how Reid made his reputation and why some groups were so determined to destroy it.

Participant in Building a Movement

No individual is crucial in a large movement. Reid, too, was not by himself decisive in the union or its recreational endeavours. The summer camp already had a season as a day camp before Reid arrived in Sudbury in March 1952. Similarly, educational community development, such as a play school and films from the public library, had been organized by the Ladies' Auxiliary and initiated by Isabella Smaller.[22]

Reid was hired after the manager of Mine Mill's camp and its halls had quit in 1951. The union executive needed help and "sent word out to trade unions in Toronto and Hamilton area to find someone capable to manage the halls and summer camp."[23] Later on, a member of the education committee explained: "It was realized by the executive board that we wanted someone with a certain education, certain qualifications ... because we had camp programs and various programs that needed someone with training and experience which he could not have gotten within the framework of the Union, but that person still had to maintain responsibility within the Union framework in putting that program into effect."[24] Mike Solski, then president of Mine Mill, stated that he "interviewed Weir Reid in Toronto and he then came to Sudbury and appeared before the Executive Board; he was approved by the board and members" at a general meeting on February 25, 1952.[25] Reid himself noted, "In the beginning I was hired to supervise the janitors and to co-operate with existing committees in various recreation programs that were then in existence and to initiate and plan new ones not only in relation to the hall but in certain community projects."[26]

When Reid arrived in Sudbury in March 1952 to take up his post as the halls and camp manager for Local 598 of Mine Mill, he found a large base he could build upon. With some fourteen thousand workers, Local 598 was one of Canada's largest union locals. In April 1952, just after Reid was hired, Nels Thibault, the president of Local 598, told a radio audience in Trail, British Columbia:

> The Mine Mill members of Sudbury have erected a monument to labour in the building of their half million dollar labour temple. This Union building at the time of its opening ceremonies was dedicated to the service of its members for education, cultural and recreational promotion ... Our Mine Mill union in Sudbury is also developing a large summer camp site in the interests of its members and their families. Our efforts in this field are receiving helpful co-operation from the Ontario government.[27]

The material foundation and the spiritual direction had been laid when Reid arrived. Similarly, Thibault emphasized union community participation and social responsibilities in 1956 when speaking to the Sudbury Chamber of Commerce: "A Union's responsibility must include recognition of assistance it can render through participation in community projects relating to health, welfare, educational and recreational needs ... Great possibilities are afforded a union to provide facilities for its own group as well as assisting in others."[28] In short, extensive support for cultural and recreational endeavours was part of the union philosophy and practice.

Reid found the rudiments of an organized workers' culture in an entertainment committee that regulated dances at the halls. That committee's records (available back to the 1940s) show that there were Saturday night dances for couples, and, later on, Wednesday dances for singles; Hallowe'en, Christmas, and New Year's Eve added special occasions. Reid would occasionally sit in on the entertainment committee meetings, as on April 12, 1953, when the group discussed the enforcement of drinking rules (Ontario law limited each person to one glass or one bottle per table), as well as how to control troublemakers.[29] The dances brought in substantial sums for the union that it could use for its charity work, such as donations to the local hospitals. In addition there were square dances organized and run by Mark

Tugby, who, like Weir Reid, would later receive a citation from the City of Sudbury for his contributions.[30] At first Reid's work included collecting the dance moneys as well as checking on the maintenance of the hall. He lived with his family in an apartment above the hall, perhaps in an attempt to alleviate vandalism that sometimes occurred when the hall was left unattended.[31] Before and after Reid's arrival, the entertainment committee also organized the Labour Day picnics and the Bernard and Barry Shows – "A Modern Cavalcade of Mirth" with midway – which Mine Mill sponsored at Queen's Athletic Field each year from 1949 until 1957.

On April 20, 1952, soon after Reid was hired, he met with the entertainment committee. "The question was raised in connection with the camp and our place in the plans laid down for summer recreation. It was expressed by Bro[ther] Reid the need for a meeting in the near future to lay down the plans for this operation."[32] Unfortunately, that promised meeting appears not to have been recorded, but a three-member camp committee was formed. Regarding that committee, a member maintained, "Mr. Reid gave the directions ... and our job was to assist in co-ordinating the work with him."[33]

Reid's work in recreation fitted into what had been established earlier in Mine Mill: the Bernard and Barry Shows since 1949, the dances since the union leased a hall. The 166-acre camp property had been bought out of building-fund donations in September 1950, and plans were under way for its development. In sports, too, he could build on the existing groups, including the Mine Mill Badminton Club and hockey teams.[34] In all these endeavours, high moral standards had been laid down: the "relaxation of ruling on jitterbugging" in May 1956 reversed a ban by the dance committee during 1951 so they could encourage younger couples to come out, but white jackets and no drinking remained mandatory for the committee members running the dances.[35] Another of Reid's duties was helping to run the halls being built in the outlying towns.[36]

Some of this work was mundane, but it required organizational skills, and the cultural events required extensive contact with the public. As he began to expand Mine Mill's cultural and recreational endeavours by enlarging the summer camp program and creating ballet and theatre groups, Reid encountered architects, newspaper editors and writers, crafts people, and others who shared his interest in the arts, religion, and literature. They respected his advice and views on cultural matters; for instance, Bette Meakes, cultural writer for *The Sudbury Star*, acknowledged his competence in drama and dance.[37] Partly because he had helped initiate cultural offerings that went well beyond the Mine Mill tradition of sports and songs, Sudbury's middle-class leaders noticed his work.[38] He helped establish the union's dance school in Garson during 1953 and then the Mine Mill Ballet at the Regent Street Hall. Reid excelled at recruiting capable, professional individuals as teachers – Nancy Lima Dent and Barbara Cook, who had trained with the National Ballet – and that helped to overcome the resistance to these endeavours in the union.[39] Reid himself wrote for the *Mine Mill Herald* in June 1957 to report on the capacity audience for the annual dance recital, on the program's innovativeness, and on the co-operative efforts of sixty volunteers, mostly from the Ladies' Auxiliary. The ballet school's formation was to have been crowned by an appearance by the Winnipeg Ballet in Sudbury under Mine Mill's auspices in January 1954.[40] Many versions of why that failed have been presented, but the dance schools were great successes. For six years, hundreds of youth received classical and other training. Evaluators were brought from across Canada and England. Reid had provided the initial force and drew support from wide sectors of the community as well as from the ladies' auxiliaries, who made costumes, ushered, and organized the events. Reid usually handled publicity and advertising as well as hall decoration.

Reid had quickly made his mark in the union and the larger community: already by 1953 he was asked to participate in the Sudbury Film Society at the Public Library, and later he advised on establishing libraries in towns close to Sudbury. Because theatre was of special interest to him, he organized the Haywood Players in 1954. They presented socially concerned plays by Barrie Stavis, Dalton Trumbo, and Arthur Miller.[41] Reid won the Quonta Drama Festival best director award in 1958 with an Arthur Miller play cast entirely of miners, who demonstrated they could compete and perform well. This initiative, too, broadened the union's involvement with the community. One executive member who supervised Reid's work testified: "A man in Mr. Reid's capacity, who is directing certain work, such as culture, art and entertainment ... has to deal with many ... different people outside the local union."[42]

How much Reid undertook and how much was a collective effort are now difficult matters to establish. A member of the entertainment committee noted that Reid assisted with the entertainment committee and "was under their supervision ... to the extent of dances and such like as that, but when it came to shows and various arts, then he was in charge of the direction of it."[43] Pressed for further information, this person stated: "Well, he worked along with the committee, in conjunction with the people on it. He put forward certain ideas and so on, and it was up to the committees to assist in every way that ... these ideas that came under the general recreational director's field to see that they were put into effect." Reid himself acknowledged the leeway he had, especially at the summer camp: "I planned and carried forth the organization and the construction program, the staff training and the program development at the summer camp, under the direction of Mr. Solski and, latterly, Mr. Racicot, and being responsible to the executive board."[44] Reid was responsible to the president and the executive, and he attended executive board meetings to give verbal reports of his activities. Later he explained: "I was in a confidential capacity. I attended board meetings; I made recommendations on policy. I also, in connection with the camp, hired and had the power to fire the staff. I trained the staff."[45]

Reid's influence at the camp was crucial to his role in Mine Mill's workers' culture. As tools for building an understanding of his involvement, the secret police reports compiled from RCMP informers prove to be less helpful than the records of Reid's trials.[46] Regardless of the sources, Reid's talents would find their greatest outlet at the camp, yet ironically his very success would bring him to the brink of ruin.

Summer Camp: Building and Destroying

To understand the summer camp is to understand important elements of Weir Reid. In 1954, for instance, he reported to the executive board on how to develop the campsite. By then he had expanded what had been a day camp into a comprehensive program for children from ages six to fourteen. Two-week blocks of organized activities and sports included "swimming, Red Cross [testing] program, Royal Life-Saving Society program, canoeing, boating, out-trips, archery, baseball, volleyball, soccer, hiking, nature study, arts and crafts, clay modelling, pottery, plaster casting, wood carving, drift wood [collecting and shaping], papier mâché, metal craft, basketry, singing, folk, square and social dancing, library, story hour and camp fires."[47] Reid himself had experience in almost all of these activities through his YMCA work or his personal interests in arts and crafts. Contemporary photos show him actively carving and sculpting with the children. Where he lacked training, he found appropriate people to help out, including his wife Ruth, who had extensive YWCA experience and worked as a volunteer. Directors and counsellors were well-trained YMCA graduates. For instance, in 1954 he recommended that Pat Craig be hired as waterfront director, which the executive approved; she had taken health and physical education at the University of Toronto. Emphasis was upon professional guidance, especially in water safety and sports, so that testing and qualification in safety and lifesaving could be taken at the camp. Counsellors-in-training came for two weeks of instruction before the six two-week sessions with the children began.

By 1954 a lodge had been constructed at the camp and Reid proposed a water filtration and sewage system. The executive agreed to build two more dormitories so that an "additional 40 overnight campers" could be accommodated. According to the *Mine Mill News* of February 8, 1954, two hundred campers were to be accommodated in ten dormitories.

By the mid-1950s an ecological program that included tree planting was under way. "Hundreds of members had given voluntarily of their time in improving the camp grounds, in landscaping and in making the camp the pride of the trade union movement," a later report found.[48] For the general membership the camp committee built a diving tower, and twenty-one picnic tables were added, bringing the total to seventy-five by 1957. Every Sunday services were held for the campers, with Protestant ministers coming to the camp while Catholics were taken to nearby churches. Under Reid's direction the camp offered a typical, but much-expanded, YMCA experience.

The camp and Weir Reid's leadership of it had been chosen as a target for attack by the White Block as early as 1955. The group attacked Reid and circulated rumours about the camp as a venue for socialist indoctrination. After the 1958 strike by Local 598 against Inco, the opposition to Mine Mill increased. The strike's effect – it undercut union solidarity – and the concerted attack by Steelworkers from outside while Catholic university "reformers" bored from within, made the camp a focus in the fight for control of Mine Mill. That put Reid in the centre of the battle for Local 598's huge membership. When the so-called "reformers," led by the Don Gillis–Ray Poirier–Don McNabb group, won election in March 1959, they had control of the Local 598 executive, aside from three members, including Reid. The Gillis group realized that if Reid continued to sit at the executive table, they would have difficulty making the changes they wanted to introduce, which included merging with the Steelworkers. Hence, among their first acts was to fire Reid as recreation and hall director without severance. He took them to court for his pay. That court case had not begun when a faked assault case heightened the tensions. Reid had supposedly placed his hand on Poirier's shoulder at the end of the May 1959 membership meeting in which his dismissal was announced. At the executive board before that meeting, Poirier had insisted that Weir's dismissal receive wide publicity. Due to that "assault," a union court hearing in June 1959 found Reid guilty, but the membership rejected that finding in August 1959 by voting to overturn the union court's finding as well as Reid's expulsion.

In September 1959 Reid filed slander charges against Gillis, McNabb, and others in the new leadership. When it appeared evident that he would

Mine Mill summer camp at Richard Lake, Ontario, in the 1950s.
Courtesy Mine Mill Local 598 (CAW)

Mine Mill unionist Bill Sorenson.
Courtesy Mine Mill Local 598 (CAW)

win the severance pay case, a jubilant Reid wrote his lawyer on December 3, 1959, that: "Tuesday's report on the assault case particularly ... has had very favourable reception ... The failure of the executive to settle the severance pay [issue] has not had a favourable reception either in the community nor among the membership."[49] Maintaining his reputation was significant to Reid, who had four children, had lost his union position, and was again forced to seek employment as a real estate agent or a recreation consultant.

Since Reid had won two rounds, the Poirier group moved to lower-level tactics. Poirier offered an exposé on Weir Reid to Toronto *Telegram* reporter Frank Drea – later a Steelworker publicity agent and an Ontario Conservative cabinet minister. Between December 22 and December 30, 1959, Drea reported Poirier's anonymous accusations that Reid was the head of a Communist cell in Sudbury, that he used the camp to indoctrinate children, controlled a group of thugs, had taken children from their parents, and had misused union moneys. All of these claims were fabricated, as Poirier admitted privately and would eventually have to acknowledge publicly when Reid took him to court.[50] However, Reid's legal actions against Drea and the *Telegram*, and then against Poirier, after Poirier's informant role became known, would take four and six years respectively to settle in Reid's favour. By then, as can be expected in slander cases, the defendant's reputation had been smeared, his livelihood undercut, and the union's cultural and recreational endeavours destroyed.

This case represents more than the victimization of a talented individual. It undercut the philosophy of all individuals having the opportunity to develop themselves spiritually and physically. That was what the camp embodied under Reid. Those values were being destroyed as the Mine Mill and Steelworkers fought each other for control of the membership. Within a few years the dance schools closed, the theatre disbanded, registrations at the camp declined, and the program was diminished. In 1962 Mine Mill lost certification at Inco, and the dances and community involvements decreased as the Steelworkers eliminated such "fringes" from U.S. "bread-and-butter" unionism. The material cutbacks reflected a spiritual demise.

When the Reids were rehired to run the camp in 1964 and 1965 – after the Mine Mill leadership had changed to a more moderate faction – they offered the same program as during the 1950s. Reid desperately sought funds and campers, even trying to support the camp by selling raffle tickets.[51] To undercut a Mine Mill revival, the same anti-Reid and former Mine Mill faction of "reformers" – who were openly supported by the Steelworkers (again led by McNabb, O'Brien, and Poirier) – published a letter in the May 1964 edition of the Steelworkers' *Searcher* accusing the Mine Mill camp of being a place of "immorality." A libel case led to a letter of apology by all except McNabb in 1966. But by then the dirty tactics had again worked and the deficit on the camp and halls ran to $40,000 per year. The lack of a large labour force, with only the Falconbridge local and friends to draw upon, plus the renewed Cold War attacks combined with competition from state-subsidized recreation, meant that Mine Mill's camp and culture faltered and disappeared in its old form. By the late 1960s Reid had won many of his libel cases, but the victories were empty ones: the opponents had undercut the social and educational activism of an alternative union.

Testimonials on the camp came from many quarters when it was later under attack. Children, councillors, and adults whose children had attended the camp remembered no indoctrination other than a few union songs being sung. Prayers and morning swims, well-organized programs, and special care from the "camp mother," as Ruth Reid was called by children and contemporaries, recurred in the many statements. In May 1959, at the first membership meeting after Weir Reid was dismissed on the grounds that a full-time director was unnecessary, many men offered "testimonies of praise" to his work. A woman added her voice in a letter to *The Sudbury Star* on May 15: "As a mother of two children who have attended the camp for the past three summers and have remained at the camp from four to six weeks each year, I can testify that every word that they have spoken is true." She pointed out that the camp held the most cherished memories for her children, while noting:

> All their outdoor activities are supervised by good qualified instructors. Every parent feels happy and much relieved when their child has learned to swim well and handle a boat expertly. My two children along with many others won their intermediate swimming certificate last summer ... The children have learned much which is to their advantage ... At no time have children been presented with pamphlets or literature, nor have they heard in any way shape or form anything pertaining to communism at the camp.

After Reid was accused of communist indoctrination and issued a slander suit against the instigators, many testimonials in his favour were collected, although because the case did not go to court, they did not become public. Carl Kudla was on the camp committee from 1953 through 1955: "He finds all the allegations about Reid as to what went on at the camp perfectly ridiculous. He found the camp well run and prizes [for competitions] reasonable, very animate in the fact that the summer camp participated in no communistic teachings or indoctrination of any sort."[52] Kudla had been a Lutheran until the strike of 1958, during which he felt the "church sold him out," and he added, "As a member of the Camp

Committee he has had no complaints from parents concerning political indoctrination of the children." A parent of four children who had been sent to the camp between 1954 and 1958 stated: "I visited the camp at least once a week while they were there and I did not observe anything untoward or unusual ... My children did not observe anything or report anything ... to indicate that they were being indoctrinated in any way."[53] Norman Jacques, who had been chair of the camp committee for three years, stated he "was quite aware of what went on at the camp. We would not have allowed any politics at the camp at all because the Union is made up of everybody."[54] A counsellor noted, "Weir made a point of seeing to it that I got the kids to church."[55] Another young man had been at the camp from 1956 to 1959 as a junior counsellor and then sports director, and had worked on the waterfront and later at canoeing. "At the camp he claims that he had never been pressured with regards to his religious beliefs in any way and similarly encountered no political indoctrination."[56]

Numerous members of the camp committee attested that no complaints had come from parents about political or religious indoctrination. Many of those who had been to the camp reported that they enjoyed camp life and had gained from it. The opportunities were evidently appreciated, because they could use their skills elsewhere: "In the summer of 1954 I was a counsellor in training and made a junior counsellor half way through the summer. In 1955 I was a senior counsellor. In 1956 I was a swimming instructor; 1957 assistant waterfront director; 1958 I was a life guard at Bell Park working for Sudbury Recreation Committee; 1959 I was assistant waterfront director on the public beach next to the Mine Mill Camp."[57] This youth, a Catholic, added that "to my knowledge no communism ideology or politics were discussed with the children at all." But the reality that all these people experienced counted for little against those who spread rumours so that, as another witness put it, "I have had some of the filthiest things said to me about Weir Reid on the job."[58]

Even while trying to destroy Reid, the Gillis-Poirier-McNabb group, in an official statement in the *Mine Mill News* on July 13, 1959, acknowledged what had been built:

> The Mine Mill Camp has now been in operation for 7 years – first as a day camp and since 1954 a co-educational resident camp for boys and girls. Each year the facilities have been improved for the children of members ... Few camps in Canada today have as good facilities as those at the camp at Richard Lake.
>
> The main building at the Camp is the Lodge. This beautiful well-equipped building consists of the main dining room, a modern kitchen, staff washrooms, First Aid room, a library, and administration quarters.

Living quarters for campers and counsellors are well constructed and screened. Good running hot and cold water, electricity and flush toilets are provided. The Craft shop is capable of providing for a varied Arts and Crafts program as well as doubling as assembly area during rainy weather.

The so-called reformers wanted only to retain the material base and did not realize that a thriving workers' culture required the spiritual content that Weir Reid and Mine Mill had so ably and diligently supplied.

Reid's Role in Context

What Weir Reid had added to the Mine Mill repertoire – recreation planning and organization, cultural events, and a breadth of vision – became most evident when he was no longer in charge. He had aimed high and tried to combine a thorough YMCA-style program at the camp with high-class cultural opportunities for the city – to bring in the Winnipeg Royal Ballet, to stage operas and start ballet schools, to develop libraries and local art programs. He staged plays such as the first, full-length production of *The Man Who Never Died* about Joe Hill. On December 22, 1954, the play's author, Barrie Stavis, wrote to Reid (who directed the Haywood Players, with Jim Tester playing Hill): "It is so fitting a commentary on our times that it is a trade union group which will give the premiere of this play."[59] With ballet schools and libraries and crafts, Reid helped to bring to Sudbury workers and their families the culture that the middle class generally thought of as its own.

Through his public presence Reid thus offered a large target to the union's opponents. To focus on that target required someone with ill intentions, because Reid had done his job well and with the support of the union leadership and membership. An examination of the executive board minutes from March 1952 to March 1959 reveals only two occasions when minor questions were raised about the running of the camp. Otherwise, there were motions passed to support the improvements and patterns that Reid suggested. The camp committee, too, approved of Reid's work and made reference to only one complaint before the 1958 strike. As well, the spectacular events that identified Mine Mill with socialism, peace movements, and communism were passed by the whole executive. For instance, the Paul Robeson concert at the time of the Eighth Annual Convention, in February 1956, was apparently arranged by the National executive.[60] The motion to show the movie *The Salt of the Earth* and to purchase a copy of this tale of workers' self-emancipation goes back to Ray Stevenson. While Reid supported progressive causes, his concerns focused more on aesthetics and creativity. During one of the slander trials, he termed himself a "sometime socialist" when asked about his political beliefs. He added, "I have

Mike Solski (left), Paul Robeson, and Nels Thibault at the Robeson concert on February 29, 1956, at Mine Mill Hall in Sudbury.

Courtesy Mike Farrell

never felt myself bound by a church or party or what is considered the right thing to do in society, but I am not a rebel."61

Reid had built well on the work of others. He had an infectious enthusiasm and the ability to draw on the strengths of a team of participants. The camp and its buildings were expanded under his direction and with Ruth Reid's dedicated support. For seven years they provided through the union a model of what was possible in recreation. Simultaneously, the city's recreation department and other organizations became involved in similar endeavours. The John Island camp and the city's swim and safety program at Bell Park both began in 1954. Mine Mill's recreation efforts had been the model, and its followers became its competitors.

Often forgotten is what Sudbury was like when Mine Mill created its camp: there was no covered arena until 1950, and there were only a few church and amateur acting groups and choirs, and a few semi-professional sporting groups. Mine Mill filled a huge void in the recreational and cultural sphere, as Reid drew workers' families into dance, theatre, crafts, and many novel sport forms for children.

What did organized workers' culture consist of in Sudbury during the 1950s? First, a distinction needs to be made between workers' culture and organized workers' culture. Together with the recreational, leisure, and educational offerings of Mine Mill, a number of other subworlds existed for and through the efforts of labourers. Pubs with one entrance reading "Men

Only" and another reading "Ladies and Gents" drew miners for regular rounds after work. A pub "culture" of loud discussion and heavy drinking prevailed. A quite different culture was formed by the almost spartan sports clubs run by ethnic groups such as the Finns. They built their own tracks for light athletics and provided their own transportation to self-organized meets. A third variant of workers' culture appeared in the unorganized activities made possible by a region full of lakes, cheap land, and materials for building private recreational facilities. This camp "culture" allegedly differed from the cottage country of the south by its emphasis upon self-built cabins and rustic outfittings.

By contrast, Mine Mill's activities fitted precisely with the organized workers' culture that authors have identified with an alternative culture allied to Austrian and German Social Democracy. In the tradition of European labour movements, Sudbury's radical union offered large symbolic actions with political overtones. This included Labour Day picnics (with rock-moving or mucking contests), gripping films, and radical folk singers, such as The Travellers and Pete Seeger. The values of world peace and class identification were writ large in its ideological assertions and cultural endeavours. Mine Mill also offered an exceptional experience to children of the miners and the community at large with the summer camp. In the early 1950s, few such activities were provided by the city's small recreation department with its underdeveloped parks and lack of financing, because the mining companies paid no local taxes.

Another aspect of the union's leisure and cultural endeavours included organized dances and a hall in nearly every mining town surrounding the city, halls used for films, dance, theatre, and games. Reid expanded upon that tradition. This triad of organized workers' cultural offerings had a slight political tinge, but it mainly offered a rational type of recreation that simultaneously fostered entertainment and education.

Organized workers' culture therefore existed simultaneously with ethnic sports culture, pub culture, and escapist family recreation. Yet within two decades, by the late 1970s, most of these "cultures" had disappeared. The ethnic sports groups' members were assimilated by intermarriage and social mobility, as well as by the competition from commercial sports housed in state-subsidized facilities. The pubs declined as the mining industry transformed the workplace and with it the labour force, so that the young boarding house occupiers decamped. During the 1980s most of the former workers' pubs closed or were renovated into middle-class bars. The escapist lake culture for families remained, but was increasingly transformed into a new cottage culture, as road access and second-generation incomes modernized the previously "primitive" world.

Mine Mill's recreational efforts disintegrated as a U.S. bread-and-butter union raided and took over most of Mine Mill's membership. Accusations of communism helped during the Cold War, as the local Catholic church and the state participated in the crusade. After the union movement split, Mine Mill still had its halls and recreational area, but not the membership to finance the community approach to recreation. Reid, as rehired recreation director, fought to regain the basis of the early successes that had come to be identified with his name, but the revived camp lasted only two seasons, 1964 and 1965, due to union deficits. The organized workers' culture disappeared, killed off by political manipulations, Cold War activists, and union infighting.

The disengagement of labour from organized workers' culture in North America occurred through very different repressive measures than those brought by fascism and war in Europe. Locally the political side of the story has been well presented, but the cultural side needs to be noted. The competition of mass commercial culture and of a changing tax base for the city's recreational involvements, too, undermined Mine Mill's alternative culture.

Mine Mill had offered workers an alternative to leisure without culture. Some individuals, the Catholic Church, and the state found Mine Mill's efforts objectionable and fought to destroy them. However, the methods of the state and church were the same as those they accused the communists of using – namely, secret police informants, lies, and authoritarianism.

Yet in the long run the organized workers' culture would probably have declined in Sudbury, just as it had earlier in Europe. A quick look at the Sudbury workplace and the working class shows the main trends: by the mid-1970s, the mine and smelter rationalization reversed the trend to an increasing number of workers; and by the 1980s, Sudbury no longer had the demographic profile of a mining centre, namely young males outnumbering young females.[62] At the same time, the cultural endeavours that Mine Mill initiated began to be offered by church groups and the city's recreation programs, with state subsidies in the form of arenas and playgrounds. Publicly fostered recreation came into place and competed with Mine Mill's offerings. Most importantly, the inroads of mass commercial culture were already undercutting the rational type of recreation organized by the union, as television, Hollywood movies, and the devaluation of education became social norms. In the union halls, organized workers' culture remains mainly as memory, similar to what numerous studies emphasize at present vis-à-vis Europe. Organized workers' culture appears to have been possible only when labour was strong, and only when aided by idealists such as Reid and supported by large alternative unions whose philosophy included community development.

Part 8

DRAWING ON THE PAST FOR FUTURE STRENGTH

Introduction

When the conference closed with a benefit banquet for a planned miners' memorial in Sudbury, Madeleine Parent and Utah Phillips, both strongly linked to Mine Mill's past, were the guests of honour. Mine Mill Hall was humming with excitement as John Lang got set to introduce Madeleine Parent, the guest speaker for evening.

Lang told how Madeleine Parent began her work with the labour movement in the 1940s, organizing textile workers along with her husband – the late Kent Rowley – in Quebec.

> This led to a number of very difficult strikes, and the struggles of the textile workers in Quebec were not only against Dominion Textile and the large textile companies. They quickly became struggles against the Duplessis government of Quebec as well. These were the seeds of the liberation struggle in Quebec, which has continued through the 1960s, 1970s, and 1980s to the present day. Many people in Ontario do not have the appreciation of the stature that Madeleine has held in both the labour movement and the political life of Quebec.
>
> In the midst of a difficult strike in 1952 the union which Madeleine had formed was betrayed by the American leadership of the Textile Workers Union of America. After that betrayal she and Kent Rowley formed the Canadian Textile and Chemical Union. Madeleine spent much of the next fifteen years working with and organizing textile workers in Ontario. During that time she and Kent were founding members and in many ways the inspiration behind the formation of the Confederation of Canadian Unions in 1969.
>
> During the strikes in Quebec Madeleine and the textile workers of Quebec received direct assistance from the Mine Mill and Smelter Workers Union, particularly from Local 598 in Sudbury. Madeleine returned that assistance when she spent a lot of time in Sudbury during the raids in 1962 and again in 1965 fighting off the Steelworkers. She worked particularly with the francophone members of Mine Mill and the francophone community of the Sudbury area.
>
> Madeleine retired, formally at least, from union affairs ten years ago, but she has continued to be active in Quebec, where she returned after her retirement. She was active in the founding of the National Action Committee on the Status of Women, where she has continued to be active, currently serving out what is likely her last term on the executive of NAC. Since leaving the labour movement, Madeleine has become extremely active in Native people's struggles in Quebec, working particularly with Native women. She has also contributed to the general popular movement in Quebec, building the resistance to the free trade agreement. So in

retirement, Madeleine amazes us by maintaining a level of activity that surpasses even that of the youngest members of the labour movement.

In 1990 Madeleine was one of ten inductees into Canada's new labour hall of fame. This is a particular tribute to Madeleine in recognition of her work with women and immigrant workers outside the mainstream of the labour movement. It also recognized her general work in bringing a critical perspective to the labour movement and to much of labour's struggles.

Singer, raconteur, and long-time "Wobbly" Utah Phillips brought the audience to its feet with his songs and stories of struggle, resistance, and occasional victory. That night he also gave another gift to Mine Millers, a gift that would change the name of Mine Mill Hall. But it is better that he tell that story in his own voice.

Chapter 20
Building a People's Movement

Madeleine Parent

When I first came to Sudbury Mine Mill in 1952, our union had six thousand members on strike in Quebec, in the cotton mills of Montreal and Valleyfield; about twenty-five hundred of these were women. Kent Rowley, our president, had phoned Mine Mill Local 598 President Nels Thibault to ask if we could come and solicit support for our strikers. Nels, who had previously met Kent at the opening of the Mine Mill Hall, was very enthusiastic and wanted Kent to come up here because he knew him to be a good speaker whom the miners respected. But Kent insisted that since there were large numbers of women in this strike, the miners should be made aware of the struggle they were waging, and that it would be better to send a woman speaker to tell about the strike and make the appeal. So I was sent up with a young woman striker from one of the Montreal mills.

Mine Mill showed a great amount of interest in the strike, in the conditions of work, in the attitude of the Duplessis government in power at the time in Quebec, and in its harassment of the textile workers. There was great sympathy for our struggle. The members voted unanimously to have collections at every payday, which was every two weeks, until the strike was over. They were as good as their word. Union stewards, shop chairs, and other activists were outside the banks on payday with their boxes and signs announcing the collection for the textile workers of Quebec. They collected an average of $2,000 every two weeks – forty years ago that was quite a lot of money. We received the money regularly throughout the strike and until the textile workers had received their first post-strike pay from the Dominion Textile Company.

A Mine Mill delegation came, walked on our picket lines in Montreal, and attended our union meetings out in a field in Valleyfield. Mike Solski was a member of that delegation, and so were Norman Jacques, Nels Thibault and his wife, who is present here tonight, and a number of other delegates. It was a great occasion for our textile workers, who knew and appreciated the support you were giving us.

This solidarity was terribly important to us, especially since we were being sold down the river by our international union. A few years later in Washington, the Senate Committee on Rackets in Unions, led by Senator Bobby Kennedy, discovered that our international union president and the international secretary-treasurer had in 1952, or after, stolen from the union treasury in order to build two expensive houses for themselves in Virginia. The Senate Committee also exposed the fact that these two men had received money from employers, including one employer in Canada, and my guess is that the employer was the Dominion Textile Company.

But it was small consolation to us, because by then the strike had been settled in favour of the corporation. The workers were prisoners of an American union, which had become a company union with a director who was a member of the secret service agency of the U.S. government, Sam Baron. The old-timers will remember Baron as having been one of the harassers of the Mine Mill and United Electrical, Radio and Machine Workers (UE) unions in the Canadian Congress of Labour (CCL) during the years of the Cold War.

Mine Mill membership meeting in the union hall in Sudbury, Ontario, during the strike of 1958.

Mike Solski Collection, Sudbury Public Library

It was years later, when Mine Mill was subjected to intense raiding by the United Steelworkers of America, that I was asked to return here to participate in your campaign. It was a great pleasure to be able to bring you the support of the textile workers, for by then we had formed an alternative Canadian union, overcoming great difficulties, particularly in Ontario. We had achieved, both at Harding Carpets in Brantford and in the Empire Cotton Mill in Welland, the best wages and conditions in our industry in the country, even though our union was a small one and very limited, espe-

In the middle of the Steelworker raids, Mine Mill unionists picket the provincial legislature for an honest vote at Inco, November 19, 1962.

Courtesy Mine Mill Local 598 (CAW)

cially in the financial resources that we could muster. But we still did better than the American unions in the industry, despite all the money they had.

I came up here gladly, addressed a number of the meetings that were held, told the story about our own Canadian union. I was given permission by the officers of Mine Mill to do some visits among the French-speaking union members in their homes. Laurie St-Jean and I organized several informal meetings for francophone miners in homes, in the Chelmsford hall, and in other Mine Mill halls. To those meetings came mainly the miners themselves, but also, on several occasions, the wives. They spoke very comfortably in their own language, dealt with the issues involved, often quite eloquently. The wives wanted to come, because in their own communities and parishes they wanted to be able to argue the position for Mine Mill against the overwhelming propaganda that was displayed against their union. They were excellent meetings, which I will remember until the day I die.

We spoke on radio and TV, on English and French programs. At Welland, where we had members in the cotton mill, we were neighbours to the Port Colborne refinery workers of Mine Mill. There again, we went to Mine Mill meetings, they came to our meetings, we were at their plant gates, they were at our plant gates, and so the solidarity between textile workers and Mine Mill members continued throughout that entire period.

Years later, when Mine Mill won an unprecedented ruling in the Supreme Court of Canada, according to which Mine Mill Local 598 *was* Mine Mill, entitled to retain its funds, its buildings, and all of its possessions, and was the continuation of the union that had been built over so many years, it was a great victory which we celebrated, along with the Mine Mill people.

It occurred to Kent Rowley, to me, and to a couple of our leading officers in the textile union that this might be the time when we could get together with some other Canadian unions and consider whether it would be feasible to develop an alliance or a council of alternative Canadian unions. Since our own textile union convention for 1967 was coming up – it was a modest convention of course, with about thirty-five delegates – we invited Mine Mill to send a couple of fraternal delegates to our convention in Brantford. Roy Scranton came from Sudbury with Laurie St-Jean, and Orville Braaten came from British Columbia. Braaten was the first president and one of the founders of the Pulp and Paper Workers of Canada (PPWC), which broke away from a corrupt American union, where the international president also stole the union treasury. The PPWC had set up their own Canadian union. After our convention we sat down, just a few of us, together with those three fraternal delegates, and considered the question whether there would be any point in setting up a council of alternative Canadian unions.

Our guests were comfortable with the idea and promised to go back to their respective unions – Local 598 Mine Mill and the PPWC – and raise the question to see how their members felt about it. We promised to discuss the idea in our own union.

As a result, there was a first, broader meeting of Canadian union representatives here in Sudbury just one year later, in 1968 at the Mine Mill children's summer camp, where we again debated the issue, and decided that 1969 would be the year of the founding convention. Delegates from the various unions – bricklayers, the Canadian Association of Industrial, Mechanical and Allied Workers (CAIMAW), electrical workers in British Columbia, stationary engineers, and others – took the idea home, the debate raged on during the year, and in 1969 in this Mine Mill Hall in Sudbury the Confederation of Canadian Unions (CCU) was born.

At that time the Canadian government had begun to publish statistics on the expenses and receipts of American unions paid out of the dues of Canadian workers. Those government figures demonstrated that Canadian union members, far from being financed by U.S. unions, were sending far more money down to the United States than they ever received back, even in years when there were many strikes in Canada. So, while the dry figures were there, and published rather discreetly, the CCU picked up the information, analysed the meaning of those figures, and publicized its analysis, drawing lessons from it.

We began to break the myth that workers in Canada were too poor, too weak, and too incapable of running their own unions. We stressed that they were, in fact, enriching the bureaucracy of American unions, and that we were far better off to use our own funds and to have our unions managed by workers elected and accountable to workers in Canada. We could obviously run our own affairs. The CCU, better than any other organization, helped to break the myth of the greater power and superiority of American unions, the myth of their greater usefulness to Canadian members.

Some people used to rationalize that relations with the American unions were only a matter of money, that they meant nothing else. I want to remind you that when the American people had the Boston Tea Party it was only a matter of money; but that issue meant a lot to them, and the War of Independence started with such an event. In any case, the money issue prepared the way for a deeper understanding as to where our collective interests lie.

On the other hand, with the social legislation that was developing in Canada in the late 1960s and 1970s (public health care, greater educational facilities), the numbers of public service workers were increasing very rapidly. They were organizing rapidly, as well. Of course, it would have been illogical for them to join American unions, so they swelled the ranks of the Canadian union forces, so that – as John Lang notes [see chapter 1] – from 1969 when the CCU was founded, when two-thirds of organized workers in Canada were in American-based unions, we have come today to the point where only a third of the organized workers in Canada are in American-based unions. That trend is bound to continue and to be reinforced. We can be proud that our CCU played an important role in the ideological process that led to the predominance of Canadian unions in this country.

There is currently, however, a change in our economic situation, one that calls for urgent and effective action. It is important for the alternative unions to recognize the significance of this change. As a result of nine years of Tory federal rule, and their free-trade policies, with their abandonment of constitutional powers, both federal and provincial, to the U.S.-Canada Free Trade Agreement, and for the North American Free Trade Agreement, this country is being brought to a situation in which our federal government is giving away our constitutional powers and responsibilities.

This increases the power over us of transnational corporations, which are using us only for their own profit, while the world is their oyster. While these corporations are being showered with government tax exemptions, government subsidies, and favours and privileges of all sorts, and while they bear a smaller and smaller share of the taxation burden, they will use us at the same time as long as it is profitable to themselves. But the corporations will then pick up all their riches, including those we showered upon them from the public treasury, to establish factories in the southern United States, in Mexico, and elsewhere where labour is cheap and workers are still suffering under undemocratic and often very oppressive conditions.

In this way, Canada is being destructured in the orientation to free trade – unfettered, uncontrolled – with no thought to retaining our wealth to develop it for the people of this country, and with no thought to restricting companies from taking out of our country everything that pays them and profits them, while leaving the empty shell behind for our people to pick up. It is obvious that our Canadian government has no plans to improve employment for better times to come.

It is all the more obvious when we look at the cutting back of the unemployment insurance plan and benefits. In a short period of time, we went from 66 percent of average earnings in unemployment insurance benefits to 60 percent, and now we've gone from 60 percent to 57 per cent, and we're on the way to 50 percent if, as intended, the government wants to level the playing field with that of the United States.

At the same time, the government has imposed drastic penalties on workers for quitting or for being fired, supposedly with cause. We all know that women, who have the largest number of precarious jobs and who are the most apt to suffer from sexual harassment in unorganized workplaces, are the ones who will have to quit. We all know that no boss is stupid enough to engage in sexual harassment in front of witnesses, so that the suffering woman is not in a position to denounce the employer, and to obtain her unemployment insurance benefits. The result is that women will suffer even more than men.

But when the government cuts so deeply into an unemployment insurance plan that is about fifty-three years old in this country, it is clear that they know that unemployment will continue and unemployment will increase. The solution to an empty unemployment insurance treasury is jobs, and they know there will not be any; therefore they are just cutting the benefits.

Until now, alternative unions have done a good job, having served an important purpose in this country. If we look at the trade union movement today, we will see mainly Canadian unions, turning in a more democratic direction. I don't speak of all of the unions, especially some of the American ones that still insist on keeping that international connection, even though they find themselves in conflict with their American union brothers over free-trade issues and other matters.

However, in terms of a Canadian trade union movement that is building, I think we should look at ourselves and see whether alternative unions are still the best policy for our members now, or whether we could do better by choosing a Canadian union that we can work with, negotiating conditions that would guarantee our democratic rights, and getting back into the mainstream union movement.

All the work that we can do, with the best of alternative unions or other unions, will not be enough to stop the growing tide of unemployment, to stop the destructuring of our economy under free trade, to stop the cutting back of our universal social programs, to stop the erosion of educational facilities for our young people. Even if we fought heroically for union contracts for our members, for the settlement of complaints, of grievances, of occupational health problems, in the process of the destructuring of this country, there are things which we cannot do alone.

The union to which I belonged, the Canadian Textile and Chemical Union – of which Laurell Ritchie is now a leader – has merged with the Canadian Auto Workers Union (CAW), having worked out a democratic arrangement whereby our union is free to bargain and make its own decisions. This has taken months of discussions in our committees, in our membership meetings, in our conventions, and months of negotiations with the CAW.

Our union has no CAW representatives as staff members: we elect and choose our own staff members and pay their salary out of a percentage of dues returned by CAW to our merged union. In this way, our staff members are responsible and accountable to the members of our union, which is now Local 40 of CAW. All of the controls remain with the union itself. We have a lot of members and officers who are women, we have a lot of members who are people of colour, many immigrant workers, and all of these people have their say within the structure of that union, now within CAW.

We also bring to CAW an awareness of the very difficult conditions and of the great exploitation of large sections of workers who have poor and insecure jobs. We have a way of talking to those workers and encouraging them to organize into this kind of a union, because it's not a union limited to higher-paid workers – namely men – but it is a union where more highly exploited people can comfortably see themselves and have their own place and voice.

Even if the whole of the trade union movement takes on the struggle over these issues with our federal and provincial governments, that also will not be enough to make the change. I am sorry to say that the Ontario government, which has chosen to make certain reforms, has not really challenged the anti-social, anti-labour, and sell-out free-trade policies of the federal government. As a provincial government it is adjusting itself to anti-people, bankrupt policies that are only going to lead to more doom, gloom, misery, and greater poverty for the people. Our united trade union movement has to spend far more time working with women's groups, anti-poverty groups, youth groups, and others that are struggling for rights in education, for job training, for a chance for young people to grow up in sanity, in short, to be able to earn a living for themselves and their future families.

We must unite with people from the discriminated minority communities. We must unite with the disabled people, who are struggling for more justice. We must unite with Native peoples, and especially Native women, who have taken on the fight against conjugal violence and incest, and the fight for the democratic development of their communities. Native women must have a strong voice and share the power to plan and administer welfare, social, and educational programs. They do not want a deal such as the Charlottetown accord, where a few powerful chiefs would institute a neo-colonial accord with a few big bosses in Ottawa and in provincial governments.

In order for the union movement to succeed in developing sound coalition work with all of these groups, the union people have to go to them, listen to their story, learn from them about their conditions and problems, and take up their cause as well. In that way we will become more credible to them, and the governments will not be able to divide them away from public-sector workers or from private-sector organized workers by saying to them, "You are poor, we've got to cut back, we'd better cut back the wages and conditions of the public-sector workers or of the miners or the auto-factory workers." They will not be divided against us if they recognize us as brothers and sisters, as friends who understand them, who hear them, who share their struggles with them.

Such solidarity won't be built overnight. We will have to overcome a lot of our unconscious, bureaucratic practices. There will be some criticism, because many of these people have been ignored for so long. But if we work in solidarity with these groups, we can build a people's movement that can develop a people's charter and people's objectives for the kind of country we want to build and where we want to live together. That will be the real challenge to the status quo of today. This is the way to build our future.

From within the larger trade union movement, we can challenge labour to develop those kinds of relations and solidarities, with thousands of democratic organizations in this country and eventually effect a real change. It won't come tomorrow, it won't come next year, but maybe we will be on the way to building something durable.

With this kind of program, we can speak of international solidarity with the workers of Mexico, who are being used against us today. Through meeting and working with them as equals, we can share our criticisms of the international corporations and hear from them about the repression of the Mexican people by the Institutional Revolutionary Party (PRI) government, about the corruption of the official Mexican trade union movement, and about the hope that their alternative unions hold for them. The alternative unions in Mexico are trying to build an honest, democratic trade union movement that will take on the more corrupt forces that the government keeps in control of the official trade union movement. With that kind of international solidarity, we'll be able to work out exchanges and plans for trading on the basis of mutual advantage for our people and for the people of the countries that we will be trading with.

It's a big challenge, but I think we should consider it – and decide whether we are going to take it on and be part of the building of a meaningful people's movement that can lead to change for the better. I think we can do it.

Chapter 21
It Never Died: How Joe Hill's Ashes Came to Be in the Sudbury Mine Mill Hall[1] One Hundred Years after the Founding of the Western Federation of Miners

Utah Phillips[2]

I was intimidated to find out that Paul Robeson had sung on this stage ... right here. We were living in Cleveland, and my mother was working for the union, and we had a radio show called "Labour Cares." It was broadcast all over the United States, and Paul Robeson would sing on it. One of the few times that my mother ever yelled at me would be, "Shut up, it's Robeson!" We'd all gather 'round the radio and listen to him sing. One of the songs he sang, of course, was Earl Robinson's "Joe Hill." Earl Robinson sang here, too; Earl was killed in a car wreck two years ago, now.

I'm from Utah. The old prison that Joe Hill was shot in, the Sugarhouse Prison, was still standing when we moved there in '47. I got the city plans so I could walk the ground in the yard there and stand on the exact same spot where that white kitchen chair was he was tied to when they killed him.

Joe was a Swedish immigrant. He learned to speak English on the tramp steamers between Sweden and Britain. Before the turn of the century, he shipped over to this country with his brother and shortened his name from Joseph Hillstrom to Joe Hill. He worked as a machinist all over the country. Some people said he could play the guitar; some said he couldn't. I've known people who knew Joe Hill, and every one of them talks about a different man. Some people say he was very mild-mannered, peaceful,

Singer-songwriter Utah Phillips performing May 1993 in the Mine Mill Hall, since named the Joe Hill Workers' Auditorium.

Courtesy Dorothy Wigmore

others say he had a terrible, terrible temper. I just don't know what to figure about Joe Hill.

He went to work in San Pedro, where he joined the union. He went down to Tijuana to fight in the Tijuana Rebellion, where anarcho-syndicalists tried to turn southern California into a commune. He was wounded in that fracas, and went to recover in Salt Lake City with the fellow workers up there. He was framed on a murder charge: they said he murdered a grocery store operator, named Morrison, and his son. Governor Spry vowed to bust the Wobblies out of the state of Utah and Joe Hill was going to be the scapegoat. Two crooked, rigged trials. Seventy-five thousand letters poured into the state from all over the world appealing for a new trial, and telegrams came from the Swedish ambassador and from President Woodrow Wilson. All to no avail. They were going to kill Joe.

Joe wrote a letter to Elizabeth Gurley Flynn, who was raising money for his defence. He said, "Lib, stop raising money for me. They're going to kill me whether I'm in jail or out. You save that money and put it to work keepin' the presses rolling, getting people into a fighting union." That's courage. He wrote himself off. He wrote a letter to Big Bill Haywood in Chicago, saying, "Bill, don't mourn for me, but organize." And then he said, "Bill, promise me one thing: that when they kill me you'll take my body over the border into Wyoming because I don't want to get caught dead in Utah."

The morning of the execution, he was taken out of his cell and tied in that chair, enraged and impatient. According to the eyewitnesses from the Salt Lake *Tribune* and the *Desert News*, Joe Hill's last true words were "Ready, Aim, Fire," as they delivered the order for his execution. That morning he'd passed a small piece of paper out through the bars to a reporter. It proved to be Joe's last will. It said:

My will is easy to decide,
for there is nothing to divide;
My kin don't need to fuss or moan,
Moss does not cling to a rolling stone.

My body? Ah, if I could choose,
I would to ashes it reduce,
And let some merry breezes blow
them to where some flowers grow.

Perhaps some fading flower then
might come to life and bloom again.
This is my last and final will:
Good luck to all of you. Joe Hill.

They took the body to Chicago, where he was cremated. His ashes were divided up into small packages with his picture and last will, and sent wherever workers were struggling, all over the world. Excepting Utah. Not to Utah.

In 1919, during the Palmer raids, the last package of those ashes was still in the office in Chicago. You don't know this. The office was appropriated because of the Espionage Act, after the First World War. That package of ashes disappeared. It finally surfaced a couple of years ago in the National Archives in Washington, D.C. We at the office of the IWW, we went after 'em, sued for 'em. We got 'em back, too. I went to the ceremony in Washington. They kept the envelope as a permanent public record; they wouldn't give us that. But they gave us Joe Hill's ashes, what was left of them, in a little cold-cream jar.

We had a meeting of the IWW. We sent small amounts of those ashes all over the United States, but not to Utah. Some of those ashes made their way up to old Art Nurse, in Missoula, Montana. He was going to take 'em down to Butte and put 'em on the grave of Frank Little, the great Cherokee Indian organizer of the IWW who was lynched for objecting to the First World War as a bosses' war. I was living in Spokane and I went over to Art Nurse's place and said to Art – he was eighty-seven at the time – "Art, did you get the ashes?"

Art said, "Yeah, I got 'em. They showed up. You wanna see 'em?" He opened his desk drawer and took 'em out, and opened a tiny package of paper, and there were Joe's ashes. Old Art Nurse took a pinch of those ashes and he threw 'em inside the hole on this guitar.

So, hundredth anniversary, at least a little tiny bit of Joe Hill really is in fact with you ... Meanwhile my home is in Utah, and my kin are in Utah, and I can't take my damned guitar there and play music with it. I have to borrow one.

NOTES

Introduction
1. M. Solski and J. Smaller, *Mine Mill: The History of the International Union of Mine, Mill and Smelter Workers in Canada Since 1895* (Ottawa: Steel Rail Publishing, 1984), 39.
2. Until 1976 the company was known as the International Nickel Company of Canada and was often referred to as INCO. Since then the offical name has been Inco Limited. Throughout this book we refer to the company as Inco.
3. *Organizing a Mine Mill Ladies' Auxiliary* (s. l.: Mine Mill, s. d.).

Chapter 1: One Hundred Years of Mine Mill
(Editors' Note)
1. CAW Local 40 comprises the membership of the former Canadian Textile and Chemical Union – a founding member of the CCU – which merged with the CAW in 1992.

Chapter 2: The Decline of Collective Bargaining in the Private Sector
1. Leo Troy, *Convergence in International Unionism, Et Cetera: The Case of Canada and the United States*, Queen's Papers in Industrial Relations (QPIR 1991-3), Industrial Relations Centre, Queen's University, Kingston, 1991.

Chapter 4: A Chilly Season for Canadian Labour
1. Eric C. Kierans, "Short Change," *Policy Options* 7, 2 (March 1986): 4–7.
2. Economic Council of Canada, *Good Jobs, Bad Jobs: Employment in the Service Economy* (Ottawa: Minister of Supply and Services, 1990), 15.
3. *Editors' Note:* With the backing of the right-wing National Citizens Coalition (NCC), Merv Lavigne, a community college teacher in Ontario, launched a legal action seeking to stop trade unions from spending money on issues and campaigns supposedly removed from the arena of collective bargaining, such as making donations to political parties, disarmament campaigns, pro-choice causes, help for striking British miners, and aid to Nicaragua. The Ontario Court of Appeal ruled that this use of compulsory union dues for political causes was not a violation of the Charter of Rights and Freedom, and an appeal to the Supreme Court met with a similar decision. The case cost the unions $400,000. See, for instance, Bryan D. Palmer, *Working-Class Experience: Rethinking the History of Canadian Labour, 1800–1991* (Toronto: McClelland and Stewart, 1992), 403–4.
4. Robert B. Reich, *Work of Nations: Preparing Ourselves for 21st Century Capitalism* (New York: Vintage Books Division of Random House Inc., 1992), 204–5.

Chapter 5: Small Unions and Dissidents in the History of Canadian Trade Unionism
1. Bryan D. Palmer, ed., *A Communist Life: Jack Scott and the Canadian Workers Movement, 1927–1985* (St. John's, Nfld.: Committee on Canadian Labour History, 1988), 92.
2. Irving Martin Abella, *Nationalism, Communism, and Canadian Labour: The CIO, the Communist Party, and the Canadian Congress of Labour, 1935–1956* (Toronto: University of Toronto Press, 1973), 21. See also Palmer, *A Communist Life*, 251–52.

Chapter 6: Le local 902 du Mine Mill
1. En français on le nommait le syndicat des travailleurs de la ville et du district de Sudbury.
2. Pour éviter d'alourdir inutilement le texte, le générique masculin est utilisé. Il est évident que plusieurs femmes étaient membres du local 902.
3. Pour des comptes rendus de l'histoire du local 598, voir surtout John B. Lang, "A Lion in a Den of Daniels: A History of the International Union of Mine Mill and Smelter

Workers in Sudbury 1942–1962," thèse de maîtrise, University of Guelph, 1970; et Mike Solski et John Smaller, *Mine Mill: The History of the International Union of Mine, Mill and Smelter Workers in Canada Since 1895* (Ottawa: Steel Rail Publishing, 1984).

4   Archives nationales du Canada (ANC), MG 28, I, 103, vol. 94, filière 6, lettre de Carlin à Conroy, le 15 janvier 1944.
5   Voir Archives de la Province d'Ontario (APO), MU 6577, boîte 10.
6   Le local 598 a été accrédité comme agent syndical des mineurs de l'Inco et de la Falconbridge le 4 février et le 8 mars 1944 respectivement suite à un vote auprès de ces derniers les 17 et 18 décembre 1943 (Inco) et le 20 décembre 1943 (Falconbridge). La première convention collective avec l'Inco a été signée le 10 mars 1944.
7   Pour un compte rendu de ce débat, voir *The Sudbury Star*, 23 mai 1944, 5; 30 mai 1944, 1; et 6 juin 1944, 15.
8   Voir *The Sudbury Star*, 26 juillet 1943, 1; 30 novembre 1943, 2; et 7 décembre 1943, 1. Voir aussi les procès-verbaux des réunions du Board of Trade, 22 janvier, 1942, 72. De plus, voir Donald Dennie, "Sudbury 1883–1946: A Social Historical Study of Property and Class," Thèse de doctorat, Carleton University, Ottawa, 1989, 366–69.
9   ANC, MG 28, I, 103, vol. 63, filière 23, 28 février 1945.
10 Voir *The Sudbury Star*, 24 juin 1946, 3. Selon le *Star*, il s'agit d'une nouvelle unité du local 598. L'entête de l'article se lit: "Form New Unit of Local 598."
11 ANC, MG 28, I, 103, vol. 85, filière 11, lettre de Harvey Ladd, organisateur du Mine Mill à Conroy, le 5 mai 1947.
12 Des références trouvées dans les archives du local 902 conservées aux Archives publiques de l'Ontario montrent que le Sudbury General Workers Union avait réussi à organiser les travailleurs des entreprises Delongchamp Cartage et Palm Dairies. Voir APO, F1278, boîte 10.
13 Solski et Smaller, *Mine Mill*, 120. Le "finding aid" des Archives publiques de l'Ontario pour le local 902 résume ainsi l'historique du local. "In 1949, Mine Mill was expelled from the CCL being accused by that body of failing to organize important segments of the industry, and of refusal to turn over jurisdiction of those segments to the United Steelworkers of America. Suspecting that the CCL might try to penetrate and make headway with union activity in the Sudbury Basin in other industries than mining, Mine Mill chartered Local 902, Sudbury & District General Workers' Union in October 1949 to work toward building and maintaining a base of support in the general trades, including taxi companies, lumbering businesses, hotels, retail outlets, metal workers and wherever else they would sign up membership."
14 Voir l'édition du 21 octobre 1949, vol. 1, no. 1, 1.
15 Ibid.
16 Selon Craig Heron, les Métallos ont été à l'avant-garde du mouvement anticommuniste à cette époque. Voir Craig Heron, *The Canadian Labour Movement* (Toronto: Lorimer, 1989).
17 APO, F1278, boîte 1, filière "Radio Lunch Strike," lettre en date du 12 mai 1950 envoyée à Al Langlois, organisateur du local 902.
18 *Local 598 Mine Mill News*, 14 octobre 1956, 2.
19 ANC, MG 28, 1, 103, vol. 94, filière 6, lettre de William Steel à Conroy, le 9 juin 1944.
20 En 1959, les bureaux du local 902 ont été déménagés sur la rue Douglas. Voir *Local 598 Mine Mill News*, le 13 juillet 1959, 6. Selon Mike Solski, ce déménagement a été orchestré par le nouveau président du local 598, M. Don Gillis. Selon M. Solski, "When Local 902 came under the fraudulent Gillis administration, one of the first moves in the conspiracy to destabilize Mine Mill was to evict Local 902 from occupancy of office space in the Sudbury union hall and to sabotage the work of the local and undermine its leadership." Solski et Smaller, *Mine Mill*, 121.
21 Dans l'édition du 18 novembre 1949, le *Local 598 Mine Mill News* a rapporté ce qui suit:

"Election of officers for Local 902, Sudbury and District General Workers, I.U.M.M.& S.W. resulted in Gordon Robinson being installed president of the new Mine Mill local, Mike Pavarnik, vice-president and Aurelle Lavigne, secretary."

22 Voir le *Local 598 Mine Mill News*, 16 mars 1953, 1. M. LaChance est demeuré agent d'affaires du local 902 jusqu'à sa fusion avec les Métallos en 1967. Il a ensuite occupé ce même poste au sein du syndicat Retail, Wholesale and Department Store Union.

23 C'est du moins l'évaluation qu'a faite un ancien président du local, M. Maurice Boissonneault, lors d'une interview par téléphone. En plus d'être président, M. Boissonneault a occupé les postes de conseiller et de président de son groupe.

24 En 1954, l'agent d'affaires du local 902, R.A. LaChance, affirmait que la négociation des conventions occupait 80 pour cent des activités du local 902. Voir APO, F 1271, boîte 3, procès-verbal du congrès du district 8 du Mine Mill tenu le 15 mai 1954 à Sudbury.

25 Selon Maurice Boissonneault.

26 La liste de ces hôtels est la suivante: Coulson, King Edward, International, Nickel Range, Balmoral, Ramsay, Queen's, Paris, Park, National, Frood, Ontario, Ledo, Prospect, Frontenac, Nickel City. Voir *Local 598 Mine Mill News*, le 30 avril 1951, 4.

27 APO, F1278, boîte 1, décision de la Commission des relations du travail de l'Ontario, 6 novembre 1950.

28 APO, F 1278, boîte 1, filière Hotels, lettre du 9 juin 1950. Au cours des années, les hôtels ont négocié en groupe sous les auspices du Sudbury Hotelmen's Association.

29 Pour des exemples de ces conventions collectives, voir celles signées avec les compagnies Laberge et Standard Dairy, APO, F1278, boîte 1.

30 En certains cas, le local 902 a mené des campagnes d'organisation pour remplacer des cellules du CCT ou de syndicats internationaux. Ainsi, les employés des laiteries Standard et Palm se sont ralliés au local 902 après avoir été membres d'une cellule du CCT. Les employés de la firme Evans étaient autrefois représentés par le syndicat International Woodworkers, ceux de Dominion Tar & Chemical par l'International Brotherhood of Carpenters & Joiners, et ceux de Delongchamp Cartage par le Canadian Brotherhood of Railway Employees. Le local 902 ne réussit pas toutefois à organiser les employés de la firme Carrington Lumber & Builders qui refusèrent de s'affilier au Mine Mill lors de la tenue d'un scrutin le 28 mai 1952.

31 *Local 598 Mine Mill News*, 31 août 1953, 3.

32 Ibid.

33 *Local 598 Mine Mill News*, 3 décembre 1953, 3 et APO, F1278, boîte 11, filière Murray's.

34 APO, F1278, boîte 3.

35 APO, F1278, boîte 3.

36 Pour une demande typique, voir celles contenues dans APO, F1278, boîte 3, filière National Grocers et boîte 11, filière Murray's Restaurant.

37 APO, F1278, boîte 3, filière I.U.M.M.&S.W.

38 *Local 598 Mine Mill News*, 29 mars 1954, 4.

39 C'est ainsi l'attitude des négociateurs pour la boulangerie Cecutti's à l'automne de 1953. Voir APO, F1278, boîte 10, filière Cecutti's.

40 *Local 598 Mine Mill News*, 21 décembre 1953, 3 et 18 janvier 1954, 1. Voir aussi APO, F1278, boîte 4.

41 APO, F1278, filière Loblaws Groceterias Contract and Renewal.

42 Entrevue téléphonique.

43 Voir *Local 598 Mine Mill News*, 17 février 1955, 3 et 29 juin 1955, 7. Voir aussi APO, F1278, boîte 14, filière Cochrane Dunlop.

44 Ce vote a été gagné de justesse 40 voix pour, 37 voix contre. Voir APO, F1278, boîte 14. Le vote a eu lieu le 2 mai 1955.

45 *Local 598 Mine Mill News*, 29 juin, 1954, 7.
46 Voir *Local 598 Mine Mill News*, 5 octobre 1955, 7 et 26 octobre 1955, 3.
47 Voir le *Local 598 Mine Mill News*, 13 mai 1957, 7.
48 *Local 598 Mine Mill News*, 15 décembre 1955, 7. Les documents ne permettent pas de connaître la suite de cet épisode. La section 78 donnait le droit à un conseil municipal d'adopter un règlement pour empêcher que des employés municipaux soient syndiqués. C'est ce droit qu'exerça le Conseil municipal de Sudbury contre les femmes mais non contre les hommes préposés à l'entretien des écoles.
49 Voir APO, F1278, boîte 4. Voir aussi *Local 598 Mine Mill News*, 13 juillet 1959, 6.
50 Il est intéressant de noter qu'en 1949, les employés municipaux de la municipalité Neelon Garson, dont Don Gillis était le maire, ont effectué un arrêt de travail de neuf jours pour protester contre le fait que la municipalité avait refusé de nommer un représentant au sein d'un comité d'arbitrage pour résoudre le cas de deux employés qui avaient été remerciés de leur service. Lorsque les employés sont revenus au travail, après avoir reçu l'assurance que ces congédiements allaient faire l'objet d'une procédure légale de griefs, la municipalité leur a remis une lettre les avisant qu'ils allaient perdre cinq jours de salaire comme punition pour leur geste. Voir APO, F1278, boîte 4.
51 *Local 598 Mine Mill News*, octobre 1950, 3.
52 *Local 598 Mine Mill News*, 25 avril 1955, 7.

Chapter 7: Mergers, Organizing, and Collective Identity

1 The research for this article was funded by the Social Sciences and Humanities Research Council of Canada, project 410-90-1446. Special thanks to Kathy Bennett and Nancy Kearnan of the CAW, who acted as resource guides throughout this project. Thanks also to Cara MacDonald, who was an excellent research assistant.
2 For a discussion of these issues, see Mary Lou Coates, "Industrial Relations in 1990: Trends and Emerging Issues" (Kingston: Queen's University, Centre for Industrial Relations, 1991), 51–54.
3 Many authors over the past thirty years have debated the issues of union size, bureaucratization, and the capacity to take collective action. See Mancur Olson, *The Logic of Collective Action* (Cambridge, MA: Harvard University Press, 1971); S.M. Lipset, Martin Trow, and James Coleman, *Union Democracy* (New York: Free Press, 1956); Claus Offe and Helmut Wiesenthal, "The Two Logics of Collective Action," in *Disorganized Capitalism*, ed. C. Offe (Cambridge, MA: MIT Press, 1985), 170–220.
4 See Offe and Wiesenthal, "Two Logics."
5 Ibid., 186.
6 Colin Crouch, *Trade Unions: The Logic of Collective Action* (London: Fontana Paperbacks, 1982), 166–67.
7 Richard Hyman, *Industrial Relations: A Marxist Introduction* (Basingstoke, U.K.: The Macmillan Press, 1975), 73–74; Colin Crouch and Alexandro Pizzorno, *The Resurgence of Class Conflict in Western Europe since 1968*, 2 vols. (New York: Holmes and Meir Publications, 1978).
8 An important contemporary example of changing union structures in response to incoming new membership groups can be seen with the changing structures that accompany massive increases in the number and mobilization of women union members. Women's committees and affirmative action programs to ensure that women become union leaders are but two examples of these changing structures. See Julie White, *Sisters and Solidarity: Women and Unions in Canada* (Toronto: Thompson Educational Publishing, 1993), especially chaps. 4 and 5, and Linda Briskin and Patricia McDermott, *Women Challenging Unions: Feminism, Democracy and Militancy* (Toronto: University of Toronto Press, 1993), chaps. 4, 5, and 6.
9 Charlotte Yates, *From Plant to Politics: The Autoworkers Union in Postwar Canada* (Philadelphia: Temple University Press, 1993), chap. 9.

10 For analysis of the restructuring of the Canadian auto industry see John Holmes, "The Globalization of Production and Canada's Mature Industries: The Case of the Auto Industry," in *The Era of New Competition*, ed. D. Drache and M. Gertler (Montreal and Kingston: McGill-Queen's University Press, 1991), 153–80; J. Holmes, "From Three Industries to One," in *Driving Continentally: National Policies and the North American Auto Industry*, ed. M. Molot (Ottawa: Carleton University Press, 1993), 23–61.
11 For Bob White's discussion of the metalworkers federation see "Canadian UAW Director's Report to Canadian Council," June 25, 26, 1983, 8–9.
12 Labour Canada, *Directory of Labour Organizations in Canada,* Ottawa, 1980, 1983, 1985.
13 CAW, Reports, Executive Board Trustees and National Secretary-Treasurer; Auditors' Reports, 1986–91, Dunwoody & Co.
14 The figure of thirty-eight thousand for new members is an approximation that tries to take into account as accurately as possible the overlap of merger data dealing with fish plants. Figures are based on calculations made on data accumulated from Reports of the Organizing Department included in National and Area Staff Reports to CAW Council, March, June, 1985; March, September, December, 1986; June, November, 1987; March, October, 1988; February, June, September, 1989; February, August, December, 1990; April, December, 1991; April, August, December, 1992.
15 Interview with Gary Fane, director, CAW Organizing Department, June 17, 1993.
16 Merger agreement between CTCU and CAW, April 22, 1992. Telephone interview with Laurell Ritchie, May 1, 1993.
17 Membership numbers are difficult to estimate accurately as membership in the fishworkers unions tends to fluctuate wildly owing to the cyclical nature of the industry and mergers are continually being concluded. In addition to CALEA, the CAW has merged with: Canadian Association of Passenger Agents (CAPA), 1987; Fishermen, Food and Allied Workers Union (FFAW), 1987; TAP (Air Portugal), 1987; IBL Industries, 1987; Coca Cola, 1988; Consumers Gas, 1988; Great Lakes Fishermen and Allied Workers Union, 1988; Canadian Seafood and Allied Workers, 1989; Brotherhood of Railway Carmen, 1990; Transportation Communications Union (TCU), 1990; Canadian Association of Industrial, Mechanical and Allied Workers (CAIMAW), 1992; Canadian Textile and Chemical Union (CTCU), 1992; United Electrical Workers (UE), 1993; Canadian Union of Mine, Mill and Smelter Workers, 1993; Canadian Railway Union, 1994; Canadian Brotherhood of Railway, Transport and General Workers (CBRT&GW), 1994; Canadian Association of Smelter and Allied Workers, 1994; PPG Glass, 1994.
18 The figure of 170,000 comes from the CAW's "Report to the National Collective Bargaining and Political Action Convention," Toronto, May 1993. This figure is substantially higher than the 153,048 reported in the 1992–93 Labour Canada *Directory of Labour Organizations in Canada.* The reason for the discrepancy lies in the additional memberships gained by the CAW in early 1993 due to the completion of the mergers with the CTCU and UE and of various organizing drives.
19 CAW, "Report to the National Collective Bargaining and Political Action Conventions," 1979, 1990, 1993. Similar figures are not available for visible minorities, but for comments on the increase in visible minorities as part of the CAW membership, see CAW President Buzz Hargrove's report to Canadian Council, June 27, 1992, 29–31.
20 For a comprehensive treatment of this argument concerning Canadian autoworkers' resistance to the terms of the postwar compromise and the continued strategic possibilities for militant action, see Yates, *From Plant to Politics.*
21 For example, see the terms of the CAIMAW merger with the CAW under the heading Article 14, Constitution, subsections (c), (d), (e); from "Terms of Merger between CAIMAW and CAW," November 1991.
22 Recent analysis of CAW staffing practices has suggested that the CAW has avoided appointing women to national representative jobs and has instead concentrated them in areas of

special assignment such as health and safety. This is likely to have less impact on rank-and-file attitudes and culture as these members are not forced to deal daily with women on issues such as wages. See White, *Sisters and Solidarity*, especially chap. 4, "Moving Up: Women into Union Leadership," 99–122, and chap. 5, "Women's Activities and Issues Inside Unions," 123–58. See also Briskin and McDermott, *Women Challenging Unions*, especially chap. 6, "Women working for the unions: female staff and the politics of transformation," 137–57, by J. Stinson and P. Richmond.

23 For discussion of district councils and their critical role in the development of the Canadian UAW, see Yates, *From Plant to Politics*. For a more general discussion of the importance of mobilizational structures in the Canadian UAW, see C. Yates, "North American Autoworkers' Response to Restructuring," in *Bargaining for Change: Union Politics in North America and Europe*, ed. M. Golden and J. Pontusson (Ithaca, NY: Cornell University Press, 1992), 119–22.

24 "Merger Agreement between CAW and FFAW," sections 2 and 5, September 1988; "Merger Agreement between CTCU and CAW," section 3, circa 1990; "Merger Agreement between the TCU and CAW," sections 3, 11, and 17, 1990.

Chapter 8: Women and the Changing Face of Labour in Northeastern Ontario

1 Unfortunately an eighth participant from the women's committee of Local 6500 of USWA representing hourly-rated workers at Inco was unable to attend on the day of the conference. This left a gap on the panel and, as a result, the discussion in this chapter does not reflect the role of unionized women who work in jobs that have been historically male-dominated in the industrial sector. We would also like to remind readers that the panel addressed the concerns of unionized women, and we recognize that the concerns of non-unionized working women have yet to be discussed.

2 See Denise Thibeault, "A Union without women is only half organized: a history of the Sudbury Mine Mill and Smelter Workers Union, Local 598 Ladies Auxiliary," unpublished paper, York University, 1987, and Meg Luxton, "From Ladies Auxiliaries to Wives Committees," in *Union Sisters: Women in the Labour Movement*, ed. L. Briskin and L. Yanz (Toronto: Women's Press, 1983).

3 Mike Solski and John Smaller, *Mine Mill: The History of the International Union of Mine, Mill and Smelter Workers in Canada Since 1895* (Ottawa: Steel Rail Publishing, 1984), 92.

4 Heather Jon Maroney, "Feminism at Work," in *Feminism and Political Economy: Women's Work, Women's Struggles*, ed. Heather Jon Maroney and Meg Luxton (Toronto: Methuen, 1987), 95; and Arja Lane, "Wives Supporting the Strike" in *Union Sisters*, ed. Briskin and Yanz, 322. See also the 16mm/VHS (73 min.) film, *A Wives' Tale*, produced by S. Bissonnette, M. Duckworth, and J. Rock (1980) and distributed by Full Frame Film and Video Distribution of Toronto.

5 Julie White, *Sisters and Solidarity: Women and Unions in Canada* (Toronto: Thompson Educational Publishing, 1993), 49–51.

6 Isabella Bakker, "Women's Employment in Comparative Perspective," in *Feminization of the Labour Force: Paradoxes and Promises*, ed. Jane Jenson, Elisabeth Hagen, and Ceallaigh Reddy (New York: Oxford, 1988), 19; White, *Sisters and Solidarity*, 46.

7 Ontario Women's Directorate, *Labour Force Infoflash*, no. 2. (September 1991): 4; Vic Satzewich and Terry Wotherspoon, *First Nations: Race, Class, and Gender Relations* (Toronto: Nelson Canada, 1993), 73. In communities such as Elliot Lake, for example, the unemployment rate is currently estimated to be at least 50 percent. See David Leadbeater and Peter Suschnigg, "Training as a Principal Focus of Adjustment Policy: A View From Northeastern Ontario," paper presented to the Canadian Industrial Relations Association, Ottawa, June 5, 1993.

8 For the City of Sudbury, the establishment of the federal government's Taxation Data Centre in 1982, the creation of the provincial tourist attraction Science North in 1984,

and the more recent transfer of the provincial Ministry of Northern Development and Mines offices are examples. See "1970s," in C.W. Wallace and A. Thompson, eds., *Sudbury: Rail Town to Regional Capital* (Toronto: Dundurn Press, 1993), 242–74.
9 White, *Sisters and Solidarity*, 59.
10 Jennifer Keck and Daina Green, "Pay Equity for Non-unionized Women: A Case Study," in *And Still We Rise*, ed. Linda Carty (Toronto: Women's Press, 1993).
11 White, *Sisters and Solidarity*, 167.
12 Ibid.
13 Katherine Scott, "Labour and the Welfare State: Labour Relations in the Community Service Sector," paper presented to the Canadian Political Science Association, Charlottetown, P.E.I., June 2, 1992.

Chapter 9: Labour Law and Fragmentation before Statutory Collective Bargaining
1 Research funding for this project was provided by a grant from the Social Sciences and Humanities Research Council of Canada.
2 For example, see Mark Rosenfeld, "'She Was a Hard Life': Work, Family, Community, Politics and Ideology in the Railway Ward of a Central Ontario Town, 1900–1960" (Ph.D. thesis, York University, 1990); and E. Faue, *Community of Suffering and Struggle* (Chapel Hill: University of North Carolina Press, 1991), 1–18. See also Joan Acker, "Class, Gender, and the Relations of Distribution," *Signs* 13 (Spring 1988): 473–97, especially p. 496, in which Acker argues persuasively that relations of distribution as well as relations of production are central to working-class life.
3 Cardinal Manning to Sidney Buxton, January 21, 1890, cited in J. Ballhatchet, "The Police and the London Dock Strike of 1889," *History Workshop Journal* 32 (1990): 54–68.
4 Claus Offe and Helmut Wiesenthal, "Two Logics of Collective Action: Theoretical Notes on Social Class and Organizational Form," *Political Power and Social Theory* 1 (1980): 67–115.
5 This is a preliminary report on a larger project that examines this period in much greater detail. The project is only partially completed and so many of the observations here are tentative. I have nearly completed a study of nineteenth-century labour law and my colleague Judy Fudge and I are just beginning a study of the period 1900–1945. For another overview, see Craig Heron, "Afterword: Male Wage-Earners and the State in Canada," 241–64; and Michael Earle and Ian McKay, "Introduction: Industrial Legality in Nova Scotia," 9–23, in *Workers and the State in Twentieth Century Nova Scotia*, ed. Michael Earle (Fredericton: Gorsebrook Research Institute, 1989).
6 For overviews of this period, see Bryan D. Palmer, *Working-Class Experience: Rethinking the History of Canadian Labour, 1800–1991*, 2nd ed. (Toronto: McClelland and Stewart, 1992), 81–116.
7 For example, see Karen Orren, *Belated Feudalism* (Cambridge: Cambridge University Press, 1991); and Robert J. Steinfeld, *The Invention of Free Labor: The Employment Relation in English and American Law and Culture, 1350–1870* (Chapel Hill: University of North Carolina Press, 1991). See also Douglas Hay and Paul Craven, "Master and Servant in England and the Empire: A Comparative Study," *Labour/Le Travail* 31 (1993): 175–84. On its use in strikes, see Gregory S. Kealey, *Toronto Workers Respond to Industrial Capitalism 1867–1892* (Toronto: University of Toronto Press, 1980), 148–49.
8 For a more detailed discussion of Canadian developments, see Eric Tucker, "'That Indefinite Area of Toleration': Criminal Conspiracy and Trade Unions in Ontario, 1837–77," *Labour/Le Travail* 27 (1991): 15–54. For a good overview of the English background, see John Orth, *Combinations and Conspiracy* (Oxford: Clarendon, 1991); and Richard Kidder, "The Development of the Picketing Immunity: 1825–1906," *Legal Studies* 13 (1993): 103–20.
9 On the United States, see Jeremy Brecher, *Strike!* (Boston: South End Press, 1987).

10. On the Knights, see Gregory S. Kealey and Bryan D. Palmer, *Dreaming of What Might Be* (Toronto: New Hogtown Press, 1987). On conflicts of the 1880s, see Eric Tucker, "The Faces of Coercion: The Legal Regulation of Labour Conflict in Ontario, 1880–1889," *Law & History Review* 12, 4 (forthcoming 1994).
11. *R. v. Gibson* (1889) 16 O.R. 704 (Q.B.D.) and S.C. 1890, c.37, s.19.
12. Craig Heron, "The Second Industrial Revolution in Canada, 1890–1930," in *Class, Community and the Labour Movement: Wales and Canada 1850–1930*, ed. Deian R. Hopkin and Gregory S. Kealey (Wales: LLAFUR/CCLH, 1989), 48–66.
13. David M. Gordon et al., *Segmented Work, Divided Workers* (Cambridge: Cambridge University Press, 1982), 100–64.
14. Douglas Cruikshank and Gregory S. Kealey, "Strikes in Canada, 1891–1950," *Labour/Le Travail* 20 (1987): 85–145, see especially p. 100.
15. Jacob Finkelman, "The Law of Picketing in Canada: I," *University of Toronto Law Journal* 2 (1937–38): 67–101, see especially pp. 83–101; A.W.R. Carrothers, *Collective Bargaining Law in Canada* (Toronto: Butterworths, 1965), 440–47 and cases cited therein.
16. *The King v. Russell* (1920) 51 D.L.R. 1 (Man. C.A.).
17. Barbara Roberts, *From Whence They Came: Deportation in Canada from 1900–1935* (Ottawa: University of Ottawa Press, 1988), 71–77.
18. William M. Baker, "The Miners and the Mounties: The Royal North West Mounted Police and the 1906 Strike," *Labour/Le Travail* 27 (1991): 55–96.
19. S.W. Horrall, "The Royal North-West Mounted Police and Labour Unrest in Western Canada, 1919," *Canadian Historical Review* 61 (1980): 169–90.
20. J.J.B. Pariseau, *Disorders, Strikes and Disasters: Military Aid to the Civil Power in Canada, 1867–1933* (Ottawa: National Defence Headquarters, 1973); and Desmond Morton, "Aid to the Civil Power: The Canadian Militia in Support of Social Order, 1867–1914," *Canadian Historical Review* 51 (1970): 407–25.
21. On the role of non-enforcement in the Rossland miners' strike, see A. Ross McCormack, *Reformers, Rebels, and Revolutionaries: The Western Canadian Radical Movement 1899–1919* (Toronto: University of Toronto Press, 1977), 39. Lack of enforcement of the Alien Labour Act had led to the failure of earlier B.C. strikes, and the labour movement subsequently campaigned for reforms. See Jeremy Mouat, "The Genesis of Western Exceptionalism: British Columbia's Hard-Rock Miners, 1895–1903," *Canadian Historical Review* 71 (1990): 313–45, see especially pp. 324–28.
22. Although there had been some attempts to exploit these possibilities in both Great Britain and Canada during the second half of the nineteenth century, success had been limited and significant doctrinal hurdles needed to be overcome. For England, see A.W.J. Thomson, "The Injunction in Trade Disputes in Britain before 1910," *Industrial and Labor Relations Review* 19 (1965–66): 213–23; and for Canada see Tucker, "The Faces of Coercion."
23. *Lumley v. Gye* (1853) 2 E.&B. 216.
24. *Quinn v. Leathem* [1901] A.C. 495.
25. *Taff Vale Ry. Co. v. Amal. Soc. of Railway Servants* [1901] A.C. 426.
26. Mouat, "Genesis"; McCormack, *Reformers, Rebels;* and Martin Robin, *Canadian Politics and Canadian Labour* (Kingston: Industrial Relations Centre, Queen's University, 1968), 53–54.
27. *Le Roi Mining Company, Ltd. v. Rossland Miners Union, No. 38* (1901) 8 B.C.R. 370.
28. *Centre Star Mining Co. v. Rossland Miners Union, No. 38* (1905) 11 B.C.R. 194.
29. The Gurney litigation did not produce reported decisions. The *Metallic Roofing* case did. See (1903) 2 O.W.R. 266 (Div. Ct.); (1903) 5 O.L.R. 424 (Div. Ct.); (1905) 9 O.L.R. 171 (C.A.); (1906) 12 O.L.R. 200 (Div. Ct.); (1907) 14 O.L.R. 156 (C.A.) and [1908] A.C. 514.
30. *Krug Furniture Co. v. Berlin Union of Amalgamated Woodworkers* (1903) 5 O.L.R. 463.

31 For references to some of these other cases and discussion of the Dominion Trades and Labour Congress reaction, see Paul Craven, 'An Impartial Umpire': Industrial Relations and the Canadian State 1900–1911 (Toronto: University of Toronto Press, 1980), 200–7.
32 S.B.C. 1902, c.66; and A.W.R. Carrothers, "A Legislative History of the B.C. Trade-unions Act: The Rossland Miners' Case," *University of British Columbia Legal Notes* 2, 4 (1956): 339–46.
33 For example, in Manitoba see *Cotter* v. *Osborne* (1908) 8 W.L.R. 451. Also, David Jay Bercuson, *Confrontation at Winnipeg*, rev. ed. (Montreal and Kingston: McGill-Queen's University Press, 1990), 45–57, argues that injunctions radicalized the Winnipeg labour movement.
34 This order was repealed a little over a month later, after the Armistice had been signed on November 11, 1918. See Bercuson, *Confrontation*, 80–83.
35 Gregory S. Kealey, "State Repression of Labour and the Left in Canada, 1914–20: The Impact of the First World War," *Canadian Historical Review* 73, 3 (1992): 281–314; Richard Fidler, "Proscribing Unlawful Associations: The Swift Rise and Agonizing Demise of Section 98," unpublished paper, 1984; and Roberts, *From Whence They Came*.
36 Kealey, "State Repression"; and Heron, "Afterword: Male Wage-Earners and the State," 249.
37 Judy A. Fudge, "Voluntarism and Compulsion: The Canadian Federal Government's Intervention in Collective Bargaining from 1900 to 1946" (D.Phil. thesis, University of Oxford, 1988), 1–22; and Jeremy Webber, "Compelling Compromise: Canada Chooses Conciliation over Arbitration, 1900–1907," *Labour/Le Travail* 28 (1991): 15–57.
38 Margaret E. McCallum, "Labour and Arbitration in the Mowat Era," *Canadian Journal of Law and Society* 6 (1991): 65–90, and "The Mines Arbitration Act, 1888: Compulsory Arbitration in Context," in *Essays in the History of Canadian Law*, ed. Philip Girard and Jim Phillips, vol. 3: *Nova Scotia* (Toronto: Osgoode Society, 1990), 303–25; Mouat, "Genesis," 337–42; *Labour Conciliation and Arbitration Act*, S.B.C. 1894, c.23. Of course, a good deal of informal arbitration and mediation occurred on an ad hoc basis.
39 *Conciliation Act*, S.C. 1900, c.24.
40 Bob Russell, *Back to Work?* (Scarborough, ON: Nelson Canada, 1990), 57–89.
41 King Diaries, cited in Russell, *Back to Work?*, 72. See also McCormack, *Reformers, Rebels*, 40.
42 Royal Commission on Industrial Disputes in the Province of British Columbia, *Report*, Sessional Paper 36a (1903), 65ff, cited in Craven, *Impartial Umpire*, 250.
43 Webber, "Compelling Compromise," 38. For a discussion of the strike itself (which involved the killing of Frank Rogers, a popular labour and socialist leader, by special police hired to protect the CPR tracks), see McCormack, *Reformers, Rebels*, 44–48.
44 Russell, *Back to Work?*, 96.
45 William M. Baker, "The Miners and the Mediator: The 1906 Lethbridge Strike and Mackenzie King," *Labour/Le Travail* 11 (1983): 89–117.
46 S.C. 1907, c.20.
47 Russell, *Back to Work?*, 107.
48 Ibid., 155–60.
49 Jeremy Webber, "The Mediation of Ideology: How Mediation Boards, through the Mediation of the Particular Disputes, Fashioned a Vision of Labour's Place within Canadian Society," *Law in Context* 7, 2 (1989): 1–23.
50 *Toronto Electric Commissioners* v. *Snider* [1925] A.C. 396; and F.R. Scott, *Essays on the Constitution* (Toronto: University of Toronto Press, 1977), 336–52.
51 See the accounts in Irving Abella, ed., *On Strike* (Toronto: James Lorimer, 1975). The end of the use of the militia did not mean that local police forces could not obtain additional assistance. For example, in the Oshawa autoworkers' strike of 1937, Premier

Hepburn dispatched four hundred provincial police officers, whom the press dubbed "Hepburn's Hussars." See Laurel Sefton MacDowell, "After the Strike – Labour Relations in Oshawa, 1937–1939," *Relations industrielles/Industrial Relations* 48, 4 (Autumn 1993): 691–711, see especially p. 693.
52 On Nova Scotia, see Margaret E. McCallum, "The Acadia Coal Strike, 1934: Thinking About Law and the State," *University of New Brunswick Law Journal* 41 (1992): 179–96; and Earle and McKay, "Introduction."
53 For a full discussion of the development of labour policy during the war years, see Russell, *Back to Work?*, 183–201; Judy Fudge, "Voluntarism, Compulsion and the Transformation of Canadian Labour Law during World War II," in *Canadian and Australian Labour History*, ed. Greg Patmore and Gregory S. Kealey (Sydney: ASSLH/CCLH, 1990), 81–100; and Laurel Sefton MacDowell, "The Formation of the Canadian Industrial Relations System During World War Two," *Labour/Le Travail* 3 (1978): 175–96.

Chapter 10: Labour Law Reform in Ontario
1 Since May 1993, when this paper was presented at the Sudbury conference, there have been some interpretations and applications of Bill 40. While some are positive (more applications for certification, some anti-scab protection), they have not undermined the critique of the fundamentals of Bill 40 offered here and at the conference.
2 *Labour Relations Act*, R.S.O. 1990, c.L-2, as am. by S.O. 1992, c.21.
3 One of those reasons was the ridiculous amount of time and effort spent on constitution-making. For instance, the Ontario NDP government proudly claimed to be the force behind the social covenant movement. This claim was an exaggeration; see H.J. Glasbeek, "The Social Charter: Poor Politics for the Poor," in *Social Justice and the Constitution*, ed. J. Bakan and D. Schneiderman (Ottawa: Carleton University Press, 1992), 115–23; but the desire to be seen as the social covenant's motivating force reveals much about this government's politics. The proposed social covenant committed itself to a decent standard of living and dignity for all, which included full employment and the right of all to engage in collective bargaining. No part of the proposed social covenant was to be justiciable, however, and, therefore, no attempt was to be made to have it enforceable. There was something hypocritical about the fierceness of the NDP's rhetorical support for this social covenant and its lack of legislative action. The Ontario NDP could have embedded the same sentiments in the Ontario Constitution or, even more directly, in Ontario's statute books. There was nothing important it sought to achieve through the social covenant package which fell outside provincial jurisdiction. The support for the social covenant proposal was meant to show that the NDP's endorsement of the new federal package was fulsome because now the refurbished Canadian capitalism could be said to have been given a human face. That is, Rae and his advisers understood the harsh philosophy of capitalism all too well. Their point was not to change it.
4 It also reflected the dominant practice, if not the law, in Ontario.
5 This is actually not very much unlike the outcome of the board's decision in the Eaton's case. It was held there that a limited right of access had to be given to make organization and collective bargaining in shopping malls a realistic possibility. To be fair, unions could not rely on this as a valuable precedent because the primary target – Eaton's – was a major shareholder in the third-party enterprise that owned the shopping mall; see *T. Eaton Co. Ltd., The Cadillac-Fairview Corp. Ltd & T.E.C. Leasehold Ltd and R.W.D.S.U.* (1985), 10 C.L.R.B.R. (N.S.) (O.L.R.B.); and the protection afforded by the board's decision may not have been available where this kind of intermingling was absent. Bill 40 is, therefore, a positive – if limited – advance.
6 The arguments that support making shopping malls open territory for organizing and picketing are that (i), legal trade union activity is to be encouraged as a matter of public policy and that (ii), it could not go on at all in shopping malls as the law stood before Bill

40 and that (iii), in any event, third-party property owners cannot have it all ways: to vigorously pretend their property is a public place on a daily basis and, then, on a whim, to say that it is private property, just as their homes are. By legislating access to shopping malls in the restrictive way the NDP did, it actually undermined this latter, and very important, pro-public space argumentation.

7   There is a jurisprudential context that gives the failure to act on these two issues particular significance. Successor rights and related employer provisions are the subject of much litigation. Recently there has been a tendency for labour relations boards to give these provisions pro-union readings, in line with the argument in the text that follows to the effect that these administrative agencies have a stake in the survival of trade unions and in their reputation as monitors of anti-collective bargaining practices. But the judiciary appears to be frowning on these expansive readings of the legislation. This is creating some hesitation in the labour relations boards. For some elaboration of this argument, see H.J. Glasbeek, "Agenda for Canadian Labour Reform: A Little Liberal Law, Much More Democratic Socialist Politics," *Osgoode Hall Law Journal* 31 (1993): 233–63. What the Labour Relations Board needed was a clear signal that its pro-union interpretations were on the right track. This was not given, leaving it to an uncertain board to determine its mandate.

8   This was a reaction to what had been a long-standing problem for unions and their allies in Ontario. Judicial and political struggles had been waged in respect of workers who had been jerked around by employers who owned large office towers and changed their cleaning subcontractors; see the Majestic Cleaners case and the fierce strike fought by immigrant women who did cleaning jobs in Toronto's tall towers. The NDP's need to act on this front to consolidate these union drives, regardless of employer opposition, was politically unavoidable.

9   Ontario Ministry of Labour, "Highlights, Labour Relations Act Reform, An Outline of The Original Proposals, The Impact of Consultation, and The Government's Changes" (Toronto, 1992).

10 Another such provision is a lower threshold requirement for an applying trade union in order to have a certification vote ordered (40 percent), although the NDP, in its efforts to keep employer opposition down, has retained the old threshold – 55 percent of cards to be signed – for certification without a vote. The change of emphasis on what is required for automatic certification when the atmosphere has been poisoned is a welcome, if minor, advance.

11 O'Grady estimates that the elimination of petitions might improve union organization, outside the construction industry, if everything goes absolutely well, by about 3,000 members every year over the average 17,000 or so in the years 1982–88. He points out that an extra 13,000 to 23,000 are needed to reverse the downward trend. More generally, he concludes that it is "undeniable" that "reform of the OLRA along the lines proposed by trade unions and their allies will be helpful." Still, that "these reforms will reverse the trajectory of decline is highly doubtful." See J. O'Grady, "Beyond the Wagner Act, What Next?" in *Getting on Track: Social Democratic Strategies in Ontario*, ed. D. Drache (Montreal and Kingston: McGill-Queen's University Press, 1991).

12 The right of domestic workers to organize is an empty one. Employers tend to have only one such employee.

13 This is true even though the anti-scab provisions, the consolidated bargaining union provisions, and the OLRB's increased remedial powers vis-à-vis unfair labour practices and bad-faith bargaining help somewhat.

14 The 1989/90 Annual Report of the Ontario Labour Relations Board recorded that the average size of the bargaining units in 573 applications that led to certification was thirty employees, the same number as in the year 1988/89. In construction, the units certified averaged seven employees, and in non-construction forty-one employees. Some 82 percent of the total certifications involved units of fewer than forty employees, and

42 percent of certifications involved units of ten employees.
15 What labour has got by dint of Bill 40 are new consultation processes that are to involve the government more directly as a facilitator. Inasmuch as an employer's insolvency leaves workers adrift with wages owed, the NDP government intervened by making, first, the taxpayer responsible to make good these losses, and second, the corporate actors and directors hardly at all; see the *Employee Wage Protection Plan* legislation. That is, no serious attempt was made to make it more costly for employers to run places down and leave workers holding the bag. By 1993 $73 million had been paid out of the plan to workers who, as a result of a corporate failure, were owed money. Not one penny had been recovered from a director.
16 Task Force on Labour Relations (Woods Task Force), *Final Report* (Ontario: Privy Council Office, 1968), paras. 271–75.
17 This is why hours of work and health and safety fights are so dramatic and important. They bring out the inherent conflictual nature of a relationship in which a subject who is a party to the contract is also its object.
18 M. Piore and C. Sabel, *The Second Industrial Divide* (New York: Basic Books, 1984). For a brief discussion of the entente in Europe and a longer one of the Canadian compromise, see D. Drache and H. Glasbeek, *The Changing Workplace: Reshaping Canada's Industrial Relations System* (Toronto: James Lorimer, 1992).
19 The classic statement is John T. Dunlop, *The Industrial Relations System* (New York: Holt, 1958). It became, and remains, the credo of liberal industrial pluralists. For an excellent historical appraisal, see J. Atleson, *Values and Assumptions in American Labor Law* (Amherst, MA: University of Massachusetts Press, 1983); for the standard Canadian approach to, and acceptance of, this liberal pluralistic tenet, see P. Weiler, *Reconcilable Differences: New Directions in Canadian Labour Law* (Toronto: Carswell, 1980).
20 Task Force on Labour Relations, *Final Report*, paras. 392–93.
21 The ally doctrine permits a trade union to use collective economic tools against businesses that carry out the functions of a legally struck primary target. The question of who is an ally for those purposes is a vexed one. What this means in practice is that workers can never be sure that they will be protected when attacking other places of business than that of their primary employers. Secondary boycotts are not tolerated by the law and the penalties are severe. The hazy state of the law is illustrated by the debates over the law's formulation, the relationships between the institutions that administer it, and the nature of the outcomes of that administration; see D. Beatty, "Secondary Boycotts: A Functional Analysis," *Canadian Bar Review* 52 (1974): 388; J. Manwaring, "Legitimacy in Labour Relations: The Courts, the B.C. Labour Board and Secondary Picketing," *Osgoode Hall Law Journal* 20 (1982): 274.
22 More than 20 percent of workers involved in strikes in Canada are engaged in unauthorized strikes; see Drache and Glasbeek, *The Changing Workplace*, n.16. Workers are not passive in the face of capital's attacks, not even when the law requires them to be so. Both narrow, self-interested resistance and wider, extra-legal political activity are part and parcel of these struggles.
23 One of the better examples of this is how the unions fought the 1975 Anti-Inflation Board (AIB) legislation. As serious hardships were imposed on workers, the union movement called for a "Day of Protest." Of course, to ask workers to strike meant that they were being asked to do something illegal, because most were locked into agreements during which they were not allowed to strike. Inasmuch as they were not bound by a collective agreement, they would be asked to take action not against their employer but against the state, a 'no-no' by dint of the law. Hence, the appellation "Day of Protest," which made it sound as if the trade union movement was about to engage in a civil liberties fight rather than economic warfare to achieve political change. Equally interesting is that, despite vociferous opposition by the union movement to the GST and the Free Trade

Agreement, the official trade union movement made no attempts to organize general strikes to stop these vicious, anti-worker policies. And there have been suggestions that Operation Solidarity in British Columbia in 1983 was defeated because of organized labour's perception that it was not ready, and/or ought not, to lead a wide-sweeping political movement; see B. Palmer, "The Rise and Fall of British Columbia's Solidarity," in *The Character of Class Struggle: Essays in Canadian Working Class History, 1850–1985*, ed. B. Palmer (Toronto: McClelland and Stewart, 1986).

24 For an insightful discussion, see L. Panitch, "Corporatism in Canada," *Studies in Political Economy* 1 (1979).

25 The attack on the public sector undertaken by the Ontario NDP government was mounted on the basis that the private sector had already suffered as a result of the rigours of globalized competition and that it was now time for the public sector to take its licks. This approach could do nothing but boost this argument and, on this ground alone, was ill-conceived.

26 Chan F. Aw, *A Dual Labour Market Analysis: A Study of Canadian Manufacturing Industries*, Labour Canada, Economic Analysis Branch (Ottawa: Ministry of Supplies and Services, 1981).

27 J. Jensen, "'Different' but not 'Exceptional': Canada's Permeable Fordism," *Canadian Review of Sociology and Anthropology* 26, 1 (1989).

28 This argument is made forcefully in H.C. Pentland, *A Study of the Changing Social, Economic and Political Background of the Canadian System of Industrial Relations*, Task Force on Labour Relations (Ottawa: Privy Council Office, 1968).

29 This general indifference to the imbalances of gendered relations in a class-divided polity was fed by the male-stream view of social relations shared by many working men.

30 This was authoritatively laid down in *Hershey's of Woodstock* v. *Goldstein* (1963), 38 D.L.R. (2d) 449 (Ont. C.A.) and, despite the embarrassing poverty of the technical and legal arguments used by viciously anti-union judges in that case, the core of the holding has never been overruled. This explains why the starting position of Canadian collective bargaining is that secondary boycotts are illegal per se. Secondary targets' freedom to trade is to trump the limited statutorily granted right of workers to strike one employer.

31 See Shalom Schachter, "Brief to the Legislative Hearings on Bill 40."

32 D. Wolfe, "The Rise and Demise of the Keynesian Era in Canada: Economic Policy, 1930–1982," in *Modern Canada 1930–1980's*, ed. M.S. Cross and G.S. Kealey (Toronto: McClelland and Stewart, 1984), 46; H.J. Glasbeek, "Labour Relations Policy and Law as Mechanisms of Adjustment" *Osgoode Hall Law Journal* 25 (1987): 179; Drache and Glasbeek, *The Changing Workplace*, n.16.

33 G. Esping-Andersen, *The Three Worlds of Welfare Capitalism* (London: Pluto Press, 1990).

34 Canada's relatively low minimum-wage provisions, poor parental-leave pay, short guaranteed minimum vacation pay, poor public-pension schemes, inferior training machinery, and failure to provide for a statutory right to sick leave led to this conclusion. The comparisons are with OECD countries; this includes the United States. Canada compares favourably only with the United States and, occasionally, Australia. The European countries generally are far more bountiful than Canada in all of these areas of the social wage, that is, in the provision of equity.

35 For a description and overview of the occupational health and safety regimes in Canada, see E. Tucker, "And Defeat Goes On: An Assessment of Third Wave Health and Safety Regulation" (paper presented at "Corporate Crime: Ethics, Law and the State" session, Queen's University, November 1992). For a statement from a conservative body that Canadian workers fare very poorly, see the Royal Commission on the Economic Union and the Development Prospects for Canada, *Final Report*, vol. 2 (Ottawa, 1985), chap. 17, where it is recorded that, in respect of traumatic injuries and deaths, Canada has one of the worst records among OECD countries; for more details, see H.J. Glasbeek, "A Role

for Criminal Sanctions in Occupational Health and Safety," *New Developments in Employment Law, Meredith Memorial Lectures 1988* (Cowansville, PQ: Les Éditions Yvon-Blais, 1989), 125. For a discussion of the continuing plight of women, see OECD, *Women and Employment: Policies for Equal Opportunities* (Paris, 1980); Isabella Bakker, "The Status of Women in OECD Countries," *Equality in Employment*, Royal Commission Report, Research Studies (Ottawa: Minister of Supply and Services, 1985), 504; J. Fudge and P. McDermott, eds., *Just Wages: A Feminist Assessment of Pay Equity* (Toronto: University of Toronto Press, 1991).

36 For an elaboration of this pro-business plan, accepted by the Ontario and federal NDPs, which were also touting a social covenant, see Glasbeek, "The Social Charter: Poor Politics and the Poor," n.2.

37 Neil Brooks, "Paying for Public Services in B.C.: Overcoming Taxaphobia" (paper presented to a conference, "Investing in People: Maintaining Public Services," March 6, 1993, Vancouver), has demonstrated that, during the 1980s, corporate income tax payments as a share of national output fell by 33 percent, from 3.7 percent of GDP to 2.5 percent of GDP. While corporate tax is not high anywhere, in other major industrialized countries of the world, as a percentage of GDP, it went up on average from 2.6 percent to 2.9 percent. This average includes the United States, where corporate taxes, as a percentage of GDP, fell; in Japan they went up 20 percent. See also Allan V. Douglas, "Changes in Corporate Tax Revenue," *Canadian Tax Journal* 38 (1990): 66; Patrick Grady, "The Distributional Impact of the Federal Tax and Transfer Changes Introduced since 1984," *Canadian Tax Journal* 38 (1990): 286.

38 But, as Brooks, "Paying for Public Services," n.44, shows, the fact that corporate taxes went up in comparable OECD countries should have made this kind of argument unconvincing, at least in logic.

39 See Brooks, "Paying for Public Services, " n.44, 2.

40 W.T. Stanbury, "The New Competition Act and Competition Tribunal Act: 'Not with a Bang but a Whimper, '" *Canadian Business Law Journal* 12 (1986–87): 2.

41 Which is not new; the idea, however, has more influence.

42 *R. v. Big M Drug Mart Ltd.* (1985), 18 D.L.R. (4th) 321 (C.S.C.); *Edwards Books and Arts Ltd v. R.* (1986), 30 C.C.C. (3d) 385 (S.C.C.).

43 *National Citizens Coalition Inc. v. A.G. for Canada* (1984), 11 D.L.R. (4th) 48 (Albta. S.Ct.); *Irwin Toy v. A.G. of Quebec*, [1989] 1 S.C.R. 927; *Ford v. ec*, [1988] 2 S.C.R. 712. Similarly, inhibitions on the investigation of corporate actors have been imposed by corporations relying on the rubric of the abstraction "freedom from unreasonable search and seizure," "protection of privacy"; *Hunter v. Southam* (1984), 11 D.L.R. (4th) 641 (S.C.C.); cf. *Thomson Newspaper Ltd v. Canada Director of Investigation and Research, Restrictive Trade Practices Commission*, [1990] 1 S.C.R. 125; or, more importantly, governments, anticipating all these potential claims, have systematically gone through their statute books and diluted laws to make them charter-proof. More significant is that it is hard to know how much legislation has not been proposed at all because of the fear of being challenged by corporations calling on the Charter.

44 Economic Council of Canada, *Good Jobs, Bad Jobs: Employment in the Service Economy* (Ottawa: Minister of Supply and Services, 1990).

45 See Economic Council of Canada, *Good Jobs, Bad Jobs*, n.51; Judy Fudge, *Labour Law's Little Sister: The Employment Standards Act and the Feminization of Labour* (Ottawa: CCPA, 1991); J. Fudge and P. McDermott, eds., *Just Wages: A Feminist Assessment of Pay Equity* (Toronto: University of Toronto Press, 1991); *Homeworkers Campaign Brief*, 1991.

46 Dave Broad, "Feminization of Labour and Casualization of Labour = More Degradation of Labour: Lions 3, Christians 0?" (Learned Societies Conference, Charlottetown, May 1992), shows how the growth of part-time work is more than a cyclical phenomenon. During recent recessions, full-time work decreased, part-time increased; but during recoveries, while full-time work increased, so did part-time work. Broad concludes that

the increasing casualization of labour is a structural phenomenon. See also H. Pold, "The Labour Market: Mid-Year Report," *Perspectives on Labour and Income* 2, 3 (Autumn 1990), Statistics Canada, Cat. 75-001E.
47 See Broad, "Feminization of Labour," n.44.
48 This is not the appropriate place to tease out yet another feature of this complex picture, but it should be noted that there are many ways in which the working classes are fragmented. Capitalism, while not responsible in the first place for sexism or racism, is always happy to exploit these phenomena. When governments intervene to tackle systemic discrimination, they ask capitalists not to create jobs but, rather, to deal out more fairly those jobs that they do decide to create. The employers' resistance to these programs are two-fold. First, there are the rednecks who want the right to discriminate. Second, there are those who protest the administrative and training costs such programs impose on them. Governments often respond by picking up some of the training costs on behalf of employers. Workers who have jobs feel themselves threatened and often make common cause with resisting employers, further splitting workers from one another. Part of this unappetizing scenario is the role of the law, which fortifies the notion that all governments should ever be allowed to do is to provide equality of opportunity – which leaves private property decision-making relatively free – as opposed to substantive equality – which requires an attack on property rights.
49 R. Freeman and A. Medoff, *What Do Unions Do?* (New York: Basic Books, 1984), is an empirical work that is often called on in this discussion.
50 For an elaboration of some of those tactics and suggestions as to how to integrate them, see Drache and Glasbeek, *The Changing Workplace*, n.16, and Glasbeek, "Canadian Labour Law: A Little Liberal Law," n.6.
51 The idea that it is not capitalism that is in crisis, but that there is a crisis of distribution, is teased out insightfully by J. Acker, "Class, Gender and the Relations of Distribution," *Signs* 13, 3 (June 1988): 473.

Chapter 11: "We're Still Here"
(Editors' Notes)
1 Mine Mill charters: Timmins Local 241 and Kirkland Lake Local 240, both in 1936.
2 The book referred to is Mike Solski and John Smaller, *Mine Mill: The History of the International Mine, Mill and Smelter Workers in Canada: Since 1895* (Ottawa: Steel Rail Publishing, 1984).
3 June Roberts was active in the long 1993 strike at the Giant goldmine near Yellowknife.
4 *The Western Federation of Miners and Canadian Union of Mine, Mill and Smelter Workers* (Winnipeg: Naylor, 1993).
5 Mine Mill union dues went into building halls for union and community activities. In the 1950s halls were built in Sudbury, Coniston, Lively, Garson, Richard Lake, Chelmsford, and Levack. During the raids by Steel in the early 1960s the union met in the headquarters of Local 902, a general workers' union organized by Mine Mill and chartered in 1949.
6 Barrie Stavis is a playwright and author of the play *The Man Who Never Died*.
7 The tapes and transcriptions of these interviews are being stored in the archives in the J.N. Desmarais Library of Laurentian University.
8 The reference is to the "Pink Slip Floyd" badges (in evidence at the conference) that represented the fight against the social contract legislation in Ontario and referred to the Ontario treasurer, Floyd Laughren, who addressed the conference on the last day.
9 The Boudreau material is in the Laurentian University Archives, Laurentian University, Extension Division Papers, Workers Educational Association files, 1958 to 1962. Alexandre Boudreau was a university extension lecturer who was influential in organizing a right-wing attack within Mine Mill. The other references are to Brian Hogan, "Hard Rock and Hard Decisions: Catholics, Communists and the IUMMSW – Sudbury

confrontations," paper presented to the Canadian Historical Association, May 1985, based on interviews with Steelworkers and Catholic priests active against Mine Mill during the late 1950s and early 1960s; and Cameron Smith, *The Unfinished Journey: The Lewis Family* (Toronto: Summerhill, 1989), especially pp. 306ff and Appendix O.
10 Steelworker radio broadcasts during the raids argued that increased pay and benefits would ensue if Steel represented miners and smelter workers.
11 *The Western Federation of Miners and Canadian Union of Mine, Mill and Smelter Workers.*
12 This is corroborated by correspondence dated October 9, 1941, from the Sudbury detachment of the Royal Canadian Mounted Police to headquarters under the subject heading "Communist Party Activity in Mine Mill and Smelter Workers Union in Sudbury, Ontario." Part of the report reads: "Arrangements were previously made with the local newspaper whereby the activities of the above-mentioned organisation should not be given any publicity either good or bad." See RG 146 (declassified information) in the National Archives of Canada.
13 Harvey Murphy (1900–77), born in Poland, was a colourful and controversial trade union leader and Communist Party member who became director of the Canadian district of Mine Mill in 1943. In the 1960s he was a key figure in the merger negotiations with the Steelworkers. See also chapter 5.
14 Bill Walsh was a United Electrical Workers organizer for about thirty years before becoming a labour consultant. He worked with Mine Mill Local 598 for many years during negotiations and arbitrations.
15 Bisbee, Arizona, is a small copper-mining town. To break a strike, the authorities herded workers into freight cars and railed them into the New Mexico desert.
16 For information on the 1917 strike at Phelps Dodge, see Solski and Smaller, *Mine Mill,* 9.
17 The reference is to how a shift was timed – when a miner arrived at the company door or at the mine face where he worked.
18 The exact site and design of the monument in Bell Park, Sudbury, have since been selected. The monument will be called the "Mining Workers Memorial."
19 Tom Taylor served as an officer and steward with Mine Mill Local 598 for about ten years and was elected president in 1962. After the merger he worked with the United Steelworkers of America.
20 At the time when the photo was taken, the beams of the central Mine Mill hall had been set up, but the rest of the building was only partially constructed.
21 This refers to the mural done by Canadian painter Henry Orenstein in 1955. The mural, commissioned by Mine Mill, is on display at the back of the central in Mine Mill's Regent Street headquarters. The mural is reprinted in Rosemary Donegan, *Industrial Images / Images industrielles* (Hamilton: Art Gallery of Hamilton, 1988), 77–78.
22 After a few years in the industry and of activity in Mine Mill, the Macks opened a general store on Kathleen Street.

Chapter 12: "The Name of the Game Is Power"
(Editors' Notes)
1 Falkowski was the health and safety representative of Steelworkers Local 6500.
2 James H. Ham et al., *Report of the Royal Commission on the Health and Safety of Workers in Mines* (Toronto: Ministry of the Attorney General, 1976).
3 Kevin M. Burkett, P. Peter Riggin, and Keith E. Rothney, *The Report of the Joint Federal-Provincial Inquiry into Safety in Mines and Mining Plants in Ontario* (s.l.: s.n., April 1981), 2 vols.
4 The McKenzie-Laskin Commission to review the administration of the Occupational Health and Safety Act was appointed May 27, 1986, by the Minister of Labour. The commission's report was made public in January 1987.

Chapter 14: "Building Tombstones in Our Lungs"
(Editors' Note)
1 Paul Weiler, *Protecting the Worker from Disability: Challenges for the Eighties* (Toronto: Ontario Ministry of Labour, 1983).

Chapter 15: Telework and the Workplace of the Future
1 Duxbury, Linda, Christopher Higgins, Catherine Lee, and Shirley Mills, "Balancing Work and Family: A Study of the Canadian Federal Public Sector" (unpublished paper, 1991; available from Dr. Duxbury at the School of Business, Carleton University, Ottawa, K1S 5B6).

Chapter 16: A Labour Agenda for Work Design
(Editors' Note)
1 In 1991 Algoma Steel of Sault Ste. Marie, Ontario, was on the brink of collapse. Since then a worker buyout, facilitated by a $110 million loan guarantee from the provincial government, has reversed Algoma's fortunes. Worker ownership has given more power and responsibility to unionized workers and replaced the traditional top-down management with joint management-union committees. Writing in the May 1994 *Labour Times* (2), Lynne Olmer stated that "even among the cynical salaried people, there is some grudging respect given to the union for keeping Algoma Steel afloat."

Chapter 18: Working Partners
(Editors' Notes)
1 All illustrations with this chapter are provided courtesy of the author.
2 Hamilton has since been chosen as the site.

Chapter 19: Weir Reid and Mine Mill
1 The author is grateful to Judith Buse and Susan Vanstone for editorial comments. General background to the issues and problems in this chapter is provided by Mike Solski and John Smaller, *Mine Mill: The History of the International Union of Mine, Mill and Smelter Workers Union in Canada Since 1895* (Ottawa: Steel Rail Publishing, 1984); Cameron Smith, *Unfinished Journey: The Lewis Family* (Toronto: Summerhill Press, 1985), esp. Appendix O; and John Lang, "A Lion in a Den of Daniels: A History of the International Union of Mine Mill and Smelter Workers in Sudbury 1942–1962" (M.A. thesis, University of Guelph, 1970).
2 *The Sudbury Star*, August 3, 1971; the article contains numerous errors but offers a positive picture of achievements. The same applies to the sketch in A. Gilbert and G. Gervais, eds., "Biographies of the Sudbury Region" (History Department of Laurentian University, Sudbury, 1980), 102.
3 *Time*, May 3, 1971.
4 The literature illustrating the nature of that culture is very large but especially pertinent is Helmut Gruber, *Red Vienna: Experiment in Working-Class Culture 1919–1934* (London: Oxford University Press, 1991); and W. Kaschuba et al., eds., *Arbeiterkultur seit 1945 – Ende oder Veränderung* (Tübingen: Tübinger Vereinigung für Volkskunde, 1991). The Kaschuba book adds to the debate about how and why organized workers' culture declined.
5 James Kidd papers, Laurentian University Library [hereafter LUL], letter to Cleve Kidd, June 26, 1955.
6 See Mollie Gillen, *The Wheel of Things: A Biography of L.M. Montgomery* (Don Mills, Ont.: Goodread Biographies, 1975), 151ff; the book also contains some fine descriptions of Norval and the local social scene. Interview with Herb Reid, March 12, 1973. In addition, the brother remembered: "He participated in high school drama, in student affairs."

Unless otherwise noted, information on Weir Reid's early life comes from this interview and an interview with Ruth Reid on April 22, 1992, and another with Ruth Reid and her sister, Margaret, on August 11, 1993.

7 The photostatic copy of Reid's General and Matriculation Courses, supplied by K. Colbran, Head of Guidance at Georgetown High School, shows that in 1937–38 he attained second-class standing in Algebra, Trigonometry, and Physics and earlier received the same in Modern History. He just passed Composition but failed Geometry, Chemistry, Latin, and French; his "plans" were stated on the reverse side of the document.

8 Weir Reid diaries, 1938–42, in possession of Ruth Reid, Sudbury; diary entry for January 11, 1939.

9 Information from Ruth Reid; for details on the bridge construction and cofferdam collapse, see Frank and Nancy Prothero, *Port Stanley: Musings and Memoirs* (Port Stanley, Ont., 1980), 54–57.

10 Reid diaries, January 20, 1938. Herb Reid suggested Weir's social conscience developed partly in response to farm foreclosures during the 1930s, when Weir's mother kept the bailiff at bay with a broom.

11 Information from correspondence of author with Registrar's Office at both universities; McMaster prepared a xerox copy of Reid's file (he obtained mostly second-class marks) and Toronto, a summary. The last entry at McMaster from December 20, 1939 (when Reid lived in Hamilton) reads: "Dropped out of attendance after six weeks on account of illness." The Toronto summary includes: "He was applying for the course in Honours Biology with the intention of becoming a teacher."

12 Reid diaries, December 18, 1938.

13 Reid diaries, January 31, 1940.

14 Interview with Ruth Reid and her sister Margaret (August 11, 1993) after they had seen a draft of this paper. They pointed to his ability to draw, sculpt, do pottery, and desire to have others try all that he did. They related how he would explain snakes to children, or pick sorrel for salad. In a group he always stood out due to his expressiveness, which apparently confounded males but made him more interesting to females.

15 A blemish on his character emerges from an incident relating to Reid's bankruptcy in 1951. The individual involved objected to Reid's bankruptcy being discharged in 1953 because "I was a minor at the time that the said Alexander Weir Reid borrowed the money from me which money was to be returned to be used by me for my education with the result that I was forced to stop school and cut short my education." Golden Collection, Toronto, "bankruptcy file." These materials were made available through Aubrey Golden, Toronto, Reid's lawyer in many of his libel and other court cases. When originally contacted, Golden did not think that any of the materials were saved, but on checking discovered correspondence plus other relevant materials in three substantial files. I am grateful for access and for permission to make copies. Hereafter cited as Golden Collection.

16 The Reid children Paul, Margaret, Brian, and Mike were born between 1946 and 1953, with Scott following a decade later.

17 Reid said in July 1969 during an interview that he met J.L. McBride at Brantford in the "very latter part of the war," by which time McBride "was a rip-roaring Tory, so that his old Labour concepts of politics were out the window." National Archives, Ottawa; copy sent to author from Miller audio collection. The suggestion of a flirtation with the Communist Party in Hamilton was made in M.D. Abrams, "Weir Reid: His Life and Times," script for Sudbury TV program (no date), 13; copy in possession of Ruth Reid. At a slander trial, Reid "stated he was a member of the Communist party in 1948 or 1949 while in Hamilton, but since that time has not been a member of the party." Quoted in *The Sudbury Star*, January 14, 1966.

18 George Prokos to Weir Reid, May 7, 1971; in the possession of Ruth Reid. Reid had made a case against reading *Time*. Prokos and Reid had met in Sarnia in the 1950s, when Reid had accompanied a baseball team. According to Prokos, Reid had influenced him greatly in life and "pitched me on the worthwhile of it all."
19 Trial Record, Supreme Court of Ontario, "Between Weir Reid v. Donald Gillis et al." before the Honourable Mr. Justice Wilson, without a jury, at Sudbury, Ontario, on November 25th, 26th and 27th, 1959, 154; hereafter cited as Trial Record, November 1959 (with identification of individual).
20 The quotation is from Judith Buse, Sudbury, who knew Reid during 1970–71, but it also reflects the opinion of many contemporaries.
21 Golden Collection, letters from J. Moore, Scarborough, Ontario, March 30, April 17, and May 7, 1959, to Reid. The letters exemplify Cold War patterns of defamation leading to job loss.
22 Information from Ruth Reid, interview April 22, 1992.
23 Deposition of Mike Solski in Archives of Ontario [hereafter AO], Solski Papers F1280, Series 2, Box 6, File 42, MU8246.
24 Trial Record, November 1959, 148 (McQuaid).
25 AO, Solski Papers F1280, Series 2, Box 6, File 42 [undated but probably 1965], MU8246; Solski says Reid applied for the position (interview, May 15, 1992).
26 Trial Record, November 1959, 155 (Reid).
27 AO, Solski Papers, F1280, Series 1, Box 3, MU8243.
28 AO, Solski Papers F1280, Series 1, Box 3, File 12, MU8243.
29 LUL, Mine Mill, Box 6, File 7, Entertainment Committee 1950–57. The minutes are cited by date of meeting from this collection.
30 AO, Solski Papers F1280, Series 2, Box 6, File 42, MU8246.
31 LUL, Mine Mill, Box 6, File 7, Entertainment Committee meeting on June 18, 1950; see also Executive Committee minutes of February 14, 1951, regarding break-in at the hall, copies in AO, Solski Papers, F1280 MU8251.
32 LUL, Mine Mill, Box 6, File 7.
33 Trial Record, November 1959, 149 (McQuaid).
34 This section draws upon the Executive Committee minutes, copies in AO, Solski Papers F1280 MU8251, September 13, 1950 (re purchase) and June 15, 1951 (re putting sand on beach); also April 23 and June 4, 1951, for examples of discussions of financial support for various teams.
35 LUL, Mine Mill, Box 6, File 7.
36 Trial Record, November 1959, 65 (Solski).
37 LUL Mine Mill, Box 45, File 7 (interview with Bette Meakes).
38 During 1957 and 1958 *The Sudbury Star* reported especially about the dance groups with many picture stories; for instance, February 20, May 18, and October 31, 1957, and March 18, May 24, and June 2, 1958; this may have been because Bette Meakes, wife of the publisher, participated in the dance group and frequently saw Reid socially.
39 Ray Stevenson informed the author on May 14, 1993, about the difficulty of obtaining support within the union for the ballet and dance schools.
40 Advertisements appeared in the *Mine Mill News* during December 1953 and January 1954, and the performance was sold out.
41 For example, Reid directed Trumbo's *The Biggest Thief in Town* on March 23, 1958, as advertised in the *Mine Mill News* on March 13, 1958. He acted in some of the plays as well.
42 Trial Record, November 1959, 54 (Racicot).
43 Trial Record, November 1959, 150 (McQuaid).
44 Trial Record, November 1959, 155–56 (Reid).

45 Trial Record, November 1959, 164 (Reid).
46 The highly edited files, which have been declassified, include one that obviously refers to Reid but has names deleted. A report of June 28, 1952, claims that Reid "has afforded the Communist movement a real stepping-stone for infiltration into the Union. [Reid] arrived in Sudbury from Hamilton, Ontario, about three months ago, and since that time, has closely associated himself with members of the L[abour] P[rogressive] Party and the N[ational] F[ederation] of L[abour] Y[outh]. He does not, however, openly associate himself with known Communists ... [though he] does meet with them privately." The reporting constable thought that Reid had great influence since he sat on the executive, could make appointments, and arranged for the Sudbury Labour Youth Club to use the union's station wagon. AC RD 146, vol. 14, File 1025-9-91043 Pt. 2.
47 List taken from advertisement for 1964 season in AO, Solski Papers, F1280, Series 1, Box 3, File 12, MU8243. Most of that program was offered from 1954 on, according to Ruth Reid. The 1955 registration form identified sports, swimming, canoeing, boating, nature study, story-telling, singing, folk dancing, arts and crafts, with an emphasis on safety and health, since counsellors all had to have Royal Life Saving Society bronze medals and St. John's Ambulance First Aid awards.
48 The report was in the response to A. Stewart's audit, which the Gillis executive of Local 598 ordered to attack its predecessors; see *Mine Mill News*, June 8, 1959. The National executive of Mine Mill appointed a fact-finding committee to investigate, and this information is from page 17 of its report, published as a pamphlet.
49 Golden Collection, Reid to Golden, December 3, 1959.
50 LUL, Mine Mill, Box 45, File 7, "Statement of Bill Stewart." Reid would eventually win the slander case against Poirier but the jury only handed out a symbolic fine, see *598 News*, February 1966.
51 LUL, Mine Mill, Box 45, File 3, "Reid," for examples.
52 LUL, Mine Mill, Box 45, File 7, "Interview with Carl Kudla."
53 LUL, Mine Mill, Box 45, File 7, "Statement of Robert Edward Jones."
54 LUL, Mine Mill, Box 45, File 7, "Statement of Norman Jacques."
55 LUL, Mine Mill, Box 45, File 7, "Statement of Sonny Robert Gowalko."
56 LUL, Mine Mill, Box 45, File 7, "Interview with Edward Kenneth Ted Loyst."
57 LUL, Mine Mill, Box 45, File 7, "Statement of Frank Fingust."
58 LUL, Mine Mill, Box 45, File 7, "Statement of William Boyuk."
59 Exchange of letters in Ruth Reid collection.
60 According to Ray Stevenson to author, May 13, 1993, Harvey Murphy was responsible for initiating Robeson's concert.
61 *The Sudbury Star*, January 14, 1966.
62 See Dieter K. Buse, "The 1970s," in *Sudbury: Rail Town to Regional Capital*, ed. C.M. Wallace and A. Thomson (Toronto: Dundurn Press, 1993), 242ff, especially pp. 246–47.

Chapter 21: It Never Died
(Editors' Notes)

1 The Main Hall of the Sudbury Mine Mill Hall was dedicated on March 8, 1994, to Joe Hill and renamed the Joe Hill Workers' Auditorium.
2 On Utah Phillips's views of IWW songs and culture, see his remarks in S. Bird et al., eds., *Solidarity Forever: An Oral History of the IWW* (Chicago: Lakeview, 1985), 24–28; on Joe Hill's ashes, see p. 234.

SELECTED BIBLIOGRAPHY

The editors assume that the reader has a basic knowledge of labour history, but recommend the following studies for background and further reading.

The most accessible and readable study, written by two conference participants, is Mike Solski and John Smaller, *Mine Mill: The History of the International Union of Mine, Mill and Smelter Workers in Canada Since 1895* (Ottawa: Steel Rail, 1984).

The local context in which Mine Mill operated is presented in C.M. Wallace and Ashley Thomson, eds., *Sudbury: Rail Town to Regional Capital* (Toronto: Dundurn, 1993).

The roles of the Catholic church, CCF-NDP leaders, and Steelworkers in fighting Mine Mill are included in Cameron Smith, *Unfinished Journey: The Lewis Family* (Toronto: Summerhill, 1989), especially the appendices.

An informative short pamphlet by a past president of Mine Mill is Jim Tester, "The Shaping of Sudbury: A Labour View" (Sudbury: Mine Mill, 1979).

The perspective of Ray Stevenson, a Mine Mill organizer accused of being a communist during the raids, but who joined the Steelworkers, predominates in a centennial booklet "The Western Federation of Miners and Canadian Union of Mine, Mill and Smelter Workers" (Winnipeg: Naylor, 1993).

The most heavily researched study is available in university libraries only: John Lang, "A Lion in a Den of Daniels: A History of the International Union of Mine Mill and Smelter Workers, Sudbury, Ontario 1942–1962" (Masters' thesis, University of Guelph, 1970).

A study of the impediments to organizing can be found in Wayne Roberts, *Miner's Life: Bob Miner and Union Organizing in Timmins, Kirkland Lake, and Sudbury* (Hamilton: McMaster University Press, 1979).

CONTRIBUTORS

KARL BEVERIDGE is an artist interested in workers' heritage. He lives in Toronto.

DIETER K. BUSE is a professor of history and director of graduate studies and research at Laurentian University, Sudbury.

KEN DELANEY is a research director for the United Steelworkers of America in Toronto.

DONALD DENNIE est professeur agrégé de sociologie et directeur de l'Institut franco-ontarien à l'Université Laurentienne à Sudbury.

HARRY J. GLASBEEK is a professor at Osgoode Hall Law School, York University, Toronto.

MIKE GROOM is national organizer for the Canadian Union of Educational Workers in Toronto.

THERESA JOHNSON is a researcher with the Public Service Alliance of Canada in Ottawa.

JENNIFER KECK is an assistant professor in the School of Social Work at Laurentian University, Sudbury.

JOHN LANG was, at the time of the conference, secretary-treasurer of the Confederation of Canadian Unions. He lives in Toronto and has written on the history of Mine Mill.

ELIE MARTEL is a former NDP member for the Sudbury East riding in the Ontario legislature.

JOHN O'GRADY is an independent consultant, working for labour organizations. He lives in Toronto.

BRYAN PALMER is a professor of history at Queen's University in Kingston.

MADELEINE PARENT is one of the founders of the Confederation of Canadian Unions and of the National Action Committee on the Status of Women. She lives in Montreal. In October 1994 she was awarded an honorary doctorate by Laurentian University.

JEAN-CLAUDE PARROT is executive vice-president of the Canadian Labour Congress and former president of the Canadian Union of Postal Workers. He lives in Ottawa.

UTAH PHILLIPS is a songwriter, singer, and long-time Wobblie living in California, not Utah!

MARY POWELL is an assistant professor of political science at Laurentian University, Sudbury.

LAURELL RITCHIE works with the Work Organization and Training Department of the Canadian Auto Workers. She lives in Toronto.

MERCEDES STEEDMAN is an assistant professor of sociology at Laurentian University, Sudbury.

PETER SUSCHNIGG is an associate professor of sociology at Laurentian University, Sudbury.

ERIC TUCKER is an associate professor at Osgoode Hall Law School, York University, Toronto.

CATHY WALKER is national health and safety director for the Canadian Auto Workers. She lives in Toronto.

CHARLOTTE YATES is an associate professor of labour studies and political science at McMaster University in Hamilton.